The
Israeli Secret
Service

The
Israeli Secret
Service

Richard Deacon

TAPLINGER PUBLISHING COMPANY

NEW YORK

First published in the United States in 1978 by
TAPLINGER PUBLISHING CO., INC.
New York, New York

Library of Congress Catalog Card Number: 78-56985
ISBN 0-8008-4266-9

Contents

1	In the Footsteps of the Twelve	9
2	Irgun Zvai Leumi Emerges	21
3	The Creation of Shin Beth	37
4	Isser Harel and the Mossad	52
5	The Lavon Affair	61
6	The Million-Dollar Spy	76
7	Global Hunt for Nazis	89
8	The Eichmann Kidnapping	103
9	Yuval Ne'eman's Technological Revolution	118
10	Nasser's German Connection	131
11	The Jew Who Posed as a Nazi	139
12	Swiss Broadside for Harel	146
13	The Case of Israel Beer	159
14	The Six-Day War	167
15	Testing Time for Shabak	186
16	Mirage Blueprints from Switzerland	203
17	The Case of the Five Gunboats	215
18	The Long Arm of the Avengers	222
19	Disaster at Lillehammer	243
20	Lessons of the Yom Kippur War	257
21	The Entebbe Raid	271
22	The Strange World of Psychic Espionage	286
Notes		303
Bibliography		309
Index		311

Illustrations

between pages 160 and 161

1   The 'Ezra' group of Poale Zion at Ben-Gurion's home town of Plonsk in 1900. Out of this developed the nucleus of an Israeli intelligence service

2a   Menachem Begin

2b   Isser Harel

2c   Shimon Peres

2d   Elie Cohen

3a   Victorino Nino, alias Marcelle

3b   Dr. Yuval Ne'eman

3c   Adolf Eichmann

3d   Israeli Police Chief Joseph Nakmias

4a   Wolfgang Lotz with Egyptian General Ghorab and Waltraud Lotz at the Cavalry Club in Cairo

4b   Israel Beer, Soviet spy

4c   General Meir Amit, former head of the Mossad

5a   Major-General Aharon Yariv, head of Israeli Military Intelligence during the Six-Day War

5b   Chaim Herzog, Director of Military Intelligence 1959–62

5c   Zvi Zamir, head of the Mossad at the time of the Lillehammer episode

6a   Two letter-bombs mailed from Turkey to Israel by terrorists. One is addressed to Dr. Yuval Ne'eman, head of Aman

6b   Two terrorist girls who took part in the Sabena hi-jacking, sentenced to life imprisonment by an Israeli military court

7a   Major-General Yitzak Hofi, head of the Mossad

7b   International terrorist Carlos (wearing beret) with the Algerian Minister Bouteflika

7c   Articles seized by the French counter-espionage service from the hide-out of Carlos-controlled Arab terrorists in Paris

8a Major-General Ariel Sharon, key figure in secret Commando operations

8b Brigadier-General Dan Shomron who headed the Commando raid on Entebbe

8c Paratrooper's Commander, Tat-Aluf Rafael Eytan (middle row, centre) explaining the activities of his corps to (from right) General Bar-Lev, General David Elazar (head of Aman) and General Rechavam Zeevi (Intelligence adviser)

Illustrations 1, 2a, 2c, 3d, 5a, 6a, 8a, and 8c are reproduced by kind permission of Camera Press Ltd.; 2b and 3c by kind permission of Thomson Regional Newspapers Ltd.; 2d by kind permission of Y. Barzray; 3a and 4c by kind permission of Associated Press Ltd.; 3b, 5b, 6b and 7a by kind permission of the Israeli Government Press Office; 4a by kind permission of Vallentine Mitchell; 4b by kind permission of Popperfoto; 5c by kind permission of the Israeli Sun Ltd.; 7b, 7c and 8b by kind permission of Rex Features Ltd.

I

In the Footsteps of
the Twelve

*And Moses sent them to spy out the land of
Canaan ... and see the land, what it is; and the
people that dwelleth therein, whether they be
strong or weak, few or many.*

(NUMBERS xiii, 17–18)

ORGANISED ESPIONAGE was an honoured and recognised profession among the Ancient Israelites, as the Old Testament bears witness, and it would therefore be fair to say that, though the State of Israel is only thirty years old, the Israeli Secret Service is one of the oldest of the world's Intelligence organisations. Only the Chinese have an older tradition of espionage. But they have had the benefit of some form of continuity; the Israelis suffered from the disadvantage of having allowed their Intelligence Service to lapse for several centuries. It is to their credit that, within a few years of having founded the modern state of Israel, they have been able to create a Secret Service which, for its size, can be classed as first-rate. Today it may be the smallest, but it is certainly the most consistently efficient in the world.

Nevertheless, in assessing the value of this Secret Service, it is important to bear in mind the paradox that it is at the same time one of the oldest and one of the youngest of all Intelligence organisations. Despite the lack of continuity, the young and sophisticated Secret Service of today owes much to the distant past. Joshua, the son of Nun, 'sent out of Shittim two men to spy secretly, saying, "Go view the land, even Jericho." '[1] And the two men found for themselves an ally in Rahab, the harlot of Jericho, who made a covenant with them. She not only sheltered them, but actively furthered their aims. But it was Moses who really initiated and organised espionage on a larger scale. It is true that he claimed

this was a divine command from God, but he laid down quite
clearly the basis for his team of spies: '. . . and Moses . . . sent
them from the wilderness of Paran: all those men were heads of
the children of Israel.'[2]

There were twelve of them in all and through them Moses
established the first positive Israelite Secret Service. Their instructions were simple and clear: '. . . spy out the land of Canaan
. . . get you up this way southward, and go up into the mountain:
and see the land, what it is; and the people that dwelleth therein,
whether they be strong or weak, few or many; And what the
land is that they dwell in, whether it be good or bad; and what
cities they be that they dwell in, whether in tents, or in strong-
holds; And what the land is, whether it be fat or lean, whether
there be wood therein or not. And be ye of good courage and
bring of the fruit of the land.'[3]

This may not have been such sophisticated advice as that given
by the Chinese espionage sage, Sun Tzu, in his *Ping Fa* in 510
B.C., but it was at least enough to ensure that within forty days
they returned with reports on a land flowing with milk and honey,
but also with warnings of what they were up against. In modern
times the Israeli Intelligence has been as receptive to bad news as
to good, which is again one of its greatest strengths. History is
strewn with Intelligence failures due almost entirely to ignoring
unpalatable facts.

If many of the recorded feats of ancient Israeli espionage consist of a mixture of fact and legend, there is a good deal of
evidence that much of Biblical origin was factually well founded.
This was demonstrated to the British Sixtieth Division in February
1918, when they were ordered by General Allenby to attack
Jericho. A brigade was directed to detach itself and capture a
small village named Michmash, and Major Vivian Gilbert, the
officer in command, was perturbed because he had little information about the terrain and the plan of attack involved storming a
steep hill on which the village was situated. Luckily, he recalled
that Michmash was mentioned in Samuel I, chapters 13 and 14:
'. . . the Philistines encamped in Michmash. . . . And between
the passages, by which Jonathan sought to go over unto the
Philistines' garrison, there was a sharp rock on the one side and a
sharp rock on the other side: and the name of the one was Bozez,
and the name of the other Seneh.

'The forefront of the one was situated northward over against

Michmash, and the other southward over against Gibeah. And Jonathan said to the young man who bare his armour, Come and let us go over unto the garrison . . . it may be that the Lord will work for us: for there is no restraint to the Lord save by many or by few. And that first slaughter which Jonathan and his armour bearer made was about twenty men, within as it were an half acre of land, which a yoke and oxen might plow.'

As a result of studying this passage Major Gilbert was able to change the plan of operation completely; instead of making a frontal attack with the whole brigade, a single company was sent to tackle the Turks.

The pass was exactly as described in the Book of Samuel and in his book, *The Romance of the Last Crusade*, Major Gilbert was able to testify to the value of ancient intelligence: 'we killed or captured every Turk that night in Michmash, so that after thousands of years, the tactics of Saul and Jonathan were repeated with success by a British force.'[4]

After the death of Herod the end of the Jewish state was in sight. The Romans gradually acquired more and more power. Despite incipient revolts, by the date of Nero's death the Roman general Vespasian had subdued practically the whole of Palestine except Jerusalem. When Vespasian eventually became Emperor he commissioned his son, Titus, to reduce Jerusalem. In A.D. 70 the Jewish state was finally crushed until its revival in 1948. The Jews were also bereft of the city of Jerusalem until they won it in the 1967 War. But for the Zealots the struggle continued in the great fortress of Masada on the shores of the Dead Sea. They held out under Eleazar, a descendant of Judas of Galilee, the founder of the movement. The Zealots were the forerunners of Haganah out of which in due course the Israeli Secret Service was born. Founded in the year A.D. 6, the Zealots who included among their number the Apostle Simon, were finally worn down by the Romans and ended their fight in A.D. 73.

From then on it was the lot of the Jews either to be exploited by their conquerors, or to move on to other lands. For those who remained there was little hope of forming any worthwhile underground movement for several centuries. For those who moved on there was a long bleak period of persecution, repression and exploitation. Not surprisingly, it was the ablest and most enterprising who emigrated and it was from among these people, who acquired their self-discipline, courage and initiative often as a direct result of the manner in which they were harried and persecuted, that many other nations recruited some of their best secret agents. In this respect the Jews can be compared with the early Jesuits who also played a part in the world of Intelligence wherever they went to settle. Inevitably, perhaps, the Jews tended to serve Protestant rather than Catholic countries, for it took them centuries to forgive, if not forget, the fact that Torquemada, the tyrannical chief of the Catholic Inquisition in Spain, declared in 1342 that the Black Death came to his country as a punishment to Spaniards for giving shelter to the Jews. It was the Puritan supporters of Cromwell who encouraged the migration of Jews to England and Cromwell's own chief of Secret Service, John Thurloe, who first appreciated the value of them as secret agents for Britain. A Jewish merchant, Antonio Fernandez Carvajal, formed a spy network for Thurloe with his correspondents on the Continent, while Simon de Caceres, another Jew, kept him informed on developments in Latin America and the Caribbean. It was as a result of information passed to him by yet another Jewish agent in Jamaica that Admiral Blake was able to capture the Spanish Plate Fleet at Tenerife.[5]

In the nineteenth century in Germany and to a lesser extent in Czarist Russia Jews were chiefly employed in the field of intelligence. In France there was a virulent anti-Semitism in the Army for very many years and it was at its worst in the General Staff. The affair of Captain Alfred Dreyfus, an officer of Jewish birth, was perhaps the supreme example of this, for it was largely because of the strong anti-Semitic feeling in the General Staff and Military Intelligence that, on the flimsiest evidence, Dreyfus was condemned in 1894 to military degradation and imprisonment on Devil's Island for allegedly offering to sell secrets to Germany. It was not until four years later that his case was re-opened, and the real culprit unmasked, but acquitted by court martial. And not until 1899 was Dreyfus brought home, re-tried and eventually pardoned.

In the light of the continual harassment and persecution of Jews throughout the centuries it is remarkable that so many of them remained true servants of their countries of adoption. Right up to World War I, with the possible exception of Russia, which was very much a special case, Jews were found to be working loyally, and often at great risk, for the nations of which they had become citizens. There were just as many serving the Central

Powers as those of the Allies and many young Palestinian Jews were officers in the Turkish Army, including Moshe Shertok (who later changed his name to Sharett), Israel's first Foreign Minister. Of course, there were exceptions, with some Jews operating as double, or even treble agents, using espionage as a profession rather than a patriotic calling. But, generally speaking, this tendency was not to be found in Britain, Germany or France, but in Czarist Russia, for it was here that Jews were still being treated with a kind of medieval savagery and herded into ghettos. Anti-Semitism was particularly marked at court and among the ruling classes of Russia in the nineteenth century, and the legend of such nonsense as 'The Protocols of the Elders of Zion' and propaganda about secret Jewish plots to dominate the world all originated there.

Consequently very many Jews joined the revolutionary underground movements that sprang up inside Russia and often extended outside that country's boundaries in the middle of the nineteenth century. Their sympathies were on the whole with the Liberals, Anarchists, Social Democrats and Revolutionary Socialists who opposed the Czarist Establishment. But while some were convinced revolutionaries and Socialists, others were more interested in personal survival and many soon learned that anti-Semitism was just as inclined to raise its ugly head inside revolutionary circles as among supporters of the Czarist regime. Suspicion, that seemingly ineradicable curse inflicted on the Russian character down the centuries, made life as difficult for the Jew among his fellow revolutionaries as it would have done in any other sphere of Russian life. If harassment ceased when the Jew joined the Revolutionary Socialists, mistrust often made him fear it had only disappeared temporarily. So there were some Jews who, as a means of surviving in this very difficult environment, sought to safeguard their existence by the perilous, yet often astonishingly successful ploy of backing both sides. One of the ways in which they could most effectively do this was by pretending to join Revolutionary Socialist, Anarchist and other underground movements and then offering their services to the Ochrana, the Czarist secret police. Many Jews became police informers in this way and their chief aim was to win the protection of the Ochrana which was in itself one means of avoiding persecution. Naturally, most of these informers merely spied on the revolutionaries and rarely became too involved with them.

Possibly this was one reason for the sudden change of heart towards Jewish Bolsheviks in the mid-twenties. However, a far greater factor was the classic case of Jewish double-dealing inside the Czarist secret police—that of Ievno Azeff. This case made as much impact in Russia as did that of Dreyfus in France. But whereas the ultimate reaction of the Dreyfus case was to the benefit of the Jews, that of Azeff was disastrously to their disadvantage. Whenever, even today, Soviet Russian officials are tackled on their harsh attitudes towards the Jews and especially to those who wish to leave the country, in private conversation they cite the case of Ievno Azeff.

The Azeff case is not in any way typical of what went on in Czarist Russia among the Jewish communities: very many Jewish informers remained loyal to the Ochrana and the Czarist state, only using their profession as a means of safeguarding themselves from persecution; many more of the Jewish community remained totally loyal to the cause of the revolutionaries. But Azeff tried to have it both ways. He will go down in history as the one double agent nobody completely unmasked. The supreme practitioner of the arts of the *agent provocateur*, he not only posed as a revolutionary while working for the police as an informer and secret agent, but actually organised assassinations of leading political figures in Russia so that he could trap the killers and their associates into being arrested and executed. For every blow he struck against the revolutionaries, he seemed to hit back equally hard against the police. Nobody else was more skilful in helping the police to arrest revolutionaries and at the same time more adept at advancing the revolutionary cause with some spectacular coup. Which side obtained the most benefit? It is still almost impossible to say, even though the whole affair was made the subject of a searching inquiry after the Revolution by the Bolsheviks. Graham Stephenson, the modern British authority on Russian history, asserts that 'it is impossible to say which side he mainly betrayed', while A. T. Vassilyev, who was chief of the Ochrana, declared that 'no clear light has ever been shed on the Azeff affair. Nor did I, during my whole period of service, ever set eyes upon any documents that might have been likely to clear up that mysterious business.'[6]

Azeff was the son of a poor Jewish tailor, born at Lyskovo in the Grodnensky province of Russia in 1869. He started life first as a clerk, then as a tutor and afterwards as a newspaper reporter before making friends with revolutionaries and subsequently offering his services to the Ochrana. He infiltrated the secret 'Battle Organisation' of the revolutionaries, and planned such assassinations as those of Sipyagin, Minister of the Interior; Obolensky, Governor of Kharkov; Bodganovitch, Governor of Ufa; Plehve, another Minister of the Interior, and the Grand Duke Sergei Alexandrovitch. But at the same time he passed on to the Ochrana sufficient information to enable them to arrest some of the actual killers, taking great care to preserve the life of his closest allies in the underground, but to eliminate all those who mistrusted him. In due course Azeff acquired supreme command of the terrorist organisation while convincing the Ochrana of his worth to the extent that his salary was raised to 16,000 roubles a year, a 400 per cent increase on what he had earned when he first worked for them. In the end he was hounded by the revolutionaries who plotted to eliminate him and equally sought by the Ochrana. But by then he had escaped from Russia. For years he kept on the move, changing his name and his hotel every few weeks, now in Italy, then in Egypt and Greece, finally settling down in Germany. There he died before World War I ended.

Purists may argue that the case of Azeff has nothing whatsoever to do with the history of the Israeli Secret Service. In one sense this is true, but as an important factor of background to the subject the Azeff affair is vital to an understanding of how such a tiny country could develop so up-to-date and efficient an Intelligence Service. Azeff was not a typical Jewish agent of the great powers prior to 1914, but his enterprise, courage, attention to detail, patience, objectivity and ruthlessness exemplify the Jewish natural talent for espionage. When the Jewish state was created after World War II, these qualities were to be found in abundance among many agents of Haganah and other Palestinian organisations; unlike Azeff, they had a burning patriotic motive for their actions.

Most of the early Jewish leaders in the fight for independence in Palestine had been in the various revolutionary movements in Russia, Poland and neighbouring countries. David Ben-Gurion, Israel's first Prime Minister and Minister of Defence, born in Poland in 1887, had been, in his teens, a member of the Jewish Socialist movement, Poale Zion, inside Poland. He had worked to make it a force in Jewish life throughout Eastern Europe, taking an active part in the Jewish self-defence organisation in the pogroms of 1905. As a result of this he was put on the Ochrana's black list and shortly afterwards went to Palestine. Professor Ben-Zion Dinaburg, Israel's first Education Minister, was born in the Ukraine in 1884 and joined the Labour Zionist Movement in Russia in 1903.

Some Russian Jews had a different story to tell. There was Joseph Trumpeldor (1880–1920), who was said to have been the only Jewish officer in the Czar's Army. He was most unusually awarded commissioned rank after the Battle of Port Arthur for exceptional bravery in action, during which he lost a hand. During the First World War Trumpeldor served in a Jewish unit fighting with the British in Gallipoli, eventually becoming some-what of a legendary figure because of his exploits in the desert. But perhaps the most spectacular Palestinian Jewish exploit of the First World War was that of the Aaronson family and their espionage activities on behalf of the British.

As already noted, the Jews were to be found on both sides in that war, but a number of the intellectuals and those who yearned for a national home sided with the Allies. Though they detested Czarist Russia, they pinned their hopes for a recognition of Zionist claims on an Allied victory with backing from the British Foreign Secretary, Lord Balfour, himself keenly sympathetic to Zionism. There were then about 80,000 Jews in Palestine and Tel Aviv had only been founded on the sand dunes outside Jaffa in 1914. Nevertheless some of the pro-Allies Jews in Palestine had evolved secret plans for trying to capture Jerusalem when the Turks retreated.

The Aaronsons were a wealthy and extremely cultured family greatly respected in their own community. They were convinced that the Allies would win and offered to set up a spy network for the British. What is more, Aaron Aaronson, the architect of this plan, not only promised to keep the British posted on Turkish troop movements, but made it clear that he and his family wanted no reward for their services. Aaronson's idea was that if the Jews patriotically offered their services free to Britain, demon-strating that they were anxious to play a part in winning the war, afterwards they would be more likely to win support for their aims. It was not an unreasonable hope in the light of the Balfour Declaration, but the Jews were soon to learn that British promises were quickly forgotten when the war was over. In fact the British authorities behaved with exceptional stupidity when Aaronson's offer was first made: they took the view that anyone who offered to spy without expecting a reward must be planted by the enemy.

Aaronson had to contend not only with British suspicion, but with the hostility of some Zionists; the latter felt that the Jewish cause might be better served by using any intelligence gleaned for their own purposes. But Aaron Aaronson was a determined young man and eventually his plan was accepted by the British. He was a botanist who had an experimental station at a place called Atlit on the Palestinian coast. It was here he set up the headquarters for his spy network. Other leading members of it were his brother, Alexander, and his sister, Sara, as well as Avshalom Feinberg from Hadera and Na'aman Belkind from Rishon. The network called itself Nili, an acronym of the Hebrew words for 'The Eternal One of Israel does not Lie'. It had its own secret code and system of communications and very soon this young and inexperienced team of spies was proving of inestimable value to the British. It so happened that a German staff officer had been given accommodation in their parents' home and, by going through his papers when he was out of the house and by asking him innocent-sounding questions, the trio obtained a wealth of information. To this was added a steady stream of intelligence gleaned from their friends, mainly young people of their own age. They suffered a serious blow in 1916 when Avshalom Feinberg was murdered by Bedouins (remarkably enough his grave was found during operations after the Six-Day War of 1967), but, though this was damaging to their communications system, Aaron Aaronson found a way round the problem. This young man rowed along the coast until he came level with the German–Turkish positions and then casually drifted towards the British lines, pulling into shore and allowing himself to be taken to the Intelligence officers for questioning.

Then in October 1917, a carrier pigeon specially trained to carry messages from Nili to the British lost its way and was trapped by the Turks. Sara Aaronson had organised this carrier-pigeon service to supplement the intelligence her brother was providing on his dangerous boat trips. The Jews were at once suspected and a round-up of them was ordered by the Turks. Sara Aaronson was one of the first to be caught. Suspicion fell on her because of the German staff officer lodged at her home and the Turks suspected that leakages of information must have come from this source. She was certainly tortured, but there was no indication that she gave anything away. It has been said that the Turks killed her; the truth would seem to be that she killed herself rather than give way under torture. One report stated that she had been whipped, burned with hot irons and had her fingernails pulled out. Ultimately her elder brother undertook a one-man mission to shoot down her tormentors. He survived the war to play a useful part in the British administration.

Thus it was that in one way or another, in one country or another, Jews, all over the world, were gaining a training and experience in espionage which was eventually to be of enormous value to them when the state of Israel was founded. Almost no other nomadic race in history has acquired such experience. It is true that the Romany tribes have for centuries served on the fringes of espionage, but they have never worked their way to the top of their profession as have the Jews. It is no mere coincidence that Sidney Reilly, perhaps Britain's most celebrated spy over the past hundred years, should have been of Jewish origin, his real name being Sigmund Georgievich Rosenblum, the illegitimate son of a Jewish doctor. Reilly went far beyond the realms of mere espionage; more often than not he was actively moulding policy as well. During the early 1920s Reilly was inside Soviet Russia as a British agent actually helping to choose and form a Shadow Cabinet for an alternative government in the event of the Bolsheviks being overthrown. Many of Reilly's machinations remain shrouded in mystery: he certainly worked for countries other than Britain, even if his main allegiance was to the United Kingdom (indeed, he always claimed in later life to be the son of an Irish sea captain!), the United States and Russia among them. It is now known that he worked for Czarist Russia as an agent while actually spying for the British inside Russia and there is still some evidence that after his disappearance in 1925 he may not have been shot by Soviet frontier guards, but actually defected to the USSR. Certainly there were some people who claimed he was still alive two years later.

However, even if Reilly survived for another few years as a double agent, he must inevitably have been liquidated by the Soviet Union well before World War II. By the late twenties the anti-Semitic drive inside the USSR had already begun. Though a large number of Russian Jews had been Bolsheviks in the early years of the Revolution and some of them attained official posts in the administration, most of them had not taken the precaution of becoming members of the Communist Party. Stalin, who was strongly biased against all Jews, used the argument that failure to join the Party should be regarded as evidence of a lukewarm attitude towards the regime. By the mid-thirties there had been a drastic purge of Jews in all walks of life in Russia. This purge, quite as much as the growing persecution of Jews by the Nazis, helped to speed up Jewish emigration from Europe to Palestine. The Soviet attitude towards Zionism was non-committal prior to the creation of Israel. Indeed the Communist Party in Palestine actually denied the principle of Jewish immigration, and in no way supported the theme of a national home. Despite this and even in the face of persecution in Russia, a number of Jews remained loyal to the Soviet regime, and pro-Marxist parties inside Palestine continued to support the Soviet Union, taking the view that it was the Bolsheviks who had rescued them from Czarist oppression and that if temporarily there was a degree of anti-Semitism, this must disappear in due course. Possibly it was also felt that, with Britain and France showing little inclination to stand out against Nazi Germany, the Soviet Union offered the only long-term prospect of rescue from European persecution. At that time the United States was overwhelmingly isolationist in outlook.

To their credit, what the Jews mainly sought for in Palestine was the creation of a democratic state. Even those who had been revolutionaries in Russia and militant socialists elsewhere sincerely wished to make the new Zionist state one that guaranteed freedom of thought and equality of opportunity with a freely elected government. It was one of the paradoxes of that period that some of the Jews who sincerely believed in and desired a form of social democracy for their own national home could at the same time serve the cause of the tyrannical Stalinist regime by acting as spies of the Soviet Union, especially in the United States. Fear may have had a great deal to do with this strange dualism: in the twenties and thirties there was a savage undercurrent of fascism, anti-Semitism and persecution in America, throwing up such dubious characters as Huey Long, a revived Ku Klux Klan and anti-Jewish forces in the Republican Party. What were Jewish immigrants to the USA, accustomed to persecution in Europe, to make of such manifestations at a time when America was showing no signs of standing up to the dictators of the European world? Almost automatically some of them—albeit a minority—reverted to their nomadic instincts, to protect themselves in much the same way as Ievno Azeff had done.

Yet at the same time it should be made quite clear that by far the greatest number of those Jews who emigrated to Palestine in the twenties and thirties and who had some experience in intelligence work, dedicated themselves totally to employing that experience towards achieving the Zionist state. For them there was no other allegiance. It is no exaggeration to say that the part they played in creating Israel was far greater than that of any of the administrators and politicians. Without that hard corps of Intelligence men working for Zionism, Israel might well never have been created.

2

Irgun Zvai Leumi
Emerges

The height will not be conquered,
If no grave is on the slope

(SHLOMO SHULSKY)

ISRAELI INTELLIGENCE really began, in an organised manner, with the creation of Jewish defence units within the organisation of Poale Zion (Workers of Zion) Party in the late nineteenth century. Inside Russia this party was positively revolutionary; in other parts of Europe it gathered intelligence on enemies of the Jews and through its defence units gave what protection it could to Jewish citizens. Later defence units were formed by Poale Zion in Palestine to give support to the Jewish immigrants from Europe as well as native Jews.

The cause of Jewish colonisation of Palestine had been given a tremendous boost in 1882 when Edmond de Rothschild, one of the less prominent members of that cosmopolitan family, made a small loan of 25,000 francs for the digging of wells in a Jewish colony. From then on he devoted himself whole-heartedly to the encouragement of colonisation, spending more than a million pounds on the purchase of land and the building of houses. But his aid went far beyond this: it is estimated that indirectly and through his influence on other people something like eight million pounds was spent on development and training schemes and self-help projects.

In 1909 a defence society named Hashomer ('The Watchman') was set up in Palestine and, as its title suggests, to some extent it formed the nucleus of an intelligence organisation. Hashomer was essentially run by revolutionary-minded Jews of varying persuasions from right-wing radicals to moderate socialists who came from Eastern Europe, but it was Marxist-orientated

Russian Jews who dominated its early councils. It had both a revolutionary flavour and a fervour of militant socialism, while seeking to protect Jewish villages from Arab attacks and to propound its own brand of Zionist-Socialism. Partly due to a belief that the British Government offered the best long-term chance of the Jews obtaining a national home (thanks to the Balfour Declaration) and partly because some of the Jewish elders grew impatient with revolutionary talk, Hashomer was disbanded in 1925, though its influence lived on.

It was in the early twenties that the far-sighted and highly civilised mind of Chaim Weizmann became a powerful influence in Palestine in moulding policy for a national home. Weizmann left his home near Pinsk to study chemistry in England in 1903. From that time onwards he became strongly Anglophil and constantly urged the view that 'if we Jews are to get help from any quarter, it will be England who, I don't doubt, will help us in Palestine.' He followed up his hunch by lending support to the Allies in World War I, giving them the formula for a new process for making acetone which, in 1916, greatly alleviated the dire shortage of explosives. By the early 1920s Weizmann had become President of the Zionist Organisation.

He was also a close confidant of the Canadian, William Stephenson, who, in World War II, was to become the key man in British Intelligence in the United States. Weizmann advised Stephenson on a large range of subjects and between the wars kept him closely informed on German scientific developments, especially in the military field. At this time Stephenson was a personal adviser to Winston Churchill on various aspects of Germany's secret rearmament and, after the Nazis came to power and when Churchill was in the political doldrums, he continued this work, supplying the Conservative rebel with much ammunition for his campaign against appeasement. Stephenson received a great deal of intelligence from Jewish scientists. This particular operation, though seemingly far removed from the story of Palestine, in the long run greatly helped Israeli Intelligence in the early days of the state of Israel. Some of these scientists who became friends of Stephenson were encouraged to develop their talents in the cause of Allied Intelligence and they not only worked for Britain in World War II, but later assisted the Israeli Secret Service.

Weizmann and Stephenson between them recruited a brilliant

team of scientists to spy on the Germans in the technological field. But Stephenson's most brilliant aide, whom he employed in his own business, was Charles Proteus Steinmetz, a Jewish scientist who had been forced to leave Germany because of his social-democratic views. Steinmetz was a man in advance of his time, especially in the sphere of electronics, and nobody was so able in analysing reports of German scientific developments and forecasting what they might mean in terms of weaponry and war potential.

From 1925 to 1929 the Jews in Palestine had a relatively prosperous time, though there was still much hard work to be done in building up their colony. It was in the thirties that the Arabs started launching attacks on Jewish businesses in Tel Aviv and Jerusalem, and gradually engaging in a guerrilla war of attrition. By then it was abundantly clear that Jews were being driven out of Germany and Austria and that some Arab leaders were not merely welcoming this trend, but actively seeking German support for their own campaign against the Jews. In this atmosphere the nucleus of an underground Palestinian Jewish Intelligence Service was created well in advance of the establishment of Israel as a state.

This underground intelligence organisation began inside Haganah, the self-defence force of the Palestine Jewish community, a body which was to become the forerunner of the Israeli Defence Force. Some of the supporters of the Zionist cause had had training in police and intelligence work. There was Bechor Shalom Shitreet, who later became Israel's first Minister of Police. He had been appointed a sub-lieutenant of Police at an early age and put in charge of the Tiberias region. By 1921 he had become Superintendent of the Fingerprints Bureau of the CID in Jerusalem; six years later he was Superintendent of Police in Tel Aviv and from 1933 onwards he had command of the Police School. But it was among the younger, more militant Jews, those who had had experience of persecution in Europe, where the organisers of the Haganah Intelligence set-up were to be found. They became more and more dissatisfied with the lack of an aggressive response to Arab attacks and, unlike the moderates, they did not believe the British would fulfil the still vague promises of a national home for the Jews. Time proved them to be right and as the British increasingly tended to try to placate both Jews and Arabs and showed no signs of relinquishing their mandatory powers in Palestine, so the militants began to acquire more authority. There were various splits inside Haganah and finally one splinter group, Haganah B, united with the youth group of Vladimir Jabotinsky to form the counter-terrorist organisation Irgun Zvai Leumi, which was in effect a para-military organisation with its own extremely well-conducted intelligence network. Jabotinsky had, like Weizmann, always believed that Britain would eventually give the Jews independence in Palestine, but by the mid-thirties it became clear to him that the British Government of that period had little intention of doing this. The British were in fact playing their ancient and dangerous game of divide-and-rule, aiming at checking Jewish immigration to Palestine, despite the persecution in Nazi Germany, in order to try to balance Jewish and Arab power. Some British administrators, civilian as well as military, had secretly encouraged Arab national-ist aspirations: if any proof of this was needed, it could be found in the slogan of the Arab nationalist movement which was whispered from one end of the country to the other—'Ad-dowlah ma'anah' ('Everything is in our favour'), which meant that the British Administration was on their side and would not seek to check them.

In this situation, with Haganah still bent on a peaceful policy and not taking the law into their own hands in the face of Arab attacks, David Raziel welded Irgun into an aggressive force. While Weizmann prided himself on his British citizenship (he only surrendered his British passport after he became first Presi-dent of Israel), the younger Jews, most of whom had had socialist or even communist backgrounds in Europe, suspected that the British ruling class and the Mandatory Authority were at heart anti-Semitic and favourably disposed both to Arabs and fascism. Even if this were not true, British actions gave ample cause for mistrust, not least the distorted reports which General Wauchope, the British High Commissioner in Palestine, sent to London. David Raziel was convinced that sooner or later there must be a showdown with the British and that obedience of their calls for self-restraint against the Arabs would only be regarded as weak-ness. He was a highly intelligent man, educated at the Hebrew University where he studied mathematics and philosophy; but he was so convinced that his people would only win and hold a national home by military means that he devoted all his spare time to studying military history, tactics and strategy. Soon he acquired so much information on military science that he was writing textbooks with Avraham Stern on small arms, teaching classes of his underground movement guerrilla tactics and how to manufacture home-made bombs. For a while Raziel cleverly fooled British Intelligence by setting up his headquarters in an exclusive girls' private school, using this as an Irgun training centre at night.

Irgun's first retaliatory attacks against the Arabs coincided with the publication of the British Royal Commission's report proposing the splitting up of Palestine into three parts—an Arab state, a Jewish state and certain reserved areas in which the British would continue to rule. If ever there was an ill-conceived compromise doomed to failure, this was it. Nevertheless, the moderate Jewish leadership under Weizmann gave the partition plan qualified support on the grounds that it was a step in the right direction. But the Arabs rejected it outright. Significantly, however, Irgun's attacks on the Arabs were countered with far more ferocity on the part of the British than had been the case when the latter were combating the so-called Arab revolt. Mass arrests were made, often indiscriminately, and prison conditions were extremely harsh.

But for the Jews there was one friend at least on the British side. In 1936 an unconventional young officer had arrived in Palestine. He was Captain Orde Charles Wingate, born in India of a military family and a cousin of the one-time British High Commissioner in Egypt, Sir Reginald Wingate. He swiftly summed up the military situation and was appalled at the failure of the British to check the Arabs' constant raids on the Iraq Petroleum Company's pipelines, which were buried only one metre underground and therefore easily and quickly located by Arab guerrillas in surprise night attacks. Wingate decided that something could and should be done about this, and, being impressed with the Jews as potential soldiers and having talked with Haganah Intelligence officers, he went to see General Sir Archibald Wavell, the Commander-in-Chief of British Forces in the Middle East. The deceptively taciturn Wavell was in an unostentatious way gifted with a lively imagination and, fortunately for Wingate and the Jews, he quickly approved the young officer's plan for co-operating with Haganah and setting up special squads of Jews to combat the Arab terrorists. For a short time Wingate was given a free hand, much to the disgust of some senior British

Army officers. He summed up his own feelings when he declared: 'When I came to Palestine I found a whole people who had been looked down upon and made to feel unwanted for centuries, yet they were undefeated and building their country anew. I felt I belonged to such a people.'

So Orde Wingate was destined to give a further boost to the organisation of an underground Israeli Intelligence. He linked the British authorities to the Jewish community in a common cause for a brief period, forming Jewish night patrols to tackle the problem of policing the oil pipelines, teaching them how to obtain intelligence on Arab movements. Such was Wingate's enthusiasm and sudden-found passion for Zionism that he went far beyond his brief. In talks with Jewish sergeants when he gave them lectures, he would preface these with a few words in Hebrew: 'we are here to found a Jewish army.' That both thrilled and inspired his listeners; it would have given some British Army officers apoplexy.[1]

Slowly the Arab attacks on the pipelines were checked. One of the guides of the patrols was the young Moshe Dayan, who worked for eight Palestinian pounds a month while attached to a unit of the British Army. He has often recalled his first encounter with Wingate and the tremendous impression this eccentric British soldier made on him and all other members of Haganah who met him. After giving one of his lectures, Wingate agreed to lead the men of Shimron on a night patrol in the Nazareth Mountains. 'It created a sensation at the time,' said Dayan afterwards. '... I doubted that he would be able to keep up the brisk pace. He seemed so fragile.... By dawn my doubts had evaporated. On my home ground this unusual British officer knew better than I what to do.... In all matters military I thought that Wingate was a genius, an innovator and a nonconformist.'[2]

It was Wingate who taught Haganah that offence was the best form of defence. He instilled into them an aggressive spirit that had previously been missing and showed them all the tricks of night-fighting, even putting tail-lights on the bonnets of patrol cars to baffle the enemy. The Englishman had a dual dream, a fanatical, religious passion for Zionism and the founding of a state for the Jews, and a patriotic belief in the British Empire. He did not find these two dreams incompatible. The one went logically with the other as far as he was concerned.

Wingate had already made up his mind that Germany was Britain's real enemy and he visualised a Jewish state, possibly linked with the British Empire in some way, as the best ally for any confrontation with the Germans in the Middle East. It is said that he had mapped out a secret plan for the creation of a Jewish army to fight alongside the British in the event of war. But soon Wingate was recalled to London and his night patrols were disbanded. He learned to his cost that he had too many enemies in Palestine, not merely among the Arabs, but among his own brother officers, some of whom behaved disgracefully towards him.

It was perhaps in Burma with his famed Chindits that Wingate, by then a brigadier-general, became best known in World War II before his tragic death in an air crash in 1944. He did not live to see the Jews gain independence, but his widow did. During the War of Independence of 1947–8, Lorna Wingate wanted to fly to a besieged Jewish settlement to give encouragement. Unable to land at the village, she attached a Bible to a parachute which was dropped to the people below. Inside was a note saying: 'This Bible represents a covenant between us in victory or defeat, now and forever.'

If Wingate had been the instigator of new techniques for combating the Arabs and had brought new ideas to the Haganah Intelligence officers, it was Sir William Stephenson who largely paved the way for a co-ordinated Jewish scientific intelligence organisation. This was started not as a deliberate plan, but almost haphazardly through a few casual friendships and then, via Stephenson, formed the nucleus of an unofficial Jewish scientific intelligence system that achieved great success both before and during World War II. It also formed the basis of the future Israeli scientific intelligence network.

The system, which began almost involuntarily, soon lent itself to the Allied cause not merely in Europe and the Middle East, but in the United States and Canada, too. It was the young Dr. Louis Slotin, born in 1912 of prosperous Jewish parents in Winnipeg, who was the forgotten hero and martyr of the quest for the nuclear weapon. Slotin, who had entered the University of Manitoba at the age of fifteen, studied at London and Chicago Universities before he became an unpaid assistant for two years on cyclotron work. Slotin knew something of what the Germans

were planning to do in this field of weaponry and his own carefully gleaned intelligence brought him into the hush-hush Man-
hattan Project for atomic research and in 1943 he went to Los
Alamos. He had begged the authorities to let him go as an observer on the raid which dispatched the first atomic bombs on
Japanese soil, but they refused. Then, in May 1946, Slotin
became a victim of radiation rays in a dangerous nuclear experi-
ment he was carrying out. Those near him at the time said afterwards that he could have saved his own life, but he preferred to
ensure the safety of others present in the laboratory. He died a
few days later.

Jewish scientists working in the defence research branch of
the French General Staff kept Stephenson informed of all
developments, taking a tremendous risk by staying on in Paris
during the German occupation. They were Dr. Alfred Eskenazy,
a specialist in electronic controls for pilotless aircraft, and Professor André Heilbronner, an expert on rocket fuels. Both men
later formed part of the Marco Polo espionage group, whose
members took code names from science fiction.

Inside Palestine any question of finding a new solution to the
Arab–Jewish problem was shelved when war was declared in
September 1939. On that very day, acting with commendable
promptness, Chaim Weizmann announced the support of the
Jewish people in Palestine for the Allied war effort. This was
swiftly followed by more than 30,000 Jews volunteering to serve
with the Allied Forces. An effort was made to create a Jewish
Legion. Early in the war Zionist leaders decided that a Jewish
armed force, serving with the Allies in the Middle East, would
serve as a useful bargaining counter with the British for the creation of an independent Jewish state when war ended. Successive
British administrators showed a singular lack of imagination at the
best and downright anti-Jewish bias at the worst in not encouraging this move. One of the main enemies of Britain was the pro-
Nazi Mufti of Jerusalem and the British even turned down a cast-
iron project by a joint Arab–Jewish team to eliminate him. Had
Wingate then been in Palestine, the Mufti might well have been
tracked down and killed. But the period between 1938 and 1943,
though bringing countless offers of help by Jews for the Allied
cause, was marked by crass stupidity by the British in their
handling of affairs in Palestine. They drove Irgun Zvai Leumi
to extremes of terrorism not originally contemplated by a series

of repressive measures. Much of the dissension was originally caused by the execution in the spring of 1938 of Shlomo Tabachnik, a Jewish youth of twenty-one who had only recently made his way illegally into Palestine from Poland. His crime was admittedly a serious one; he had fired on an Arab bus after witnessing several Arab attacks on his village. Nobody was injured, but Tabachnik was hanged just the same, despite worldwide appeals for clemency.

On the eve of war the British Government had introduced a new White Paper proposing that in the next five years a total of only 75,000 Jews were to be allowed into Palestine and after that immigration was to cease. Even a moderate Zionist such as Vladimir Jabotinsky, who had expressed revulsion for assassination methods, came out in support of Irgun. There were some sporadic attacks by Haganah against certain British buildings in Palestine, but these were met with far greater ruthlessness than the British had shown against the Arabs. David Raziel, head of Irgun, and his deputy, Avraham Stern, were both arrested. Irgun's reply was to extend their propaganda into Europe, to launch a newspaper which was clandestinely circulated in Poland and other Eastern European countries.

The assassination of Lord Moyne, who had been Colonial Secretary in the British Government after the death of Lord Lloyd, has often been referred to as one of the blackest deeds perpetrated by Irgun. Indeed, after it occurred, some moderate Zionist leaders, including even Ben-Gurion, seized the chance to denounce Irgun and co-operate with the British. Yet no man did more than Moyne to exacerbate relations between Britain and the Palestinian Jews and to take no pains to hide his anti-Semitism. Tolerated under the Churchill Government, which was surprising enough, he survived politically to emerge as British Resident Minister in Cairo. Two examples of Moyne's intransigent attitude to the Jews were his sabotaging of the scheme for a Jewish unit within the British Army (supported by Churchill and Eden initially) after an officer had actually been appointed to command it, and his refusal to allow a Jewish ship carrying refugees from Rumania to put in at a Palestinian port in 1942. The ship, which had been forced to put in at Istanbul because of engine trouble, carried 760 refugees. When Moyne refused entry, the Turkish authorities ordered the ship to return to Rumania, having her forcibly towed out into the Black Sea. The ship blew up and sank. These incidents may not excuse the killing of Lord Moyne, but they do a great deal to explain it.

It is not surprising that many Jews in Palestine and far beyond its borders still wondered whether the British Government was not harbouring Nazi sympathisers. The truth was that Lord Moyne was frequently operating in direct opposition to Churchill's own wishes. Indeed Churchill himself wrote to Moyne in 1943, making it abundantly clear that he was personally hostile to the White Paper limiting Jewish immigration introduced by the Chamberlain Government: 'I have always regarded it [the White Paper] as a gross breach of faith. . . . My position remains strictly that set forth in the speech I made in the House of Commons in the debate on the White Paper. I am sure the majority of the present War Cabinet would never agree to any positive endorsement of the White Paper.'

The assassination of Lord Moyne was carried out with sophistication and cool planning by an extremist group known as LHI (Lohamei Herut Israel), a dissident group which was called the 'Stern Gang' by the British because it was led by Avraham Stern. The latter's commanding officer in Irgun, David Raziel, was released from Acre Prison by the British who, when the pro-German revolt began in Iraq in 1941, asked him to go to Iraq to arrange and command guerrilla actions behind the lines. Raziel, a soldier and a patriot, unhesitatingly agreed; he was killed in a bomb attack before he was able to start his work. If the British had been wise, they would have made an approach to Avraham Stern immediately after Raziel's death. Cynically, they regarded Raziel as expendable, and it was this which made Avraham increasingly bitter. He had always urged carrying on the fight against the British even in the middle of the war against Hitler, but after Raziel's death he insisted that the real enemy was not Hitler's Germany, but Britain. Stern, a scholar who was also a poet, being the author of 'Anonymous Soldiers' the battle hymn of Irgun, decided to test his theories. In the summer of 1941 he set in motion a devious plan for making a deal with Hitler. It was not such an insane scheme as it sounded: indeed, it was a plan which showed the hall-mark of the astute intelligence mind. Stern's plan was to turn Hitler's anti-Semitism to the advantage of the Jews. Hitler wanted to be rid of the Jews; all right then, the Palestinian Jews would help him to achieve this and at the same time make things awkward for the British. What Stern required was a bargain with Hitler for him to send a fleet of ships containing tens of thousands of Jews into the Mediterranean not merely to sail for Palestine, but to break the British blockade and upset all the Royal Navy's dispositions. If it succeeded, tens of thousands more Jews would reach Palestine; if it failed, then the propaganda value against Britain might force them to reconsider their priorities.

First of all Stern dispatched Naftali Lubentschik to Syria, then controlled by the Vichy French Government, to establish contacts with the Germans and Italians. Lubentschik was arrested and this preliminary plan failed. Stern was, however, unshakable in his determination once he was convinced of the value of an idea, and he next sent Nathan Friedman-Yellin, his closest colleague, to start negotiations. But Friedman-Yellin was also arrested in Syria en route for Rumania. Stern's scheme was conjured up in a mood of reckless bitterness and, though having a certain logic, took no account of logistics in wartime. Shmuel Katz summed up the fatuity of it when he wrote that Stern's plan was one 'born of desperation. It failed to see the overriding, all-embracing menace of Nazism to the survival of our people. . . . An agreement with Hitler was impracticable; to make the scheme feasible Hitler would have had to remove from his forces in North Africa the shipping on which they were dependent for their supplies, which in turn meant that he would have had to give up North Africa altogether.'[3]

Stern was relentlessly hunted down by the British. Finally, in February 1942, he was located by British police in a flat in the middle of Tel Aviv and reported to have been 'shot while trying to escape'.

Nevertheless, during World War II the aid which Britain obtained from the Jews was of almost inestimable value. It was not merely what the scientists achieved in terms of intelligence, but the activities of those on active service. It was during World War II that many of the Jews who eventually formed the nucleus of the early Israeli Secret Service learned what intelligence was all about and developed a technique that was in many ways superior to anything possessed by the great powers. Above all they learned how to win against tremendous odds, and this is just what their successors have been doing ever since. Without the assistance of the Jewish Agency scientists the Allies might well not have won the war before the end of 1946, or might even have lost it. Certainly their role in helping not merely to win it, but to develop the nuclear deterrent for the Western Allies has never received adequate acknowledgement. And without that deterrent World War II might easily have turned into World War III, with a confrontation between the West and Russia before 1947.

It was not only in the laboratories, but on the battlefields, too, that Jews played a remarkable part in this war. Two in particular deserve singling out—Jack Nissenthal and Peretz Rose. Nissenthal was the son of a Jewish tailor who had settled in London after escaping from Poland. Highly intelligent, quick-witted, disciplined and brave, he became one of the younger members of Sir Robert Watson-Watt's radar and electronics research team. He was temporarily attached to the RAF with the rank of sergeant and was specially selected to take part in the Dieppe Raid because he had detailed knowledge of radar. The task assigned to him was to go ashore and, within a relatively short time, locate the enemy's equivalent of the cavity magnetron upon which the flexibility of radar depended. The object was to compare British and German radar.

The name of this operation within an operation was Jubilee and in many respects it was more important than the Dieppe Raid itself. What is interesting is that the name Jubilee was chosen because of its Jewish associations and the fact that it owed its origin to Jewish enterprise. Sergeant Rose had been an electronics and communications expert for the Jewish Agency and its secret organisation within Haganah. He came from Germany originally and had been called in to interrogate a captured German electronics expert. From his shrewd and knowledgeable questioning Rose deduced that the Germans had radar stations all along their European coastal 'wall' and that the chief of these was at Dieppe. Other refugee German scientists had indicated to Sir William Stephenson that the Germans had made great strides in radar. Later, when Peretz Rose retired to an Israeli settlement near Haifa, he declared that 'the code name Jubilee came out of a discussion with Stephenson, Chaim Weizmann and other Jewish leaders. Weizmann, as a scientist, was in touch with Germans on matters like the atomic bomb. . . . I regarded him as the man working for a Jewish national home. Somehow we got talking about Jewish Biblical traditions. If ever Hitler was destroyed and Europe liberated, it would be like that Biblical period when slaves are freed and the land restored to its rightful owners—the period the Jews traditionally call Jubilee.'[4]

Rose and Nissenthal were accompanied on their mission by an FBI agent and a number of Canadian Army sharpshooters who had strict instructions to shoot both men dead if they were in danger of being captured by the enemy. It was felt that their combined knowledge was far too important to risk any chance of either man talking after being tortured by their captors. There was a ruthless brutality about the British attitude to these two brave men that must have made them feel they were operating against the threats of their own side and the enemy. Both of them luckily survived; they went ashore and reached the radio-detection station above Dieppe Harbour. The aim was to demolish the radar after key pieces from the unit had been removed.

Neither Rose nor Nissenthal were awarded any medals for their splendid work which ultimately made the invasion of Normandy by the Allies a much less costly operation than it would otherwise have been. Both men were exceptionally shabbily treated by the British.

It is important to stress these examples of the inestimable services rendered by many Jews to the Allies in World War II not only to show that they had earned some special recognition when peace came, but also how failure to acknowledge the part they had played and a refusal to do anything about a national home drove them to extreme measures.

In the Special Operations Executive organisation alone Jews played a prominent part. Professor M. R. D. Foot, in his official history of the SOE, tells how Peter Churchill when landed by submarine in France 'recruited George Levin as his second-in-command in Lyons, the hub of his circuit; Levin like himself was a Jew, and they recruited several Jewish friends, notably two Racheline brothers. As Jews, they all ran bigger risks than gentiles in working against the Germans, but were even more determined anti-Nazis.' Foot also makes the point that some of SOE's enemies took malicious pleasure in the knowledge that a few of its staff and agents were of enemy nationality: 'most of these had some Jewish blood,' he writes, 'this made them thoroughly anti-Nazi and their efficiency was beyond question in every case.'[5]

People like these and others who had served in Sir William

Stephenson's Intrepid network spied for, fought for and helped to establish the state of Israel after World War II. Swiftly Irgun began to extend its tentacles to America and Europe. In 1944 Hillel Kook, an active Irgun member, went to the USA, under the name of Peter Bergson, to set up the American Emergency Committee for Zionist Affairs and, more especially, the Bergson Group, which was partly propagandist and partly a miniature Secret Service in the USA, enabling Irgun agents to glean political secrets from both the White House and the State Department.

Between 1945 and 1947 there was something like total war between Irgun, Haganah and LHI on the one hand and the British in Palestine on the other. But it was Irgun who set the pace. Towards the end of the war there had been some diplomatic blunders by the British which were not properly seen as such at that time. One was the disastrous intervention of Brigadier-General Spears and his policy in the Lebanon and Syria which managed at one and the same time to alienate both the Jews and the French. This resulted in a warm relationship between the Israeli Freedom Fighters and the French Government immediately after the war. There was also the failure by the British Government, despite pleas from many quarters, to launch a rescue operation to the Nazi concentration camps before the war was ended. Marshal of the RAF Sir Arthur 'Bomber' Harris declared afterwards that a rescue plan was 'perfectly feasible, but I was never asked to undertake it.' What the British never realised—at least in the heady days of victory—was that while they might have won the war against the common enemy, the Jews, the Poles and countless others for whom they were supposed to be fighting had been decimated, exterminated and left without hope.[6]

Irgun's chief aim after the overriding priority of creating the state of Israel was to step up immigration into Palestine. The organisation for smuggling Jews out of Europe and North Africa to Palestine was strengthened. At the same time Haganah sabotaged ships used by the British to deport Jews from Palestine. It was a highly efficient operation, starting in the Displaced Persons Camps in Europe, where the escape of Jewish inmates was implemented, the caring for them in transit centres and bringing them to embarkation ports whence they were shipped to Palestine. It was a plan which would have frustrated any but the most determined organisation, for, while occasionally a refugee ship would evade the British patrols, the great majority were stopped and taken to Haifa and the passengers sent to Cyprus. Irgun meanwhile built up its organisation inside Europe, thus paving the way for an ultimate intelligence network for the future state of Israel.

France became a central base for Irgun activity. Here the Jews were helped partly by a sympathetic attitude of consecutive French governments towards their aspirations as well as by receiving the active support of those of their race who had gained knowledge of underground organisation work in the Resistance. Prominent among these was Madame Claire Vayda, an ex-Resistance fighter who, though not a member of Irgun, lent them support and lobbied for the Zionist cause in government and other circles. The top Irgun officer in France was Dr. Shmuel Ariel, and their key man in Italy was Yaacov Tavin, who had taken a degree in philosophy at the Hebrew University before becoming head of the Irgun Intelligence Department in Palestine. Tavin operated under a number of aliases, being known as 'Pesach', 'Eliezer' and 'Eli'. In many respects he was even more outstanding than the handsome and formidable Menahem Begin, the co-ordinating genius of Irgun, especially in Europe. Tavin not only proved to be a brilliant organiser of intelligence and operations in Italy, but was a first class recruiter and trainer of agents.

It was Tavin who was the prime instigator of the bomb attack by Irgun agents on the British Embassy in Rome, which had become a symbol of opposition to Jewish immigration, much of which passed through Italy en route from northern and eastern Europe. Immediately the embassy was blown up Irgun issued a communiqué announcing the opening of a new and more ruthless campaign against the British, indicating that this would be developed inside Britain.

Irgun's terrorist campaign horrified many Jews just as much as it angered the British people. Moderate Jews realised that Britain, as the mandatory power in Palestine, had an unenviable task in trying to maintain a balance between Jews and Arabs. But it was far too late for moderation to succeed in Palestine. As in Northern Ireland, a running political sore had been allowed to fester for too long. From the point of view of the Jews (and here even their moderates were wrong) only aggressive action could at this stage ensure the setting up of a Zionist state. Ernest Bevin, the British Foreign Secretary, was not so much anti-Semitic as stubborn and he was unfortunately backed by the pro-Arab lobby which has always existed within the British Foreign Office itself.

Irgun's threats to carry out a terrorist campaign in London created considerable alarm and hysterical stories appeared in the British press, but in fact Irgun's terrorist activities were well controlled, disciplined and rarely indiscriminate. Never were they on anything like the senseless, purposeless scale of attacks by Northern Ireland terrorists against women and children as well as men. Even the bombing of the King David Hotel in Jerusalem was planned with care and precision, being directed against only the south wing where the Military Government operated. Some eighty lives were lost, but this was due chiefly to British officials ignoring a warning given to them by an Irgun agent just under half an hour before the explosion.

Perhaps the most spectacular of Irgun's operations was the destruction of twenty-two RAF planes on the ground at Kastina airport. By 1947 Irgun had proved that it was the focal point of the fight for independence and had won grudging respect even from the British. Had Irgun stepped up their terrorist campaign, it might have been counter-productive. But, whatever the pros and cons may have been it cannot be denied that their actions were usually against specifically military targets and not too costly in loss of life.

Irgun's law was that of an eye for an eye and a tooth for a tooth, but they did not go beyond this. Their enemies have said that they who opposed Hitler used Hitlerian methods. Not so. The Nazis would take scores of innocent civilian hostages and shoot them for the loss of a single member of the SS. When a seventeen-year-old Jew was sentenced to eighteen years' imprisonment and eighteen lashes for carrying arms, Irgun warned the British not to carry out the flogging, but made no reference to the sentence of imprisonment. The Irgun soldier was flogged and within forty-eight hours two British officers were kidnapped by Irgun agents and given eighteen lashes each before being released.

That was the difference—a very great difference—between Irgun tactics and those of Hitler and his minions.

3

The Creation of
Shin Beth

*There will come about an age of small and in-
dependent nations whose first line of defence will
be knowledge.*

(CHARLES PROTEUS STEINMETZ)

THE FOREGOING QUOTATION was written by a Jewish scientist
who believed, even in the late twenties, that liberty was exemplified in the small nations who struggled for independence. But he
believed even more strongly that only by a ruthless dedication to
knowledge (by which he meant intelligence) could such nations
hope to survive. It was Steinmetz who encouraged Jewish scientists in Germany and elsewhere to acquire this specialised knowledge, if necessary by espionage, subterfuge and cunning, if they
wished to see the Jews survive as a free people.

It was through Steinmetz's teaching, his constant urging for
the quest for knowledge that Jewish intellectuals came to be
brought to work on the decoding of enemy signals in World War
II. They were among the people who decoded German signals in
what was known as the Enigma Chain.

Hebrew literature is filled with examples of ancient forms of
cryptography and code systems of letter substitution dating back
for centuries. Hebrew numbers, like Roman numbers, were
written with the letters of the Hebrew alphabet and the sub-
stitutes were chosen from the first nine letters of the alphabet so
that they would add up to ten. There are countless examples of
cryptograms in the Bible and even the meaningless names Shad-
rach, Meshach and Abednego are believed to be a code for the
names of real kings or leaders. The skill of cryptanalysis has been
handed down for generations among the Jews and doubtless

during the long centuries of persecution the preservation of codes and ciphers was invaluable to their scholars.

During the last few years of the struggle against the British prior to the granting of independence to Israel, the nucleus of a Secret Service had already been forged for the nation to be. It consisted partly of the ablest of those Zionists who had undertaken Intelligence and Resistance work of various kinds in World War II, but in the main it comprised the intelligence-gathering organisations of Haganah and Irgun Zvai Leumi.

Just as it was out of the secret army of Haganah—Zva Haganah Le'Israel—that the Israeli Defence Force developed, so it was from such organisations as the Mossad Le Aliyah Beth (Institution for Intelligence and Special Services), the Shai and the Rekhesh that the Israeli Secret Service emerged. The Mossad Le Aliyah Beth, out of which the Mossad of today grew, was founded as a secret army in 1937, created by Haganah mainly for carrying out the large-scale 'illegal' immigration known in Hebrew as *Ha'apala*. The Mossad was largely the inspiration of Eliahu Golomb and Shaul Avigur. Gradually, however, the tasks set for it increased and eventually included espionage, especially overseas, the procuring of arms and counter-espionage. Also, though not generally appreciated at the time, the hierarchy of the Mossad kept a close watch on breakaway, extremist Jewish movements in Palestine.

It was at Golomb's home in Tel Aviv that the Mossad was planned. It should be stressed that it was essentially a Haganah institution which had no links with any extremist movements. At the same time that the Mossad was set up, a miniature 'naval base' was established in secret at Caesarea for Palyam, which became the maritime branch of Palmach, which provided the striking arm of Haganah. Later this was a centre for the training of personnel to man the refugee-carrying ships. Golomb died before the Mossad developed into a powerful Secret Service in miniature, but as early as 1942 some carefully chosen men and women— forty in all—attended a secret course at Mikveh Israel, an agricultural school outside Tel Aviv. These members of the Mossad were coached in map-reading, marksmanship, cryptography and the planning of escape routes.

Shaul Avigur was born in Dvinsk in Latvia and he emigrated to Palestine in 1912. He was one of the founders in 1940 of the Shai, an underground intelligence service for Haganah. The word Shai was an acronym of the Hebrew for 'Information Service'. Avigur was assisted by Yehudi Arazi (later commander of Shai in Europe) and David Shaltiel. The Mossad depended heavily on Shai, especially for the screening of Haganah members, checking their credentials, keeping a watch on Arab agents (with some of whom they established secret contacts) and also informing themselves on British Special Branch Police activities. Yehudi Arazi himself not only joined the Palestine Police, and so kept a watch on British intentions, but was an adviser on Arab movements, as well as keeping in close touch with Rekhesh, Haganah's own arms and munitions procurement branch. Shaul Avigur later became an adviser to Israel's first Prime Minister.

Shai was astonishingly efficient and without it the Mossad could not have carried on as well as it did. The upper echelons of Shai comprised some of the best brains in intelligence and at the same time extended its network to include thousands of volunteers and freelance agents. Usually when any Intelligence Service increases its organisation to this extent, it risks running into trouble. The organisers of Shai were clever enough to reduce this risk by setting up their own counter-espionage section. Without any aid from any other organisations Shai set out to screen all its many informers and to eliminate the untrustworthy. At the same time it established a British Department which was charged not only with obtaining information on British plans, but with ensuring that false information was planted on British GHQ.

Shai agents were everywhere—in the customs, the police, the postal services and offices dealing with transport. The result was that the Arab guerrilla forces had far more of their arms seized than did the Jews. Shai was kept well informed on all Arab arms caches. When there was a question of smuggling arms into the country, it greatly aided Rekhesh, ensuring that their agents in customs connived at the entry of munitions. Yet another of Shai's activities was the setting up of the 'Voice of Israel', Haganah's secret transmitter, which was a constant source of irritation to the British.

During World War II Haganah had actively co-operated with the British against the Germans in the Middle East and at the same time had, towards the end of the war, surreptitiously 'acquired' substantial amounts of small armaments from the British Army and from weapons abandoned in various parts of the Middle East. British security in guarding against such tactics had been very lax. But immediately after the war Rekhesh set out to buy surplus arms from European countries. In this task Rekhesh was greatly assisted both by the Mossad and Shai. Meanwhile Palyam had been recruited for tasks in Europe, some of its members being used to act as mates to the various foreign captains of illegal immigrant ships. Their real duties consisted of keeping a close watch on the captains to ensure there was no double-crossing. Later the Palyam was to form the basis of Israel's first Naval Intelligence Service.

As the Second World War drew to an end the plight of Jews in near-by Moslem states became more serious. In Iraq there were vicious anti-Jewish pogroms and it became necessary for the Mossad to extend its network. Jewish soldiers in Allied armies were used to smuggle in refugees in the back of their lorries and even Arabs were paid by the Mossad to guide Jews across the northern borders into Palestine. More than 8,000 Jews from the Arab lands alone entered the land of their fathers.

Discreet diplomacy, not only by the Mossad and Rekhesh but by some of the top men in Irgun Zvai Leumi as well, had ensured a sympathetic hearing for Israel's cause from the Italian as well as the French authorities. Secret transmitters were set up in Bari, Naples and elsewhere in Italy, which was made a centre for Mossad operations. Their headquarters was established in 1945 in the back room of a Jewish servicemen's club in Milan. Meanwhile another network was set up in France under the command of Shmarya Zameret, who controlled a whole network of secret bases on the French Mediterranean coast from Marseilles.

Before the end of the war in Europe it had been decided that Italy must be the main staging-post for 'illegal' immigrants to Palestine. It was with this aim in view that one young Mossad agent was given a small sum of money and told to find his own way to Europe to organise escape routes through Italy. He took a few companions with him and they travelled to Italy in a British troop ship as members of the Jewish Brigade. On arrival they received help from other Palestinian Jews working for the Allies and Italian Partisans engaged in rounding up Germans. By the time the war in Europe had ended this small group had set up escape routes from Rumania and Yugoslavia to Florence and Pisa. Finally, they bought the hulk of a small, but unfinished fishing craft and eventually made it seaworthy. Yigal Allon writes that 'living on canned food and biscuits donated by the Jewish

Brigade, holding on to their still unspent precious £100, and relying for identification on papers they had forged in the back of a car adroitly turned into a mobile forger's studio, the trio attended to the final preparations: a motor had to be bought for the fishing boat, water had to be obtained and the minimum of food."[1]

This craft, named the *Dallin*, but nicknamed 'The Nutshell' by the Mossad members, eventually took off for Palestine with thirty-five refugees aboard. She was the first of many such craft; altogether more than 40,000 Jews were rescued by the Mossad.

A secret store for the purchases of surplus war material was also set up in Milan. Patiently at first, and in small quantities at a time, the majority of these arms were smuggled into Palestine during 1947. It was estimated that by the end of that year 193 Bren guns, 1,500 rifles, 378 sub-machine guns and more than a million rounds of ammunition had been received by agents of Haganah and Irgun Zvai Leumi.

David Ben-Gurion, the outstanding genius of Haganah, had long foreseen that, even if the state of Israel was created, the new nation would face constant threats from some of the surrounding Arab nations right from its inception. Once independence was won, the real struggle would begin—the War of Independence with the Arabs, which actually began in sporadic fashion before Israel came into being. To stand up to this menace not only were large stocks of arms needed, but the creation of an Israeli Air Force. With this in mind Ben-Gurion persuaded various wealthy Jewish industrialists, mainly American, to raise not only capital, but to provide equipment for the establishment of an arms industry in Palestine. One of the side effects of this drive was the creation of Bedeh Aircraft, which later changed its name to Israel Aircraft Industries.

In the early stages Czechoslovakia was earmarked as the most promising source of supply for arms, not only because it was an arms-producing country, but because at that time it was freer from Soviet domination than any of the other Soviet bloc countries of Eastern Europe. Nevertheless it still required Secret Service style activities to plan the purchase of such arms. The Palestinian Jews were helped by a former German Jew who had been one of a number of such Jews specially recruited by Admiral Canaris as agents for his *Abwehr* (German Secret Service) mainly to enable them to escape to foreign lands. Canaris disapproved of the Nazis' treatment of the Jews and he also thought highly of them as Intelligence agents, but his surreptitious generosity was one of the factors which cost him his life when the Nazis finally arrested him. A team of four men was also sent from Palestine to Prague in December 1947, with the express purpose of negotiating arms purchases. Leader of this group was Ehud Avriel, who was given a forged identity document showing that he was Herr Ueberall, an agent of the Swiss Government. In Prague Avriel made contact with two Haganah resident agents, Uriel Doron and Pino Ginsberg. Together they approached the Czechoslovakian Ministries of Defence and Supply and within two months had concluded the first major arms deal.

The Czechs were eager for such a deal because Haganah had arranged through its American network for payment to be made in dollars, the currency for which everyone clamoured in postwar Europe. But what surprised the Jews was that the Russians gave tacit approval to the undercover deal. It was the first sign that the Russians, who had always been indifferent if not actually hostile to the idea of a Jewish national home, were prepared to support the clamour for independence in Palestine. The Communist Party in Palestine had opposed Jewish immigration and the Soviet decision in 1947 to vote for the establishment of a Jewish state at the United Nations came as a surprise to the Jews themselves. The Soviet Union was in fact the first nation to give diplomatic recognition to Israel. There was nothing genuine about this seemingly sudden conversion; it was merely that the Russians deliberately exploited the situation to weaken British influence in the Middle East and to try to drive a wedge between British and American governmental views which had been at odds over Britain's Palestinian policy. The 'honeymoon' with Russia did not last for long. The initial indications of Soviet insincerity came when Israel sent her first ambassador, Mrs. Golda Meir, to Moscow, and there was a spontaneous demonstration by Russian Jews on her arrival. Soviet officials were not merely dismayed by this, but were anxious to clamp down on any indication by Russian Jews that they were different from other citizens of the Soviet Union. Within months a new anti-Semitic campaign had been launched and Soviet Jews were instructed that they were to have no links with their co-religionists in Israel or elsewhere. Soon, with the encouragement of Stalin himself, Jewish organisations and individual Jews were openly and officially condemned as 'enemies of the state'.

Much of Haganah's Secret Service was devoted to arms purchases and smuggling in the late forties. Munya Mardor was appointed as the director of the underground network for the dispatch of arms from Czechoslovakia. He was given *carte blanche* by Ben-Gurion to travel wherever necessary in Europe and to organise the long and hazardous pipeline for smuggling the arms out of Czechoslovakia, then via the American zone of Germany into Belgium, whence they went by sea to Palestine. To sail from Belgium to Palestine without being trapped and stopped by the Royal Navy, busily engaged in policing the Mediterranean for immigrant traffic, required considerable ingenuity on the part of the agents of Haganah and Irgun. The most dangerous activities were handled by men in the Rekhesh branch who, in the early stages of their arms procurement campaign, concentrated on obtaining explosives only, as these were cheap, fairly easily stolen or obtained by bribery, and simple to carry. As security was tightened up so explosives were more difficult to obtain in Palestine and great ingenuity was shown by the Rekhesh men who bribed Arabs to let them have small quantities of a special explosive ingredient which they used for firing the cannons to mark sunset at Ramadan. Eventually secret factories for the making of explosives were set up in Palestine.

Overseas Rekhesh men indulged in some daring coups such as looting arms from moving trains and raiding stores for rifles. Italy was the source of a great deal of the armaments obtained, including shells and guns recovered from sunken ships close in to the coast. Yehuda Arazi was one of the most successful Mossad leaders in Italy. He was primarily concerned with arranging arms supplies, mainly concentrating on Milan, but with cells set up in Bari and Naples and with radio links to Istanbul, Athens, Marseilles and Paris. Having escaped from Palestine, where he was wanted by the British authorities, Arazi turned up in Italy wearing the uniform of a Polish airman and made his headquarters at a farm outside Milan, using the code name of 'Alon'. He obtained false papers, set up a bogus military camp of his own and even managed to obtain Army petrol for his secret organisation. Arazi was outwardly a debonair, swashbuckling character who made friends easily, but underneath was a cool, calculating manipulator who maintained radio contact with Palestine via some roundabout routes, arranged that each Palestinian Jewish unit stationed in Italy should deliver to him a fixed levy of petrol and other fuels and enable him to take over any jeeps or trucks which they left behind when being demobilised.

The obtaining of arms for the Jews was always fraught with difficulties, in addition to which they had to contend with a constant watch by the Royal Navy throughout the Mediterranean. During this period the author of this book was a foreign correspondent covering the whole of North-West Africa, based on the then International Zone of Tangier. In the course of my journalistic duties I saw a great deal of the undercover work in which secret agents of the Israeli cause involved themselves to ensure a safe passage for both arms and immigrants.

Even in the autumn of 1946 Tangier in particular and North Africa in general had become a centre for 'illegal' immigration, partly of European Jews who found it relatively easy to obtain admission to the International Zone and partly of North African Jews, some of whom feared the granting of independence to Arabs in Morocco and Tunisia and others who were encouraged to migrate for the sake of the Zionist cause. In Algeria the situation was made easier for the Jews by the connivance of gendarmes and custom officials who at that time were in sympathy with the French police strike.

One of the stories I filed at this time told how 'responding to an urgent request to protect British property, the Royal Navy frigate *St. Bride's Bay*, carrying a detachment of the Liverpool Scottish Regiment, arrived at Tangier from Gibraltar. . . . The action follows Arab demonstrations throughout the week in the International Zone, resulting from the mobilisation of troops in the Spanish Zone [of Morocco] and the arrival of Goum troops in Tangier. Members of the Moroccan Independence movement . . . protest against Jewish refugee arrivals in Tangier.'[2] It was a story which was emphatically denied in London both by the War Office and the Foreign Office, but nonetheless was printed by the *Sunday Times*. The fact was the British were made to look fools by sending over a ship when there was no sign of any real threat to Consular or other British property. What was omitted from the story, which brought upon my head the wrath of the British Consulate-General in Tangier, was that British Intelligence in the area had been totally panicked by false information about an Arab rising planted by Jewish agents to distract the British from certain small ships which at the same time were slipping through the Straits of Gibraltar with arms for Haganah.

Tangier was at that time administered by a Portuguese admiral and was run by a Committee of Control comprising British, Belgian, Dutch, French and Spanish representatives. During World War II it had been one of the world's chief spy centres and in the immediate post-war years was one of the easiest places in which to plant false rumours, largely because of the presence of a large number of freelance spies (most of them serving more than one country) who feared being made redundant and were anxious to capitalise on any scare which would make espionage worth while again. Jewish agents took full advantage of this state of affairs. They had a small but efficient organisation in Tangier, which was a vital transit point in their arms traffic because it was opposite the port of Gibraltar. This organisation had two purposes: first, and perhaps most effective, to mislead British Naval Intelligence in Gibraltar, and, secondly, to receive and re-route arms supplies. One day custom officials in Tangier seized a large quantity of Commando-type knives with 'WD' (War Department) markings, which had been smuggled in from Antwerp. Police inquiries revealed that these and other consignments of arms, including machine-guns, were intended for an agent of the Mossad (not Irgun Zvai Leumi, as was reported at the time).

By mid-1947 arms traffic through the Straits of Gibraltar had reached considerable proportions. I wrote in a dispatch on 1 June 1947, that information concerning the traffic 'was responsible for the special ordinance allowing the Governor of Gibraltar to detain any ship suspected of being engaged in illegal immigration and gun-running to Palestine. The seizure this week of the ship *Colony Trader*, flying the Costa Rican flag, was the first step in a carefully laid plan to suppress the increasing traffic. Key ports in the business are Gibraltar, Tangier and Oran, where there is a Jewish immigrant colony awaiting passage to Palestine. Many boats used for arms running and immigrant carrying are ex-Royal Navy craft recently disposed of by the Admiralty. A number of purchases of the boats were made through the International Exchange Market in Tangier, where dollars were paid for the craft. British Intelligence sources now have adequate proof of how Admiralty agents have been deceived by the buyers. Arms, including machine-guns, ammunition and bombs have been traced from Eire, Central America and Belgium, shipped by coastal cargo vessels through the Mediterranean. The arms are transferred at night to a ship in Tangier harbour.'[3]

All this was part of the Tangier-based organisation's plan to hoodwink the Royal Navy which had hitherto only kept a look-out for ships actually sailing from Belgian ports. By transferring arms at night from one large ship to two or sometimes even three quite small craft the planners of these clandestine operations were able to disperse their arms and often slip through the Navy's net.

With the exception of Czechoslovakia the Mossad and Rek-hesh found it extremely difficult to obtain arms from the Iron Curtain countries. Willy Katz, a Mossad agent, was sent to Rumania towards the end of 1947 to seek the aid of the formid-able Anna Pauker, then First Secretary of the Communist Party and every bit as tough a leader as any of the heads of Communist governments in Eastern Europe. There were long delays in nego-tiations, vague hints that perhaps next week something might be done, and in the end nothing at all was offered. Much the same story was true of Poland, Bulgaria and Hungary. The Mossad set up a special headquarters in Istanbul to try to make undercover arrangements with certain Iron Curtain countries.

It proved even slower and harder work to create an effective Israeli Air Force. When, after Israel was created, the War of Independence with the Arabs began, the latter had a hundred aircraft and it was not until January 1948, that the Israeli Air Force started its career with eight light aircraft that had been clandestinely acquired. One amusing sideline on the secret attempts to build up the force is the story of how the RAF (Palestine) disposed of twenty-five aircraft as scrap, little knowing that the dealer who bought them was an undercover agent of Haganah. They were dismantled and the various parts and sections used to build up eighteen new planes.[4]

Meanwhile Shai was operating in Palestine itself with a superb counter-espionage set-up. It owed much to the initial work of Yehuda Arazi before he went to Europe, but in the last two years of the British mandate it functioned like a well-oiled machine. One of Shai's most devastating achievements as far as the British were concerned was its patient acquisition of the British CID's 'black book', or dossier of literally thousands of suspected Hag-anah, Irgun and Mossad agents. This carefully compiled book was intended for instant use when the order was given for a round-up of Jewish terrorists. Using agents they had carefully planted within the clerical staff of the Palestinian Police, Shai obtained a few pages at a time of the 'black book', had them copied and returned to the CID files. It was a slow process, but it meant that the British had no idea what was going on. A secret room for cameramen and typists was set up for handling the information contained in the dossier; all those listed were warned of what was happening and told to move to new addresses, or go underground completely.

'We could not have succeeded quite so well without the help and connivance of a very friendly Englishman inside the CID,' one of the Haganah agents told me. 'It was slow work, but we completed it before the British gave the order for a round-up. That attempt at a round-up was almost a total flop.'

Even General Barker, the GOC British Army in Palestine, admitted ruefully afterwards that 'both Haganah and the Shai caught us napping. They had a brilliant intelligence service.'

Ben-Gurion's greatest achievement when Israel was established was the unifying and nationalising not only of the Haganah secret army units, but all guerrilla forces into the Israeli Defence Force. At the same time he combined the offices of Prime Minister and Minister of Defence in Israel's first government, and from this unique and all-powerful position set about creating the nation's Secret Service. Ben-Gurion was realistic enough to know that Israel would face considerable Arab opposition for the first few years of her existence so he concentrated on ensuring that the Army received the best possible personnel as regards its leaders and senior officers. Consequently the Ministry of Defence suffered somewhat from not having men of the same competence and experience. They were mainly politicians and some of them gave Ben-Gurion management problems.

This did not matter much as long as Ben-Gurion was at the helm, for he not only dominated the Ministry of Defence, but had his own specially close relationships with the Army chiefs. One of his aims was to prevent the Army from becoming politically-minded or in any way linked with political intrigues; he had seen how the French Army had become demoralised and corrupted through the political machinations of a few of its generals. It was Ben-Gurion himself who made all the appointments from the rank of lieutenant-colonel upwards to Chief of Staff, a post which eventually became one of greater importance and influence than that of the Director-General of the Ministry of Defence.

Nobody was more anxious than Ben-Gurion to ensure that Israel's image to the outside world was made to appear moderate, sober and civilised. Wisely, he took the view that one way of ensuring this was to keep a tight control of the newly created Secret Service. Bomb attacks against the British had not particularly alienated world opinion; many French and Italians and perhaps even more Americans openly sympathised with the Jews, and of course the revelation of the horrors of the Nazi policy of extermination had made world opinion generally, excepting the Arab world, favourably disposed to the new state. But the assassination of Count Bernadotte, the UN mediator, suspected of being anti-Jewish, was a different matter. The outside world saw Bernadotte as a genuinely unprejudiced mediator anxious only for a peaceful settlement and at that time the United Nations was actually respected as the new peace-making force. But Bernadotte had not in fact shown the kind of impartiality one would expect from a mediator: he had actually modified his plans by suggesting a United Nations regime for the city when he was informed that some Jews regarded him as a British agent. In September 1948, Count Bernadotte was shot dead while travelling through Jerusalem by car. His assailants were never caught. The British believed that members of the extreme LHI (Lohamei Herut Israel) group were responsible and so did some Israelis. Dr. Dov Joseph, the Military Governor of Jerusalem, announced that the LHI was to be rounded up. Moshe Dayan, then a colonel, sent in troops to carry out these instructions. Hundreds of LHI members were arrested.

However, it was by no means certain that the killing of Bernadotte was the work either of LHI or Irgun Zvai Leumi, or any other extreme terrorist movement. On the Tangier intelligence grapevine at that time there was a strong rumour that Bernadotte was killed as part of a Soviet Secret Service plot to sabotage UN influence in the Middle East and that they had dispatched two Bulgarian Jews to Palestine for this purpose. Israeli Secret Service reports on this subject were vague but not without some substance. But with the state of Israel only a few months old at that time, and relations with Russia still relatively friendly on the surface, Israel did not wish to risk exacerbating an already difficult situation. There was another overriding consideration—the need for improving Israel's image—and this was given the utmost priority by Ben-Gurion. The killing of Bernadotte gave him the chance he had been waiting for, a good excuse for clamping down on and winding up LHI and Irgun. He dealt with LHI first and then turned his attention to Irgun. On 20 September 1948, Yigal Yadin, who was then Chief of Staff, issued this order:

'The Irgun Zvai Leumi in Jerusalem must accept the law of the State regarding the Army, enlistment and arms.

'All members of Irgun liable for mobilisation must join the Haganah Army of Israel.

'The law applying to the Irgun is the law applying to every other Jew.

'If within twenty-four hours beginning today at 1200 hours, you accept the terms: disband the Irgun Zvai Leumi and its special battalions, hand over arms and join the Haganah Army, none of you will suffer for the infringements you have hitherto committed against the law of Israel and you will be treated like every other Jew.

'If within the time stated you do not fulfil the demands of the Government, the Army will act with all the means at its disposal.'

While this decree and the rounding up of the LHI was of inestimable value to Israel in presenting a more orderly face to the rest of the world (not least to those overseas Jews who were not Zionists), these two acts were of paramount importance to ensuring the total integrity and discipline of the new Israeli Secret Service, founded personally the following year by Ben-Gurion. There is some dispute as to which section of the Secret Service came into being first. The old Mossad was merged into the new and official Mossad, but the emphasis in the early stages of the Secret Service was placed on counter-espionage and it was for this reason that Shin Beth (an abbreviation of Sheruth Bitakhon, meaning Security Service) was created. It was primarily aimed at spy-catching, but swiftly developed into the most efficient intelligence-gathering organisation concerned with the Arab world. It soon won the respect of other secret services who found that within a few years the Israelis were far better informed on what was really going on in Egypt, Iraq, Syria, Jordan and Saudi-Arabia than were the great powers themselves.

When Irgun was disbanded, all other unofficial groups disintegrated. Originally the intention had been that if the Irgun would disband and its members enter the Israeli Army, '... the Irgun units would remain intact within the Army and their integrity would not be disturbed.' The disbanding of Irgun was actually resented by a large proportion of the population who believed that, under the command of Menahem Begin, Irgun had won the fight for independence on its own. Ben-Gurion feared the establishment of a group within a group, especially in any Secret Service, and it was for this reason that he delayed the establishment of all sections of the new Secret Service until 1949, after the total disbandment of Irgun, when there was no prospect of any attempt by individuals to create their own pocket of intelligence within the national Secret Service. This could have been disastrous. Ben-Gurion's foresight in this respect and the care, ingenuity and organisational genius he personally displayed in creating Shin Beth marks him out as one of the outstanding political masters of the world since World War II. What Ben-Gurion feared, too, was not so much the domination of Shin Beth by the fanatics of Irgun and LHI, but the exploitation of such dissident voices by outside influences, not least by Soviet Russia. Early in 1948 there had been evidence that Russia was manipulating some Jewish fanatics and that this had led to temporary hesitations in the USA about the administration's pro-Jewish policy in the Middle East. Somebody in the Pentagon had overreacted to this information and had decided that to back the Jews was to play into the hands of the Russians. James V. Forrestal, the US Secretary of Defence, had hinted in private conversations that it might be necessary to abandon support for the Jews to concentrate all efforts against the Russians. In public he expressed this somewhat differently, telling a Senate Committee that 'partition [of Palestine] would endanger American oil resources'.

So Ben-Gurion's plan to recruit most of the personnel for the creation of Shin Beth from Haganah was intended to ensure that Haganah men were put in key positions. At the same time he was enough of a realist to know that there was an enormous amount of talent inside Irgun and even LHI which needed to be harnessed in the cause of the new state. He was determined not to lose the services of such people. So he set in motion a systematic screening of members of both Irgun and LHI with a view to recruiting their best and most reliable and disciplined agents, some in Shin Beth, others in the various branches of the Secret Service. As a result it could be said that within a year or two of its inception Shin Beth in particular and the Israeli Secret Service as a whole comprised the most brilliant team of spies and Intelligence organisers from the combined ranks of Haganah, Irgun and LHI, including a diverse range of talents from professional saboteurs, passport and document forgers to communications experts and code-breakers.

Though from time to time, even in the ranks of Jewry, there have been critical murmurings that some of the personnel of the Israeli Secret Service have been recklessly piratical in some of their actions, there is no doubt that Ben-Gurion's policy of selection was wise. Few Secret Services succeed one hundred per cent unless they have some spark of aggression. This was particularly true of the British Secret Service up to the late twenties; after that it gradually lost its capacity to be feared by its adversaries, though that fear lasted long enough to frighten even the Nazis in the vital 1940 to 1941 period. Without a measure of bold, aggressive action in the field of secret service, Israel might today be in a far weaker position. Breaking the rules, even breaking the law, have proved justified, if one accepts the validity of Machiavellian principles. And a tiny nation surrounded by enemies living almost permanently under threat of war needs to have such principles if only to ensure its existence.

4

Isser Harel and the Mossad

*Arab enmity has helped the Zionists to maintain
what too often disappears in other revolutionary
regimes—an atmosphere of 'permanent revolution'.*

(AMOS ELON IN *The Israelis, Founders and Sons*)

INTERNAL SECURITY and the smack of firm government were
the primary needs of the new state of Israel and to this extent the
Secret Service was first actuated by domestic considerations. But,
as the state, unlike most nations achieving independence, was
actually baptised by fire, the fire of the enemy and the War of
Independence with the Arabs, it swiftly became essential to
develop an overseas intelligence service.

The obvious answer to this was more or less a ready-made one:
to expand the Mossad. Since its inception, as a branch of Haganah, the Mossad had performed the role of foreign intelligence-
gathering to perfection. It was true that this was principally
concerned with illegal immigration and supporting the case of
Zionism, but an existing foreign intelligence service of any kind
was of paramount importance in 1948–49. The Mossad was
almost purpose-built: it was the orthodox foreign intelligence wing
of the old Haganah. The only problem was to extend it quickly
and efficiently and to apply it towards intelligence on Israel's
numerous enemies.

The Israelis knew perfectly well that this was not simply a
matter of obtaining intelligence from inside Arab countries,
many of which at that time—Algeria, Morocco, Tunisia, Libya,
Aden, Egypt—were still more or less under the domination or
protectorship of Britain or France. The new Secret Service needed
to be kept up-to-date on the various shifts in opinion and policy

in the British and French Governments, to have agents in London and Paris, Rabat, Tunis and Algiers no less than Cairo, Damascus and Teheran. They also needed to keep a watchful eye on developments in the United States and Russia. But first of all the Mossad had to be weaned from being the instrument of an underground movement aimed at immigration, and the winning of nationhood to the more formalised espionage service of a nation threatened by war.

Israel needed what would have seemed impossible to any other new nation—a first-class, aggressive secret service which could put itself on a war footing from its inception. While the War of Independence continued Israel faced not only the hostility of the Arab world, but a growing hostility inside Russia. That honeymoon period of seeming friendship which had so surprised Israel when the Soviet Union backed her cause in 1947 at the United Nations swiftly soured. An anti-Zionist campaign was stepped up in the Soviet press, Jews in Russia were sacked from key posts and very few Jewish technicians were left in positions of any influence. The truth was that once Israel was created it no longer had any value to the Soviet Union except as an area in which they could foment further trouble, embarrassing the Western powers in the process. It was soon clear that the Soviet Union was putting increasing pressure on Russian Jews who wanted to emigrate to Israel and very few of these were allowed to go. But many managed to leave Bulgaria, Hungary, Poland and Rumania.

In 1949–50 the Mossad, which had excellent agents in Teheran and Istanbul, had news of Russian espionage directed against Israel. There were attempts by the Russians to infiltrate Israel with a few non-Zionist Jews from Bulgaria and Rumania, having very carefully brain-washed them beforehand. For there still remained a small number of Jews who looked upon the Russians as their saviours from Nazism and who remained devoted to the Bolshevik revolution. They were subtly persuaded that the kibbutzim in Israel were 'labour camps' and that some Zionists had collaborated with the Nazis during the war, citing the case of Avraham Stern, but totally distorting the latter's motives. In October 1952, Hagop Antaryessian, a 28-year-old Armenian living in the Old City of Jerusalem, was arrested and charged with spying for Russia. It was stated at the preliminary hearing that Antaryessian had been under surveillance by the security authorities since he returned from Soviet Armenia eighteen months previously. On an earlier occasion he had been picked up and held briefly in Jericho for attempting to cross into Jordan over the Allenby Bridge. Further inquiries revealed that he was transmitting secret information about Israel to an agent in the Soviet Embassy in Beirut where he had travelled on a number of occasions.[1] It was obvious from information picked up in Istanbul that some of this Russian intelligence was being passed on to the Arabs.

Thus the Israelis were fighting an espionage war on two fronts —against the Arabs and the Russians. There was also a third, if somewhat shadowy enemy, the ex-Nazi fraternity who had escaped to other parts of the world. Most of them had gone to the countries of Latin America, a few to Spain and Ireland and many to the USSR. Evidence poured into Mossad headquarters from all over the world that hundreds of Nazis who had been instrumental in the policy of exterminating the Jews had slipped away to safety. The fear then was that somehow they would acquire sufficient power and influence to continue harrying the Jews and to urge the destruction of Israel. To Anglo-American ears this may have sounded like paranoia now that the war had ended. To the Jews and to all those Belgian, French, Czech and Polish people who had suffered in concentration camps and who dreaded the rise of Nazism in some other guise in Germany itself, the fear was a very real one. Apart from this there were disturbing stories from Washington of certain American generals who were so alarmed at the stepping-up of the cold war that they would gladly make a deal with any ex-Nazi if he would support them against the Russians.

The outstanding man in the Israeli Secret Service in these early days was Isser Harel, more usually known as 'Little Isser', not so much because he was short and thin and had somewhat of a pinched look, but to distinguish him from 'Big Isser' who was originally regarded as a likely candidate for the post of chief of the Mossad. 'Big Isser' was a dynamic, thrustful character named Isser Be'eri who was imbued with all the toughness and ruthlessness of the pre-Independence days, but was said to lack a sense of diplomacy. From February 1948 until November 1949, he was commander of Shai. There had been political scandals surrounding Isser Be'eri, whose methods were sometimes blatantly opportunist even by the abnormal standards of the intelligence world. He was said to have faked evidence against an

Israeli politician on the grounds that the latter was a threat to national security and to have had a man shot for simply intending to cross to the enemy lines. No doubt some of the allegations against 'Big Isser' were exaggerated, but he drew far too much attention to himself for an intelligence chief. While being groomed for the top job he was swiftly replaced on the orders of Ben-Gurion himself. And the man who stepped into his shoes and was also involved in the creation of Shin Beth was a man who habitually wore sandals, 'Little Isser' himself.

Isser Harel was born under the name of Isser Halperin in Vitebsk in Central Russia in 1912. Unlike many of the other Jewish immigrants from Russia Isser's family was not associated with the Bolsheviks or even the Mensheviks. They were orthodox Jews with a small but prosperous business which was drastically taken over by the Revolutionaries after the events of 1917. By 1922 the family business was confiscated in the name of the state and the Halperins moved to Dvinsk in Latvia. All this made young Isser an ardent Zionist; no doubt he realised that the nationalisation of small businesses was often a Bolshevik excuse for anti-Semitism.

Some of the family emigrated to Palestine in the late twenties and in 1931 Isser followed and joined a kibbutz, the family name then being changed to Harel. Quick-thinking, nimble, bursting with energy and always engaged in some form of work, the young Harel soon made his mark. 'He had quite an authoritative manner even as a very young man,' said one who knew him as a keen agricultural worker in those days. 'We used to tease him about his small stature and broad shoulders and "Napoleon" was one of his many nicknames. Some called him "Napoleon" Harel others "Little Isser" and some "Isser the Terrible", presumably because he came from Russia and was compared jokingly with Ivan the Terrible. He always took life seriously and never wasted words. Almost every sentence was like a terse command. But you must not think he wasn't popular. He had a certain way with him that won him friends and he was often able to make us do whatever he wanted. That is why later on he made such a good spymaster.'

Isser was also quite a good businessman, for he set himself up in business to help pay the fares of other members of his family to emigrate to Palestine. He joined the ranks of Haganah who in 1942 ordered him to join the locally recruited auxiliary constabulary in Palestine. He was dismissed by the British for insubordination and then joined the Jewish settlement police force. From 1944 onwards he was head of the internal department of Shai, so establishing himself as an excellent intelligence executive. Soon afterwards he was promoted head of the whole Tel Aviv section of Shai and his work in that sphere won him the respect and friendship of Ben-Gurion. It was 'Little Isser' who organised many of the intelligence coups against the British, including the obtaining of the CID dossiers. 'Isser makes his own rules as he goes along,' Ben-Gurion once declared, 'but he nevertheless respects the law of Israel.' Certainly during his long career with Shai Isser Harel had often ploughed a lonely furrow, establishing close contacts with both the Arabs and the British to further his intelligence work. Often he would make forays on his own into Arab settlements. He had a remarkably astute grasp of the intricacies of the Arab mind and could often anticipate to an uncanny degree exactly what their next move would be. Just before and just after the granting of independence to Israel Harel was mainly concerned with military intelligence and he obtained documentary evidence of Egyptian intentions, both political and military.

Ben-Gurion found Harel to be not only a good collector of intelligence, but a brilliant interpreter of it. It was on the strength of the latter quality that Ben-Gurion singled him out as the head of Shin Beth, in charge of counter-espionage. The actual operational work of this department and the names of its executives have always been masked in far greater secrecy than that of the Mossad. This is not surprising in that the Mossad has often had to take greater risks, almost inviting publicity, whereas Shin Beth has been able to maintain its anonymity and to guard the identity of its chiefs more effectively. Before Harel became head of the Mossad in 1952, being given the military rank of colonel, Reuven Shiloah (formerly known as Zaslany), a senior Foreign Ministry official who died in 1959 following a car accident, had presided over a kind of unofficial Mossad-type establishment.

The War of Independence between Arabs and Jews delayed Ben-Gurion's plans for re-organising the Intelligence Services of Israel. These were not fully implemented until 1953, when the Prime Minister decided that their whole structure needed tightening up and defining more clearly.

The Secret Service had three main branches, though it also

had a number of 'unofficial' tentacles which reached out overseas into all spheres of life, scientific, industrial, military and purely informational. The oldest intelligence link of all—the Mossad— was preserved more or less intact, probably because its roots were firmly with Haganah. For a while it also took over completely the duties of the pre-Independence Rekhesh, but its prime function was and is the organisation of a world-wide intelligence network outside Israel. The Mossad is still the most feared of all branches of Israeli Intelligence.

Shin Beth was in one sense at the administrative apex and grouped around it were the Mossad and Aman. Ben-Gurion wanted to keep it that way and it was for this reason that when he appointed Isser Harel as chief of the Mossad, he ordered his nominee to keep a watchful eye on internal security and counter-espionage as well. As has been indicated already, Shin Beth is primarily a counter-espionage organisation, even though as a title it is sometimes erroneously applied to the Israeli Secret Service as a whole, confusing its functions with those of the Mossad. This is partly because the very name of Shin Beth is regarded as the quintessence of security efficiency overseas, but also because the Israeli habit of using abbreviations and contractions of words in the titles of their institutional organisations leads foreigners into errors of interpretation. Shin Beth is not a purely counter-espionage service in the sense that DI5 and the FBI are, but is also entrusted with the collection of a certain amount of military intelligence and, in this way, is linked with the Directorate of Military Intelligence which evaluates and interprets all such information. But the purely counter-espionage section of Shin Beth is Sheruth Bitakhon Klali, more usually known as the Shabak.

Ben-Gurion himself was—fortunately for the new state—the world's ablest Prime Minister in assessing a secret service and, above all, appreciating what it was all about. It is not generally realised that he had made a study of the strengths and weaknesses of other powers' intelligence services. He did not want a monolithic organisation combining espionage and counter-espionage such as that of the KGB, but nor did he want espionage and counter-espionage to be so totally divorced as they have been in Britain. Ben-Gurion aimed at a compromise and, certainly in 1952, this was the one which gave Isser Harel a watching brief over the one department and total control of the other.

Thus, in his re-organisation of the Secret Services in 1952–53, two distinct units were created, each being totally independent of the other, while permitting exchanges of information and a certain amount of co-operation and inter-relation. Emphasis was publicly and rightly placed on the first of these units the Directorate of Military Intelligence; the other unit, Shin Beth, and its associated agencies, including the Mossad, operated in the shadows and covered a multiplicity of tasks. The Mossad can be compared with the British DI6, or the American CIA, whereas Aman is really an external collector of purely military intelligence linked to the DMI. Yet to a certain extent the Mossad and Aman co-operate, especially on the collection of intelligence on armaments, logistics and enemy defence works.

In the plans he laid down for the structure of the Secret Service as a whole Ben-Gurion provided for autonomy for its respective military and non-military branches, while allowing enough flexibility for effective co-operation, something that has baffled most of the great powers at one time and another. He may not have achieved perfection, and there were clashes between the military and the civilian sections from time to time, but these were far fewer than they would have been but for Ben-Gurion's sound judgment in the beginning. The buck stopped at two men, the Director of Military Intelligence and the Memuneh, who was titular head of the civilian section of the Secret Service. This was the post which Harel filled with such distinction for fifteen years. In effect, the Memuneh is chief executive of the Secret Services as well as head of the Mossad. He is also chairman of the committee comprising the heads of all sections of the Secret Service and is responsible directly to the Prime Minister. In this respect Ben-Gurion decided that he would borrow from the tradition of another democracy, the British, as the head of DI6 is personally responsible to the Prime Minister. In recent years some British Prime Ministers have tried to push this responsibility on to their Home Secretaries with disastrous results. Ben-Gurion would never have stood for any buck-passing such as this.

The post of Memuneh became more powerful than that of the Director of Military Intelligence because the man who held it could extend his brief both to espionage and counter-espionage, to collecting military intelligence and co-ordinating all the security services. The Memuneh was, in fact, very nearly a law unto himself, or as near to that as it is possible to get in a democracy, with unspoken powers to break the rules from time to time.

But Israel has on the whole managed to solve remarkably well the problem of remaining a jealous guardian of democracy, while giving autocratic powers to her Secret Service chiefs. The rule has generally been that, if such a chief breaks the rules and gets caught without being able to justify himself to the Knesset, then out he goes. Though secrecy has been preserved as far as is possible in a democracy, the post of Memuneh has more than once come under considerable criticism from some politicians and even some generals. A close parliamentary watch has always been kept by members of the Knesset on this office and more than once departmental heads have been dismissed or forced to resign.

Isser Harel was for years able to get away with a great deal of unorthodox and even questionable activities in his Secret Service work by reason of his close friendship with the Prime Minister. He always seemed to know just how far to go and how to use his undoubted talents for diplomacy in coping with awkward questions from the parliamentary committee responsible for scrutinising Secret Service costs.

Meanwhile the Mossad and Aman began to develop their contacts overseas, leaving Shabak, to tackle the problems of internal security. Harel's plan was to ensure that the Israeli Secret Service had a global outlook and to prevent it from being regarded as a minor parochial institution in the Middle East. Here the nation owes Harel an enormous debt. Right from the beginning Isser Harel thought of Israel's problems as global problems and he made the Secret Service respected by the great powers and feared by Israeli's enemies. 'You tell me our job is only to watch the Arabs,' he once replied to a critic. 'I will tell you our job is to watch who are the allies of the Arabs. And there are plenty of them all round the world—in Latin America just as much as in Moscow.'

The Aman also extended its network overseas and concentrated on organising a world-wide industrial espionage network which proved invaluable in the years ahead. The Aman's title is yet another abbreviation, the full name being Agaf Modiin (Information Bureau). In effect it is the Israeli Army's external intelligence service, though it is much more enterprising and adventurous than the military intelligence services of most other powers. It would not be making too flattering a comparison to say it is a kind of low-profile Fourth Bureau of Russia, which is primarily the Red Army's intelligence organisation. Aman includes all military and other Service attachés overseas, has its own press and information service and is also responsible for imposing censorship regulations concerning anything connected with the Army and internal security. Every foreign correspondent in Israel has to work through this organisation, though on the whole interference is minimal. One point worth noting is that the Israeli Secret Service as a whole and the Aman in particular regard Service attachés rather more seriously than, say, the Services of Britain and the United States. In Israel anyone who becomes a Service attaché is regarded as somebody worth grooming for promotion, very often for a high intelligence post. A number of men who have acquired posts at the top of the Intelligence Services in recent years have all had experience as attachés, Brigadier-General Herzog, who was military attaché in Washington, Brigadier-General Aharon Yariv, also in Washington, Brigadier-General Zvi Zamir, military attaché in Britain, and Yuval Ne'eman among them.

The strength of Shin Beth and the whole of the counterespionage service owes much both to the Mossad and Aman. No counter-espionage service in the world has a greater problem than Israel, for as that nation has developed through the immigration policy, so too, paradoxically has that policy posed a security problem. It was always possible for spies to be infiltrated into the new state as immigrants, and the Russians succeeded in doing just this. At the same time inside Israel are nearly half a million Israeli Arabs, all of them speaking more or less perfect Hebrew and offering every opportunity for the infiltration of Arab spies. This situation is not made any easier by the fact that some of these are loyal Israeli subjects, even members of the Israeli Army. But for this reason Shin Beth has three sections to cope with the questions of infiltration, an Arab Section, which is concerned chiefly with security among Israeli Arabs, an Eastern European Section, mainly watching for Soviet Spies, and an anti-Terrorist Section which is permanently on the alert for the investigation of reports of terrorism or the suspected presence of terrorists. Linked to Shin Beth is also the Reshud, which is very similar to Britain's Special Branch at Scotland Yard and was in fact largely based on their methods. Reshud performs the same functions for Shin Beth as the British Special Branch does for DI5, keeping a watch on underground terrorist organisations and making arrests on the evidence gathered by Shin Beth agents.

5

The Lavon Affair

... the operations of the espionage establishments
have provoked events to the point where the
governments which they were created to serve
have either teetered on the brink of disaster or
actually fallen ... in Israel, during the 1965 elec-
tion campaign, David Ben-Gurion and Levi
Eshkol still fought over a decade-old intelligence
scandal known as the Lavon Affair.

(DAVID WISE AND THOMAS B. ROSS IN
The Espionage Establishment)

IN JULY 1952, General Neguib overthrew the monarchy in Egypt, exiled King Farouk and in 1953 proclaimed the country a republic with himself as President. It was not long before the Secret Services of the Western powers were being tipped off by some of their most respected agents (curiously enough mainly agents whose 'covers' were with one of the major oil combines) that Neguib would not last and that the man they should back, the man who was the true friend of the West, was Lieutenant-Colonel Gamal Abdel Nasser. It was one of the most skilfully worked propaganda exercises of recent years. It fooled the Secret Services, deceived both Britain and the United States and helped to pave the way for the overthrow of Neguib early in 1954 and the smooth transition to power of the ambitious lieutenant-colonel.

Disillusionment was swift, but it came too late both in Britain and the United States. Sir Winston Churchill, then an ageing Prime Minister long since past his best, together with Anthony Eden, his Foreign Secretary, went to Washington for talks with President Eisenhower and John Foster Dulles, the arch cold war warrior of American diplomacy. Dulles had largely fallen for the pro-Nasser propaganda; he actually regarded Nasser as a bulwark for the Western World against communism, providing the

'imperialist British' would get their troops out of Egypt. Within
a matter of weeks agreement was reached, after a certain amount
of American pressure on Britain, and after talks in Cairo, the
Churchill Government gave the Israelis real cause for concern by
promising to withdraw all their troops from the Suez Canal Zone.
Until that moment Israel's relations with Britain had been
greatly improved since independence. The old enemy, Ernest
Bevin, the Labour Government's pro-Arab Foreign Secretary,
was dead, and with Sir Winston Churchill back in power Israel
had an understanding and sympathetic ally in Downing Street.
But now there were signs of a general softening up of opinion in
the West in the hope that the cold war was drawing to an end.
Mossad agents reported back to Cairo that American opinion
had veered over to the support of Nasser and that, with the British
troops leaving the Canal Zone, it was only a matter of time before
Nasser would take over the Canal and blockade Israel and the
West.

Tel Aviv was kept exceptionally well informed on developments and had no doubt whatsoever that a new Middle East
crisis was building up. At the same time it was clear that aid for
the Algerian and Tunisian terrorists fighting for independence
was coming from Egypt and that Cairo Radio was deliberately
inciting them. This information had been available in Paris for
the previous three years, but nothing had been done about it.
French governments had pursued their colonial policy with one
eye on America, and the State Department's backing of the
Egyptian Government had scared the Quai d'Orsay into ignoring
many unfriendly acts from Cairo which should have been answered with firmness. Mendès-France, the new Prime Minister of
France and himself a Jew, though sympathetic to Arab aspirations, had no such inhibitions. As both Foreign Minister and head
of the Government he was able to tackle the problem with greater
authority and he lost no time in putting the responsibility firmly
on Cairo. The Egyptian Ambassador was summoned to the Quai
d'Orsay where the Prime Minister delivered a strong note of protest against the Cairo Radio broadcasts. 'The "Voice of the
Arabs" broadcasts from Cairo have incited the North African
populations to revolt, insurrection and even murder,' he declared.

This had some effect. Gamal Abdel Nasser instructed the state-
controlled Cairo Radio to tone down its campaign against French
policy in North Africa. But, as the Israelis knew full well, this was

Special Services Unit]. I thought it should be used only in time of war and remain dormant in peacetime. Since he was the Minister and insisted on the right to meet with senior officers without my participation, and at times even without my knowledge, I warned one of the responsible officers in the Unit to be wary of Lavon's eagerness to activate it.'[1]

Dayan may have been writing with hindsight, but the general opinion both at the time and at various inquiries since has been that Lavon was anxious to take over military policy-making himself and to by-pass the high command, thus upsetting the delicate balance between the politicians and the Army which Ben-Gurion had so carefully nurtured. This resulted in various personality clashes, not only between Lavon and Sharett, whose tactics were criticised by the Defence Minister, but between the Minister and the Director-General of the Ministry and also the Chief of Staff. Lavon was always wanting to take decisions without even consulting his Chief of Staff and on one occasion Dayan sent in a letter of resignation, but was persuaded to withdraw it.

Lavon had had hardly any experience at all of defence matters when he became Minister. Possibly he felt he must assert his authority from the beginning because he realised that he was flanked by two old and wise hands in Dayan as Chief of Staff and Shimon Peres as Director-General. But the faults were not wholly on Lavon's side and even the most thorough secret inquiries into his conduct of affairs revealed that not one, but many people contributed to the disasters of 1954 which proved a body blow to the Secret Service. Perhaps the fairest summing-up of the whole business was that of Amos Perlmutter, who commented that Lavon 'did not link up well with the Army, but he became embroiled in security misfortunes not of his own doing, which in the end cost him his career.'[2]

The truth is that, while Lavon was undoubtedly responsible for the use of the Special Service Unit and for intensifying border raids against the Egyptians, it was not only the Ministry of Defence which was involved in the 'security misfortunes', but Shin Beth as well. There ought to have been close co-operation between Shin Beth and the Ministry of Defence with a tight political control of the whole highly dangerous operation. In Ben-Gurion's time, when the Prime Minister was also Defence Minister, this would undoubtedly have been achieved. With Lavon at the helm there was a recipe for disaster in the fact that he was prone to make his own decisions without consulting others, while some of those he might have consulted withheld their confidence from him. Even though Dayan and Peres favoured a policy of militancy against the Arabs, including border raids, while Sharett was all for conciliation and caution, Lavon failed to ally himself with the Army chiefs. Possibly he sought allies inside Shin Beth or the Mossad, or other sections of the Secret Service.

During 1954 a series of espionage and sabotage operations by Israeli agents inside Egypt and Syria ended in total disaster and a round-up of the carefully constructed Israeli spy network in Egypt. All the work of the previous four years was almost totally destroyed and new networks had to be built up again at enormous cost in time and money.

Dayan had wanted personally to control the border raids and presumably any sabotage operations linked with them. Lavon not only wanted to direct these himself, but to have access to the sabotage files prepared by Army Intelligence officers. These files had originally been compiled with Ben-Gurion's full approval.

Meanwhile a plan was worked out to blacken Nasser in the eyes of the Americans and the British by a series of bomb attacks on such premises as those of the US Information Centre in Cairo, the British Council and various offices of British and American firms in Egypt. The raids were to be carried out by a special group of Israeli secret agents comprised entirely of Egyptian Jews and given the code name of 'Unit 131'. They were to be disguised as Arab terrorists and everything was to be done, including the forging of documents, to implicate the Egyptians as the real culprits of the whole plot. The documents were to be leaked into the hands of the American CIA. This highly dangerous, politically outrageous and criminal operation directed against two friendly powers was perhaps the most Machiavellian conception of Secret Service activities to be put into action in peacetime. It is certain that the Prime Minister, Moshe Sharett, would have vetoed it and so, too, would a number of other politicians and even some generals. Some of them would have been horrified at the sheer criminality of it all. However, in looking at this objectively as a student of Secret Service histories rather than as an orthodox historian concerned with ethics, one must concede first of all that the Israelis were, if not at war, at least the target for an undeclared war by the Arabs, including a blockade of their shipping. They were not only faced by the prospect of the British pulling their troops out of the Middle East for ever, but of the Americans refusing to supply Israel with arms because of the Eisenhower administration's lunatic policy of appeasing the Arabs. Israel faced friends who were, in effect, not all that much better than enemies. And nobody knew better than Israel's Secret Service that the Arabs, led by Egypt, still hankered for revenge and the destruction of their country. Therefore in the context of a somewhat desperate *Machtpolitik*, making allowance for the fervent patriotism of a young nation fighting for its life, there might have been some justification for such tactics.

Wisely, it was soon decided that the targets to be selected for the bomb attacks should be wholly American and not British. There seemed to be no point in running the risk of alienating two friendly nations, if the plot should by a mischance be discovered. It was also felt that the British counter-espionage would be more likely at that time to detect Israeli undercover sabotage tactics than would the American. But what really encouraged the Israelis to go ahead with this plan were vague promises of assistance and absolute security by one of their own men who was working for the CIA.

Shin Beth and the Mossad were certainly involved in the plot and a superficial glance at the situation may make it hard to see how the Army should have been directly involved. But the subsequent blame for the series of disasters was most unfortunately pinned on the Ministry of Defence. The Secret Service managed to preserve its anonymity in the whole affair. Yet this was a sabotage operation to be carried out by spies, not soldiers in uniform, or, for that matter, soldiers out of uniform. Moshe Dayan has this to say on the subject: 'In the latter half of July, 1954, while I was on a three and a half years' visit to the Army bases in the USA, the [Special Services] Unit initiated an operation which thereafter was always referred to as "the security mishap". A detachment carried out a few small-scale sabotage actions in Cairo and Alexandria. The result was the arrest and trial of eleven of its members. Some were sentenced to long terms of imprisonment. The tragic climax was the suicide of one member and the execution of two others on January 1, 1955.'[3]

It would appear that the man who most strongly supported the sabotage plan was Pinhas Lavon who perhaps ultimately paid the penalty for trespassing on a sphere which was strictly that of the Secret Service rather than Military Intelligence. His adversaries both in the Knesset and the Ministry of Defence were all for answering rebuffs from Washington by winning co-operation with France. Lavon believed that in the long-term there was not much to be gained by this policy. He pointed to the instability of the French government in those days.

Lavon believed it was much more important to do everything possible to reverse the trend of Anglo-American politics—to stop the withdrawal of British troops from the Canal Zone and to curb the American flirtation with Nasser. The Minister of Defence had good cause to advance this thesis because Mossad agents had reported the imminent departure of British troops from Egypt long before this had been officially announced. But unfortunately for Lavon he had not enjoyed the best of relations with Isser Harel and little help was forthcoming from that direction. It was for this reason that Lavon turned to the Special Services Unit (the MTM, Makhleka Letafkidim Meuhadim) and to the albeit silent co-operation of Colonel Benjamin Givli, of Aman.

The task of master-minding the sabotage plot was given to Colonel Abraham Dar, who used the name of John Darling when outside Israel, claiming to be the representative of various British commercial interests. He had an extensive network in Syria as well as in Egypt, but he seems to have ignored warning signals of a drive by all Arab nations to track down Israeli agents as early as 1951. There had been an attempt by the Iraqi authorities to frighten many professional Jews in their country into emigrating to Palestine. Then the Iraqis arrested two Mossad agents in Baghdad, Shalom Tzalh and Joseph Bazri, and several others were caught soon afterwards. By 1954 the Dar network had become extremely vulnerable and far too large. Apart from suspected treachery on the part of one of the chief Israeli agents there was considerable laxity among the other agents. Elie Cohen, for example, who later became a top Mossad agent in Syria, but who was then unconnected with any Secret Service work and was working as a book-keeper in Alexandria, was informed about the plot against the Egyptians and even given some documents concerning it. On that occasion he showed a greater sense of security than the professionals. Elie Cohen realised, even as an ordinary citizen, that the Egyptian Jewish network was dangerously near to being compromised.

'Unit 131' comprised Dar himself, Paul Frank, his number

two, and, at the head of the Cairo section, Dr. Moussa Marzouk, a doctor at the Jewish hospital in the Egyptian capital, and at the head of the Alexandrian section was Samuel Azzar. These were the key members of the Unit and the liaison officer between the two sections, linking them up with Dar, was an attractive young nurse working with an English firm at Heliopolis, Victorino Nino. Dar himself was an Aman agent working under the direction of Colonel Benjamin Givli, who was Chief of Military Intelligence from 1950–55. This brilliant young officer was the son of a veteran Palestinian farmer, born at Petach Tivka in 1919. He was one of the up-and-coming new school of Intelligence officers who seemed likely to rise to the peak of his profession. Givli had been in Haganah as a youth, working in the Jewish settlement police and joining Shai in the forties. In 1948 he became commander of the Jerusalem area for Shai.

Benjamin Givli was one of the judges in the field trial of Major Meir Tubiansky, who in 1948 was sentenced to death and executed immediately for allegedly having passed military information to the British staff of the Jerusalem Electric Company, who were said to have been acting on behalf of the Arabs. The court was then presided over by Isser Be'eri who, a year later, when a review of the case found Tubiansky to have been innocent, was sentenced by court martial to one day in prison and was then immediately reprieved by President Chaim Weizmann. In 1949 Givli became deputy chief of Aman, and shortly afterwards he was sent to Britain for military studies and then to academic studies at Princeton University in the USA. Thereafter his progress was rapid, and in 1954 he became head of Aman with the rank of brigadier-general. Thus he was closely concerned with the secret sabotage plot. It was, however, a very loose relationship between Aman and the network under Colonel Dar and difficult to know exactly where the role of the military ended and that of Secret Service agents began. Nor is it even clear what happened after Colonel Dar had signalled to Tel Aviv that all was ready for the plan to be implemented.

It was at this juncture that other Israeli agents, specially trained in the arts of sabotage and handling explosives, were sent to Egypt to reinforce 'Unit 131'. Somebody somewhere gave the order for the plan to be put into operation. But the plot proved to be a total catastrophe. Some bombs were planted in the United States Information Offices in Alexandria and Cairo, but none of them exploded and the rest of the plan was never carried out. That there was some amateurish bungling in the team was clear enough, but there was treachery too. Later it was learned that Paul Frank, who was Colonel Dar's key man in Cairo, had betrayed details of the whole operation to the Egyptians. The entire network of Egyptian Jews in both Alexandria and Cairo was rounded up. Two were hanged in Alexandria—Samuel Azzar, a schoolteacher, and a young Jewish girl—while eight others, including Victorino Nino, were imprisoned. Some of these were never heard of again.

But there was an even more serious casualty in the Intelligence ranks. Max Bennett, an Aman operative, with great experience as a spy both in Europe and the Middle East, was arrested by the Egyptian police because his name had been given to them by one of the network. Following prolonged torture in a Cairo prison, Bennett committed suicide to prevent himself from giving away information. The death of this agent, who had been born in Germany, was a tremendous loss. He had emigrated to Palestine with his family in the thirties, studied as an electrical engineer and then joined Haganah. Speaking both English and German, he had at various times posed as one of both races, one of his favourite covers being that of a commercial traveller. Bennett had been an Israeli agent in Germany, Austria, Iraq, Syria and Egypt, being particularly effective in obtaining military intelligence. One of his greatest coups was to strike up a remarkable friendship with General Neguib as a result of which much useful intelligence was passed on to Tel Aviv. Bennett was one of the first men to warn Israel of the imminent rise to power of Nasser, of the changes in American diplomatic policy in the Middle East and of the presence of pro-Soviet traitors in the British Foreign Office and Secret Service. He was on the point of alerting Tel Aviv about Kim Philby only a matter of hours before he was arrested.

Paul Frank, as he was known in Egypt by the name he used on his British passport, had formerly been a member of Palmach. His background is still somewhat of a mystery and a secret which has been closely guarded by Shin Beth. Some give his name as Hans Hoffman, others identify him as Avni Weisenfeld, though the latter is almost certainly one of many names he went under. During his stay in Egypt he had been won over to the side of the Egyptians by Colonel Osman Nouri, head of the Military Intelligence Service in Cairo, a brilliant counter-espionage expert who later became Egyptian Ambassador to Nigeria. Nouri was far and away the best intelligence operative Egypt had in those days and his links extended to Baghdad and Damascus as well as to Bonn and Vienna. He was also the chief architect of Egypt's intelligence network in Europe. Later he played a prominent part in organising the revolutionary coup against the Imam in the Yemen and the Egyptian invasion of that territory.

There was no indication at the time of the fiasco in Egypt, later to be generally known as the Lavon Affair, that Paul Frank was a traitor. He and Colonel Dar were the only two who managed to escape from the country in time, Frank going to Vienna while preserving what seemed a sound enough cover story. In fact he had played a very dangerous game with remarkable coolness. The Egyptian police had been partly alerted to the bomb plot by finding one of the plotters with a smoking incendiary bomb in his trousers pocket. Events moved so speedily that Frank himself was taken to the police station for questioning. Despite the other arrests, but presumably with the backing of Colonel Nouri, he was released the following day. No doubt he deliberately allowed himself to be arrested, but it was a desperate gamble all the same.

When it became known, or suspected, that Israel's Egyptian * network had been unmasked by Nouri's counter-espionage team, the whole business blew up into a tremendous political row. Members of the Knesset demanded an immediate investigation into what some regarded as a colossal blunder by the Intelligence Services and others denounced as an act of criminal folly. But the mystery as to who was responsible was not so easily solved. Shin Beth kept silent, but the Ministry of Defence could not dodge the issue: the facts, contradictory as they were, seemed to be that while the senior Army officer responsible for sending the signal to Cairo, giving the go-ahead for the plan, insisted he was given his orders orally by the Minister of Defence at a meeting with nobody else present, Lavon himself testified that the officer in question acted entirely on his own responsibility.

The Prime Minister set up an *ad hoc* two-man committee to investigate the disaster and the all important question of who gave the order. Lavon supported the Prime Minister in this instance, as the two members of the committee were a former President of the Supreme Court and the first Israeli Chief of Staff. In the meantime the Lavon Affair began to take on something of the aura surrounding that other controversial espionage *cause célèbre* involving a Jew—the Dreyfus Case. It remained a secret to all except those in government or Ministry of Defence circles for a long time, but eventually it split the nation apart politically, just as the Dreyfus Case had done in France, cutting across party lines and creating considerable acrimony, with Lavon and his supporters on one side and Shimon Peres and Moshe Dayan on the other, the latter having the backing of some, but not all of Ben-Gurion's supporters. The row waged furiously inside the Cabinet, the Ministry of Defence and in homes and cafés. But at least the scandal demonstrated to the world that democracy was very much alive in Israel and that not even the most unscrupulous of Secret Services or Defence Ministries could get away with a blunder of this kind. Even the policies of Ben-Gurion came under fire because he was associated with the strategy of retaliatory raids against the Arabs.

Lavon claimed he had carried out an independent inquiry into what had happened, but the committee do not seem to have heeded this. Certainly they did not support the Minister of Defence, but instead adopted an unhelpfully neutral position. They expressed their opinion that it was not possible to say with any certainty who gave the original order to the Cairo sabotage team. This left Lavon in a dangerously untenable position. He tried to overcome this problem by seeking the Prime Minister's approval for a re-organisation of the Ministry of Defence, which would have meant the dismissal of the Director-General and some of the Intelligence officers involved in the disaster. But Moshe Sharett declined to accept this proposal.

Eventually the pressure on Lavon became too great. In February 1955, he resigned and the old warrior, Ben-Gurion, was recalled from the kibbutz to which he had retired, to take over the portfolio of Minister of Defence once again. Sharett himself managed to remain unscathed by all this and so retained the premiership. The full details of the Egyptian scandal were kept from the Israeli public. They knew at the time there had been a major blunder, but the Lavon Affair was classified as top secret: too many members of the hierarchy were involved for it to be otherwise.

Later in 1955 there were general elections in Israel as a result of which Ben-Gurion once again became Prime Minister, still retaining the post of Minister of Defence. One of his first acts was to remove the senior Intelligence officer involved in the Lavon Affair from his post. Gradually more information about the scandal came to light. Colonel Nouri, the Egyptian Military Intelligence chief, had been sent to Bonn where he was actively concerned in conducting Secret Service activities with the connivance and assistance of General Reinhard Gehlen, the West German Intelligence chief. The treacherous Israeli agent, Frank, was still working with Nouri, but both the Mossad and Shin Beth were on his track. By 1957 they had a complete dossier on all his activities and, having caught up with him in Vienna, lured him back to Tel Aviv. There he was brought to trial and sentenced to twelve years' imprisonment, a mild punishment for one who had caused so much misery to those of his own race. This trial in 1960 not only threw fresh light on the Lavon Affair, but stirred up the embers of controversy in the Knesset the following year, having such an effect in the political arena that even so powerful a statesman as Ben-Gurion was injured to the extent of being forced to dissolve the Knesset and hold new elections. The scandal boomeranged on the Prime Minister, for his party lost five seats.

Towards the end of the summer of 1960 Pinhas Lavon sought an interview with Ben-Gurion about the 1954 disaster, claiming that there was new evidence which would prove conclusively that he had not given the vital order for the sabotage plan to be put into action. He asked to be exonerated. Ben-Gurion declined to do this and there was an acrimonious relationship between the two men, with Lavon arguing that Ben-Gurion was personally hostile to him. However, Ben-Gurion agreed to refer the matter to a more or less informal inquiry into Lavon's new evidence, which included testing the reliability of another Intelligence officer. The Prime Minister was very reluctant to do anything which would make a public issue of the affair once again. It was agreed to try and get a positive opinion as to who really gave the order and General Chaim Laskov, the new Chief of Staff, was ordered to investigate charges against a number of Intelligence officers.

Ben-Gurion summed it up as follows: 'I have implicated Lavon and it is not my duty to exonerate him. If somebody else implicated him, his responsibility is not within my authority.'[4] This may have seemed mere sophistry to some, but Ben-Gurion was in a very difficult position. Nobody, not even the Chief of Staff, was anxious to give a positive opinion and eventually the matter was referred to a Cabinet Committee. A majority of Ministers decided not to set up a judicial commission of inquiry, but to appoint a committee of seven Ministers to report on the subject. At the end of December 1960, this Committee presented their report and offered three opinions: (1) Pinhas Lavon had not given the original order and the sabotage action had been implemented without his knowledge or authorisation; (2) the Committee could not determine what were the exact working relations in the Ministry of Defence in 1954; (3) the Committee accepted the Attorney-General's report that certain documents presented to the 1954 Committee were forged.

The Cabinet accepted this report after some heated debate, at the end of which there were four abstentions in the voting, Ben-Gurion and Dayan (then in the Cabinet) being among them. Ben-Gurion said he would not accept the Cabinet Committee's decision as binding on him, holding that there had been a miscarriage of justice. He said that he would only accept the decision of a judicial hearing. His resignation followed soon afterwards.

Thus the Lavon Affair petered out in an unsatisfactory manner, with nobody on any side coming out of it with much credit. It had resulted in a shake-up both in the Ministry of Defence and Shin Beth in the period between 1954 and 1961. A number of senior officers, including the Director of Military Intelligence, resigned. Perhaps the unhappiest result was the way in which it cut short a promising and indeed outstanding career in Intelligence, that of Colonel Givli. He was appointed chief of Northern Command and in 1956 was commander of the Golani Brigade in the Sinai campaign. In 1959 he was acting commander of Central Command, but it is said that Ben-Gurion refused to have him promoted to Major-General because of the Lavon Affair. Soon afterwards he was appointed military attaché to the United Kingdom and the Scandinavian countries. Upon retiring from the Army he pursued a highly successful career in business and today is managing director of Shemen Israel Oil Company and also deputy chairman of the Israel Export Institute.

Out of the depressing story of the Lavon Affair there gradually emerged a distinct pattern of improvement in the administration of the Secret Service as a whole. Obviously the relations between the Ministry of Defence and the extra-mural forces of Intelligence and other branches of the Secret Service had been far too loose.

There had been too much of giving orders by nods and winks, of turning a blind eye, of taking dangerous risks and mixing politics and espionage. If, of course, the 1954 'adventure' had worked, and nothing had been suspected, all might have been well, though it is doubtful if even bomb attacks on American installations would have changed US policy to any great extent. For that reason alone the sabotage plan was a mad one and not worth the risk. But perhaps because it was discovered, a great many other 'adventures' which might have led to more serious trouble were checked.

Co-operation between the Ministry of Defence and the Aman were at last clearly defined and the Memuneh was given greater powers of co-ordinating and controlling other branches of Intelligence. A much tighter rein was kept on all aspects of espionage and counter-espionage. The Israeli Secret Service had started life with a burst of uncontrolled enthusiasm and, when caught red-handed in unauthorised acts, some personnel behaved in a highly reprehensible manner in trying to pin the blame on others. Amos Perlmutter, an authority on Israeli military history, wrote that efforts were made to implicate Lavon with responsibility for the fiasco: 'some Intelligence officers even forged documents and testified against him before the committee. At the same time Shimon Peres, in his testimony before the committee, concentrated upon Lavon's incompetence as Defence Minister. In this way hearings were turned from a challenge to the Army Intelligence Division's competence and responsibility for the fiasco into Lavon's trial. In vindictive testimonies both Peres and Dayan strayed from the fiasco to comment on Lavon's incompetence as Defence Minister . . . . the 1954 Committee reached no conclusions and condemned no one, not even the cabal of intelligence officers who actually plotted the dismissal of Lavon, although it did note that some documents were forged and that one of the intelligence officers lied to the committee.'[5]

6

The Million-Dollar
Spy

*The Israelites had a perfect system of intelligence
on Egypt. They knew the secret codes of our air
force and our armoured corps.*

(MOHAMMED HASSANEIN HEIKAL,
editor of *Al-Ahram*)

TOWARDS THE END of the fifties Israel was shocked by a series of
revelations of Arab espionage plots directed against the nation.
Though the counter-espionage teams had done their work thoroughly, it was again agreed that the best form of defence was
attack and, as a corollary to this, that the best places in which to
attack were at the heart of the enemy—Cairo and Damascus.

To achieve any spectacular success in these two capitals the
Israelis needed first-class agents who could not only pass as Arabs,
but had talents exceptional enough for them to be accepted in
government circles. This was not as difficult as it might seem to
the uninitiated, for the Israelis themselves—except for the native-
born—came from as many as sixty-two different countries and
ranged from fair-haired, blue-eyed Nordic types who would pass
for Germans in Cairo to dark-skinned aquiline Jews who had
lived in such territories as Morocco, Tunisia, Egypt and Aden
and who spoke fluently the actual dialects of Arabic in those
countries. Thus Israel acquired a reserve of agents who could
easily be infiltrated into a wide range of territories without anyone noticing.

At the end of 1959 the Mossad was particularly anxious to
recruit a highly intelligent and resourceful agent with the kind of
background which would enable him to be undetected in Arab
territories. Mossad recruiting staff were looking for somebody who
could produce brilliant results quickly; they were prepared to

wait a year or two, but after that they expected and indeed demanded a major break-through.

The quest for such a man was extremely thorough and long before the first approaches were made to him the Mossad officers had been impressed by an accountant who was working in a relatively insignificant job in the supply department of a Tel Aviv firm. His name was Elie Cohen.

Born at Alexandria in 1924, the son of Saul and Sophie Cohen, who had emigrated there from Aleppo in Syria before the First World War, Elie had been brought up in the Jewish Quarter of Alexandria. His parents were relatively poor, but Elie had not only been a promising pupil at his school in the Jewish Quarter, but had gone on to a French high school in Alexandria with the aid of a grant, and afterwards to Farouk University for two years. But it was not until he had started work as a salesman in a clothing store to help support his family that he first learned Hebrew.

When the state of Israel was established his family left Egypt and moved to Israel, but Elie remained behind in Alexandria presumably to carry on with his studies. He worked as a bookkeeper until the time of the Suez Campaign of 1956. When the Egyptians began to take a harsh line with native Jews following the withdrawal of the Anglo-French forces, Cohen, who was a dedicated Zionist at heart, emigrated to Israel. But he did not settle down well in his new home and, surprisingly for one who was both intelligent and quick-witted, he was often unemployed. He spoke and wrote Arabic fluently and was as much at home in an Arabic as in an Israeli environment; it was also noticed that he was extremely observant and had an exceptional memory.

'There is a clerk in an office down the street who is just the chap we are looking for,' reported the Mossad agent to his chief.

'Why do you find him so exceptional?'

'He is meticulously honest, he has a quick brain and a memory like a computer bank. And, above all, he is what you call a quiet patriot. Not one of your noisy ones who shout the odds. To see him, to listen to him, you would think he was just another Arab who had strayed into Tel Aviv.'

'Maybe he is.'

'Oh, no, though he would pass for a Syrian any day and speaks like one, he is a Jew one hundred per cent. What is more he was one of the very few who weren't caught by the Egptian police in that disastrous action of ours in Alexandria and Cairo in 1954.'

'Tell me more. How did he escape?'

'Well, this chap wasn't in our organisation, but he knew all about it—the plans to blow up the libraries and other institutions. No doubt at all he at least thought the plans were half-baked and he was sceptical about what they would achieve. But he kept faith. He acted coolly and efficiently when he was told by an Egyptian police friend of his that the ringleaders had been arrested. He didn't lose his head, or fear being involved himself and inform on his friends. He went straight home, destroyed some incriminating evidence and, when the Egyptian secret police eventually came to question him, they found nothing and he was set free. But the point is that he stood up to interrogation.'

'But he will be on Egyptian police records?'

'Yes, but his identity can be changed. He recently got married, but I don't think it matters. There is one snag, however. He doesn't want to change his job, not even for more money. All he wants is to settle down.'

What happened then is not quite clear. Certainly a short while afterwards Elie Cohen was dismissed from his job along with a few other clerks on the grounds that the firm had to make economies. Whether or not his particular dismissal was engineered by the Mossad is uncertain. But it was almost immediately after this, sometime in 1960, that Elie Cohen was recruited as a secret agent, ostensibly for the Ministry of Defence, but actually for the Mossad. And it was his previous association with Israeli agents in Alexandria, tenuous though this link was, that decided the Secret Service recruiters to enlist him. It was felt that any Jew who had become enmeshed in that disastrous campaign of terror and yet managed to survive unscathed must have a cool head and the kind of luck all good agents need.

For several months Cohen was given intensive training for a major espionage assignment. This was tough, realistic, but practical and more concerned with the minutiae of an agent's daily life than the kind of theory which is expounded by some intelligence instructors. His pay was increased and Cohen was happy enough to be able to provide more comforts for his young wife, Nadia, than he had been able to dream of previously. As far as his wife was concerned Elie had a job at the Ministry of Defence. Neither of them discussed his work and Elie was a typical, home-loving husband, fond of his children as they arrived—first a son, then two daughters. His training period was a particularly happy time, the excitement of the new job, the satisfaction he gained from being praised as an apt pupil and, for the time being, the knowledge that each night he was at home with his family.

It has been said that his training was realistic: it was in fact, as is the case with all the crack agents of the Mossad, realistic to the point of testing Cohen's reactions to the ultimate in physical endurance. In this respect Israeli agents are far more professional, much tougher and more resilient than the secret agents of other democracies. One can compare them with the KGB, not with the British Secret Service or the CIA. An Israeli secret agent owes almost everything to the example of his predecessors in the underground of Shai, Irgun Zvai Leumi and the original Mossad.

The Mossad at that time urgently needed a highly skilled operator in Damascus and it was soon decided that Cohen was the man to be groomed for this post. As he had been in Egypt before and actually interviewed by the Egyptian secret police, it was felt that Syria would be safer as a first mission. But, remembering how the whole ring of agents in Egypt had been rounded up in 1954, and how they had all confessed under torture, Cohen's spy-masters were ultra-cautious before sending him on a major assignment and gave him local ones first.

The Mossad's aim was that Elie Cohen should make friends with the most influential members of Syrian society. One test set was for him to make such contacts in Jerusalem where Syrian businessmen often stayed at the King David Hotel. It was soon made abundantly plain to him that he was to pose as a Moslem and a Syrian. In vain he pleaded to be allowed to return to Egypt, a land he felt he knew much better. The Mossad's response was that Egypt was far more efficient in checking on its citizens and visitors than other countries in the Middle East. In Syria, which was becoming increasingly important, Elie would much more easily avoid recognition or detection.

The last few months of Elie's training were spent in improving his knowledge of the Moslem world, developing to perfection the Syrian accent of his Arabic and learning his new identity as Kamel Amine Tabet, a Syrian subject.[1] False papers were issued to him and a complete, detailed story woven around his new identity. His father was Amine Tabet and his mother's name was Sa'ida Ibrahim. Both parents were Syrian, but he was born in Beirut where his father was in the textile business. To make it more difficult for checks on Elie to be made by the Syrian authorities, it was planned as part of the cover story that his uncle had emigrated to Argentina immediately after World War II and that soon afterwards he asked Elie to take up a post with him. So in 1947 Kamel Amine Tabet emigrated to Argentina with his father and had a textile business in Buenos Aires. That business subsequently went bankrupt and Kamel worked for a while in a travel agency going into business on his own account. Elie's immediate assignment was to go to Argentina and build up his cover story and career from there.

In contrast to some of the Russians' long-term planning in espionage, the case of Elie Cohen may be said to have been conducted at reckless speed. The Russians would send a man overseas and leave him dormant to build up his own cover over a period of ten or even twenty years, as they had in the case of Gordon Lonsdale. But for the Israelis time was not on their side: they needed as near perfect a cover as possible, but results at all costs within a year or two at the most. The intensified training for this attempt at 'instant' intelligence was as thorough as it could be in the circumstances, but it could not extend to detailed instruction in the Koran and the Moslem religion. Cohen was, however, thoroughly experienced in the arts of deciphering and composing coded messages, in micro-photography and radio transmission before he left Tel Aviv.

As far as his wife was concerned, Elie had to go to Argentina to make purchases on behalf of the Ministry of Defence and the Israeli Foreign Office. To complete the picture of the typical Syrian Elie grew a heavy moustache. Then, armed with a false passport in his new identity, he went first to Zurich, then on to Buenos Aires.

The Mossad network in Buenos Aires, and indeed throughout Argentina, was already highly efficient and, while mainly geared to tracking down and keeping watch on ex-Nazis, was able to cope with all manner of espionage problems. Another resident Mossad agent was assigned to discreetly help and advise Elie on his role as a member of the Syrian community in the Argentinian capital. An apartment in Buenos Aires was rented for him and, cautiously at first, Elie set about making influential friends in the Syrian community. With ample funds at his disposal this was not too difficult. But it took all Elie's flair for making himself popular to win over the leading members of that community, and more importantly to make friends with Syrian Embassy officials. The

Mossad made the latter task easier by keeping him closely informed on their latest intelligence on political developments inside Syria with the result that Elie often seemed to the Embassy officials better informed than they were themselves. Through the support of the Syrian military attaché in Buenos Aires Elie was able to join the Baathist Party. By the end of 1961 he had won innumerable friends among the Syrian community, he had made himself accepted as a fanatical Syrian patriot and an enemy of Israel and he paved the way to further favours by making generous donations to Arab charities.

Early in 1962 the Mossad made plans for Elie to begin his espionage assignment. He was instructed to go to Syria and, by using the contacts he had already made through his influential friends in the Syrian community in Buenos Aires, to ingratiate himself with government circles in Damascus. But his first problem was to smuggle into Syria the do-it-yourself spy kit with which the Mossad had supplied him: this consisted of a miniature radio transmitter, receiving set, codes, invisible inks and other gadgets. By this time a close watch was kept on all people, even Syrian nationals, coming into Syria by the normal air routes. Elie made the trip first by plane to Italy and from then on to Beirut by a slow boat. From there he was helped across the Lebanese–Syrian border by a friendly Arab, but not without having to part with substantial bribes before being allowed through the customs without opening up all his luggage.

Once in Damascus Elie made his bid for swift recognition in high places by two ploys; first, by posing as a convert to the Baathist cause who had returned to the home of his fathers to do what he could for his country, and again by spending freely in an ostentatious manner in this same cause. The money came from Israel but via a bank in America. Most professional spies aim at being unobtrusive and ordinary; Elie, desperately needing quick results, had no alternative but to play his role entirely the opposite way. It amused him that one of his earliest hazards was that of the marriage brokers. More than once some intermediary for a wealthy Syrian merchant inquired whether he would be agreeable to marry a daughter who had probably never been consulted as to her wishes. Elie adroitly, but never impolitely, managed to disengage himself from any such propositions. After all, he required to retain his bachelor status as far as Syria was concerned if only to ensure that he could transmit information on his radio set to Tel Aviv without being disturbed by a suspicious Moslem wife.

Having installed himself in a luxurious villa in Damascus, Elie talked rather more about business deals than actually making them, but he made enough import–export transactions to impress the local merchants and also pleased many of their wives by importing presents of mink coats from France. This was a touch of genius on the part of Elie, who seems to have been able to read the minds of women with extraordinary accuracy without ever getting himself involved with them.

Then came an opportunity which he seized with alacrity. Elie was asked to give talks on their Spanish programme by the directors of Radio Damascus; these were to be beamed to Syrians who had emigrated and based on material supplied by the Syrian Ministry of Information. It was a chance which Elie was quick to accept, for not only did it give him easy access to the Ministry of Information and other ministerial sources, but it provided him with the chance to slip through coded messages to Israel in his broadcasts. Now Elie had a valuable and seemingly secure two-way system of communication with Tel Aviv through Radio Damascus and by sending out similar material in the form of micro-dot messages hidden inside backgammon sets which he sent to his friends in Argentina.

The Mossad headquarters in Tel Aviv were soon alerted to the importance of Elie's broadcasts to which they always listened in case he should casually insert a coded message into his text. This was not too difficult as nobody in Damascus had any reason to suspect the brilliant Arab propagandist whose talks earned him the highest praise from the Syrians. Meanwhile Cohen also maintained permanent contact with Israel by the radio set which he kept hidden in his bedroom. This eventually proved to be his fatal mistake, for no agent should keep his radio transmitter and receiving set in the same place for too long. Sooner or later it invites disaster. But probably Elie was lulled into a false sense of security by the apparently lax counter-espionage precautions of the Syrians.

Elie had done a certain amount of work while in Argentina helping other Mossad agents to trace Nazi war criminals hiding in that country. It was useful work which was well appreciated in Tel Aviv and, according to some accounts,[2] he was also asked to make similar inquiries about a former war criminal living in Syria under an assumed name. But this is not altogether confirmed by other sources.

T. E. Lawrence once said of the Arabs that they can understand black and white, but never the shades in between when it comes to assessing a situation or an individual. Elie had played the role of a fanatical, pro-Baathist, anti-Israeli Syrian patriot; this was something which the Arab mind could understand and accept unquestioningly. A more subtle approach would have caused the Syrians to view a supposedly wealthy Arab more critically. After all, full bellies are rarely fanatical. But it was by playing on the theme of his own personal integrity and commitment to the pan-Arab cause that Elie came to be accepted and given confidences which another wealthy Syrian might not have received so easily. Elie made a point of constantly urging the building of stronger defences against the Israelis and of trying to convince the military junta that much more needed to be done if Syria was to survive a surprise attack. He made some of the senior officers feel almost guilty. Anxious to justify themselves, they not only made him an honorary major in the Syrian Army, but willingly suggested showing him just how good their defences were. They took him into forbidden military areas in order to reassure him that all was well.

Among the close friends he made in Damascus were Salem Saif, a Radio Damascus announcer, Magd al Ard, an important merchant, various colonels on the General Staff of the Syrian Army, Abdullah Hashan, editor of *Arab World*, and General Amin el-Hafez. He obtained quite an important post in the Baathist Party hierarchy and through this was given various unofficial tasks by the Syrian Prime Minister, Salah Bitar. He accompanied the Prime Minister on visits to Cairo and other Arab capitals and was present on a number of occasions at confidential talks between various Arab leaders and their military commanders. The picture he obtained not merely of Syrian plans, but of those of Egypt and other Arab countries as well, was as complete as Tel Aviv could possibly have desired.

Elie extended his contacts by giving the impression that he was always able to produce desirable females to brighten up a party, or to minister to the nocturnal needs of a lonely senior officer. But even in this role Elie acted with discretion, playing the part of the reluctant friend rather than the eager pimp: the more he needed to pick the brains of a senior Syrian officer the more he chose a girl who could play hard to get. Sometimes, almost impudently, but at the same time to allay suspicion, he chose girls working as secretaries in the Ministry of Defence. In this way he obtained intelligence which ranged from the latest development in Baathist politics, attitudes towards Egypt and the latest defensive plans. Few agents have been able to weigh up so swiftly and to analyse and transmit accurate interpretations of both political and defence matters so ably as Elie.

His apartment in Damascus became a meeting place for senior Syrian Army officers seeking a night out with courtesans. Such intimacy loosened many tongues in high places. Elie was told how a network of subterranean tunnels had been built in which Syrian soldiers were stationed all along the Israeli border. He was even taken to see them. Soon he was able to transmit to the Mossad in Tel Aviv details of all the Syrian border fortifications, figures of the strength of the forces manning them and the general viewpoint of the Syrian Army *vis-à-vis* Israel. He had access to the most senior officers of the Syrian Army almost any time he wished.

A moment arrived when Elie had such a mass of detailed information and, arising out of this, so many complex questions which his masters in Tel Aviv needed to put to him, that he had to return to Israel. Telling his friends in Damascus that he had to make a quick trip to Argentina, Elie flew to Buenos Aires, stayed a few days making contact with Mossad officers there, then returned to Europe and from there unobtrusively set out for Israel. He was able to give the Mossad not merely an analysis of Syrian Army strengths and dispositions, but an accurate forecast of the strength of the Baathist Party and future political trends.

Shortly after he returned to Syria in 1963, again by a roundabout route, a Baathist coup was launched in Damascus. Amin el-Hafez became President and a number of Elie's closest friends were appointed ministers. His fanatical devotion to the Baathist cause had paid off. From then on Elie was able to entertain leading ministers and Baathist leaders at his villa and he was privy to even more governmental secrets. The Baathists were not nearly as security-conscious as they were to be after 1966, when the extreme left-wing of the party staged a counter-revolution to grasp power for themselves from the bourgeois and often corrupt elements who had previously dominated the Baathists.

As time passed Elie had to step up his broadcasts to Israel and spend longer periods at his transmissions. Daily the risks grew greater. By the spring of 1963 he was obtaining as much information as it normally takes a dozen agents to acquire, and in much quicker time. There were radio messages on the latest armament purchases, minute measurements of tunnels and border posts, Cabinet secrets, snippets of information on what other powers were doing, including the Russians, and with the full story of how Kim Philby, the British traitor, had made his way across Syria into Turkey and from there to the Soviet Union. It is probable that at that time the Israelis knew more about Philby than did the British Secret Service and certainly much more than the CIA, some of whose agents had had instructions to eliminate the former British Secret Serviceman. Elie Cohen knew Philby's exact route into Russia; he had developed an almost photographic memory to absorb topographical details so that he could supplement his radioed intelligence with detailed sketches of locations of Syrian Army outposts and the topography of the areas.

Elie Cohen was one of those allowed to make a tour of these outposts along the Syrian–Israeli border during the visit to Syria of General Ali Amer, Commander-in-Chief of the United Arab Republics Command. It was during some of these tours of fortifications that Elie rashly allowed himself to be photographed as one of the official party. It is true that he did this in the belief that later he would be able to capitalise on being photographed in such distinguished company, but he overlooked the fact that these photographs found their way back to Egypt and that Egyptian scrutiny of them was carried out by their counter-espionage department. By this time Elie's confidence must have exceeded his discretion. Many months later an old Egyptian friend of his reported to the Egyptian secret police that he believed the photograph was that of an Egyptian Jew with whom he had been at school thirty years before. The final mistake was made not by Elie, but by someone in Tel Aviv who was also over-confident. Some snippets of Elie's intelligence had been passed on by the Mossad to the Voice of Israel. It was not long before even the somewhat lax Syrians realised that there must be a traitor in their midst, or, alternatively, an enemy agent.

Suspicions of espionage inside Damascus soon created tensions in Syrian governmental circles. Elie was quick to sense that attitudes were hardening, that officials were becoming cautious and suspicious and that there was obviously a spy hunt going on. It was at this moment that it would have been wise for the Mossad to have called a halt and ordered him to leave Tel Aviv probably permanently. What weighed against such a decision was that the name of Kamel Amine Tabet was too well known for him suddenly to disappear without a lot of questions being asked. The truth was that if Elie had to be recalled, he would have to maintain his cover for some time in a place like Argentina where he would still use the name of Kamel Amine Tabet.

On the other hand the Mossad could argue that right up to the moment he was caught Elie Cohen provided them with new and vital intelligence. One of the last of these all important transmissions was the news that the Syrians were planning to send teams of saboteurs into Israel.

But by this time the net was closing around Elie. The Syrians had been zealously hunting for months for the traitor in their midst. Certain senior officers had begun to have doubts about the gregarious Kamel Amine Tabet and then came a report from the Egyptians about the photograph which had been identified as that of Elie, despite the moustache which he now wore. Early one morning, while he was tapping out a message to Tel Aviv, security agents led by Colonel Ahmed Swidani, Syria's Chief of Counter-espionage, burst into his villa and arrested him in the act.

Elie had been quick enough to warn Tel Aviv that he had been caught by stepping up the pace of his last broadcast, a pre-arranged signal in the event of his arrest. Radio Damascus also announced the capture of Kamel Amine Tabet, naming him as one of Israel's top agents. There was consternation among Elie's many Syrian friends who hourly feared they, too, would be picked up for questioning. In governmental circles there was alarm at how Egypt would react to the news that the Baathists had been harbouring a man who was Israel's most important spy in Damascus. It was known then that many Egyptian top officials were dissatisfied with the Baathist leadership. But what really worried those in the government and close to the President was how many senior Baathists might be involved. For this reason it was decided that Cohen would not be tried in public, but in camera, though Syrian authorities seem to have been divided in opinion as to the wisdom of this course.

There was never any doubt as to the course the trial would

take, despite every effort made by Israel to try to ensure Elie was adequately defended. French aid was sought by the Israelis who briefed two distinguished Paris advocates, Batonnier Paul Arrighi and Maître Jacques Mercier, on behalf of Elie's wife and family. But the Syrian authorities were adamant in refusing any facilities to the two Frenchman. So outraged were these lawyers that when the trial ended and Elie had been sentenced to death along with two Syrian associates, they published a letter which they had sent to the Syrian President protesting that, despite repeated assurances, they were kept from seeing Cohen, from attending the court and from appealing and seeking clemency for their client. The procedure, they said, was 'a defiance of all moral rules'.[3]

Through intermediaries Israel secretly offered Syria a cheque for more than a million dollars, plus army lorries, tractors and a large quantity of medical supplies in exchange for Elie's life. They managed to start secret talks with Syrian officials and even stepped up their offer to include the handing over of ten Syrian spies captured during the last few years. Never in history has so much been offered to save the life of a single spy. But for the fact that so many highly placed Syrians were involved, it is just possible the offer might have been accepted. But the hierarchy of the Baathist Party knew full well that if Elie were freed, some of the left-wing of the party would insist he had been saved by traitors inside their own ranks.

Elie Cohen was hanged in the public square of Damascus on 18 May 1965. He was buried in the city that afternoon and appeals for his body to be returned to Israel were ignored by the Syrian authorities. 'There is no doubt that he was tortured beyond belief,' said Maître Mercier. 'That is why his body was not sent back to Israel. His body was mutilated and as good as dead long before he died on the scaffold.'

Consternation in the ranks of the Syrian Government at the revelations of Elie Cohen's friends in the Army and the Baathist Party led to a wave of anger among the people. There were vociferous demands for those who had confided in the Israeli spy to be punished. Elie's exploits led directly to the collapse of the Government, the disgrace of a number of Cabinet Ministers and the arrest of more than sixty Syrian Army officers, seventeen of whom were found guilty of conduct prejudicial to the safety of the state and in due course put to death.

It was Elie's widow, Nadia, who had the last word on the

whole affair. 'Something inside me whispered that the day my husband would become a public personality was rapidly approaching.

'I said goodbye to him in the last days of November 1964, with a clear feeling that this would be our last meeting. When they informed me two months later that he had been caught, my heart ached, but I was not surprised.

' "Your husband was a hero," they said. "His exploits will go down in history." When the Six-Day War ended I knew that indeed that's what he was and that history will remember him.'4

7

Global Hunt for Nazis

*It's all in the present, what they did is not a
matter of old history, and cannot be. Once you
could say that a mass murderer was a sick man,
but now we have a type beyond our judgement,
the man murdering from his desk. They have de-
valued human life and that is why I want life
imprisonment for them. To redress the moral
balance.*

(SIMON WIESENTHAL)

ONE NIGHT in November 1948, a heavy sack plopped into the
moonlit waters of Tangier Bay from a house overlooking the
harbour. Inside it was the body of Countess Marguerite d'Andurain, widow of the Vicomte Pierre d'Andurain, and for many
years a notorious intriguer in Middle Eastern affairs.

Two months later Casablanca police heard the strange tale of
the Countess's end from Hans Abel (who had been living under
the alias of Renato Poncini), a young ex-Gestapo agent. According to Abel, it was he who disposed of the Countess after kicking
her downstairs at her villa. He was the last of many men in her
life. What mystified many people was why Abel should confess to
this murder when the body of the Countess was never found.

Abel and his girl friend, Hélène Kultz were caretakers on the
Countess's yacht *Djeilan*. She had come to Morocco, said Abel,
to help smuggle ex-Nazis living in Spain via the port of Tangier
to Latin America. Inquiries by the French police showed that the
Countess was also interested in trafficking in Congolese gold.
Hans Abel and his employer had quarrelled when the middle-
aged Countess discovered that her lover was paying more attention to the younger and more attractive Hélène Kultz. After killing
the Countess Hans Abel sold the yacht's stores and some fittings
to a Tangier dealer and then fled with Hélène to Casablanca.

It was partly through this affair that the Israeli Secret Service got their first break in tracking down ex-Nazis and war criminals to Latin America. Marguerite d'Andurain was the daughter of a French magistrate and even as a girl of seventeen had won a reputation for herself as a beauty and a wit. She then married Vicomte Pierre d'Andurain, a French nobleman with a passion for the Middle East. In 1918 they travelled to the Lebanon and started trading in pearls. Marga, as she was known to her friends, learned Arabic and loved to dress in Arab garb. She led a strange enigmatic existence, often alone in the remotest parts of the territory, always dominating the men, European or Arab, who came her way. She bought the Grand Hotel at Palmyra in the Syrian Desert, 120 miles from Damascus, changing its name to the Hotel de la Reine Zenobie, becoming known to the Bedouins as Queen Zenobie.

At some time during the period 1918 to 1925 Marga d'Andurain became involved in the world of espionage, most probably in the first place as an agent for the French. She met Lawrence of Arabia, is said deliberately to have set her cap at him, but that women-shy masochist fled from her in terror. Then she had a love affair with a Colonel Sinclair of British Intelligence, who was later found dead in Damascus, his death being attributed to suicide. In 1925 Marga divorced her husband and married a Wahabi sheikh named Suleiman, who took her, secretly disguised as a man, to Mecca to gratify her wish to see the Kaaba, the sacred black stone in the mosque in that holy city. There are various versions as to what happened as a result of that trip. One was that she was discovered on the pilgrimage, arrested and sentenced to be stoned to death, but that the intervention of King Ibn Saud saved her life. However, it is also said that when Sheikh Suleiman locked her up in his harem at Jeddah she revolted and that within a few days her husband had died of poisoning. It is quite certain that Suleiman died, but what is not clear is whether Ibn Saud saved her from being sentenced to death for poisoning her husband, or for travelling to Mecca.

Strange as all this may sound outside the pages of Ouida, the life of Marga d'Andurain followed an increasingly bizarre pattern. Within a short time she returned to Palmyra and re-married the Vicomte in 1937. Within two months of her re-marriage the Vicomte d'Andurain was found dead in the grounds of the Hotel de la Reine Zenobie with seventeen knife-wounds in his back. Two men were arrested, one of whom was stabbed to death in prison before he could talk. Still handsome, the widowed Countess mixed espionage with dubious business deals. She smuggled gold into France, traded in forged passports and frequented the best hotels from Nice to Cairo. At the outbreak of World War II she was in Paris where she did some petty spying for the Nazis, who seem to have paid her badly. By 1945 she was living in a flat which her nephew, a young Parisian lawyer named Raimond Clérisse, had lent her. When Clérisse wanted his flat back there was a quarrel. Shortly afterwards the young lawyer was found writhing in agony and, in the presence of Marga and a servant, he accused the Countess of having given him poisoned chocolates. He died and Marga fled from Paris. A few months later she was arrested in Nice and charged with complicity in his murder, but at her trial she was acquitted.

Since that day Marga was reputed to have been on the death lists of various powers and organisations. She had many enemies, including a Soviet agent who was said to have been shadowing her for several months prior to her death. What had caused the Secret Services of a number of countries to take an interest in her was undoubtedly her role as a friend of ex-Nazis and her attempts to smuggle them out of Europe. It was an Israeli agent in Tangier who, by making inquiries about the Countess, first discovered the traffic in Nazis and just how many of them were getting through to Latin America. Today this agent is a banker in Europe and he has never taken full credit for his initial role in helping to launch a global hunt for the Nazis by the Israelis. But without his initial work and diligent probing Eichmann and many others might never have been caught.

Indeed, at that time many Israelis did not take seriously reports that prominent ex-Nazis were being smuggled incognito out of Europe to Argentina, Paraguay, Uruguay and even Brazil and Peru. It was X——, the Israeli agent in Tangier, who tracked down Hans Abel in Casablanca. Without his prompting it is doubtful if any arrests would have been made for the murder of Marga. There were some who believed that as her body was never found she was still alive and had staged her own death. Nevertheless Hans Abel was sent to prison for twenty years, and there seemed to be no doubt whatsoever of his guilt. Both he and Hélène Kultz had forged Swiss passports on them when arrested.

Shortly before she disappeared the Countess d'Andurain had

applied for a visa to visit Gibraltar in her yacht the *Djeilan*, but this had been refused mainly on account of her association with the Nazis. But X——, who had excellent contacts among the British Security Forces in Gibraltar, made a trip across the Straits from Tangier and learned that this woman was deeply involved in the Palestinian conflict on the Arab side. As proof of this he was given photo-copies of a number of documents alleged to have been stolen from the Countess, including a highly confidential and incriminating letter to her from King Abdullah of Jordan. On the strength of this X—— made further inquiries and in the town of Tetuan, then capital of the Spanish Zone of Morocco, confronted a Spanish accomplice of the Countess d'Andurain and obtained from him a list of the names of more than thirty Nazis who had passed to Latin America through the Countess's network.

It was some time before all this information filtered through to Tel Aviv and even then, largely because X—— was not a senior Mossad agent, there were demands for further checks before any action was taken. What mostly concerned the Intelligence executives was whether the Nazis escape network would reveal any indications of a renaissance of Nazism and fascism in Europe itself, if in fact, there was any evidence of a neo-Nazi party underground in Germany or elsewhere. It was for this reason that the Israelis were slow to act in tracking down and capturing ex-Nazis: they were afraid that any premature move on their part might prevent them from finding out who were lending support to these war criminals.

Perhaps in the light of the past thirty years this may seem to have been a case of the Israelis being obsessed with Nazism and having a totally unwarranted phobia about the renaissance of that creed. But at that time there were a number of reasons why not merely the Israelis, but other races as well, needed to be vigilant in this respect. Under cover of stamping out communism, in the name of the cold war and even the sometimes bogus cause of defending Western civilisation, a number of Western nations were establishing some highly questionable relationships with former Nazis. One of these strange relationships that especially worried the Israeli Intelligence was that of General Reinhard Gehlen, formerly Hitler's Intelligence chief, with the American CIA. As a lieutenant-general and military intelligence expert in World War II, Gehlen had collected an abundance of data about Russia. When he realised that the war was on the verge of being lost, he packed this data in his luggage and left Berlin for Bavaria where he waited until the first US Intelligence officer arrived to inter- rogate him. Gehlen was soon able to make a deal with the Americans and he made such an impression on them that he was able to launch a new anti-communist intelligence organisation financed by the CIA to the tune of £200 millions.

One of the earliest reports the Israelis had on the whereabouts of prominent ex-Nazis was that Martin Bormann had fled to Latin America. At first they became more convinced of the truth of this because Gehlen had told the Americans quite a different story which one of the Mossad men in Germany had ferreted out. Gehlen claimed to produce 'evidence' that Martin Bormann was killed in Berlin in 1945. Was Gehlen lying to protect Bormann? The Israelis became even more suspicious when Gehlen later declared that Bormann was a Soviet spy, still alive in Moscow. Gehlen then swore that Bormann actually became a Russian spy as early as 1941 and that at the end of the war he defected to the Russians. But more than this the Israelis were gravely concerned about the evidence sent them by Mossad agents that Gehlen was making undercover deals with Nazis who were hiding out in various parts of the Middle East—Cairo, Damascus and Bagh- dad. Over and above all this was the horrifying thought, that in the name of defending Western civilisation against communism, one of Hitler's leading generals had gained a position of great power not only with the American CIA, but ultimately as new head of West German Intelligence under Dr. Adenauer, having managed to cast suspicion on Dr. Otto John, who, after the war, with full British approval, had become head of West German counter-espionage. What helped Gehlen back to a position of complete power in West Germany was when in 1954 John went from West Berlin to East Berlin—by his own account after being drugged by a Soviet agent, by other accounts as a defector. He escaped to the West in December 1955, and was tried and sen- tenced to four years' imprisonment for treasonable falsification. Dr. John was released in 1958 after the remainder of his sentence had been suspended. There is little doubt that he had been framed over a long period.

It was current political anxieties rather than any particular phobia about Nazis which in the early fifties led the Israelis on a world-wide hunt for Nazis and war criminals. Only after the actual hunt had been fully launched did an element of vengeance enter into it. But by that time the Israelis had complete dossiers on these war criminals and they were deeply shocked by what they learned.

'We were even more shocked,' X—— told me, 'when we learned that the escape of these criminals had been actively aided not only by adventurers like the Countess d'Andurain, some members of Franco's entourage and various Vichy Frenchmen, but also by people in the Vatican City. One of the clues I picked up when looking into the d'Andurain case was that some of these escaping Nazis were actually getting refugee passports from Vatican relief centres.

'The name of Eichmann cropped up early on in the war trials at Nuremberg and gradually we had reports from people who had escaped from the concentration camps who told of his butchery. But outside Israel the world at large had hardly ever heard of him. As far as most of the Western powers were concerned, Eichmann, the worst war criminal of them all, was the forgotten man. It seems ridiculous that Hess, who spent so much of the war in captivity in Britain, should be jailed for life and that a monster like Eichmann should go free.'

Otto Adolf Eichmann was born in the Rhineland in 1906, the son of a book-keeper who was also a devout Evangelical Christian. The family moved to Austria and in 1932 Eichmann joined the Nazi Party and soon became a member of the Austrian SS. Before the war Eichmann was put in charge of the Jewish emigration office in Vienna at a time when the Nazis were expelling Jews from the territories they held after having stripped them of their cash and property. From Vienna, where his ruthless efficiency won him praise from the Nazi hierarchy, Eichmann was sent to Prague to carry out the same work. Later, when war had broken out, he was charged with the task of deporting Jews from the Greater Reich to ghettos in Poland, and finally given overall responsibility for carrying out what the Nazis euphemistically called the 'Final Solution', in other words, the solution of the 'Jewish Problem' by the extermination of that race. Though only a lieutenant-colonel in the SS, Eichmann had extraordinary powers, extending even to France, Italy, Hungary and Rumania. He created around him a huge staff of bureaucrats.

It was he who organised the gas ovens and the speediest methods of carrying out the mass murders of Jews. But he was always careful to cover up his own activities and to ensure that the blame went to somebody else. Gerald Reitlinger cites an example of this on 16 July 1942, at the Vélodrome d'Hiver, a Paris sports stadium, when 'some 7,000 people were in this stadium, mostly women and small children who had been unable to escape a mass round-up of Jews. They were kept there for five days without food. There was one water hydrant and two doctors. A dozen people went insane, several women gave birth to children and thirty died.

'The purpose of this delay before entraining for the gas chambers was to find out from Eichmann what was to be done with the children. And it took all that time for Eichmann to cover himself up. On the fifth day the ruling arrived. The children were to be separated from their parents and kept at Drancy until trains were ready to take them to the gas chamber some 900 miles away. In one of the box cars returning empty through Belgium it was reported a few weeks later that the bodies of 25 children had been found aged from two to four. At Auschwitz it had not even been thought worthwhile removing them from the train.'[1]

Eichmann, cautious in most things and at all times ensuring that what he carried out was approved from on high, set about his work with a fiendish relish. It was the fact that he was sufficiently alert and conscious of his evil-doing to try to cover himself at all times which totally damns him. But if proof is wanted that he actually enjoyed his 'work', it is provided by Dieter Wisliceny, another mass murderer who was executed in Czechoslovakia. Describing his elusive and almost unknown chief, Eichmann, Wisliceny said of him: 'He told me he did not care what happened if Germany lost the war. He said he would leap into his grave laughing because the feeling that he had five million Jews on his conscience only filled his heart with gladness.'[2]

But so well had Eichmann covered his traces that some people in Israeli Intelligence believed he was dead. X——himself declares that 'information I passed to Tel Aviv in 1949 that Eichmann was almost certainly somewhere in Latin America and that it was known he had headed that way was received with incredulity.'

All that was then known for certain was that on 8 May 1945, Eichmann had been captured by US forces in Austria. By that time he had discarded his SS uniform and personal documents and was wearing the uniform of a private in the Luftwaffe. He gave the Americans a false name, though this was not discovered at the time. After that there was no news at all of him. Some reports reaching Israel suggested he was dead, others that he had escaped from an American camp. All that seems certain is that there was a lamentable failure on the part of the Americans either to track down Eichmann, or even to check on the identity of the 'Luftwaffe private' they held.

'Even as early as 1945 there was a special Jewish unit in Europe trying to track down war criminals, with Eichmann their especial quarry,' declared X———. 'The trouble was that so many conflicting reports came through that Tel Aviv became sceptical. The Latin American report that I made was discounted because at that time some believed that Eichmann had made full use of his Arab contacts [he had been a close ally of the Mufti of Jerusalem] to find sanctuary in Kuwait.'

There were, of course, many other Nazis who were being hunted down and a great deal of spade-work on all this was carried out by a man outside the Israeli Intelligence, but who, nevertheless, was able to be of great assistance to them. This was Dr. Simon Wiesenthal, who was himself practically the sole survivor of all his family from the 'Final Solution'. Simon Wiesenthal's father had actually been a cavalry officer in the Emperor Franz Josef's army, a rare honour for a Jew in those days. In World War II some of the Wiesenthal family were killed by Germans, others by Russians. He was himself taken to a concentration camp and in April 1943, stripped naked and rounded up by the SS in the sandpit where executions were carried out. At the last minute he was fortuitously saved. In 1945 when the Americans entered Mauthausen, corpses were lying around where they had fallen and Dr. Wiesenthal was a third of his normal weight when he was rescued.

Wiesenthal has been hailed as the man who tracked down Eichmann, but he himself makes no such claim, though from his office in Linz where he set up a centre to help refugees and amass evidence to hunt down war criminals he worked ceaselessly to get a lead on the elusive mass killer. Perhaps his most valuable contribution to the ultimate location of Eichmann was the watch he kept on Eichmann's wife and family. As a result of this he was able to prove that Eichmann was alive and well somewhere and in touch with his wife so that Frau Eichmann's claim to be a widow had to be officially denied by the Austrian Government.

Wiesenthal's Jewish Documentation Centre in Vienna became the nucleus of a private Secret Service charged with bringing ex-Nazis and war criminals to justice. He began building up files on them immediately after the war, first for the American War Crimes Office and then for his own centre, which was supported by funds from Austrian Jews. Within a few years Dr. Wiesenthal had established informants all over the world: 'from Scotland to South America,' he said once, 'each day I get between twenty-five and thirty letters giving information. None of it is paid for. If you pay for information, it is not information, it is business.'[3]

Unofficial help was given to him by a number of governments, for over the years the doctor acquired a reputation for integrity and justice as well as efficiency. The government which he has found most helpful in more recent years has been that of Holland, though in the immediate post-war period many war criminals were actually protected by some Dutch politicians. It was Dr. Wiesenthal who tracked down Erich Rajakovic, the ex-SS officer who was dubbed the 'Eichmann of Holland', and he was personally responsible for bringing 3,500 war criminals to trial in the immediate post-war period. But he had persevered with this work ever since, despite the fact that in 1965 the Statute of Limitations preventing the prosecution of war criminals after this date automatically came into force. The year before that he stated: 'I have in my files complete dossiers on 22,500 more murderers and torturers still to be brought to book.'[4]

All this may suggest that Simon Wiesenthal is a humourless, fanatical man interested only in vengeance, his mind dwelling eternally on the past. Any such deduction would be far from the mark on almost every count. He is in fact a jovial man who often laughs heartily and is possessed of a keen sense of humour. He was born at Lemburg, which used to be in Poland, but is now in Soviet Russia and one can understand how he feels when he says: 'Before the war there were 150,000 Jews in Lemburg; after the war there were 500. I was one of the survivors. That is why I do this.'

Single-minded he certainly is, for he has sacrificed a career as an architect to undertake this one-man crusade against ex-Nazis. But he is a logical man whose eye is as much on present events as on the past. It is probably in part at least due to his influence and work that the Statute of Limitations was extended after 1965, thus enabling him to bring to justice such men as Franz Stangl, former SS commander of the Polish concentration camp at Treblinka, who was extradited from Brazil in 1967. As to the present day, Dr. Wiesenthal is seriously concerned at the fact that Soviet Russia and some of her communist allies in Europe have not only given sanctuary to war criminals, but provided them with key jobs. He alone has effectively put the spotlight on Soviet connivance at Nazi extermination practices, producing an extensive dossier on the subject. It was Dr. Wiesenthal who uncovered the fact that thirty-nine former Nazi propagandists were holding key positions in East Germany in 1969, and that they had masterminded a violent anti-Jewish campaign in the press of that country. Further inquiries revealed that more than 600 ex-Nazis held jobs inside the East German communist regime and that the Polish secret police had been conducting a Jewish witch-hunt for some few years past.

Dr. Wiesenthal's work has not been carried on without dangers to him personally. He has received no less than a hundred threats on his life during his post-war campaign against the Nazis. Yet he has never asked for police protection. In November 1975, Dr. Bruno Kreisky, the Austrian Chancellor, accused Wiesenthal of having been a Nazi agent himself during the Hitler era and of having 'indulged in Mafia methods' in tracking down Nazis. He even implied that Wiesenthal had been involved in an espionage case concerning a former Austrian secret police official and that he had spied for the Czechs. The Chancellor's astonishing attack followed Dr. Wiesenthal's denunciation of a former SS officer, Dr. Friederich Peter, who was head of the right-wing Austrian Freedom Party. Dr. Peter had had the offer of the Vice-Chancellorship made to him in return for a promise to support Dr. Kreisky's Socialists if they failed to gain a majority. It was then that Wiesenthal produced German war diaries which showed that Dr. Peter had served in the special SS brigade set up by Himmler to round up and massacre the Jews.

Wiesenthal replied to the Chancellor's allegations by threatening a libel action and eventually the matter was settled out of court, but his row with the Chancellor was damaging all the same and shortly after this the Nazi-hunter announced that he was considering retiring. But it is hard to believe he will ever give up while such arch war criminals as Joseph Mengele (now living in Argentina) and Walther Rauff, head of the gas execution squad and now living in Chile, remain safely out of range of justice.

The capture of Stangl was perhaps his greatest triumph and, though he received co-operation from the Israeli Intelligence, the actual arrest of the Nazi cost Wiesenthal a considerable sum of money. The wily doctor has often relied on the fact that sooner or later Nazis will fall out with each other and then one of them will come to him and pass on a dossier on the other. So it was with Stangl: an ex-Gestapo official in South America gave the first tip-off that the former Treblinka Camp chief was employed at the São Paolo Volkswagen assembly plant in Brazil. Wiesenthal arranged for a bogus telephone call to be made by a nurse at a local hospital to the car plant, asking for the ex-SS man to come to the accident ward immediately as his daughter had been injured in a car crash. When Stangl arrived Brazilian detectives were waiting to arrest him. But apart from this final subterfuge to trap Stangl before anyone warned him of the net about to close in on him Wiesenthal had to make all manner of diplomatic contacts both in Brazil and the United States.

One of the factors which slowed up the long hunt for Eichmann was the mystery surrounding the whereabouts of Martin Bormann. The Israelis had a shrewd idea that if they could find the Deputy Führer, Martin Bormann, they could find Eichmann, as it was generally suspected that the former had helped the latter to escape. But conflicting stories on Bormann's whereabouts made this increasingly difficult. X—— claimed to have learned that Countess d'Andurain had been one of the principal figures in the network which brought Bormann from hiding in Europe to safety in Latin America. But Tel Aviv was sceptical about his story at that time because of the theory that he had gone over to the Russians.

'Eventually I, too, became sceptical,' says X——. 'I was quite certain there was an escape route, but from what I gathered from an ex-crew member of the Countess's yacht, *Djeilan*, I became convinced that the story about Bormann still being alive was played up by various people for different reasons. This crewman told me that the people organising the escape route used the name of Martin Bormann as a kind of red herring to detract attention from other Nazis who really were slipping through the net. This suited the few remaining Nazis well because they believed that the story of a living Nazi leader in exile, ready to return at the right moment, would keep hopes alive among their dwindling membership. As for the Russians, they found it was a useful story to keep Bormann alive as part of the cold war propaganda. As for General Gehlen, what was one to make of a man who first produced "evidence" that Bormann was killed in 1945 and then, years afterwards, claimed he was a Soviet spy, still alive in Moscow?'

False reports on Bormann abounded and even Dr. Wiesenthal, who followed the Bormann manhunt for years with the keenest interest, was sure at one time that he had gone to South America. At first it was thought he had gone to Argentina, then, as the hunt for him speeded up, experts were convinced he had moved to another Latin American country. In 1967 Wiesenthal stated: 'The tracking down of a single man using eight to ten aliases, who has unlimited funds, and who is surrounded by friends anxious to protect him, in an area as large as South America, has no precedent, except in the case of Eichmann. But I would say it would be worth while to make inquiries among the gigantic coffee plantations in the vast jungle area of Tingo Maria in Peru.'[5]

But by 1974 Wiesenthal had changed his mind completely. Asked what had happened to Bormann, he replied: 'Definitely dead. Suicided on May 2 or 3, 1945.'

Professor Tuviah Friedman, Director of the Nazi War Crimes Centre in Israel, who spent fifteen years tracking down Bormann and Eichmann, claimed in an interview in 1960 that Adolf Eichmann, making full use of his extensive contacts in the Arab world, first escaped to Kuwait, believing that he would be much safer there than in any other part of the world. It was a foolish belief because, as Eichmann soon discovered, there were many Arabs prepared to betray him for a price. He moved from one Middle Eastern country to another, always in terror of being captured and smuggled across the border into Israel. In fact, Eichmann did not have to worry about Arabs alone; Israeli agents were even then hunting him down inside Syria and Kuwait. Professor Friedman, whose role in tracking down Eichmann has been somewhat neglected by most writers on the subject, said that Eichmann 'had at his disposal no fewer than seventy passports of many nationalities. They included some in Jewish names [he spoke Hebrew and Yiddish perfectly], and he used whatever passport suited the circumstances and his purpose. Our great difficulty in establishing the identity of the man we believed to be Eichmann was the fact that since 1942 he had either not been photographed or else all negatives and pictures had been destroyed. Nor did his signature appear on any documents. Eichmann invariably gave orders by telephone.'[6]

It is necessary to examine carefully the cogent reasons which the Israeli Secret Service had for tracking down and capturing Eichmann more than any other war criminal. Eichmann was not only the supreme war criminal of them all as far as Israel was concerned, with millions of deaths due entirely to him, but he was practically unknown to the rest of the world. Eichmann had worked in almost total anonymity and even the references to him at the Nuremberg trials did not attract more than passing interest in the non-Jewish world. But, over and above this, there was the undeniable fact that by 1960 political developments generally had been adverse for Israel. The Suez adventure had found them completely let down by Britain and France in an ignominious retreat in the face of bluffing and threats by the United States and Russia (neither would have carried out their threats, if that bluff had been called, as Russia was confronted with the Hungarian revolt and Eisenhower was always no better than a paper tiger). Nasser had established himself as a Middle Eastern dictator with visions of a mighty Arab empire. But beyond all this was the fact that the world had begun to forget about war crimes and concentration camps; some of the politicians and writers had even played down these ghastly deeds and suggested that there had been gross exaggeration about the extent of the decimation of the Jewish population in Europe. What was needed was a full scale trial of a man such as Eichmann so that it could be demonstrated to the world at large that the enormity of the Nazi crimes was beyond belief.

For the Israeli Secret Service, with the help of various private agencies such as Wiesenthal's one-man organisation and Professor Friedman's War Crimes Centre, had already amassed all the evidence required to condemn Eichmann and many others as well. The folly of the Nuremberg trials was that too many people who need never have been put on trial were actually sentenced to death, while the real criminals got away scot free. And ever since there had been a reaction against the mishandling of the Nuremberg trials which had tended to hide the horrors perpetrated in the concentration camps. For when the Nazis found that it took too long to burn up the mass graves and that the carbon-monoxide chambers required too many buildings, it was

Eichmann who came up with the ultimate solution for speedy extermination of his victims—his own brain-child and master-piece, the Zyklon B Chambers with linked crematoria, reducing to bone-meal, mattress-hair, gold dental fillings and vapour 24,000 Jews a day.

The theory in Tel Aviv was that if Eichmann could be brought to justice the publicity resulting from the trial would be of tremendous value to Israel. 'Once this is done,' said Professor Friedman, 'anti-Semitism will have been killed in Europe for the next twenty-five years. It is not realised that the murder of 20 millions, including six million Jews—in eighteen occupied countries—was the work of not more than 200 top rank SS and Gestapo officers, headed by Muller and Eichmann.'[7]

In the final reckoning both Wiesenthal and Friedman were unlucky in that, having trailed Eichmann for fifteen years, they had no part in his capture. It was the patient pertinacity of the special unit of the Mossad, continuing the work begun by the Haganah underground unit charged with tracking down war criminals in 1945, which finally made a break-through. As the special unit delved deeper for evidence that would convict Eichmann, if ever they caught him, so they became more and more convinced that here was the supreme war criminal as far as the Jewish people were concerned. The evidence uncovered by the Mossad agents shows that Eichmann was so virulently anti-Semitic that he could not tolerate orders from Hitler himself which would have enabled 8,700 Jewish families to be saved. In 1944 Hitler had agreed to permit the emigration of 8,700 Jewish families from Hungary, if Admiral Horthy, the Regent, would permit him to take the remaining 300,000 Jews in Budapest. Even this concession angered Eichmann and he planned to intercede through Himmler for a reversal of the order: this was clearly proved in a telegram to the Foreign Office in Berlin on 25 July 1944, from Colonel Veesenmayer, Reich Plenipotentiary in Budapest. It was evidence such as this which drove the hunters of Eichmann relentlessly on, switching their attentions from Europe to Argentina, where a unit was specially established to carry on the search in that country.

In the end Eichmann was given away by his mistress and his son's girl-friend, but it was a senior official of the West German Government who eventually enabled the Israeli Secret Service to plan the kidnapping of Eichmann.

8

The Eichmann Kidnapping

*'Operation Eichmann' had to be performed. The
fact that it was necessary to take Eichmann out
of Argentina caused us a great deal of inner conflict. My mind was by no means easy about the
need to carry out a clandestine action in the sovereign territory of a friendly country.*

(ISSER HAREL)[1]

JULES LEMOINE, a former crewman of the *Djeilan*, provided the
first clue as to Eichmann's final destination. He had left the ship
at Tangier and disappeared into the interior of Morocco because
he feared that Abel and the Countess had been plotting to kill
him at sea on the grounds that he knew too much. Lemoine
reported that 'a certain important Nazi' was waiting in the
Vatican City to obtain a refugee passport for Argentina under the
name of Ricardo Clementi.

'He swore that this was the man's real name,' said X——,
'and that he had it endorsed on a Vatican identification paper, and
for this reason I was not inclined to take the matter too seriously.
We had not then realised how many secret sympathisers with
the Nazis there then were in the Vatican City. It was only later
we learned that there was a pro-Nazi 'unit'—call it what you will
—inside the Holy City and that the Pope himself deliberately
turned a blind eye to their activities. It was big Vatican business
and their bureaucrats were taking a rake-off for the Nazi big-fish
being smuggled through. In the end the Mossad obtained a complete dossier on the Vatican's undercover operations in the late
forties and early fifties in smuggling ex-Nazis out of Europe to
the safer fascist states of Latin America.'

The name given—'Ricardo Clementi'—was not quite accurate
anyhow. The pseudonym which Eichmann actually used when
he escaped from Austria to Italy was Ricardo Klement and thus

it was spelt on his refugee passport, endorsed by the Vatican, identifying him as a mechanic, born in Bolzano, Italy, of German parentage. Only years later was the name of Ricardo Klement linked up with that of Ricardo Clementi.

But in the end it was a high official of the West German Government who enabled the Israeli Secret Service to kidnap Adolf Eichmann. Precise information on the Nazi's whereabouts was supplied by Dr. Fritz Bauer, Chief Prosecutor of Hesse Province, who had obtained the information in the utmost confidence from the West German Secret Service following their interrogation of two agents of a Nazi escape organisation. They supplied all the data about the escape networks, secret funds and the hiding places of some of the war criminals. Dr. Bauer, a Jew himself, decided to pass this information on in the utmost secrecy to the Israeli Secret Service, but he also insisted on not revealing the names of any of his informants which meant that the Israelis had to follow up his tip more or less from scratch. Bauer had been a judge in Stuttgart until the Nazis came to power; imprisoned for a year by the new regime, he moved to Denmark. In 1940 when the Nazis seized that country, he was again arrested and sent to prison for three years. Eventually he escaped to Sweden. When he returned to Germany after the war he not unnaturally wished to see as many Nazis as possible tried for crimes they had committed. The information he had obtained about Eichmann was just what he wanted.

Dr. Bauer's intelligence was passed to the Ministry of Foreign Affairs in Tel Aviv by an intermediary Dr. Shinar, who was head of the Reparations Mission in West Germany. It was Walter Eytan, Director-General of the Israeli Foreign Ministry, who telephoned Isser Harel with the tidings that at last there was a 'lead' on Eichmann.

There had been many disappointments in the quest for Eichmann. On countless occasions Isser Harel had been given what promised to be a firm clue to his whereabouts; but invariably when the Mossad followed it up, it turned out to be a dead end. As Harel himself said: '... we kept getting tips about places where he was supposedly hiding, but in each case investigation ended in disappointment, and what's more, we couldn't even find definite proof that he was still alive.'[2]

It was towards the end of 1957 that Dr. Bauer's tip was passed on to Tel Aviv and immediately Harel, whose professional instincts told him that this time there was a substantial clue, set in motion what became the best organised kidnapping by a Secret Service in modern history. The pros and cons of the action by the Mossad will be argued about by historians and politicians for generations to come and there will be those who condemn the action and those who support it. What should be made clear is that this was not just an act of revenge. Harel himself has said that initially he had some qualms about the illegality of the action, though none about the moral issues. 'The proper procedure would have been to advise the Argentine authorities of our suspicions that a German immigrant resident in a suburb of Buenos Aires was the war criminal Adolf Eichmann and then to wait for the prolonged legalities entailed in extraditing him either to Germany or to one of the other countries where he was wanted. But how could we know that Eichmann himself would wait?'[3]

This was the crux of the matter. Apart from a prolonged legal wrangle with an element of doubt as to whether he would actually be extradited, there was the probability—indeed, the near certainty, that Eichmann himself would go to ground and escape elsewhere long before extradition could be enforced. Eichmann, who had taken such extraordinary precautions to escape from Europe and create a new identity in Argentina, would not tamely await arrest. In any event there was a Nazi escape route still in operation and his German friends in Argentina would ensure that he got away in a new disguise to Paraguay, Uruguay, Peru or elsewhere. Thus Harel was determined that he would personally direct the whole operation right from the checking up on the Bauer report and the actual location of Eichmann, down to his kidnapping and transportation to Israel. And Harel was the ideal man to carry out such an assignment, not merely because of his record as a first-class Secret Service director, but because he was such a close friend of Ben-Gurion.

Harel had the right blend of ruthlessness, cunning and diplomacy and in most accounts of the kidnapping of Eichmann it is the subtle diplomacy of the Israelis which has been overlooked. From 1950 to 1960 they had relentlessly followed up every clue as to the Nazi's whereabouts, but when it actually came to the moment of decision they showed consummate diplomatic skill in winning over a trusted team of Argentinians as allies and, by doing so, minimising the risk of any serious political trouble with the Argentinian Government during or after the kidnapping.

Eichmann had arrived in Buenos Aires towards the end of the summer of 1950: his *cédula de identidad* was given to him by the Argentinian police on 3 August of that year. Even after putting several thousand miles between himself and Europe and being surrounded now by Nazi friends, Eichmann continued to maintain a low profile, changing his address frequently, and he was always suspicious of any strangers in the vicinity. In 1952 he went to live in the Argentinian province of San Miguel de Tucumán and at that time he seems to have changed his profession, listing himself as a cartographer. It was this change of occupation which attracted the attention of the Argentinian secret police who soon discovered that the man calling himself Ricardo Klement was Adolf Eichmann. The secret was known only to a few and, though no effort was made to exploit the discovery, from that time onwards Eichmann was subjected to surveillance.

Aware that he was still far from being safe from arrest, Eichmann tried to settle in other parts of South America. For a while he evaded his watchers, but what he had not counted on was that one or two Argentinian democrats also shared his secret with the police. When he returned to Argentina a few years later, believing he had probably thrown his watchers off the scent, he looked forward to a peaceful reunion with his family. For two years after he arrived in Argentina his wife, Vera, unobtrusively slipped away from her home in Vienna and went to Buenos Aires by a roundabout route.

The Israelis had been anxious to locate Vera Eichmann for a very long time. They had checked on a variety of reports all to no avail. The cover story put out by friends on her behalf was that she had married an American and left Europe. The Israelis suspected that it was a cover story and that the 'second husband' would turn out to be none other than the first. Therefore one of the most vital tasks of the Mossad was to keep a constant watch in Vienna for her eventual return. They had learned that her passport, issued in her maiden name of Veronika Liebl, was soon due for renewal and that to comply with Austrian and Argentinian formalities she would have to apply in person in Vienna.

When Vera Eichmann duly appeared in the Austrian capital Mossad agents shadowed her by night and day. One of them followed her back to Argentina. It was the first real success the Israelis had had in following up the Bauer tip. One of the difficul-

ties which confronted the Israeli agents in Argentina was in ensuring a hundred per cent accurate identification of Eichmann.
This was mainly due to the fact that very few photographs of him
existed: he had always shied away from the cameras even during
the hey-day of the Nazi movement and towards the end of the
war had systematically destroyed any photographs of himself he
or his family possessed. It made the quest for Eichmann 'like that
of a blind man being sent to locate the enemy', said one Mossad
operator.

The information which Harel had was terse and sparse enough;
on the other hand, as he himself pointed out, at least it was lucid
and positive. Dr. Bauer's informants had not given the alias being
used by Eichmann, but they had passed on an address—'4261
Chacabuco Street, Olivos, a suburb of Buenos Aires'.

Harel sent one of his key professional agents to Buenos Aires,
giving him more or less a free hand in dealing with the situation.
In his account of the whole operation Harel describes this man as
'Yoel Goren, an experienced operations man who, before joining
the Service, had spent quite a lot of time in the Latin American
countries as the representative of a private company and still
spoke some Spanish.'[4] In fact, as Harel himself makes clear in a
preface to his book, it was then essential for security reasons to
preserve the anonymity of the team engaged in the hunt for
Eichmann and the name 'Yoel Goren' is a pseudonym. Only one
name was revealed in the book—that of Shalom Dani, who has
since died, who joined the team of investigators as the all important expert in forging documents and passports.

One important reason for the guarding of the identity of
members of the Israeli team is that a number of them had close
business and other associations with Argentina and other parts of
Latin America. But it was almost equally important not to reveal
their true identities because this would spotlight their friendship
with certain Argentinian citizens who had played a role in capturing Eichmann. Nazi vengeance was still dealt out to anyone who
tried to probe too deeply into their extensive colony in Latin
America. The leader of the team also used the name 'Zimmerman'
as a result of which the unit in Argentina was sometimes referred
to as the 'Z Team'. He had a reputation for versatility in disguise
and imagination in conducting investigations and it has been said
that he could, if necessary, speak English with a Welsh accent,
learned no doubt in the Welsh–Argentinian colony of Patagonia.

The team of operatives was young and enthusiastic and they soon traced the address where Eichmann was said to be living and ascertained that the woman supposed to be his second wife was undoubtedly Vera Eichmann. The sons of the Klement family were also undoubtedly sons of Eichmann. What was not certain was whether Ricardo Klement was Adolf Eichmann. After Vera had been followed back to Buenos Aires from Vienna there was no doubt at all that she was Adolf's wife. But, although each piece of evidence collected pointed more strongly to Klement being Eichmann, there was still a slight chance that her cover story was true and that he was her second husband. And one serious doubt lingered: Ricardo Klement appeared to be a much older man than Eichmann.

To try to establish Klement's identity positively meant that the agents had to take many photographs of the man with concealed and long distance cameras to avoid detection. These photographs, taken from every conceivable angle, had to be printed off and dispatched to Tel Aviv. There, laboriously, the prints were shown to former inmates of concentration camps who had actually seen Eichmann. Some prints were sent to Vienna and places in Germany for an attempt at identification there. In far too many cases there was a total failure to identify Klement; some gave a positive 'no', saying that this man looked far too old to be Eichmann; others could not be sure; only a few declared he was the Nazi and there was an element of doubt even then. For often it turned out that those who claimed to identify him had only seen Eichmann for a few brief minutes in their lives.

The nightmarish horror of botching the whole operation and kidnapping the wrong man made Isser Harel hold back until the very last minute. In the matter of Eichmann's identification he was a perfectionist and, to be fair, he had no desire to send the wrong man to the gallows. Then, suddenly and unexpectedly, came one of those lucky breaks which make or mar Secret Service work. The agents who had been photographing Klement had been specifically told to record every unusual detail and to report any little incident, however trivial. Some agents photographed him surreptitiously while he was walking from his place of work, the Mercedes Benz car factory in the Suarez district of Buenos Aires, to his home. One snapped him coming out of a shop bearing a bouquet of flowers in his hand.

The leader of the team spotted this photograph and immediately wanted to know whether it was significant. Another Israeli agent who had been stationed in an apartment on the upper floor of a building opposite the Klement home, keeping watch with a pair of binoculars, reported that Klement took the bouquet into his house. The team leader, having had this further confirmation of what he suspected, looked at the date in the calendar. The day on which Klement took the bouquet home was 21 March, the anniversary of Eichmann's marriage to Vera. With a triumphant grin on his face, he declared to his fellow agents: 'This is it! This is far better proof than any identification of photographs. The answer is very simple: why should the second husband of Mrs. Klement want to commemorate the anniversary of her first wedding? There can be no doubt this is the man we are looking for.'

The good news was flashed to Tel Aviv by pre-arranged code immediately. Meanwhile the team in Argentina discussed the best method of kidnapping Eichmann. There was also the problem of how long they could ensure absolute secrecy of their plans and prevent him from learning or even guessing what was afoot. For one or two mistakes had been made by the team, mistakes no professional agent should have risked. Once they realised the extent of the photography that would be required for Eichmann's identification they should have set up their own developing arrangements for security purposes. Instead, as they had had very little experience of photography, they gave the films to a firm to be developed. It was with a sense of panic that they learned that the firm did not carry out its own developments and printing, but passed orders on to an outside photographer and that they had not only asked for the film to be developed, but for prints and enlargements as well. For a few hours the Israeli agents suspected that the film might well have fallen into the wrong hands. However, all was well and, apart from the lucky break of the bouquet incident, firmer confirmation of photographic evidence was soon available. This was made possible by 'blowing up' photographs of Klement to take account of facial measurements and minor idiosyncrasies and then comparing these with 'blown up' prints of the very few photographs obtainable of Eichmann of twenty years earlier.

Another important clue to his identity had come to the Israeli Secret Service from Lothar Hermann, a German half-Jew who had gone blind in Dachau concentration camp and now lived in

Argentina. Hermann's daughter had become very friendly with Nikolaus Eichmann, Adolf's son. Because he talked freely about his hatred of the Jews and made comments such as 'Hitler should have finished them all off', the girl mentioned this to her father. He in his turn asked his daughter to describe what the boy's father (Klement) looked like. From the description she gave, Herr Hermann was convinced he must be Eichmann and it was from this source that Dr. Bauer's first tip had come.

Another tip came from a former German mistress of Eichmann. She had actually followed him to Argentina, been brutally discarded and had then taken a job working in a restaurant close to the Mercedes Benz factory. According to Victor Alexandrov, an Israeli journalist, this woman 'revealed Eichmann's address to a Georgian Jew named Adolf Tauber, known under the pseudonym of Anastasse Beridze',[5] who was a Mossad agent. But the German woman was also an informant of an anti-Nazi group of Argentinians.

It was this group who greatly aided the Israeli agents when they went out to Buenos Aires. In fact, without in any way detracting from the skill and pertinacity of the Israelis, it is perhaps fair to say that the whole operation of capturing Eichmann could never have gone so smoothly, possibly never even have succeeded, without Argentinian help and, above all, the unofficial co-operation of the Argentinian Intelligence Service and secret police. The latter had been keeping a close watch on known ex-Nazis in Argentina since the mid-fifties, though mainly for reasons of internal security. Since the end of the Perón regime there had been a strong demand in police and intelligence circles for a check on the known association of members of La Arana, a political organisation, and former Nazis and Italian Fascists. Investigations revealed that among the ex-Nazis was the man who went under the name of Ricardo Klement.

The Israeli team had heard about the Argentinian Intelligence discoveries before they went out to Buenos Aires, even though no information had been given them officially. But up to 1960 they thought that the Argentinians had merely flushed Eichmann out of Argentina into Bolivia. What they did not know was that after adopting a number of aliases in Bolivia and Paraguay he had returned to Argentina. Once the Israelis established discreet and unofficial contact with the Argentinian team they soon put two and two together—that Ricardo Klement of Buenos Aires and

Rodolfo Spee of Bolivia were one and the same man. Naturally the hierarchy of the Argentinian Intelligence was soon informed that the Israelis had made contact and from that point onwards business was conducted, not through the normal ambassadorial and ministerial channels, but through the respective Intelligence Services.

It was not difficult to do business. Eichmann's presence in Argentina was a source of embarrassment to the Argentinian government. While he was relatively safe under the old Perón regime, when this was overthrown in 1955, Eichmann's existence in Argentina was mildly precarious at the very best. It was for this reason he had decided to try his luck in Paraguay or Bolivia. His former contact in the Perón police, Ante Pavelic, a Croatian Nazi, was no longer in any position to help him. The Frondizi regime loathed the ex-Peronist secret police and, secretly, the Argentinian government preferred not to be asked to extradite Eichmann. They knew that not only would it present internal political problems, but that Eichmann's friends would almost certainly smuggle him to a place of safety before any extradition order could be made. So intimation was given to the Argentinian Intelligence merely to keep a watch on the Israeli team and, in a strictly confidential memorandum referring to 'the presence of Israeli Commandos in the Republic of Argentina', they were told to refrain 'from acting against them, except to keep the situation under control'.

In strict terms of protocol the Argentinians remained neutral, neither giving the Israelis any positive help to track down their quarry, nor in any way obstructing them. But in effect this neutrality was of great help to the Israeli team. There is little doubt that Harel's secret diplomacy, a certain amount of bargaining on intelligence matters and the benevolent attitude of President Frondizi were all factors conducive to the success of 'Operation Eichmann'.

What the Argentinians feared, almost as much as the Israelis, was that Eichmann would be tipped off about the Israeli presence and suddenly disappear. For this reason the Argentinian Intelligence issued an order that Ricardo Klement was to be shadowed day and night by their agents. This order was made as early as September 1959. On the ninth of that month Commander Jorge Messina, Director-General of the Argentinian Central Intelligence body, stated in yet another memorandum that Ricardo Klement 'has been seen with another high-ranking Nazi in the neighbour-hood of La Gallareta, in the province of Santa Fe. The description of that other man corresponds to that of Joseph Mengele.'

Thus it will be seen that the Argentinians were fully alerted to the presence not only of Eichmann, but other Nazis, at a very early stage and several months before Isser Harel ordered the Commando team into Buenos Aires. It is probable that Dr. Bauer had had some kind of unofficial confirmation from Argentina that his other information about the whereabouts of Eichmann was true.

Nevertheless it should not be thought, as has been suggested in some quarters, that the Argentinians deserved all the credit for finding Eichmann. It is very doubtful if they would have been so eager to keep watch on him but for the known presence of the Israeli team. And it should also be remembered that Israeli agents in Argentina had been quietly active for long before Isser Harel dispatched his special investigation team. On the other hand the diplomatic links of Ben-Gurion and Frondizi, with Harel actively co-operating with the Argentinian Intelligence, undoubtedly paved the way to a successful conclusion of the whole affair.

Harel decided that it was essential for him to go to Argentina to supervise the operation for kidnapping Eichmann and taking him to Israel. Meanwhile he chose his task force of Secret Service Commandos with great care, relying on men who had already proved their courage and initiative in the ranks of Haganah, the Palmach and other pre-Independence organisations. The leader of the group was one who had been blooded in Palmach at the age of eighteen and who had been personally responsible for destroying British radar apparatus on Mount Carmel. In later operations he had distinguished himself by directing troops on night operations in battle areas. Altogether there were eleven members of this Commando team, which included a doctor and the forgery expert, Shalom Dani.

Various means of transporting Eichmann to Israel were considered. Harel first thought of sending an Israeli ship to Buenos Aires, but this plan was finally dropped on the grounds that the voyage would take too long and calls at ports en route would present security problems. It so happened that in May 1960, Argentina was due to celebrate the hundred and fiftieth anniversary of her independence, and Israel, in common with other countries, had been invited to send a delegation for the occasion.

So Harel devised a plan by which Israel sent a special plane to Buenos Aires taking the delegation along with some of the Commando team suitably disguised either as airline employees or personnel attached to the delegation.

There is no doubt that the Argentinian Secret Service guessed that when Eichmann was kidnapped the Israelis might try to smuggle him on to the El Al plane, but they made no attempt at interference. Yet they seem to have known the names of at least some of the Israeli task force, which in their Intelligence reports they named as 'the Special Brigade of Blue Falcons', for they recorded that the leader of the team was Yehuda Simoni.[6]

The El Al plane was a Britannia aircraft of British manufacture which left Tel Aviv on 11 May and arrived in Buenos Aires the following day. It was scheduled to return on 13 or 14 May, with the proviso that an excuse of minor repairs could delay it another day if absolutely necessary. Meanwhile the leading members of the Commando team were already in Buenos Aires ready for the signal telling them to kidnap Eichmann. Included in the team was the one man who could most reliably identify him; it was not so much a question doubting whether the man they were kidnapping really was Eichmann, as whether at the last moment somebody else might be substituted for him. For if anybody wished to make mischief against the Israelis, all they had to do was to use a man posing as Eichmann as a decoy, to create a scandal of international proportions. So, the Commando was armed with the minutest details of Eichmann's description down to the size of his shoes, the circumference of his head, and to such distinguishing marks as a scar above his left eyebrow, a blood type tattooed under the left armpit, which was official procedure with SS officers, and an appendicitis scar. As soon as Eichmann was captured Harel's orders were that a thorough examination of the man was to be carried out for identification purposes.

The date set for Eichmann's capture was 10 May, two days before the El Al plane was due to arrive. Shalom Dani, had already flown into Buenos Aires with all his equipment disguised as that of an artist; brushes and canvases peeped out of his luggage. He got through customs without any difficulty, though he had to pay excess on his luggage. Born in Hungary in 1928, Shalom Dani had seen the Germans take over his country in collaboration with Admiral Horthy and his father sent to Belsen concentration camp, where he died. Shalom himself managed to escape to Austria where he lay low until he was able to get away to Palestine in an illegal immigrant ship. He had had a long career in Israeli Intelligence and was a past master at forging documents. Isser Harel has said of him that he was 'an essential member' of the team, 'a skilled craftsman in that delicate art, the forging of official documents of all kinds, especially identity papers. . . . his ability to do his work at any time, under any conditions, made him a shining example to his fellow workers.'[7]

Within a few hours of arriving in Buenos Aires Dani had set up his equipment in a secret hideout and was busily at work. He was a compulsive worker at whatever task he took up. The Mossad had employed him in various parts of Europe and when he wasn't concocting bogus identification papers, he was devoting himself to his hobby of making stained glass. By this time, however, it had been decided to make the deadline for capturing Eichmann 11 May, hopefully narrowing the time in which he would have to be held captive in Argentinian territory before being put aboard the Israeli plane. The hideout for holding him had been carefully chosen and was reasonably safe.

Eichmann left his home in Garibaldi Street as usual on the morning of 11 May to go to work. From that moment all his movements were closely observed by three members of the Israeli team. It was already approaching dusk when he left his work to return home by bus. In a car parked near to the bus stop by Eichmann's home, key members of the Commando team were sitting, waiting.

Just before 6.30 p.m. the bus appeared, slowly passing the parked car and making its usual stop. Luck was with the team: Eichmann was the only passenger to get off the bus. While one team member started up the car, another approached Eichmann on the pavement as he walked towards his home. Swiftly, a third man got out of the car and moved towards him. The kidnapping was the work of seconds; the judo training of the Commandos ensured that. There was one brief scream from Eichmann as he was seized and then silence as he was bundled into the car. Again luck was with the kidnappers as nobody was about at the time.

The whole operation took about half a minute. Two men held Eichmann down on the floor of the car while the third drove off to the hideout. During the journey there was a brief stop to change the car's number plates; then they drove straight into the garage of the 'safe' house and Eichmann was taken into the house via a passage-way.

He was undressed, medically examined, and only after he had been thoroughly checked over was he questioned as to his identity. He made no attempt at evasion; he admitted that he was Adolf Eichmann and that he had come to Argentina in 1950 under the name of Ricardo Klement. Within minutes the news was flashed to Tel Aviv by a pre-arranged code.

Isser Harel had taken every precaution in his planning against last minute obstacles. He had even forseen the possible need for moving Eichmann to yet another hide-out and a suitable place had already been prepared. But all went according to plan. The worst phase of the operation was, however, waiting for the propitious moment when their prisoner could safely be taken to the El Al plane. For various reasons this involved a wait of a whole week which was much longer than Harel would have wished. What would happen if Eichmann's wife and family reported the matter to the Argentinian police, or, even worse, made his disappearance public by giving information to the press? What would happen if other Nazis hiding out in Argentina attempted to launch a counter-coup, perhaps a bomb attack on the Israeli Embassy? And could the Argentinian Intelligence be relied upon? Would one of their agents tip off the Nazis?

In fact the Argentinian Intelligence had already kept a fairly close watch on the Israeli operation even down to locating the 'safe' house where Eichmann was held. And in a subsequent interview with the German weekly magazine *Quick* Nikolaus Eichmann, Adolf's eldest son, stated that 'for two days we searched for him [Eichmann] at police stations, hospitals and mortuaries. In vain, needless to say. And then we understood that he was being held captive. A Peronist youth group put themselves at our disposal . . . we became more bitter. The wildest deeds were planned during those hours. The leader of the group said: "Let's kidnap the Israeli Ambassador. Let's take him out of town and torture him until your father comes home." The plan was rejected. Some suggested blowing up the Israeli Embassy.'

So Harel's fears were fully justified and the week of waiting must have seemed as long as a month to the Commando team, some of whom spent the time trying to track down the elusive Dr. Joseph Mengele, the notorious Auschwitz camp doctor, but without success. On the afternoon of the departure day Eichmann was given an injection which made him drowsy. A carefully compiled cover story had been backed up by Shalom Dani's documentation: the sick passenger was a man who had been seriously injured in a car accident a few days before and there was even a medical certificate to show that he was fit to travel by air, though owing to head injuries it was important that he be disturbed no more than absolutely necessary. All that Shalom Dani had to do was to provide some additional documentation and to have Eichmann's photograph transferred to these papers.

Eichmann was carried to a waiting car and driven off to the Buenos Aires airport. Some of the team posed as male nurses, others as relatives of the sick passenger. Soon the Nazi Jew baiter was taken on to the El Al plane and that night it took off for Israel, halting only at Dakar to refuel en route for Tel Aviv. On 23 May David Ben-Gurion, the Prime Minister, announced to a crowded Knesset that Adolf Eichmann had been found, 'is already under arrest in Israel, and will shortly be put on trial under the Nazi and Nazi Collaborators (Punishment) Law, 1950.' It was perhaps the most sensational and unexpected announcement ever made to the Israeli Parliament and Moshe Pearlman, formerly adviser on public affairs to the Israeli Prime Minister, wrote: 'The House was electrified. For several seconds there was a stunned silence. Suddenly, from all parts of the chamber, came a roar of applause. Rarely had the Knesset been so moved. The murderer of their people had been caught. He would be brought to justice.'[8]

Yet without the secret co-operation of the Argentinian Intelligence the kidnapping of Eichmann would have been a much more difficult proposition. Certainly it could not have been carried out with an Israeli plane; the Commando team would have had to wait for a suitable opportunity of smuggling him on to a specially chartered boat in the middle of the night. Nevertheless the presence on that plane of the Israeli Foreign Minister, Abba Eban, General Meir Zorea, of the Israeli Army, and Yehuda Yaabi of the Office of Cultural Affairs, was a great aid to this kind of Secret Service diplomacy in which the Israelis are particularly skilled. At first Ben-Gurion merely announced that Eichmann had been caught and was 'under arrest in Israel'; he did not say where he had been captured or how. It was not until early in June 1960, that Israel officially told Argentina that Israeli 'volunteers' had kidnapped Eichmann in Buenos Aires. This disclosure was made in a note replying to an Argentinian request for clarification of reports that Eichmann had been kidnapped by Israeli Secret Service agents. Though there had been predictions of a breaking off of diplomatic relations between Argentina and Israel, the whole affair swiftly simmered down, and it is perhaps significant that there were far more vociferous protests about the Israeli action in Britain and some European countries than in Argentina.

Eichmann was duly brought to trial and on 12 December 1961, was convicted on all fifteen counts made against him. These included charges of deporting more than half a million Poles, and 14,000 Slovenes, causing the killing of millions of Jews and being party to the murder of tens of thousands of Gypsies and ninety-one children from Lidice. He was sentenced to death by hanging and, after his appeal had been rejected by the Israeli Supreme Court, the sentence was duly carried out on 1 June 1962.

9

Yuval Ne'eman's
Technological Revolution

*Because Israel is a small country surrounded by
enemies and dependent upon swiftly mobilised
military reserves rather than professional forces,
it has to rely more than most lands on accurate
intelligence and its appreciation. The costly process of calling up troops disrupts normal economic
life and is avoided unless there is grave danger.*

(C. L. SULZBERGER)[1]

ISRAEL HAD MAINTAINED throughout the 1950s the excellent
relations with France which had been developed during the
immediate post-war years when Haganah used France as a base
for some of its underground activities. This co-operation had extended to the realms of intelligence and it was especially useful in
the sphere of naval intelligence, thanks very largely to a sympathetic arrangement made by a former Palyam officer with
Admiral Pierre Barjot, which was of enormous value to Israel at
the time of the 1956 drive against Egypt. This relationship between Israeli and French Intelligence Services was to continue
for several years.

It was the Israeli Intelligence's links both with the French
Secret Service and the American CIA that kept them informed
on British plans at the time of the Suez crisis of 1956. 'We always
knew the British would chicken out,' declared one Mossad agent,
'because the British Cabinet were behaving all the time as though
they were not only frightened of their own shadows, but of one
another. The truth was that there were too many humbugs in the
Cabinet, too many hypocrites who would be glad enough to take
all the credit if the Suez invasion had gone well, but would rat
on the Prime Minister the moment things went badly. For this

reason, as we learned from our CIA contacts, some members of the British Cabinet were not told of the invasion plans. The CIA knew more about British planning through their contacts with the SIS than some Cabinet Ministers in London. Our help from the CIA, given unofficially, was the only aid we got from the United States at that time. Eisenhower was taking every opportunity of telling us not to endanger the peace, but doing damn all about the uprising in Hungary.'

Yet despite the hostility of the Eisenhower administration to the 'Suez adventure', the CIA secretly sympathised with Israel at this time, especially those among them who had had first-hand experience of the appalling leakages and trail of treachery in the ranks of British Intelligence—the SIS, and especially Naval Intelligence.

But the Suez débâcle created by the Anglo-French withdrawal from the Canal Zone after their abortive landings, taught Israel the lesson that in future she must go it alone and rely entirely on her own efforts. There is little doubt that if the British Government had not lost its nerve, the French could have been persuaded to press on at least for long enough to topple Nasser. And it was Nasser who more than anyone else needed to be toppled at this time as far as Israel was concerned. The fatuous argument of the Suez apologists has always been that, even if Nasser had been forced to resign, there was nobody else to put in his place.

British statesmen, especially those who belonged to the Tory Government of those fatal years, when the seeds of disaster and decadence were sown in Britain, have always lied their heads off in an attempt to pretend there was no collusion with Israel at the time of Suez. Moshe Dayan makes it clear enough in his biography that he, too, is exasperated by the contumacious lies by British statesmen on this subject. 'Britain's Foreign Minister [Selwyn Lloyd] may well have been a friendly man, pleasant, charming, amiable. If so, he showed near-genius in concealing these virtues,'[2] writes Dayan in commenting on the craven deviousness of the British in the talks with the French before the Suez invasion was launched. Dayan should know: he was there to observe the behaviour of the perfidious Albions.

It was in this same year that the Israeli Secret Service acquired the services of a man who was to revolutionise their military intelligence and pave the way to the astonishing victories of the

Six-Day War as well as providing the additional security so vital for a nation surrounded by potential enemies. He was Yuval Ne'eman, born in Tel Aviv in 1925, educated at Haifa and the Imperial College, London, where he took his degree of doctor of science. Having attended the Ecole de Guerre in Paris, Dr. Ne'eman, who had served with the Israeli Defence Force in the War of Independence in 1948, began to take a keen interest in the technological aspects of military warfare and especially the new science of computerology. He was deputy commander of the 'Givati' Brigade and joined the Aman in 1954. At that time military intelligence was largely dependent on the laborious process of awaiting reports from individual agents and sifting through the information thus gleaned in a leisurely fashion. Dr. Ne'eman found it to be totally inadequate for a young nation, without allies, hemmed in on all sides by openly antagonistic states and confronted with the prospect of a cock-a-hoop President Nasser who, having seen the inglorious retreat of the British and French from Suez, was now openly preparing for an ultimate war with Israel. 'Egypt may have taken a drubbing from us in 1956, but she is recovering faster than you think,' declared Ne'eman. 'We can only cope with this very real danger by being better informed, and informed more quickly by our Military Intelligence than the Arabs. We cannot afford to wait until someone smuggles through a report from Cairo or Damascus, useful though that undoubtedly is. One day our survival may depend upon whether we get instant intelligence on a particular topic. Remember, Egypt or Syria can strike at us within a matter of minutes in the air and of mere hours by land.'

Perhaps no nation in modern times has required a steady stream of 'instant intelligence' such as Dr. Ne'eman visualised in the mid-1950s. Though the Mossad provided a compendious amount of information from inside enemy territory, the Israeli Army still needed not only instantaneous intelligence on all enemy moves of a military character, but the means of analysing and interpreting these with equal rapidity. As a result of Ne'eman's promptings, the scope of Aman widened considerably, so that during the sixties and seventies it has played an increasingly vital role. Fortunately the Aman has only had to cope with one potential enemy the whole time—the coalition of Arab states supporting Egyptian intervention against Israel leaving the Mossad and the other Intelligence Services to keep an eye on the machinations of Moscow. But although it has extended its espionage techniques into the sphere of computerology, the Aman has never neglected such ancient procedures as intelligence obtained from agents and, often equally important, from prisoners-of-war. Israeli methods of interrogating prisoners-of-war from Arab countries are remarkably efficient and based on a careful study of Arab psychological processes.

Dr. Ne'eman was determined to re-organise Aman so that technologically it was on a footing with that of the American Intelligence Services, though not, of course, on the same costly global scale. It was no easy task for a scientist to tilt with the generals, especially as the Aman had had a reputation for being essentially the preserve of the soldiers. Nevertheless Israel has always chosen very carefully those of her generals who have been given high posts in Intelligence and all of them have been versatile men who have since proved equally efficient in the worlds of business, broadcasting and literature. One such was the General Y. Harkabi, a specialist in philosophy and Arab literature at the Hebrew University in Jerusalem; another was Brigadier-General Chaim Herzog, who later made a name for himself in legal circles, as a broadcaster, an author and in business. Ne'eman himself never became chief of Aman, but he was its *éminence grise* and the most brilliant brain ever to be associated with that Service, as well as being its outstanding innovator.

Yuval Ne'eman had shown early promise as a brilliant mathematical pupil at the Herzlya School in Tel Aviv; at the age of fourteen he had passed the most advanced examinations and by nineteen he had taken a degree at Haifa. His companions affectionately nicknamed him 'The Brain', but they were apt to underrate the quiet courage and physical will-power of this slight, silent and shy young man. They laughed when he decided to join the Israeli Forces in the War of Independence—'what is he going to fight with? His slide-rule?' they asked—but he surprised them all. He rose to the rank of lieutenant-colonel and was a highly efficient officer. But every time there was a lull in the fighting Yuval Ne'eman was back at his books, making copious notes and never wasting a moment. As a mathematician he began to see military tactics in terms of the slide-rule and the calculating machine. As one who had spent part of his childhood with his family in Egypt, where he attended a French school, he also had a knowledge of the Arabs. Ne'eman had also broadened his horizons after the War of Independence by going to France to study at the Ecole de Guerre, afterwards joining Aman. By 1954 Yuval Ne'eman was second only to Colonel Benjamin Givli in the Service and he survived Givli's departure to become deputy to the new chief of Aman, Yehoshafat Harkabi.

Dr. Ne'eman insisted that the Ministry of Defence needed computers for the collection and analysis of military intelligence. The main objection to the installation of these was on the grounds of cost, though there were a few old-fashioned generals who maintained that the traditional methods of obtaining military intelligence were good enough. 'They might be today,' replied Dr. Ne'eman, 'and they might be just as good tomorrow or next year, but in ten years' time, if we haven't got computers and electronic watch-stations in Sinai, we shall be doomed.'

Fortunately Ne'eman and the new head of Aman saw eye to eye. Yehoshafat ('Fatti') Harkabi was the son of a judge, who had studied philosophy, history and Hebrew language and literature in Jerusalem. In 1943 he had joined the second Jewish battalion in the British Army as an education sergeant. After his discharge he continued his academic studies and trained in the first cadre of Israel's future diplomats. Eventually he became head of the Israeli Foreign Ministry's Asian section and then liaison officer between the Foreign Ministry and the Army. He was a member of Israel's delegation to the Rhodes armistice talks in 1949 and participated in secret talks with King Abdullah of Jordan. After specialised scientific studies in France he was appointed head of Aman, which post he held until 1959.

It was perhaps unfortunate for Ne'eman that he was known to be not only a compulsive reader of comic-strips (one of the few relaxations he allowed himself), but also an avid collector of them. For his critics seized on this as evidence of his eccentricity and unworldliness and as at this time the science fiction comic strip was coming into its own, they accused him of borrowing ideas from the fertile minds of the strip-writers. It was a grossly unfair suggestion, for Ne'eman had by diligent study actually projected orthodox computer and electronic methods into the then still experimental field of intelligence. If the battle for freedom in the West is to be won eventually, it will be partly the result of Ne'eman's brilliant break-through in the field of 'instant intelligence' upon which today the security of the whole of the Western World depends, especially in the computerised tracking

of nuclear submarines. But Ne'eman's main concern in the early
1950s was with nothing so sophisticated as this: he wanted a daily
appraisal of the military and naval dispositions of Israeli's potential enemies which would give his country the all-important
advantage of time in the intelligence field. He had one argument
that appealed not merely to the military, but to civilian Cabinet
Ministers who were concerned with the economic progress of the
young country. He was able to point out that, though the permanent army of Israel was only about 80,000, one-seventh of the
country's total Jewish population of two and a half millions was
on the reserve and liable to be called up. Thus he drove home the
point made in the quotation from C. L. Sulzberger in the *New
York Herald Tribune* which appears at the beginning of this
chapter. Ne'eman's trump card was the fact that any call-up of
the reserve forces, based on dated intelligence, or inaccurate
analysis of intelligence, when moves by the enemy were suspected,
could be far more costly to the economy of Israel in its disruption
of production than the installation of computers.

These arguments proved decisive in winning over some of the
Cabinet, but Ne'eman was also given firm backing by Moshe
Dayan, then Chief of Staff, who had the imagination to see what
computers could do for the defence of his country. Dayan over-
came objections inside the Ministry of Defence by enlisting the
aid of Ben-Gurion in championing the Ne'eman cause. He also
arranged for Ne'eman to be posted temporarily to London as
military attaché in 1958 so that he could devote more time to
scientific research and take his doctorate in physics. Dayan's
imaginative support for Ne'eman was in many respects one of his
outstanding services to his country while he was at the Ministry
of Defence.

Yet even while Ne'eman was winning his battle for the installation of computers for analysing and documenting intelligence on
a day-to-day basis and for the setting up of electronic intelligence
devices, he was also concerned with Israel's research into nuclear
power. He was soon appointed director of the industrial branch
of the Committee of Atomic Energy as well as controlling a
research laboratory (Nahal Sorek) for the application of nuclear
physics for military purposes. It was at Nahal Sorek, close to the
small town of Dimona in the Northern Negev Desert, that Israel
developed her nuclear power potential. Here a small nuclear
reactor was set up. In terms of military value its rating of six

thermal megawatts was negligible, but it served as an invaluable training ground for scientists and technicians.

Thanks largely to the initiative of Yuval Ne'eman Israel later created a large reactor, also at Dimona, which had an output of twenty-four thermal megawatts and thus could produce sufficient plutonium per year to make one bomb of a yield similar to that used on Nagasaki. This was the situation in 1972 according to the most careful scientific predictions, and there is little question now that in nuclear know-how Israel has the edge on her enemies. This success can be attributed to Aman's influence on military thinking and is perhaps the first example in modern times of an Intelligence Service actually paving the way to military experimentation. But it was also the product of that close co-operation between the Israeli and French Intelligence Services which lasted for so long. Far too often General de Gaulle has been wrongly personified as being hostile to Israel and biased towards the Arabs. Nothing could be further from the truth. This is not to say that de Gaulle, especially in the latter period of his presidency, did not see himself as a dispassionate arbiter between Jews and Arabs, but his sympathies with Israel and with French Jewish politicians were always marked. When Pierre Mendès-France was for a brief time Prime Minister of France it was de Gaulle who lent his support and advice in the background. The Dimona reactor was built with French co-operation and the bilateral arrangements between the two countries have remained secret ever since.

It has been argued that Israel has shown an ambivalent attitude on the question of nuclear warfare and has been excessively secret on the subject of her own nuclear research. What else could be expected of a small nation hemmed in by hostile states who were themselves receiving support from a nuclear power, the Soviet Union? Israel also had to consider not merely the possibility, however remote, of requiring possession of an atomic weapon, but of supplies of the raw materials for its production. For this reason diplomatic and highly secret talks were carried out with the French and the Belgians to ensure supplies of plutonium from Gabon and the Congo. The quest for plutonium and uranium were also the reason for close diplomatic ties with South Africa.

In the beginning of his work for Aman Dr. Ne'eman counted on a large organisation of talented technocrats to carry out the necessary research and preliminary work in starting a computerised intelligence set-up. He had to rely on a team of students in cybernetics from the United States, most of them Harvard-trained. But it can be said that the Ne'eman technique was much more sophisticated than anything which British business at its highest levels was reaching in the technological revolution of the later fifties. It was, in fact, far more advanced than anything achieved among European powers in computer intelligence and comparable on a modest scale with the development of electronic espionage by the Pentagon, NSA and the Naval Intelligence Service of the USA.

It was after the 1956 War with Egypt when Israel advanced into the Sinai Peninsula and captured a large number of prisoners-of-war that Ne'eman was able to put his computers to their first effective test. All information gleaned from interrogation of the thousands of Egyptian prisoners was fed into the computers and analysed. 'This information,' wrote Steve Eytan in *L'Oeil de Tel Aviv*, 'coded and immediately available, was regularly supplemented with up-to-date data, enormously facilitating preparations for the 1967 conflict. And after the Six Day *blitzkrieg* there were copious amounts of information for the electronic brains to absorb.... The prisoners taken in 1956 swelled the coffers of Israeli intelligence considerably. The Egyptian officers and non-commissioned officers were neither cowards nor traitors, and few furnished real military information. But there seemed little to fear from the charming fellow who slipped in a number of apparently harmless questions while chatting over a pot of tea.... Usually the prisoner is happy enough to take advantage of this pleasant interlude in the monotony of detention life. And the information is digested by the insatiable computers. A finger on one button will tell the specialist whether a particular soldier is pliable or a hard case, prudent or headstrong, honest or corrupt.'

In short, the analysis of prisoner-of-war intelligence was extended from the realm of facts into that of psychology, on the very sound thesis that it was essential to know one's adversary. Aman built from this not only a dossier on prisoners-of-war who had been questioned, but on every Egyptian officer from the time he left his military academy. Nothing was missed; every item of intelligence on his career was fed into the computers—where he was posted, how he was promoted, what seemed to be his speciality and so on. Much of this intelligence was merely a question of gleaning information from Egyptian newspapers or military gazettes. But as a result of this the Ministry of Defence could call

at any moment for an up-to-date assessment of any Egyptian or
Syrian commanding officer on any part of the front facing them.
This again was to be of tremendous value in calculating the
probable moves of adversaries in the Six-Day War in 1967.

The Ministry of Defence benefitted in a wide range of targets
from the scientific intelligence projects of Aman. What Ne'eman
started others followed up with even more astonishing ideas. Very
soon Israel was to have the most forward-looking, sophisticated
and *avant garde* intelligence system in the world. Only its small-
ness as a nation limited the effects of this astonishing technological advance which has filled the Russians with a secret admiration,
even if tempered with exasperation, for Israeli techniques. Apart
from the computer bank of instant and up-to-date intelligence
carefully analysed, the striking power of Israel's espionage system
was perhaps best exemplified by their electronic watch-stations
and the adapting of mobile electronic 'watch-systems' for probing
enemy territory. Israeli patrols were sent into the desert and the
no-man's-land between Israel and her Arab neighbours with
electronic recording devices which could be secretly attached to
the enemy's telephone cables and enable them to be tapped. It
was much the same technique as that used by the Arab gangs who
pre-1939 cut the oil pipes buried a few feet under the ground.
Tapes attached to the gadgets on the cables recorded all that
passed on the telephone lines and these were collected by subsequent patrols. They also placed at strategic intervals highly
sensitive apparatus which could pick up conversations in enemy
camps half a mile or so distant.

The Ne'eman innovations revolutionised the process of gathering military intelligence in Israel and, far from making the old-
fashioned individual spy redundant, it provided him with more
missions and more precisely defined targets for espionage. Photographic and radar intelligence were developed along parallel
lines with the watch-station systems used by the USIB in America
and during the past twenty years there have been instances of
Israel providing such intelligence for the United States and vice
versa. It is well known that the US satellite photographs of the
Suez Canal and other sectors of the Middle East have enabled
the Pentagon and the State Department to be forewarned of the
approach of new crises in the Middle East. The vast amount of
data obtained by Aman through PHOTINT (photographic
intelligence), ELINT (electronic intelligence) and RADINT

(radar intelligence) has meant that the Ministry of Defence has required trained reserves of personnel skilled as data analysers and processors, cryptanalysts, traffic analysts, photographic interpreters, and specialists in communications, radar and telemetry who can make sense of a conglomeration of words and figures that might otherwise bog down a whole Ministry, strangled in tapes and paper, within a few weeks. At the same time the Israelis have occasionally had unofficial assistance from the CIA who have leaked data gleaned by means of wide-angled cameras from photographic satellites.

Today Israel is still benefitting from the assistance it has received in its electronic watch-stations in Sinai from American specialists seconded by NSA and the CIA. The Arabs were slow in appreciating the extent to which Israel had forged ahead in the intelligence world of computerology, but though Israel's Secret Service is still by far the most efficient in the whole area of the Middle East, some Arab states are now developing their own counter-measures. President Sadat of Egypt, himself a former secret agent, has re-organised the Moukhabarat-el-Amma (the Presidential [civil] Secret Service) and the Egyptian Military Intelligence, the Moukhabarat-el-Kharbeya, giving full rein to his old colleague and trusted adviser, General Hosny Mubarak, who is keenly interested in the development of electronic spying devices. The Saudi Arabian Secret Service, though small, benefits from the phenomenal wealth of this small oil state: it is equipped with all manner of electronic devices and a computer service, supplied by the United States. But Israel has managed to retain her lead in this field and will almost certainly continue to do so: she has been exceptionally fortunate in having a great reserve of talented young scientists and in inheriting the know-how in electronics from such men as Jack Nissenthal and Peretz Rose.

If those generals of the early 1950s thought Yuval Ne'eman was bringing spy fiction to life with his demands for computerised intelligence, one wonders what they would have thought about some of the more recent innovations of Israeli military intelligence. One of the most fantastic of these has been the training of pigeons by Israeli psychologists so that they enable Arab military installations to be pin-pointed.

The birds were equipped with electronic signalling devices so that their location in hostile territory could be monitored by

technicians in Israel. This project, which was the subject of intensive research, was carried out in a specially created unit at Tel
Aviv University under the direction of Dr. Robert Lubow, who
worked on similar animal-training programmes at the Land Warfare Laboratory in Maryland, USA. The project was financed by
a special Israeli Air Force contract.

The pigeons were kept without food until their weight was
reduced by some twenty per cent. It was judged that at this
weight they would be acutely hungry and desperately eager to spy
out food, while retaining efficiency. The theory was that, when
released into flight, they would depend for their food supplies on
being able to distinguish between the markings across the desert as
to which were natural parts of the environment and which were
man-made and therefore, presumably, close to stocks of food. It
seemed a highly questionable proposition, but, according to Dr.
Lubow's report *The Perception of High Order Variables by the
Pigeon*, 'the birds can fairly easily spot the difference between
the straight lines and symmetrical curves of human construction
from the more random outlines produced by nature. Building
upon this basic difference, the objective is to train the pigeons to
identify specific types of military installations such as runways,
fuel-tanks and ammunition dumps.'[3]

Thus once the Sinai-spying pigeon saw such an installation
from on high, it immediately swooped upon it in quest of food,
and the pigeon's flight and movements would be watched on a
screen. The scanner would then assume that the pigeon had
located something of importance—roads being built, buildings
erected, or missile sites developed. The exact site would be pin-
pointed on a map and compared with up-to-date maps of the
same area. If the pigeon had made its swoop or swoops in an area
previously free of any man-made constructions, then the Intelligence Service would be alerted to make further inquiries, or even,
in exceptional circumstances, to order an 'air strike' depending
on the military situation prevailing at the time.

Dr. Lubow had already worked on the application of dogs for
military purposes and the Israelis are very proud indeed of their
corps of mine-spotting dogs. He had also worked with Dr. E. Carr-
Harris, the acknowledged world authority on animal training for
military purposes, at the US Air Force Avionics Laboratory.

Nor has scientific method been neglected in tackling the
problems of counter-espionage. Internal security has always posed

a major problem for the Israelis for it is easy enough for enemy agents to be infiltrated to join the 300,000 Israeli Arabs in the territory, all of them speaking Hebrew. To check the credentials of more than a million Arabs on the west bank of the River Jordan and in Gaza has been particularly difficult in view of the 'open door' policy of General Dayan. But in the early 1970s a new device was tested on a small hill overlooking the Allenby Bridge in Israel: it was the most sophisticated of all lie-detectors.[4]

This device was—to give it its technical description—a microwave respiration monitor, and it was designed for screening the countless Arabs who crossed the bridge. Israeli secret police train the device direct at the solar plexus region of any immigrant. While soldiers at the crossing-point question the Arabs, the monitor machine records by microwaves playing on the stomach the breathing rate of each individual. If the device shows that any one Arab is breathing faster than normal, then the secret police telephone to the soldiers to hold him for further questioning. Development of this lie detector has enabled the Israelis greatly to speed up and strengthen their interrogation processes by eliminating the majority who might otherwise waste the soldiers' time and pin-pointing the likely suspects.

Where the Israelis have made what may be an even more important break-through is in their scientific espionage network behind the Iron Curtain. Not even the Americans have achieved quite so much success in keeping abreast of the Soviet Union's new scientific espionage and counter-espionage techniques, some of which are alarmingly menacing in the hidden threats which they pose for the future. The Israeli Secret Service backroom boys are often able to make extraordinarily accurate predictions of what the Soviet Union is likely to do next in this respect, sometimes basing their findings on the most slender of reports by Mossad or other agents. One report from Rumania told how the Russians were carrying out experiments on frogs which had been subjected to microwaves: the pulses of the frogs were synchronised to a microwave signal. Radiation was beamed to the chest area and the frogs were killed.

In Tel Aviv this information was passed to a number of experts who came up with various answers as a team. They were unanimous that these experiments could point in two directions: first, that the Soviet scientists were aware of the biological effects of low-level microwave radiation and their application as an offensive weapon; secondly, that the Russians were probably experimenting with the development of a system for disorientating or disrupting the behaviour of individuals, even perhaps as an aid to interrogation.

Promptly the Israelis studied the reports circulating in Washington and the Pentagon about the alleged Russian use of microwaves being beamed against the US Embassy in Moscow. From these they were alerted to a deadlier menace—the prospect that eventually microwaves could be so controlled and adapted to put thoughts into the human mind.

This last somewhat macabre glimpse of the horrific development of scientific espionage and counter-espionage exemplifies more than anything else the constant need for the Secret Services of the free world to be on the alert for any new technique likely to be employed against them. Electronic espionage and counter-espionage are now in the forefront of the war of deterrents and the Israelis are determined to keep abreast with West and East alike in this respect. Hence the liaison with such bodies as the US Land Warfare Laboratory in Maryland, with various radar research firms and Aman's keen interest in the vast range of electronic devices coming under such obscurantist technical titles as 'personal identity verification systems' and 'perimeter intruder systems of microwave energy'.

This is almost back to that realm of science fiction mentioned earlier in this chapter. But the harsh truth is that it is now fact, not fiction and whoever slips behind in the race is a certain loser. As for Yuval Ne'eman, he has carved for himself and his country a very special niche in the highest scientific circles of the world. This Professor of Physics and head of the Physics Department of Tel Aviv University has made his mark in the Western World. His research work has been greatly admired both in Europe and the USA, where he has been Director of the Centre for Particle Theory in Texas and visiting professor at the Californian Institute of Technology, which is perhaps one of the most illustrious of its kind in the world. In 1969 he was awarded the Albert Einstein Prize for achievements in theoretical physics, the first time this had been won by any scientist other than an American. Without his drive and imagination Israel would never have obtained the military superiority which she won with such ease in the sixties: this was achieved largely because of the excellence of Israel's military intelligence and drawing the right deductions from it.

10

Nasser's German Connection

Aircraft industry in North Africa requires technical advisers. . . .

(Advertisement appearing in German
newspapers, 1958)

IT WAS SHORTLY AFTER the seizure of the Suez Canal by President
Nasser that the Israeli Secret Service first had intimations that ex-
Nazi technocrats were being recruited for work in Egypt—work
that was directed against the state of Israel.

The earliest intelligence on this state of affairs came as a result
of Mossad inquiries about Nazis escaping from Europe and it was
somewhat of a shock to learn that, while some were bent solely
on living anonymously in hiding in South America, others were
once again pledged to attacking their old adversaries, the Jews.
At first the information was vague and sketchy; all that was
known for certain was that some Nazis who had been in the
Gestapo and in aeronautical research had gone to ground in Arab
countries under Arab names and that they were actively helping
the Egyptian Government and Army.

Isser Harel ordered an immediate investigation of these reports
both in Cairo and Bonn. Back from Cairo came news that a
number of Germans met almost every day at the Löwenbrau
Brewery in the Twenty-Sixth of July Street in Cairo. The agent
reporting this was instructed to keep the place under surveillance
and to arrange for the Germans to be followed to their homes. As
a result it was learned that shortly before King Farouk was
deposed a German named Dr. Wilhelm Voss had arrived in Cairo
to seek work in the munitions field. Since then he had been engaged by President Nasser to take charge of the production of
small-calibre rockets, and, so it was whispered, he was shortly to
be given a much bigger assignment.

Now Voss had been an executive with the Hermann Goering

munitions works in Germany and also manager of the Skoda works in Czechoslovakia during the German occupation, so he was a figure to be reckoned with. This could mean only one thing— that Nasser was deliberately engaging ex-Nazis for military purposes. There was swift confirmation of this: Nasser had appointed Voss as director of CERVA, the Egyptian organisation set up to make tactical rockets and engaged as his assistant Professor Paul Goercke, an electronics specialist who had worked on the V1s.

The implications of even this modest item of intelligence were indeed alarming for the Israelis. It pointed to Nasser acquiring the kind of technical know-how which Egypt had never before possessed and to a new drive against Israel. There could be no question as to what those rockets were to be used for: it could only be the destruction of Israel. Harel was determined to track down the Nazis being engaged in Egypt and to use every wile to sabotage Nasser's plans for employing the Germans. Fortunately the Israeli Secret Service has always had excellent contacts and agents of its own working in foreign Intelligence Services. Occasionally these people are actually double agents, but more often they are sympathetic Zionists who are loyal and patriotic citizens of other nations. It would be unfair to describe these men as double-dealers, for it is very rarely today that Israel's interests are not more or less identical with those of the Western World and there is no record that in serving Israel surreptitiously any of these people have betrayed secrets vital to their own country. These double agents are to be found mainly in the USA, France and Germany, though there are some in Italy and Austria. There are many others behind the Iron Curtain, as Moscow is only too well aware. But that is another story and, of course, when they serve Israel they are certainly taking the risk of betraying Soviet interests.

But to assess the technical ability of these Nazi specialists in the aeronautical and munitions field, the Israelis needed to get reports from their contacts in the USA, from men who had access to the pro-West German scientists working over there who would know all about men like Voss and Goercke. There was a certain amount of bartering of information and the Israelis are past-masters at the game of exchanging intelligence.

During the build-up to the Suez Crisis of 1956 when Israel was planning to invade the Sinai Peninsula, an unexpected bonus came to Shin Beth and the Mossad. A German adviser who had been engaged on Nasser's personal intelligence service also worked for the Gehlen Organisation, that post-war intelligence conglomerate which, led by General Reinhard Gehlen, had powerful American backing through the CIA. This German adviser was actually at work assessing Israeli military moves when he received from the Gehlen Organisation a questionnaire seeking information on Egyptian matters. Believing that the Gehlen Organisation and Nasser shared the same ideals and goals, he answered all the queries and sent the questionnaire back to Germany. Little did he know that his opposite number was an American officer who had asked for the information solely for passing on to Israel. He was a Mossad agent!

The Israeli Secret Service determined to investigate the ex-Nazis in Egypt by further infiltration of the Gehlen Organisation, making use of its contacts in Cairo. For while some in the Organisation were aware of the Israeli links, the men in Cairo were quite unaware of what was happening. A further probe was carried out in Paris by alerting a Mossad top agent inside the French Secret Service. France was then still a member of NATO and the Mossad man had access to an exchange of military intelligence circulating between NATO members.

In terms of conventional warfare Israel was in 1956–58 vastly superior to Egypt and it was in a desperate effort to catch up that Nasser planned to build his own rockets and, if possible, nuclear weapons. From West Germany came clippings from a number of newspapers carrying the advertisement quoted at the beginning of this chapter: 'aircraft industry in North Africa requires technical advisers . . .' Tel Aviv at once suspected that the industry was probably CERVA and that the advertisement emanated from Voss and Goercke. Soon the Mossad had a long list of names of ex-Nazis who were either 'technical advisers' to the Egyptian Army or 'specialists' attached to Nasser's secret police.

Some of these were regarded as Arabs and had adopted Arab names and habits. A man named Mohammed Hassein turned out to be none other than Jurgen Knetch, former Nazi cultural officer in Montevideo; another calling himself Mohamed Akbar was really SS Lieutenant Ulrich Kraus. Leopold Gleim had been Gestapo chief in Warsaw, while Oscar Dirlewanger and Willi Brenner had been in charge of the concentration camp at Mauthausen. These men and others had congregated in a suburb of Cairo where their rallying figure was Dr. Johannes von Leers, who had been one of Dr. Goebbels' chief assistants in the Propaganda Ministry and was one of the most virulent of anti-Semites. Some of these Germans had been smuggled into Egypt on the network set up by the Countess d'Andurain, but it was not until the early fifties that Germans started arriving in droves in Egypt, including such men as General Wilhelm Fahrmbacher. It was about 1956 that Dr. von Leers reappeared in Cairo as Professor Omar Amin: his work for Nasser was part intelligence and part propaganda. It was the odious Omar Amin who started up the campaign of blackmail against Israeli trade and firms, extending his smear tactics to Jewish firms in all parts of the world. This campaign was particularly designed to appeal to the new emerging nations of Africa.

Denis Sefton Delmer, one of the ablest British newspaper correspondents in Germany in the inter-war years and who was engaged in countering German propaganda during World War II, has told of his own investigation into 'the activities of that little group of Nazi fanatics who escaped to the Middle East after Hitler's collapse' and worked for Nasser. In 1962 he wrote: '. . . my Israeli friends produced a file with full details of Nazis who now have Arab names, live in Cairo and are instructing the Egyptians in the techniques of the Gestapo and the Abwehr. The Israeli officials even presented me with the photographs of a correspondence that had been passing for four years between a Nazi in Cairo and another at Wiesbaden in Germany. The Nazi in Cairo was Dr. Johannes von Leers whom I first met in Berlin many years ago when he was an "expert" in Dr. Goebbels' Ministry. . . . The Nazi in Wiesbaden was Karl Heinz Priester, a publisher producing books and pamphlets for the racist Neo-Nazis of today.

'The Leers—Priester letters start just after the seizure of the Suez Canal in 1956, run on through 1957 and 1958 right into the summer of 1959. They stop only with Priester's death. . . . I was dumbfounded when I saw this material. It means that someone working for Israel was—and no doubt still is—in a position to intercept letters passing between Egypt and the German Federal Republic—two states with which Israel has no diplomatic relations [today Israel has an embassy in Bonn]—photograph whatever correspondence interested him, and then pass on the letters to their destination without the correspondents being any the wiser.'[1]

I quote this statement by Delmer as supporting evidence of my claim that the Israelis infiltrated every possible source that would lead them to the unmasking of the Nazi scientists, soldiers and adventurers who served Egypt. Whether they could intercept mail in Egypt as well as Germany is a matter of conjecture, but they certainly had a tight watch on correspondence from Egypt coming into Bonn and Pullach, where Gehlen had his head-quarters. For the record, Delmer expresses the opinion that 'these intercepts have been passed to Israel by an intelligence officer of Zionist sympathies belonging to one of Germany's NATO allies —most probably the French—who in the ordinary course of his duty had access to intercepts made by the German Security Service tapping mails and telephones in Germany.'[2]

One of the arguments used by Western appeasers of Nasser, whether of the Eisenhower–Foster Dulles type, or the misinformed executives of the oil companies, was that any move to oppose the Egyptian President would only push him into the Soviet camp. At that time Nasser was very far from being a Soviet sympathiser: he instinctively turned to the Germans. What the West did not realise was that Nasser was not unlike the Mufti of Jerusalem who had been such a firm ally of Hitler. One of the men who replied to the advertisements placed in the German press (answers had to go to a Zurich accommodation address) was Ferdinand Brandner, a former SS colonel who was an aeronautical con-struction specialist. He was eagerly accepted by the Egyptians on the basis that he would recruit other German specialists to work for them. Soon the Israelis were on the trail of the intermediaries being used by the Egyptians for these undercover deals: they were led to the offices of an unostentatious business man in Zurich who was part Swiss and part Egyptian.

A close watch on the intermediary's moves and those of Ferdinand Brandner revealed that Egypt was engaging Germans not by the dozen, but by the score; Brandner alone interviewed no fewer than 220 Germans for work there. All this gave rise to some concern as to whether a new Neo-Nazi movement was not being built up on the basis of a secret alliance with Nasser. This might in retrospect seem fanciful, but in 1958–59 it was a distinct possibility. Then there had been no complete *rapprochement* between Israel and West Germany and there was still a large question mark as to which way Germany would go politically. Nor had all the ramifications of the Gehlen Organisation been fully probed. It was still feared in Tel Aviv that with Gehlen as head of the West German Secret Service there might well be an anti-Semitic element influencing policy within that Service, especially as it was now known that Gehlen had actually advised Nasser on the organisation of the Egyptian Secret Services. There was indeed every reason for Israel to infiltrate the Gehlen Organisation not merely to obtain information on Egypt, but to keep a close watch on how West German Intelligence was functioning and how strong were its links with the CIA.

Ironically, much later Gehlen was able to boast not only how he had advised Nasser on intelligence matters, but also infiltrated an Israeli spy into Egypt. But, as will be seen, the credit he took for this belonged not to him, but to the Mossad. It ill behoved Gehlen to brag about his espionage triumphs, for, while they were spectacular for a short period, they soon turned into total disaster when he overreached himself. In the fifties Gehlen was the Americans' main instrument in waging the cold war. He brought off many remarkable coups such as helping to organise the Berlin Rising in 1953 and the Hungarian Revolt in 1956. He also infiltrated hundreds of spies into the Soviet Union. But Reinhard Gehlen did not reveal his failures in his memoirs;[3] the truth is that the arch-infiltrator was himself infiltrated. Not just by a few Israelis (they did him no harm anyway), but by the Russians. Gehlen was over-confident; he pushed one too many infiltrators to the other side. One of them went over to the KGB and after that the Russians just let the Gehlen agents pour in and, as early as 1951, they quietly 'blew' the Gehlen Organisation. They took over his agents and using them against Gehlen slowly but surely placed their key men in vital positions inside his Organisation.

The Egyptians extended their German connection in the late fifties and in November 1959, contracts were signed by the Egyptian Government and Willy Messerschmitt in Munich. The man who signed this hush-hush contract on behalf of Egypt was Aldin Mahmoud Khalil, chief of the Egyptian Air Force Intelligence. While Messerschmitt's factories were building aircraft for NATO, the aeronautical genius of Germany also had interests in Spain and Switzerland and he was quite willing to extend these to the Middle East as well. Another capture for Cairo was Eugen Sanger, director of the Jet-Propulsion Study Institute in Stuttgart, who had long been experimenting in rocket research. He was one of the leading exponents of rocket-building for launching earth satellites. Thus by 1960 Egypt was full of German scientists, technicians and engineers. Messerschmitt alone sent out more than a dozen engineers and Sanger took with him many of his most promising young pupils at the Stuttgart Institute. All the projects being undertaken by the German scientists and technicians were top secret and given code numbers. The latter were, however, used so ostentatiously that in messages intercepted by the Israelis they stuck out like obvious codes. It was the task of Mossad agents to find out what the mysterious numbers '36', '135' and '333' stood for.

They knew that CERVA had ceased to exist because the Egyptian High Comand had rejected the idea of giving the Army tactical rockets. But they also learned from agents in Germany that a company named INTRA had been set up in Munich to purchase electronic equipment and engines of a kind that suggested they might be used for a certain type of rocket. Aman had the specialists who could evaluate this. What was more significant was that Paul Goercke was associated with this company. The numbers '36', '135' and '333' were in some way connected with what INTRA was doing.

Other reports from Zurich, Basle, Paris and Cairo suggested that the Egyptians had set up a vast undercover purchasing organisation for aircraft components. The clue to this seemed to lie in a mysterious institution which a talkative Egyptian was apt to refer to as the 'Caballistics'. He was asked what he meant by this odd word.

'Are you like myself a student of the occult?' inquired the Mossad agent who had been posing as an astrologer to the Egyptian.

'Oh, not at all,' replied the Egyptian. 'I am merely trying to make a pun in English. Not a very good óne, I am afraid.'

'How do you mean?'

'Oh, it doesn't matter. I have just mixed up the two words "cabal" and "ballistics".'

The Mossad man did not press him any further. The Egyptian had been educated in England and was obviously a sophisticated individual who would soon become suspicious of any probing questions. Later the Israeli discussed the probable meaning of the pun with a colleague.

'Well, you can pretty well bet that it refers to ballistics, probably in its old sense of projectiles. As to "cabal", it could mean either a secret organisation to do with ballistics, which could mean rockets, or the "mystery ballistics". Either way it seems to me that he must have been talking in a broad sense. But I have come across another clue. Some of the Egyptians who are out at Heliopolis talk of the *Thalathat*. As they used this phrase while gambling, I thought they meant it in a gambling sense—"the Threes". Now I think there must be a link between the *Thalathat* and your "caballistics".'

'Ah, now we are getting somewhere,' replied the Mossad man. '*Thalathat* could be "333", the three threes, and that could mean some kind of code number for a rocket centre. Come to think of it, there is a three in each of those three codes—"36", "135" and "333". Let us now see what kind of sense that makes in reference to the intercepted messages.'

It did not take long for Tel Aviv to unravel this enigma. '333' was eventually identified as a highly secret rocket testing ground in the desert not far from Heliopolis. '135' proved to be an establishment set up outside Cairo by Ferdinand Brandner, while '36' was a factory outside Cairo where, under the direction of Willy Messerschmitt's technicians, components for supersonic aircraft were being made. This intelligence soon revealed to the Israelis the extent of German aid, but it also brought a modicum of comfort. Despite all this effort, the Egyptians still did not have a comprehensive aircraft component industry. They depended entirely on foreign aid.

From then onwards it was not difficult for the Mossad to create a detailed picture of what the Germans were doing in Egypt. While the vast majority of Egyptians, including those of the upper middle classes, were relatively poorly paid, the German scientists received handsome salaries and were given magnificent villas. Their opulence was visible to all, including their gallivantings and parties in Cairo and at the Heliopolis Sporting Club. There was little problem in keeping them under observation. And apart from that, by this time an occasional ascending rocket was clearly visible at least from the outskirts of Cairo and in the vicinity of the German colony.

I I

The Jew who posed as a Nazi

*Whate'er he did was done with so
much ease,
In him alone t'was natural to please.*

(JOHN DRYDEN)

YET ANOTHER ISRAELI SPY who successfully infiltrated Arab
government offices and military establishments and gained accept-
ance in enemy territory was Wolfgang Lotz, whose colleagues at
one time nicknamed him the 'Champagne Spy' on account of his
dispensation of this drink to loosen tongues. When one considers
the activities of Elie Cohen and Wolfgang Lotz and the quantities
of intoxicating liquor which flowed at their parties, the Israelis
might be forgiven a certain amount of cynicism about Moslem
taboos on alcohol.

Wolfgang Lotz, like another celebrated spy before him—the
British agent, Sidney Reilly—was half Jew and half Gentile.
Born at Mannheim in Baden-Württemberg, West Germany,
in 1921, he was the son of a theatrical impressario who died at an
early age. His widow, being Jewish, was dismayed at the changed
conditions of life after the Nazis came to power and these feelings
must have been conveyed to her young son who seems to have
embraced the ideals of Zionism when he was barely in his teens.
They emigrated to Palestine in 1933. There, while only a boy of
sixteen, Wolfgang joined Haganah and learned something of the
arts of underground fighting, while at the same time studying at
an agricultural school where he gained his diploma. He also
acquired a Hebrew first name, Zeev. When World War II broke
out he volunteered for service in the British Army, was accepted
and trained as a Commando. He showed adaptability, initiative
and courage and soon rose to the rank of quartermaster sergeant,
taking part in the Desert War in Egypt.

During this period Wolfgang perfected his English and by the end of the war spoke fluent German, English, Arabic and Hebrew, an excellent combination of languages for an Israeli agent in the late fifties. For a time he worked at an oil refinery in Haifa, but during the War of Independence he joined the Israeli Army and was gazetted as a lieutenant. His record during these years was quite exceptional: he served in the crack Golani Brigade which defended the northern front and was more than once commended for outstanding services. After the War of Independence he gained rapid promotion, eventually achieving the rank of major and Intelligence Officer of his regiment.

Lotz's linguistic talents had been noted, but so, too, had his blond hair and Nordic appearance. He would have passed for one of Hitler's perfect Aryan types any day. The Military Intelligence Section also took into account his courage and enterprise and in due course a dossier on this officer found its way on to the desk of the chief of the Mossad. Wolfgang Lotz was just the man they were looking for—somebody who could eventually infiltrate the German scientists' colony in Egypt and report back to Tel Aviv exactly what they were doing.

In selecting Wolfgang Lotz for this mission there was excellent co-operation between Aman and the Mossad. It is in this inter-Intelligence Services co-operation that the Israelis have an edge over even the leading Western powers. If Lotz had been in British Military Intelligence, especially in peacetime, he might have languished at a desk for years without DI6 ever knowing what a splendid overseas agent was being wasted. It was some time after the Suez War of 1956 that Lotz was interviewed for this assignment and told that it meant his posing as an ex-Nazi.

There was something unique in the annals of espionage about the cover story built up for Lotz. He was ordered to retain his own name and to keep his early history as near to the truth as possible. This meant that he was furnished with his own original birth certificate and identification documents, but his mother's Jewish origin was removed from the papers. The story of his emigration to Palestine was blotted out, but the Mossad provided him with the cover story that he was an officer in Rommel's Edelweiss Corps during the Desert War. As Lotz had fought in the desert on the British side he at least knew enough about the terrain and nature of the war to be able to talk about it credibly. In the event of any unexpected difficulties occurring he was also given a second cover story—that he had fought with the Germans on the Russian front. His absence after the end of the war was to be explained that, as a Nazi, he had found it difficult to be accepted in the new Germany and had no desire to be converted to a democrat. So he had emigrated to Australia, but had not enjoyed life out there and determined to return home.

It was a complicated cover in many respects and only a consummate actor and alert personality could have got away with it for as long as Lotz did. Even then it would have been extremely difficult for him to have penetrated so deeply into Egypt's top military circles and to have won the confidence of the German scientists without the aid of the Gehlen Organisation in West Germany. The Israelis had established first rate contacts inside the very organisation which in the beginning they had suspected might be directed against themselves. Israel has gained its pre-eminence in the world of intelligence by its subtle blend of espionage and diplomacy and by convincing the Secret Services of the Western World that they all share a common interest. For this reason not only has Tel Aviv become a kind of international exchange for secret information for Western Powers, but Western Intelligence chiefs, while outwardly maintaining a strict neutrality towards Israel, nonetheless look upon her as a secret ally who should be unofficially helped whenever possible. In the late fifties this help came abundantly from both the CIA and the West German Intelligence Service, with the tacit approval of General Gehlen himself.

Lotz, armed with various papers, was first sent to a special training camp in Bavaria which came under Gehlen's direction. His blond good looks enabled him to pass as a German without any difficulty and, after having been schooled in the techniques of espionage, he was sent to Egypt, carrying letters of introduction from former high-ranking German officers which had been provided for him by General Gehlen. Once in Cairo he posed as a fun-loving sportsman who had made a substantial amount of money in Australia and now wanted to spend some of it. The Egyptian counter-espionage and police authorities were perfectly satisfied and Lotz passed all tests and interrogations without trouble. One certain avenue to make friends in the German colony in Egypt was through a mutual interest in riding and horse-racing. Lotz used the ample funds with which he had been provided to start a riding school and stud farm in the high class suburb of Zamalek. He was an accomplished rider, though this was a recreation for which he had shown no particular enthusiasm previously and had in fact been the result of a crash course in equestrianism. But he had acquired some knowledge of stud farming while at his agricultural college.

Unlike Elie Cohen, who had been instructed to obtain quick results, Wolfgang Lotz was given a whole year in which to lie low and simply concentrate on making as many friends as possible among the circle of ex-Nazi officers and scientists. He gave the impression of having been a fanatical Nazi, of being nostalgic about the Third Reich and a great admirer of Nasser. Although more or less fulfilling the role of a 'sleeping agent' and not then engaged in active espionage, Lotz managed to collect quite a lot of intelligence in that year, at the end of which he went back to Germany and was there debriefed by an officer of the Mossad.

While in Egypt he had struck up a close friendship not only with some of the ex-Nazi scientists at the rocket and aircraft research establishments, but several of the senior officers in Nasser's Army and on the President's personal staff. What intrigued him was the extent of the Egyptian Intelligence network's activities in Germany and Switzerland: he had detected the links between Ferdinand Brandner and Hassan Kamil, the Egyptian Swiss in Zurich. Also Lotz had discovered that, since the fall of President Perón in Argentina, a number of Germans had left that country to seek safety in Egypt. Among these was one Kurt Tank who had first gone back to Germany, but failed to get work there and gone on to India to help make that country's first jet-fighter. Notwithstanding the entry of these specialists into Egypt, the Arab Republic's rocket production plans ran into serious trouble towards the end of 1959. There were problems at the Messerschmitt establishment, as a result of which a number of technicians were sacked, and some of the German experts had their contacts abruptly cancelled. It was because the Egyptians were making desperate efforts to catch up with Israel in air power that a new quest for talent was launched in Germany and Switzerland. One of the reasons for Lotz's return to Germany was to help Mossad European agents trace the several links in the chain which extended from Cairo to the Stuttgart Institute and undercover companies in Switzerland.

The Mossad experts in assessing the requirements for developing cover stories were firmly of the opinion that it would be a great asset to Lotz and lend more plausibility to his status if he could have a perfect Aryan wife. The Israeli Secret Service has in its relatively short existence shown real genius in its ability to create good covers for its agents, equalling the Russians in this respect. However, the Russians, who believe that the Western World is doomed anyhow, are prepared to wait years for results and they are perhaps ultra-cautious in building up a cover for an agent. But, because Israel is a small country, surrounded by enemies and often desperately in need of intelligence, her Secret Service has developed a talent to obtain top secrets speedily. As we have already seen from the case of Elie Cohen, they dispatch an agent into the highest circles of an enemy country as quickly as possible. It is true that they were prepared to wait one year for Lotz to 'play himself in', but that was all.

So a wife for Lotz was regarded as being one means of strengthening his hand. There was, however, a problem: he was already married, not to any Aryan-type German, but to a typical Hebrew-speaking Israeli girl, by whom he had had two children. Discreet arrangements were made, the requirements of the security and honour of Israel were cited, and back in Israel a faithful and patriotic wife eventually accepted the situation, while her husband agreed to be 'married' to an attractive Nordic blonde named Waldraut Neumann. The marriage took place in Munich, after which the apparently radiantly happy couple went back to Cairo to live in a handsome villa on the outskirts of Heliopolis. It was during the next six months that Wolfgang acquired for himself in underground circles the nickname of the 'Champagne Spy'. His parties were noted for the amount of champagne dispensed and Lotz himself made no secret of the fact that it was his favourite drink, whether at home, at the Gezira Sporting Club near the Pyramids, or the Cavalry Club.

But if Lotz's life may sound like that of the spy of old-fashioned fiction, it was nevertheless sheer hard work. By now he was left in no doubt at all that, for the quantity of money which Israel was giving him to spend, they expected results quickly. They not only wanted details of all Egyptian rocket plans, but maps of the various secret establishments, names of technicians and, above all, enough evidence to be able to launch a diplomatic campaign to force the German technicians out of Egypt.

Like Elie Cohen in Damascus, Wolfgang Lotz lost no time in making friends among the highest-ranking Egyptian officers. These included Colonel Abdel Rahman, the deputy head of the

Egyptian Military Intelligence, Admiral Fawzi Moneim, General Fouad Osman, chief of security for Egypt's rocket sites, General Salaam Suleiman and the General of Police, Youssef Ghorab. Many senior officers attended his riding-school and took lessons: the fees were not excessive and there was the attraction of champagne parties afterwards. Lotz was greatly helped by his German 'wife' on these occasions and she flattered and delighted the Egyptian officers. One officer who occasionally attended these parties and probably prefers to forget the fact today was Colonel Ahmar Sadat, who was then chairman of the National Assembly and is now President of Egypt. Sadat was a great admirer of Rommel and Wolfgang Lotz made a point of reminiscing about the German general in conversations with him.

Lotz was provided with a radio transmission set which he is said to have concealed in a weighing-machine in his bathroom. Once he was firmly established as an agent with a wealth of intelligence to pass on, he kept Tel Aviv regularly supplied with this. It should not be thought that the entire Gehlen Organisation knew of Lotz's masquerade (that was a secret kept only to the few members who were also agents of Mossad). The top man of the West German Intelligence Service in Cairo was himself completely ignorant of Lotz's true identity. He suspected that Lotz might be an agent, but thought he was probably a Briton or American using a West German name as a cover. With his wide range of contacts Lotz was able to provide the Mossad with economic and political intelligence as well as a detailed dossier on what the ex-Nazis and other German technicians were doing. The Israeli agent made such a close friend of General Fouad Osman that he was let into all manner of military secrets. Later, when it seemed evident that Egypt was seeking Russian aid for the development of her rocket programme, Lotz was able to confirm this by getting an invitation from the general to tour the SAM rocket bases and see the launching pads in Sinai and on the Negev frontier. On this occasion Lotz took an enormous risk, but it paid off. He had given all his friends to understand that he was a compulsive amateur photographer and he asked Fouad Osman if he would care to pose in front of one of the new rockets on its launching pad. He got permission and his picture!

Most important of all, however, Lotz had surveyed the postal facilities accorded to the German colony near the rocket sites. As a result there was a carefully planned surveillance of mail passing between this colony in Egypt and various addresses in Germany; sometimes mail and parcels were intercepted in one country, sometimes in the other. Any correspondence was photocopied and parcels and letters were forwarded on as though nothing had happened. It not only gave the Israelis all the information they wanted, but addresses of the scientists' German relatives. The stage was set for confronting the West German Government with a sensational dossier and a demand for the recall of these technicians. Or, if that tactic failed, then more ruthless methods must be used. For time was no longer on the side of the Israelis: Nasser had achieved with German aid what he could never have hoped to do on his own—the production of an effective rocket for his armoury. But this was not all. For early in 1962 reports had come through to the Mossad that the German scientists were working on even more terrible weapons to be used against Israel, involving bacteria and chemical warfare.

One report was that a young German woman chemist had arrived in Cairo and that Dr. Hans Eisele, who had been a doctor in concentration camps, was installed at the '135' establishment and was possibly engaged in research for germ warfare. This news was ominous, but still vague and conjectural. However, in the same year rather more factual and alarming evidence was received from a former Austrian Wehrmacht officer who had been living in Cairo. He informed the Israeli Secret Service that he had proof that German scientists were perfecting a 'horror bomb', a cheap and small nuclear weapon, but one which contained the dread elements of strontium 90 and cobalt 60, and which, if dropped on Israel, would pollute the atmosphere and the soil and in a slow, insidious way cause thousands of deaths.[1]

While the Israelis were totally satisfied with the accurate and extremely factual information which Lotz was sending them from Cairo, they were somewhat chary of these other reports. Opinion both inside the Israeli Cabinet and the various branches of the Intelligence Services was divided as to whether to accept this information as being true without further verification and confront the West German Government, or to wait until proof was certain just in case there was a subtle plot to trick the Israelis into making claims which would easily be disproved. This became a major political issue in Tel Aviv.

12

Swiss Broadside for Harel

*'Ibis' and 'Cleopatra' were projects with the in-
tention of destroying Israel. That is why we had
to act.*

(ISSER HAREL)

'IBIS' AND 'CLEOPATRA' were code-names for some of the projects
being run by German scientists in Egypt in the early 1960s. These
were especially concerned with the top secret plans for creating
terror weapons which, it was hoped, could be used to blackmail
Israel into surrender. 'Ibis' was a plan devised to inject missiles
with cobalt 60 and strontium 90 atomic waste, while 'Cleopatra'
was in essence a poor nation's atomic weapon. In fact, by this
time much of the research work of the German scientists had
broken down and numerous failures had been recorded and, as
later Isser Harel had to admit, neither of these two projects had
much technological substance. But he was not to know that at the
time. As far as Harel was concerned, they 'were projects with the
intention of destroying Israel. That is why we had to act.'[1]

Harel was all for a carefully organised Secret Service action
which would frighten the German scientists out of Egypt. The
moderate members of the Israeli Cabinet, and this included Ben-
Gurion himself, were at that time anxious to restore normal relations with West Germany, to bury the past and create an accord
with the post-war democratic West German Republic. They did
not want anything which would hinder this development; they
hoped that diplomacy could be used to persuade the West
German Government to recall the scientists in Egypt.

But, argued Harel, with considerable logic on his side, however
much they might wish to be able to recall their own nationals,
the West German Government had little power to do so. Here

was a serious threat to Israel's very existence and something had to be done about it. Indeed, it would be a criminal folly not to act. There were also reports that phials of a nerve gas, Tabun, developed by the Nazis during World War II, had been experimented with in Egypt, though there was no confirmation of this during the 1960s.

It was the old question of whether Machiavellian tactics are ever justifiable. And in this instance it could legitimately be argued that there was a strong case for adopting such measures. Alas, for Isser Harel, some of his aggressive tactics went sadly astray and in the end the 'threat to Israel' proved to be somewhat of a damp squib. But this is being wise after the event. In 1962–63 the threat seemed real enough and Harel, no doubt fortified by his success in kidnapping Eichmann, thought he could get away with strong-arm measures. He was in his own way meticulously scrupulous in a very difficult post, and would not have retained the confidence of Ben-Gurion for so many years if it had been otherwise. One example of his scrupulous insistence on there being no abuse of the system was when he sacked an agent for using a free cinema pass to entertain his girl friend, when he was intended to detect Russians making exchanges of papers in the back row of the stalls. Harel had always accepted without question that he was answerable to the civilian power and on countless occasions refused to take advantage of the various privileges which his position conferred on him. But at the same time he could and did operate ruthlessly and in 1963 he went far beyond his actions of the Argentinian adventure in conduct which was certainly illegal and in some cases criminal by international standards. But he took the view that Israel was actually suffering from all the disadvantages of an undeclared war by Egypt and that on such occasions 'you have to break the law, but you do the very minimum'.

The Israeli Government had already made approaches to the West German Government about the German scientists in Egypt and had given them ample evidence on which to assess the situation. And perhaps where Isser Harel may have overstepped the mark was in not making allowances for what the West German Government had been able to do. They had responded in a friendly manner and had actually put considerable pressure on the Stuttgart Institute which was subsidised by the Bonn Government. The Federal Republic had ordered Eugen Sanger and his research students to return to Germany and declare their contracts null and void. Sanger complied and was appointed director of an aeronautical study-centre in West Berlin. On the other hand some of his assistants refused to leave Egypt and other Germans filled the places of Sanger and those who had complied with the request from Bonn. Thus, in effect, the West German Government's influence had been minimal and the Israelis were not altogether happy about the attitude of the West German Defence Minister, Strauss. Harel in particular was irked by the slow process of what he regarded as somewhat futile diplomacy and by 26 July 1962, his mind was made up by the news that Egypt had launched two rockets in a demonstration staged in front of Nasser. An official communiqué stated that Egypt had two new long-range missiles—'Al Kahir', with a range of 350 miles and 'Al Zafir', with a range of 175 miles. There was no mistaking the implications of this. From then on the Israeli Secret Service went into action.

Harel hadn't waited until the Egyptian announcement about their new missiles before making plans. He regarded the Swiss–Egyptian Hassan Kamil as one of the most dangerous and elusive of Israel's enemies and for months had kept watch on this mysterious businessman's movements. Israel's relations with Switzerland have always been uneasy and sometimes, under the guise of neutrality, the Swiss authorities have appeared to be more hostile to the Israelis than to any other nation in the world.

There may have been faults on both sides in the development of this situation, but the facts speak for themselves: on countless occasions the Swiss have arrested Israelis, or taken action against Israeli citizens, whereas all too often they have remained inactive in the face of Arab terrorism, or threats of this. But something of this lack of reciprocity between the two nations dates back to World War II when, in parts of Switzerland, there was a good deal of support for the Nazis. Indeed, in German Switzerland it was sometimes said of them that they were more Nazi than the Nazis. Even during the immediate post-war years when the Zionists were building up an underground movement in Europe, they found it almost impossible to do much in Switzerland. Shmuel Katz stated that the 'Irgun representative in Switzerland was Rammy (David Danon), a medical student at Geneva, who after active service in 1944 had been spirited out of Palestine.

Another Irgun member, Reuben Hecht, was in Basle. In the end the plan to attack British installations in Switzerland was abandoned. My own discussions with Rammy, a survey of conditions in Geneva and Basle, a two-day investigation in Berne by Hecht convinced me that any operation there would be too complicated and hazardous.'[2]

In 1962, a series of mysterious incidents occurred in Switzerland, Egypt and Germany, all of which pointed to machinations of the Israeli Secret Service. The first took place in July when Hassan Kamil chartered a plane to take himself and his wife from the island of Sylt close to the Danish–German border to Dusseldorf. Just before the plane was due to leave Kamil had to cancel his trip, and his wife travelled on alone. The plane crashed in Westphalia a few hours later, the pilot and Madame Kamil were both killed.

This aroused comparatively little interest outside intelligence circles even though the cause of the accident was never discovered for certain. But the next incident at Munich on 10 September 1962, was rather different. The wife of Heinz Krug, the manager of the INTRA office in the Schillerstrasse (suspected of having been used as a purchasing agency for electronic equipment and rocket motors by the Egyptians), reported to the Munich police that her husband was missing. Inquiries were made and it was ascertained that earlier that day he had been seen leaving his office with another man whom an Egyptian airline hostess reported as looking like an Israeli. Forty-eight hours afterwards Krug's car was found abandoned some distance out of the city. It was rumoured that he had been kidnapped.

The next events happened within a few days of each other. Wolfgang Pilz, one of the German technicians in Egypt and a leading rocket authority, had taken the place of Sanger in directing research. On 27 November 1962, his secretary opened his mail and came across a parcel on which was the address of the supposed sender—a barrister in Hamburg. She started to open the parcel without any hesitation: it blew up in her face and for several weeks she was in a Cairo hospital.

This was the first of a series of letter-bombs. The next day a parcel, this time apparently from a bookshop in Stuttgart, was received in another of the secret offices of the rocket researchers. It exploded killing five Egyptians. The message was clear: the German scientists were being threatened with death if they did not quit Egypt. Other parcels arrived during the next two days and they were handed over to experts for examination without being opened. It was found that they contained books filled with explosive devices.

Notwithstanding the speculation as to who might have posted the parcel-bombs, the Egyptian authorities made no statements on the subject and merely alerted their own Intelligence Services. Later there were other reports from Egypt and Germany that members of the families of German scientists had received anonymous telephone calls warning them that, unless the technicians and rocket experts left Egypt, action would be taken against them. But it was whispered in Beirut, perhaps one of the best listening-posts on Middle Eastern imbroglios at this period, that the KGB had moved in on this Israeli operation and were anxious to turn it to their own advantage. This could well have been true, as it has been impossible to trace whether all the anonymous telephone calls originated from Israeli agents, and it would have been in the Russians' interests to see the German experts disappear from Egypt so that they could increase their own influence in that sphere.

The next victim of this war of nerves was Dr. Hans Kleinwachter, a laboratory technician who was an authority on rocket construction. In February 1963, he left Egypt for a brief visit to Germany where he still maintained his own research laboratory at Lorrach, close to the Swiss frontier. One day while he was driving along a narrow lane near his home a car suddenly swerved in front of him, forcing him to stop. There was nobody else about at the time. Afterwards Dr. Kleinwachter described the incident as follows. 'I could see there were three men in the other car. One of them got out and walked towards me. I was somewhat uneasy as it seemed to me that there was something sinister about the chap and the others were obviously watching my car and not speaking. As the man drew level with me he just said: "Can you tell me where Dr. Schenker lives?" I suppose this was intended to disarm me into thinking it was just an innocent inquiry. Before I could say a word he whipped out a gun fitted with a silencer and pressed the trigger. I was lucky. The bullet broke the windscreen into small pieces, but it did not harm me. By a miraculous chance it buried itself in my thick winter scarf.'

The marksman ran back to the other car which promptly drove off. Later the police found it abandoned only a short distance from the scene of the attack. It was presumed that the three men made their getaway in another car, probably across the Swiss border. The only clue was a passport, bearing the name of Ali Samir, said to be a member of the Egyptian Intelligence Service, which had been left in the abandoned car. But this was almost certainly a deliberately planted false clue, as it was later established that Ali Samir had been in Cairo at the time. None of this made much sense to the investigators, who included German and Swiss police as well as some European Secret Service operators. Certainly nobody believed that the Egyptian Secret Service had organised this operation against Dr. Kleinwachter, for the Egyptians had no quarrel with him, though naturally some of the press played up the story of the Ali Samir passport. Yet though the impression was given that the shooting had been bungled, it seemed highly unlikely that a skilled 'hit team' would miss their man at more or less point blank range. Therefore the presumption must be that the Israelis only wanted to frighten Dr. Kleinwachter and to remind him that he was a marked man unless he pulled out of Egypt permanently. In short, to frighten was better than to kill. But the false clue of the passport seemed a little clumsy; why not choose a bogus Egyptian name, not that of a man who could be proved to have been in Cairo at the time of the attack?

While the German police were investigating this affair, a final incident occurred which resulted in a great deal of publicity for the whole question of German scientists in Egypt, and made the secret Egyptian horror weapons designed for use against Israel front page news throughout the world. This time the incident occurred inside Switzerland where the small but efficient Intelligence Service had already been alerted to what was going on not only across the border in Germany, but in the various undercover offices set up in their own territory by people working on behalf of the Egyptians. It did not take the Swiss police long to ascertain the links between recent events in Germany and what was going on in Switzerland. They suspected that the getaway car driven off after the attempt on Dr. Kleinwachter's life (if it really was a genuine attempt) had made its way into Switzerland, probably crossing the border long before the Kleinwachter affair had been reported to the German police. Then on the day before Mardi Gras in 1963 the Swiss police received a tip from Germany that Israeli agents were suspected of having moved to Switzerland.

They based this surmise not merely on the Kleinwachter case, but on the fact that the daughter of Paul Goercke, the German scientist who had helped the Egyptians, had received a threat from an Austrian, Otto Frank Joklik, that if her father did not desist from making weapons for use against Israel, action might be taken against him and his family. It was believed that Joklik had then disappeared into Switzerland. Somewhat firmer evidence, however, came from the Freiberg police that Heidi Goercke had received an anonymous telephone call asking her to make a rendezvous with two men at a hotel in Basle. The German police believed there was an element of threat behind this proposed rendezvous.

At this time Arab money was being deposited in safes and numbered accounts in Swiss banks. New Arab banks were also being opened up in the country. Some of these funds were 'funk money' placed by Arab potentates who wished to safeguard their future against possible take-overs or coups. But a great deal was money set aside by various factions of the guerrillas who had been fighting for independence for Algeria. Behind the scenes there was much manoeuvring for power and in a subtle way the Swiss bankers were fully aware that life would never quite be the same again. They had weathered the storms related to all the Nazi loot which had been stowed away in their country and they were fully cognisant of the many Secret Service funds which in one form or another were paid out by all the great powers in Switzerland. But now there was a new element—the organised Arab campaign against Jewish capital and business, one which sometimes took the form of threatening financial sanctions against any country which showed a bias towards Israel. By this time the Swiss were extremely anxious not to offend the Arabs. The quest for Israeli agents, therefore, although there was no evidence that they were operating on Swiss territory, was seen partly as a means of demonstrating to the Arabs the scrupulous 'neutrality' of the Swiss.

An Egyptian–Algerian intelligence cell had been established in Montreux during the early sixties. It was directed at pressurising the Swiss into some semblance of a pro-Arab stance. Knowing full well that the Swiss, who worshipped neutrality in much the same way that some people worship God, would never officially agree to any pro-Arab or anti-Israeli policy, the pressure was cunningly designed to influence not governmental circles, but banks, police

and the Intelligence Service. At the same time attention was paid
to the elements of pro-Nazism who had been prominent in
Switzerland in World War II. It was a tip-off from an Algerian
agent in Montreux which informed the Swiss police that Otto
Joklik was an Israeli agent who was plotting to destroy the offices
of Hassan Kamil. In fact Otto Joklik, an Austrian scientist and
a former Wehrmacht officer, was an implacable enemy of the
Nazis and only a year previously he had offered information to
the Israelis about the German scientists in Egypt. Indeed, Joklik
was the man who had given the most alarming details of the
strontium-cobalt bomb.

It was late in February 1963, that the prosecutor's office in
Freiburg-in-Breisgau in West Germany asked the Basle authorities
to put under surveillance the meeting planned for 2 March at the
Drei Koenigen Hotel in Basle, between Fraulein Heidi Goercke,
her brother, and Dr. Otto Joklik, who was to be accompanied by
an Israeli national, Joseph Ben-Gal. According to the information
accompanying this request, Joklik had himself once worked for
the United Arab Republic Government, and his name was said
to have been mentioned in Munich in 1962 in connection with
the disappearance of Dr. Heinz Krug and with the attempted
murder of Dr. Kleinwachter, both of whom were working in
Egypt with Goercke. So on the day of Mardi Gras in March
1963, Swiss police in civilian clothes kept watch at the hotel in
Basle. The West German police had advised Heidi Goercke to
keep the appointment, assuring her that the Swiss police would
keep watch all the time and ensure her safety. In the light of the
Kleinwachter affair it was a decision which must have required
some courage on her part. She took her younger brother with her
for company and together they sat down in the hotel lounge where
a microphone had been concealed in a lamp close to their table.
Meanwhile police were seated nearby.

Eventually Joklik arrived accompanied by another man who
said he was an Israeli. Joklik did most of the talking, once again
stressing that if Goercke persisted in his work for Egypt, he was
running very grave risks. There was still an implied threat, but,
if anything, it seemed rather less sinister than previously. Heide
Goercke wondered why she had been asked to go to Basle for a
mere repetition of the previous hints of trouble and danger for
her family. But the object of the exercise was clear: she was to use
her influence to persuade her father to leave Egypt.

The two men left the hotel and went to the railway station where they took a train to Zurich. The Zurich police were telephoned and were waiting for them when they arrived. Then they followed them to a restaurant near the lake where people were attending the masked Mardi Gras ball. Joklik and his companion had a drink together and then left the restaurant and went their separate ways.

Joklik went back to the railway station where eventually he was arrested, while his companion walked towards the Israeli Consulate. Before he had time to enter its doors and so be safely inside Israeli territory, the police stopped him and asked to see his passport. This he produced, showing his name was Joseph Ben-Gal, and claiming to be a civil servant in the Israeli Ministry of Education. Strictly speaking, Ben-Gal had every reason to claim some form of diplomatic immunity. In any event it is surprising that as he had not actually committed any offence other than the fact that he was accompanying Joklik, which was hardly a crime, the Swiss police should have arrested him. The case of Joklik was somewhat different as there had been complaints about him from the German police.

The Swiss authorities must have been somewhat perplexed as to what to do next for, after questioning the two men, they kept them in custody for two weeks before announcing on 15 March 1963, that two agents of a foreign power were being charged with making threats to Fraulein Heide Goercke. The Basle prosecutor's statement added that 'according to the investigation so far, the contention made in Tel Aviv that it was Fraulein Goercke who organised the meeting at the hotel, and that this was no more than a frame-up, must be rejected as totally incorrect.' Swiss newspapers reported that Joklik had previously been expelled from Switzerland for trying to induce Swiss scientists to work for Israel. It was also said that Hassan Kamil had been one of the instigators of Swiss action against these two men. Certainly the West German police suspected them of having been involved in the attack on Dr. Kleinwachter, as they applied to the Swiss for their extradition to Germany.

The trial opened at Basle on 10 June 1963, Ben-Gal being charged with conduct prejudicial to the liberty of the individual, while Joklik was charged with being an accomplice and of 'repeated violation of the interdiction on his entering Swiss territory, to which he has been subject since February 1960'. At

the same time the Swiss rejected a request for the extradition of
Ben-Gal and Joklik to West Germany.

It was the publicity surrounding this case that created difficulties for Isser Harel. Ben-Gurion had been doing his best in secret
diplomacy with the West Germans to seek their aid in getting the
German scientists out of Egypt. At the same time he had also
been anxious to improve relations between his country and Bonn.
The ageing Chancellor, Konrad Adenauer, was himself eager to
see these relations put on a better basis. It was true that not much
had been achieved, but the scandals of recent events in Germany
and Switzerland, which swiftly became publicised through the
trial of the alleged Israeli agents, inevitably made matters worse.
In Israel all this news was received by the public with mixed feelings of alarm, anger and renewed clamour for bringing war
criminals to justice. In other parts of the world there was criticism
of illegal activities by the Israeli Secret Service and allegations of
terrorist tactics. A certain amount of damage was done to Israel's
standing abroad. This was especially true of the reports that an
Israeli secret society, code-named 'Gideon', was responsible for
the letter-bombs sent to Egypt. For soon there appeared in the
press lurid reports of attempted kidnappings of German scientists,
of virus bombs being manufactured in Egyptian laboratories and
some highly coloured accounts of the planning of a death-ray to
wipe out Israel.

Harel did not deny the charges made against him, as many
Secret Service chiefs might have done. There was no disowning
of the Israeli agents, even if there was no admission of guilt. But
during the trial of Ben-Gal and Joklik at Basle there was suddenly
a marked change in the atmosphere of the court. Originally,
many had been surprised that Switzerland had not just allowed
the two men to be extradited to West Germany. It is possible, of
course, that this extradition request was a half-hearted one and
that the Bonn Government was not particularly anxious to be
seen prosecuting Israeli agents. But it was the atmosphere of Swiss
hostility to the Israelis that changed almost overnight. Somewhere
along the line secret diplomatic exchanges must have been carried
out, because unofficially the Swiss Intelligence seem to have been
told in advance that there was going to be a change in the direction of the Mossad and that no further actions concerning the
German scientists would be conducted on Swiss soil. For the
prosecuting counsel at the trial gradually played a less belligerent

role and it was obvious that he had been instructed not to over-
state his case.

Whatever may be argued for or against Isser Harel and the
Mossad operations of this period, there can be no denying that
the defence of Ben-Gal and Joklik was skilfully employed in
obtaining the maximum publicity for the presence of the German
scientists in Egypt. Some indication of the importance the Israeli
Government attached to the affair was the presence in Basle of
David Landor, head of the Government Press Office, and of
Gabriel Bach, an assistant prosecutor at the Eichmann trial, who
attended as an observer.

No doubt most nations would have insisted that absolute silence
be preserved and nothing admitted, even in mitigation, as to what
the two men had been about. But, by allowing the defence to
make public so many proofs of the activities of the German
scientists in Egypt, Israel not only gained the kind of publicity
she wanted, but assisted the cause of the two men. During the trial
an order by Wolfgang Pilz for the purchase of 900 pieces of
rocket mechanism and 2,700 gyroscopes was produced by counsel.
The document on which this was written clearly indicated that it
was for equipping 900 rockets which were to be mass-produced at
the '333' factory.

Joklik himself claimed that he had left his job with the UAR
Government in Egypt because he had gained the impression that
the 'de facto intention of the Egyptians was the extermination of
the Jews'. He alleged that Dr. Wolfgang Pilz, head of the team
of German scientists engaged by the UAR Government, planned
to provide the rockets being built in Egypt with capsules containing radio-active strontium and cobalt. The prosecution's case was
that Ben-Gal then joined the Israeli Secret Service and came to
Europe.

The lawyer representing Heidi Goercke told the judges that
the radio-active substances listed in facsimiles of what were
alleged to be orders and inquiries made by the Egyptian authorities were in quantities suitable for hospital purposes only. Joklik,
when questioned by the judges, said he had ordered radio-active
materials through a firm in Brunswick. At first he thought these
were for medical purposes. Professor Walter Binder, of Berne
University, estimated that the quantity of cobalt 60 mentioned
in the documents would be sufficient to contaminate the atmosphere over Israel to a height of one kilometre for at least five years

with a concentration of 'fifty times the genetically tolerable maximum dose'. His report did not, however, mention how this concentration could be created over Israel without equally endangering neighbouring Arab countries. But this omission did not deter Joklik from claiming that the 'project involving cobalt 60' which Egypt was planning was 'a threat not only to Israel but to various European capitals'.

In fact, the case for the defence regarding the possibility of such use of chemical warfare was extremely flimsy, but it had its effect in the amount of propaganda which Israel was able to extract from the trial and probably even alarmed the Swiss. For from then on the prosecuting counsel bent over backwards to be fair to the accused. He even went so far as to say he 'fully appreciated Israel's anxiety for her very existence in the light of these revelations', and added that Ben-Gal's intentions had been 'honourable'. The judges gave them a sentence of two months, which, as both men had been in custody for more than three months, meant they were released immediately.

Meanwhile after an irreconcilable conflict between Isser Harel and Ben-Gurion, Harel had resigned from his post as Intelligence chief. The two men who had so greatly respected and admired one another had finally parted ways. Harel was quite unrepentant and maintained that if his tactics had brought things out into the open, no great harm had been done and that many important people who were apt to forget there had ever been any Nazis had now learned just what these men were still doing. 'I had the support of most of the Cabinet,' he claimed, 'but I couldn't stay if I disagreed so profoundly with the Prime Minister.' As to his tactics in employing such gangster methods as letter-bombs and threats to the German scientists, he is reported as having made the comment: 'There are men who—it is a Biblical phrase, and I am not quite sure of it in English—are marked to die.'[3]

Ben-Gurion, however, put the need for better relations with Germany above any arguments on the pros and cons of Secret Service policy. Unquestionably ever since that day these relations have improved and anti-German propaganda has disappeared from the Israeli press. The Bonn Government did its best to discourage its nationals from taking scientific posts in Egypt which might be linked to military work, but it could do little more than hope to persuade people to return. A few of the scientists did, probably more from fear of reprisals than at the behest of the

Bonn Government. Ben-Gurion, however, could point to the fact that some of the information about what the German scientists were doing was grossly exaggerated, possibly untrue. The American CIA took this view. There was a good deal of doubt about the reliability of Joklik's evidence. He had originally gone to work on the secret weapons projects in Egypt and claimed that he only decided to leave Cairo because he felt a terrible guilt at being implicated in a plot to destroy the Israelis. Perhaps, but he must have heard of the fact that the Israelis were prepared to pay well for the right kind of information. At his trial it was also proved that he had lied about his scientific qualifications. Even Harel had to admit that ultimately Joklik's information was not altogether technologically sound.

13

The Case of Israel Beer

The life of the secret agent is dangerous enough, but the life of the double agent is infinitely more precarious. If anyone balances on a swinging tight-rope it is he, and a single slip must send him crashing to destruction.

(SIR JOHN MASTERMAN IN *The Case of the Four Friends*)

THOUGH MOST OF ISRAEL's counter-espionage was concentrated on threats from Arab neighbours during the period up to 1965, it had already become evident that the Soviet Union had increasingly been indulging in espionage against the new Jewish state and actually using Israel as a base for its agents.

It was, of course, not too difficult for the Russians to slip in an occasional KGB man among the small number of Soviet citizens who were allowed to emigrate to Israel. Invariably they would choose a Russian Jew who spoke Hebrew fluently and was able to pose as a Zionist. Very few such Jews were prepared to betray their co-religionists, but the few who did created enormous trouble for Israel. From 1948 until 1967 the Russians were extremely active in Israel and employing not only disloyal Jews, but spies planted in embassies and in one instance a key agent inside the Israeli Foreign Office. Curiously enough, though a number of Jews have successfully posed as Moslems in the spy game, few Arabs have successfully posed as Jews. Nor have the Russians attempted to make use of Arab agents in this way. The reason seems to be that the Russians have found they cannot trust the Arabs and prefer Jewish agents who, of course, can also keep them informed on Arab matters.

Between 1956 and 1957 a steady stream of anti-Semitic propaganda poured out from the Soviet press. Those in Israel who had believed that the cold war had ended and that there would be a more favourable climate for Zionism in Russia were swiftly disillusioned. More Jews were dismissed from key posts in the USSR and from 1957 onwards the Soviet press and radio gave accounts of how individual Soviet migrants had been bitterly disappointed with Israel. They called the institution of the kibbutz a 'labour camp'. Israel was even condemned for having 'collaborated with Nazism in the past'—a total lie, but an example of how Soviet propaganda works, for they fastened on to the single incident of the war-time attempt to do a deal with the Nazis on the subject of Jewish immigrants. Russia also accused Israel of whitewashing the Third Reich by accepting reparations from West Germany.

In November 1958, the Israeli Government announced that the largest espionage network then so far discovered in Israel had been liquidated by the security police. This involved Israeli Arabs and their relatives in Jordan, as well as infiltrators who crossed the border from Lebanon. Ten Israeli Arabs were arrested, though it was believed at the time that far more were implicated. Their activities dated back to 1956, with some interruptions, as a result of counter-measures adopted from time to time by Israel's security services.

Two brothers, described as belonging to a prominent family in Western Galilee, were reported to have written confessions in which they expressed regret for what they had done, after at first denying all accusations against them. They had both crossed into the Old City of Jerusalem in January 1957, and, according to the Government statement, the elder was contacted by a Syrian agent named Achmed Daoud Azia, who lived in Lebanon but came to Jordan to recruit agents among Israeli Arab pilgrims. The two brothers agreed to work for Azia and when they returned home were contacted by another agent living in Acre, who received information from one of the brothers (a teacher) and was able to move around the country in spite of restrictions on the movements of Arabs. The Acre agent was visited by Syrian infiltrators, who collected maps, Army periodicals and other material prepared for them, and in exchange handed over money and further instructions. The names of the Syrian infiltrators, who were the ringleaders in this network, were Hassan Abd el

The 'Ezra' group of Poale Zion at Ben-Gurion's home town of Plonsk in 1900. Out of this developed the nucleus of an Israeli intelligence service

Top left: Menachem Begin *Top right:* Isser Harel
Bottom left: Shimon Peres *Bottom right:* Elie Cohen

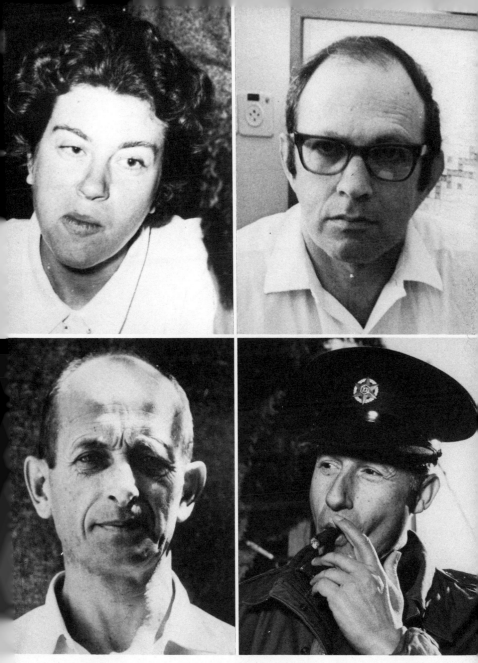

Top left: Victorino Nino, alias Marcelle *Top right:* Dr. Yuval
Ne'eman *Bottom left:* Adolf Eichmann *Bottom right:* Israeli Police
Chief Joseph Nakmias

Left:
Wolfgang Lotz with
Egyptian General
Ghorab and Waltraud
Lotz at the Cavalry
Club in Cairo
Bottom left:
Israel Beer, Soviet spy
Bottom right:
General Meir Amit,
former head of the
Mossad

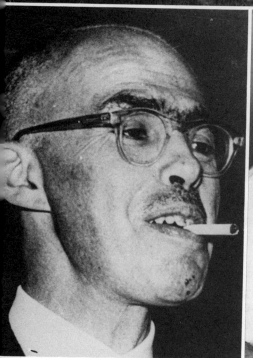

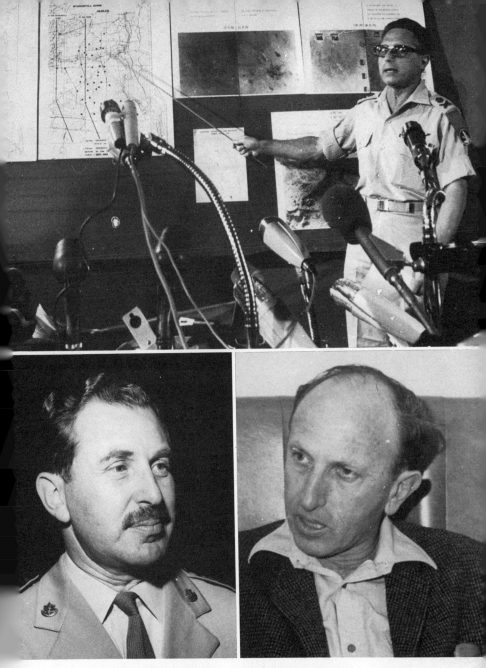

Top: Major-General Aharon Yariv, head of Israeli Military
Intelligence during the Six-Day War *Bottom left:* Chaim Herzog,
Director of Military Intelligence 1959–62 *Bottom right:* Zvi Zamir,
head of the Mossad at the time of the Lillehammer episode

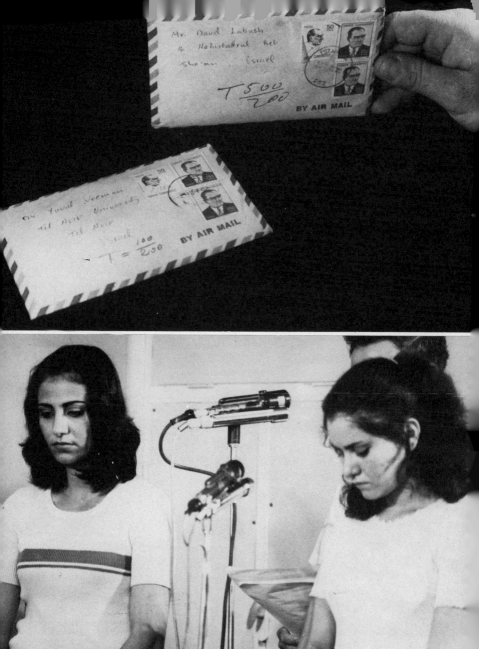

Top: Two letter bombs mailed from Turkey to Israel by
terrorists. One is addressed to Dr. Yuval Ne'eman, head of Aman
Bottom: Two terrorist girls who took part in the Sabena hi-jacking,
sentenced to life imprisonment by an Israeli military court

Top left: Major-General Yitzak Hofi, head of the Mossad
Top right: International terrorist Carlos (wearing beret) with the
Algerian Minister Bouteflika *Bottom:* Articles seized by the
French counter-espionage service from the hide-out of Carlos-
controlled Arab terrorists in Paris

Top left: Major-General Ariel Sharon, key figure in secret
Commando operations *Top right:* Brigadier-General Dan Shomron
who headed the Commando raid on Entebbe
Bottom: Paratrooper's Commander, Tat-Aluf Rafael Eytan (middle
row, centre) explaining the activities of his corps to (from right)
General Bar-Lev, General David Elazar (head of Aman) and
General Rechavam Zeevi (Intelligence adviser)

Hassied Hassan, Ali Arbush, Maflah el Muad, Hassan el Makdah and Kassam el Hayek.

Though the Israelis were a little slow in tracking down this network and in realising what was going on, once they detected one spy they wisely waited to round up the whole network before taking action, with the result that, in the end, they not only knew the ringleaders, but their contacts and those in the villages of Araba and Mugar who had sheltered the infiltrators, or knew of the spying, but had not informed the authorities as required by law.

There was no connection between this spy ring and any of the Soviet activities inside Israel, but it was about this time—towards the end of 1958—that the Israelis first came on the trail of Soviet agents operating inside their territory. The USSR not only operated with their own agents, but also directed espionage inside Israel through the secret services of Poland, Rumania and Czechoslovakia. One of the first of these communist agents to be suspected was Aharon Cohen, who in 1962 was sentenced to five years' imprisonment for passing secret information 'to the agents of a communist power'.

Aharon Cohen was a Middle East expert of the left-wing Mapam Party in Israel. He had a good record of service to his country both as an ordinary citizen and a politician, and this undoubtedly saved him from a much heavier punishment and was a factor in the decision of the Supreme Court to commute half his sentence when he made an appeal in September 1962. At his trial in Haifa it was stated that the agent to whom Cohen passed information was 'a representative of a scientific research mission', but that Cohen was well aware of the nature of the mission and the agent's activities. Information had been passed to the agent over a period of fourteen months. The trial was held *in camera*.

While Israeli Intelligence officers were on the trail of Aharon Cohen and beginning to realise the extent of Russian, Polish, Rumanian and Czech efforts to spy on Israel, they came quite unexpectedly, through a report from a Mossad agent, on the disturbing news that there was a nuclear scientist in their midst who was passing information behind the Iron Curtain. Numerous cases of Eastern bloc espionage had been uncovered by the Shabak during the late fifties and early sixties, but only about eight of these were brought to trial and publicly revealed, largely because the highly efficient Shabak and their allies in the other branches of the Israeli Secret Service were able to exploit the captured agents and 'turn' them against the enemy. In some instances this was not difficult to do as the Israelis found they were dealing with somewhat unwilling spies who had been bullied into working for the Eastern bloc through blackmail, or threats made against their relatives if they did not agree to undertake missions for the communists.

By this time the Israelis had borrowed something of the 'Double-Cross System' which was so brilliantly handled for 'turning' enemy agents by B1A of the British Intelligence in World War II. One or two Israeli Intelligence people had actually had first hand experience of the working of this system. But, as Sir John Masterman, who played a vital role in B1A, stated, the game of using double agents is a dangerous one. 'Running a team of double agents is very like running a club cricket side,' he wrote. 'Older players lose their form and are gradually replaced by new-comers. Well-established veterans unaccountably fail to make runs, whereas youngsters whose style at first appears crude and untutored for some unexplained reason make large scores.' The Israelis soon learned that it was the minor agent who often turned out to be the astonishingly successful double agent and some of those they 'turned' not only fed back false information behind the Iron Curtain, but actually managed to help penetrate the Intelligence Services of Poland and Czechoslovakia and in at least one instance of Russia itself.

Nevertheless during the early sixties Israel suffered two serious set-backs in this war of espionage. Each instance proved a substantial victory for the Soviet Union. The first case was that of a middle-aged Sudeten German, Professor Kurt Sitte, who held an important research post as a nuclear physicist and specialist in cosmic radiation at the Institute of Technology at Haifa. Here was a spy at work over a long period in a vitally important establishment inside Israel. He was a threat not merely to Israel, but to the United States and the whole of Western Europe.

Sitte was born in Czechoslovakia, but although a Sudeten German, the one race in that country Hitler had pledged himself to rescue, he had shown himself to be a friend of the Jews during the war. He had actually helped Jews to escape from Czechoslovakia, both as a member of the Underground Movement and as an inmate of a concentration camp. Undoubtedly it was while showing these sympathies that he was recruited by the Russians as an agent. No doubt it was the Russians who urged him to ensure that he became a citizen of the West German Federal Republic. This may have been a useful cover for a Soviet agent in many countries, but it was not perhaps the best for one operating in Israel. After the war Sitte worked at the universities of Edinburgh and Manchester between 1946 and 1948, and later taught at Syracuse University in the USA. He joined the Haifa Institute in 1954 and for a period of over four years had been furnishing intelligence from Israel to the Soviet bloc. In this instance it was the Czech Intelligence Service who employed him and his actual date of recruitment by them goes back to his time in a Buchenwald Prison Camp where a Czech communist cell had been set up.

Some of the work Sitte had been carrying out at the Haifa Institute was on behalf of the United States Air Force, for he was highly regarded as a scientist on both sides of the Atlantic. He was eventually trapped by the Israelis and charged on seven counts with transmitting secret information to a foreign power. On 7 February 1961, he was jailed for five years. It is interesting to note that at his trial his defence counsel, Mr. Jacob Saloman, put forward the plea that Sitte had not been motivated by financial gain or ideological identification with the power he served, but by concern for members of his family still living in the country for which he spied. Censorship in Israel usually prohibits naming the country for which a defendant is alleged to have spied. In the case of Sitte he faced a maximum penalty of life imprisonment, so that the actual sentence of five years was remarkably lenient.

It was the second case of Eastern bloc espionage which not only seriously injured Israel, but compromised the Western powers and damaged the Prime Minister himself. In its impact on Israel the case of Dr. Israel Beer can only be compared to that of Kim Philby in Britain. But it was much worse than that because Israel, unlike Britain, was living permanently on the brink of war.

Israel Beer was born in Austria and he claimed to have fought in the *Schütbund*, the Austrian Socialists' own armed force, in the uprising against Dollfuss in 1934 and later to have fought in Spain during the Civil War as a battalion commander in the International Brigade. There is little doubt that Beer, unlike Sitte, had become a communist agent at about the same time as Kim

Philby and that his whole life was dedicated to the cause of the Soviet Union and her satellites. Soon after the Nazis took control of Vienna in 1938 Beer went to Palestine as a refugee. He joined the Haganah almost immediately afterwards, was highly regarded for his services during the underground fight against the British and he served with the Israeli forces in the War of Independence of 1948. Beer became one of the youngest lieutenant-colonels in the Israeli Army and at the same time he acquired a considerable reputation as a scholar, being chosen to write a history of the War of Independence. Yet all the time he was acting under the instructions of Moscow and keeping the Centre (the KGB Head-quarters in Moscow) informed on all manner of top secrets from Tel Aviv as well as a wealth of intelligence on other countries, too.

Beer became the principal aide of General Yigal Yadin, at that time Chief of Staff of the Israeli Army, and latterly one of the country's foremost archaeologists. Thus he had access to all manner of military secrets. But even this did not satisfy this ambitious agent in his quest for perfection. He extended his influence to all branches of life in Israel. In the cultural sphere he became head of the Faculty of Military History at Tel Aviv University, while remaining on the Army Reserve. As he was working on his history of the War of Independence as well, his University post gave him access to historic archives at the Ministry of Defence, but there is little doubt he delved into far more up-to-date and prohibited items. Dr. Beer published a number of books and articles on military themes both in European and Israeli publications. He visited Europe on various occasions, lecturing before military groups in West Germany and Sweden, and in his contacts with NATO military leaders was able to pick up further intelligence.

Even this was not enough promotion for Beer. He ingratiated himself with members of the Israeli Cabinet and especially with Ben-Gurion. It was probably the one mistake in his life which Ben-Gurion most regretted, for Beer was eventually made deputy chief of Aman and liaison officer on intelligence to the Defence Minister, Ben-Gurion. At the time of his arrest in 1962 he was even described inside Israel as a 'close adviser to Ben-Gurion', though a Government spokesman was quick to reply that Ben-Gurion had not seen Beer since May 1960, when they merely discussed the official history of the War of Independence. Never-theless the affair caused a considerable political scandal when

Beer appeared before the examining magistrate in Tel Aviv in April 1962.

Various rumours were bruited around the capitals of the world after Dr. Beer's arrest. It was reported that he had been an observer at NATO manoeuvres in West Germany, though this was denied by the West German Government. On the other hand Dr. Beer was so well known in many European capitals that it is almost certain that he was in a position to have obtained NATO secrets. But most Tel Aviv sources at the time of his arrest insisted that it was not the counter-espionage service of a NATO power which had exposed him, but that the Israelis claimed to have discovered his activities themselves when a foreign agent who was being trailed led them to Beer. Many documents were taken from his rooms when he was arrested and there was an intensive questioning of Ministry of Defence personnel with whom he had been in contact.

Although the Israelis finally tracked him down themselves, the first real hint that Beer might be implicated in espionage came from the British Secret Service, who, more than once have given the Israelis vital information. It is also probable that the Shabak had confirmation of the British evidence from the CIA otherwise they might have continued to refuse to believe that their trusted professor was a Soviet agent. Much of the British information on Beer came as a result of the revelations of the treachery of George Blake as well as from the interrogation of defectors from the Soviet bloc. E. H. Cookridge goes so far as to say that Israel Beer 'might never have been unmasked had it not been for a communist defector, Colonel Michael Goleniewski, of the Polish Secret Service, who contacted the CIA in West Berlin. His disclosures shook several espionage services to their foundations.'[1]

Ironically enough, it may even have been the KGB who decided that Israel Beer's usefulness to the USSR was coming to an end and somebody within that body deliberately planted evidence to incriminate the historian spy. There were some indications that this was the case. During his trial, in which details of the charges were kept secret, some curious comments were made in the summing up. The trial was conducted behind closed doors, but the public were admitted for the pronunciation of the sentence. In sentencing Beer to ten years' imprisonment, the court found that he had transmitted information calculated to impair the security of the state, but conceded that his motive had initially been to promote its welfare, but that he had become 'inextricably enmeshed in the network of a foreign agency'. The judges acquitted him on two counts of obtaining secret information, but convicted him of transmitting it. He was also found guilty of maintaining contact with a foreign agent over a fairly long period.

Yet the court found that Dr. Beer had neither treason nor monetary gain as motives, and also dismissed the prosecution's contention that he had been spying since 1953: 'we are inclined to believe that his motives in establishing contact with a foreign agent had been concern and fear for the welfare of the state,' the three judges declared. 'The accused believed that his solo activities would bring about new relations with another country for the benefit of Israel. However, the theoretician tripped up when he encountered a man of action—a foreign agent whose motives were plain.' The court added the somewhat ambivalent rider that 'no individual could enter such an adventure without the knowledge of the appropriate authorities, even if he believed that they were not doing enough in a certain direction.'[2]

Thus there is more than a hint even from the Israeli side that Dr. Beer may have spied for Russia originally from purely ideological reasons, but that latterly—presumably during the period he was betraying Israeli secrets—he was doing it in the belief that in the long run he was helping Israel. The same parallel has been made by some apologists for Kim Philby, but such sophistries do not alter the basic fact that the crime is still one of treason. The brilliant military historian and analyst may well have held the naïve belief that the Soviet Union could be won over as an ally of Israel, but when naïvety goes to these lengths people need to be protected from it. Beer died four years later in his prison cell, a totally disillusioned and defeated man. He may even have realised that the KGB had abandoned him.

14

The Six-Day War

*All I can say is [at the end of the Six-Day War]
that the role of Intelligence had been all as
important as that of the Air Force or the
armoured corps.*

(MOSHE DAYAN)

THE THIRD WAR to be fought between Israel and her Arab
neighbours in under twenty years lasted only six days—from
5 to 10 June 1967. It was also Israel's third victory, but this time
a far more decisive one.

If Israel was technically the aggressor, it might perhaps be
fair to note that in both the world wars, it was Britain who
declared war on Germany. The parallel between Israel and
Britain is not illogical: in each case the nation which took the
initiative was the victim of constant aggression and threatening
tactics which were all just short of war. Indeed, the case in Israel's
favour is perhaps even stronger. Neither in 1948–49, nor in 1956,
were any peace terms negotiated. Admittedly Israel had built up
her own forces to achieve great technical superiority over the
potential enemy, but so, too, had Egypt, Syria and their allies.
Gamal Abdel Nasser had never made any great secret of the fact
that he wanted to see Israel crushed, though many of the Western
powers still pretended otherwise.

Yet even the Israeli Cabinet itself was divided on the wisdom
of going to war against Egypt. It was Dayan and the vast majority
of the Israeli people who wanted to see a clear-cut victory and an
end to the years of tension, just as in 1939 it was Churchill and
the British people and not the Chamberlain government who
wanted war against Germany. The Israeli Army, backed by
Aman, became increasingly doubtful of the wisdom of the post of
Prime Minister and Minister of Defence being held by the same
man. The Army made no move to challenge the Cabinet, but put

pressure on the Prime Minister to act. It was this pressure on the Mapai Party leadership which finally brought in Moshe Dayan as Minister of Defence. Unusually, too, it was Ben-Gurion who opposed the 1967 war, fearing Soviet intervention, while Levi Eshkol, the new Prime Minister and no soldier, backed it.

But the stark truth was that through their Secret Service network the Israeli Cabinet were forced to realise that further delay in confronting the Arabs would see their position of strength slowly whittled away. Israel had long been denied use of the Suez Canal (a serious economic blow) and then on 17 May 1967, Nasser had demanded and obtained the withdrawl of the United Nations Emergency Forces from the Gaza Strip. Having achieved this much, he responded by closing the Gulf of Aqaba to Israeli shipping.

Israel had long known from the lessons of 1956 that it was not enough to wage and win a war against the Arabs, but that to ensure survival and an end to a situation of incessant crisis, she needed to win total victory within a few days. If the war went on longer than a week, she knew perfectly well that the United Nations would try to enforce a cease-fire, undoubtedly on unsatisfactory terms for Israel. It was because the pressing need was for a swift and total victory that intelligence on the enemy needed to be comprehensive, detailed, up-to-date and infallible. And if ever a war was won on a magnificent intelligence system, the Six-Day War was it.

The Israeli contribution alone was a magnificent effort for a small power and never before equalled in history. At the same time the Israeli Secret Service, in order to achieve the kind of victory Israel won, needed absolute perfection in military intelligence. This could only be guaranteed by the Secret Service entering the field of diplomacy and winning co-operation from other powers. The British had, unofficially, helped on a few occasions, as has been seen in the previous chapter, but they were not altogether trusted because of the constant leaks of intelligence from Britain to the Soviet Union. Also the Israelis knew all about Kim Philby; after all Philby's first wife, Litzi Kohlman, was a Viennese Jewess, and the Mossad's network of contacts had long since enabled them to trace his links with communism as a young man. But the main assistance the Israelis gained in the field of intelligence was from the Americans and the French.

On the American side the Israelis had won a certain amount of unofficial support from the CIA even during the Eisenhower era. The CIA had been realistic enough to realise that the Eisenhower appeasement policy towards the Arab world would ultimately be disastrous for every American interest, military or economic. For this reason they had maintained a policy of allowing all intelligence operations in Israel to be carried out entirely by the Mossad. In short, what this meant was that the CIA had no office or station chief in Tel Aviv, but that certain officers in the US Embassy there co-operated with the Mossad. In theory this entailed an exchange of intelligence between the two sides and in practice this worked rather better than one could have expected normally. The key figures in this arrangement were originally Isser Harel, Ephraim Evron, who later became deputy Israeli Ambassador in Washington, and James Angleton, chief of the CIA Counter-Intelligence.

Angleton, having seen the folly of the US foreign policy during the abortive Suez operation, decided to counteract the State Department's bias towards the Arabs by close co-operation with Israel. It was he who first saw the need for a new policy in the Middle East and safeguards against increasing Russian influence. He and Evron worked well together and, as a result, the CIA helped Israel with technical assistance in the nuclear field. Evron was eager to grasp this opportunity for he had been one of the prime instigators of the aggressive challenge to the US policy of friendship for Nasser in the events which led up to the Lavon Affair in 1954.

Evron lay very low after the Lavon Affair, but he was instrumental in paving the way to a reversal of the pro-Arab policy which for a while dominated American thinking, not only under Eisenhower, but also the Kennedy administration. What helped Evron was the evidence he was able to produce not only for the CIA, but the State Department too, of increasing Russian involvement in Egypt. Early in 1967 he had been able to reveal to the CIA that the Soviet Embassy in Egypt was filled with spies (some of whom were unmasked in June 1967), as well as providing evidence of the Russian spy ships' tactics in the eastern Mediterranean both against Israel and the US Sixth Fleet.

For a brief period Ephraim Evron was Israel's most powerful figure in Washington, more highly regarded than the Ambassador, and welcomed as a collaborator and Mossad liaison officer to the

. For years the tentacles of the Israeli Secret Service had
hed out into all walks of American life, not in any sinister
, as was sometimes alleged by her enemies, but in a quietly
persistent manner which embraced making friends and influencing
people, establishing opinion lobbies and gathering intelligence.
This influence extended into the US Congress and the Senate,
the Pentagon, the defence and electronic industries, the research
laboratories and such Jewish-oriented organisations as the Anti-
Defamation League, the Jewish Defence Committee, Bonds for
Israel and the Federation of Jewish Philanthropies. Some of these
bodies have served as fronts for intelligence-gathering and there
are few of the important Congressional Committees which do not
possess one member or staff-assistant who does not feed the Israeli
network relevant material.

There may be occasional rumbles of criticism in the USA
by those who feel that this Israeli influence is all pervading,
but in the years just prior to the Six-Day War such complaints
were largely muted because the Mossad had had a great deal to
offer the Americans in intelligence which directly concerned the
USA. This information finally convinced not only the CIA but
the State Department as well, especially Eugene Rostow and
his brother Walt, who became President Johnson's adviser on
national security. Walt, in fact, urged on the President a view
which was shared by the CIA and the Israelis alike. Indeed, the
pendulum swung so far the other way in Washington that, by
the end of 1965, there was even pressure inside the CIA for
launching a coup in Egypt to get rid of Nasser. While it was
realised that Nasser's standing in the country was far too strong
to make such a coup feasible, the view began to develop that a
military defeat for Egypt might bring about his downfall.

All this took place about the time that Ahmed Shukeiry, head
of the recently formed Palestine Liberation Organisation, was
forging an alliance with Nasser with wild promises that Tel Aviv
would be totally destroyed and the Jews driven out of Palestine.
Various highly secret meetings between CIA area representatives
in the Middle East and members of the Israeli Secret Service
were held with the object of co-ordinating both policy and
intelligence-gathering. Among those who directed these meetings
were James Angleton, Ephraim Evron, Meir Amit, the new head
of the Mossad, and Brigadier-General Yariv, Director of Military
Intelligence.

Both the latter were newcomers to the hierarchy of the Israeli Secret Service. Meir Amit had been born in Tiberias in 1921 and as a native-born Israeli had been educated at the agricultural college of Givat Hashelosha, becoming a member of the Elonim kibbutz. Like so many other members of the Israeli Secret Service he had been an active member of Haganah, serving as a deputy commander of the Golani Brigade in 1948. After being wounded in action during the War of Independence he was given command of the brigade in 1950, after which he became head of Operations and served in Military Intelligence. During this period he paid a long and fruitful visit to the United States which lasted for two years. He made several useful contacts in high places and especially in the Intelligence world. On his return to Israel he was rewarded by being appointed chief of Aman in 1961 and two years later, after the resignation of Isser Harel, he became head of the Mossad. It was a singularly apt appointment at this juncture when it was important to have the closest possible relationship between Aman and the Mossad.

Meir Amit was fortunate in that he was able to strike up an excellent relationship with his successor at the head of Aman, Brigadier-General Aharon Yariv. Both were Army career men, both had been born in the same year, and in many respects their methods and approach to intelligence were similar. Theirs was an invaluable combination for the security of Israel. Yariv was born Aharon Rabinowitz in Moscow, the son of a children's medical consultant, who later moved to Berlin and Latvia. The father was murdered by the Nazis and Aharon emigrated to Israel at the age of fourteen. He joined the British Army in World War II and served in the Buffs, soon proving himself a dedicated soldier and rising from private to sergeant. At the end of the war Rabinowitz was sent to Cyrenaica on an OCTU course. He returned to the Army as an officer in the First Battalion of the Jewish Brigade and when the war ended held the rank of captain.

Once out of the Army he became active in the ranks of Haganah and attended the Jewish Agency's Political Department School for Advanced Studies. He then worked under David Shaltiel, head of Haganah Intelligence and later a general in the Israeli Army. In 1950 Rabinowitz was promoted to lieutenant-colonel in the Israeli Army and in the same year, a few days after his wedding, he was ordered to go to France to study at the

French Ecole de Guerre. He was the first of a number of Israeli officers to be sent abroad for training. At that time David Shaltiel was Israeli military attaché in Paris.

Shaltiel and others had marked out young Rabinowitz as a future executive in some branch of the Israeli Secret Service and it was probably because of this that he was given so many administrative posts when what he yearned for was command of a battalion. Slimly built, of medium stature, with light brown hair, this young officer changed his name to Yariv when he was sent to Washington as military attaché in 1957. He remained there for three years and, like Meir Amit, established an excellent working relationship with various Americans. When he returned to Israel he was made Officer Commanding the Golani Brigade for a short period and then transferred back to Military Intelligence, becoming its head in 1964.

'I have never in my life had a more difficult but more engrossing assignment,' he said at the time. 'It acts like opium. It exercises a growing fascination on one. One can get drunk on intelligence work, but one must never lose sight of the other side as well: that the purpose of one's work is to help operations, that you must always be at the service of the Chief of the General Staff and the state.'

These two men—Meir Amit and Aharon Yariv—played a prodigious part in the preparations leading up to the Six-Day War and it was this highly successful combination which produced the vital information for a swift victory. They built on and developed the techniques which Yuval Ne'eman had introduced. The achievements of the Six-Day War were due to seventeen years of accumulated and carefully tabulated intelligence work. In the *Atlantic Monthly* of September 1967, Barbara Tuchman wrote that 'Brigadier Yariv was the key man in Israel's army. He could deal with 150 pressmen at a conference, talking non-stop without giving away any secrets.'

Yariv was that rarity among intelligence chiefs—a man highly popular with journalists and, not least, with foreign correspondents with whom, within limits, he spoke freely in Hebrew, English, French and German. He eschewed ostentation, living and working in a modest semi-detatched house in the suburbs of Tel Aviv, his office consisting of a small desk in a corner of the split-level dining-room.

*

High among the bonuses which Amit and Yariv received in this period were the reports from Elie Cohen in Damascus and Lotz in Cairo. Lotz continued to play his role of fanatical ex-Nazi and Jew-hater. From the microfilms of the Sinai defences which he had smuggled out of Egypt to his messages on the location of the SAM rocket sites and information on what the Russians were doing, Tel Aviv had as clear a picture of what was going on in Egypt as in Syria.

Eventually Lotz was caught in 1965 though the circumstances leading up to his arrest are not altogether clear. One version is that he was unlucky and arrested not on suspicion, but by a chance police call. The East German leader, Walter Ulbricht, was due to visit Cairo and the Egyptian secret police were making routine calls at houses along the route on which Ulbricht was to drive with Nasser. When a servant admitted the police officers they were amazed to find a wireless transmitter, cipher and code books and other paraphernalia of espionage lying around in Lotz's study. This sounds a less plausible story than that of Elie Cohen, who was trapped in similar circumstances. If it were true, then Lotz was an incredibly careless agent, which seems unlikely in view of his long record of meticulous service. Cohen may have been careless, but one could be fairly sure that after the manner in which he was caught in possession of a transmitter, Lotz would have been advised of these risks. Another version is that Lotz was betrayed by one of his colleagues in the Gehlen Organisation. This is probable, for by this time the Gehlen Organisation had been infiltrated by the Russians. One of the chief men in Gehlen's team who had been won over by the KGB was Hans Joachim Geyer, who worked for the East Germans by night and for Gehlen by day. So it is more than likely that information on Lotz was passed to Cairo by the East German secret police prior to Ulbricht's visit.

Lotz was ruthlessly interrogated by the Egyptians with all the methods of torture their secret police normally apply in such cases. He denied being an agent of the Israelis, said as little as possible, but hinted that he might be working for the West Germans. Throughout his daily interrogations Lotz kept remarkably cool and shrewdly played along with his captors. He did not look like a Jew and, because he was not circumcised, the Egyptians did not suspect him of being one. But it was, of course, obvious that he was a spy: the only question was whether he was solely a spy for the Gehlen Organisation or for Israel as well. But eventually even Lotz, when confronted with evidence of his activities, could hardly deny any longer that some of his information had gone to Israel. Had the Egyptians known he was a Jew, he would undoubtedly have been executed. As it was, he escaped with life imprisonment, while his 'wife' was sentenced to three years. Their period of imprisonment was to some extent made tolerable by the interest taken in them by the West German Consulate whose representatives visited them regularly. Waldraut Lotz found herself in the same prison as Victorino Nino, who was one of the victims of the Lavon affair.

Yet all the splendid work of such ace agents as Lotz and Cohen and very many other reports from Mossad agents were enhanced by the follow-up carried out by Meir Amit and Aharon Yariv. Every suggestion of Yuval Ne'eman was examined and in most cases put into practice. Highly sensitive listening devices were developed which, planted within a mile of enemy military camps, enabled the Israelis to pick up conversations. Egyptian telephone lines were tapped in military areas; new photographic equipment for aerial reconnaissance was used as well as new techniques for jamming enemy radar. These innovations largely explained the Israeli's astonishing success in the Six-Day War. On top of all this was the intensive interrogation of Egyptian prisoners-of-war taken during the 1956 campaign. The information gleaned from this enabled the Israelis not only to obtain a veritable treasure house of factual information, but a psychological portrait of the Egyptian army. This was achieved not so much by what the Egyptian prisoners revealed in genuine military intelligence, which was negligible, but by building up a picture from seemingly innocent questions. These might be about food rations, or how long it took a reservist to get from his home to his unit, how often a soldier saw his family, where he went to school, or what his hobbies were. In this respect the Israelis had patiently developed a technique that had not been employed in any other Secret Service except that of the Chinese. This was made possible largely by the use of computers which enabled thousands of seemingly unimportant answers to simple, non-military questions to be analysed and applied to military problems. What emerged from this analysis was a complete picture of the whole set-up of the Egyptian Army, from what regions the personnel came, how they differed in outlook from one area to another, which units were treated best and which suffered from bad commanders, who had considerate officers and which units were suffering from lack of supplies, as well as educational qualifications of officers and men. The characters of individual commanders were analysed and their weaknesses noted. But without computerisation any such analysis would have been almost impossible.

Speed in intelligence communications has been of crucial value to the Israelis. Both the Mossad and the Shabak have made the utmost use of the latest equipment from ultra-modern installations for the interception of high-speed radio traffic and electronic computer machinery for the breaking of secret ciphers to the new reflector microphone for monitoring conversations. In addition the Israelis have on their Secret Service staffs men trained in the best cipher-breaking techniques of the West. When a *coup d'état* occurred in Syria in 1961, and Syrian Army officers revolted against Nasser, agents of the Mossad had actually predicted this and were able to get news to their headquarters in Tel Aviv before anyone else in the world knew about it.

But the volume of work and intensive calculations needed for the proper evaluation of all intelligence were more than the Israeli computers alone could cope with. As the amount of intelligence received grew so there was a need for spreading the load as far as computerisation was concerned. And it was in this sphere that the Israelis then required either collaboration or unofficial assistance from other powers. During both the de Gaulle and the Giscard d'Estaing regimes there have been times when France has appeared to go out of its way to support the Arabs and to put unfair restraints on the Jews. But throughout the whole of the post-war period Israel has maintained excellent unofficial links with the French Secret Service and the French Navy. These links date back to the immediate post-war years when the French Government was sympathetic towards Haganah and local police commissioners in the French Mediterranean ports even collaborated with Palyam agents sponsoring the illegal immigration of Jews to Palestine. This measure of co-operation with the French had continued after the Suez débâcle and had been maintained in the early years of de Gaulle's presidency. The Mossad-French Intelligence collaboration had probably been at its peak at the time of Suez, but it was still effective in the early sixties.

One of the key figures in this Franco-Israeli co-operation had been Brigadier-General Chaim (Vivian) Herzog, an officer highly popular in Western circles who had been sent on a special assignment to France in 1961. Born in Belfast in 1918, the son of the Rabbi of Ireland, he had spent his childhood in the small Jewish community in Dublin, being educated there at Wesley College and later in London and Cambridge University. The young Herzog showed prowess as a bantam-weight boxer and at rugger and cricket. In World War II he joined the British Army and, having passed through Sandhurst, was given various appointments in Army Intelligence until he was promoted to captain and joined General Cunningham's staff.

Herzog belonged to the first British division to land in Normandy and, as a major, later served with the Occupation Forces in Germany. 'I was one of the last British officers to examine Himmler just before he committed suicide,' he declared on one occasion. Afterwards he was so highly regarded that he was appointed district governor in occupied territory responsible for two and a half million Germans. After his war service, when he went to Israel, Herzog was made head of the Intelligence Department of Haganah because of his experience in this field. From 1950–54 he was the Israeli military attaché in Washington, covering Canada as well. On his return to Israel he held the post of Commanding Officer of the Jerusalem District (1954–57) and then of the Southern Command (1957–59). In 1959 he was appointed Director of Military Intelligence, being one of Yariv's predecessors. During this period he actually learned to fly, such was the importance he attached to being able to make a more accurate personal assessment of air intelligence reports.

During World War II Herzog had been highly regarded as an Intelligence officer as General Sir Brian Horrocks himself testified when he visited Israel in 1954, telling Israeli officers, 'We had an excellent Intelligence officer in the war. He is one of your men now and you are extremely fortunate to have him.'

It was a just tribute, for while he was chief of Aman, Brigadier-General Herzog was able to bring into play all those talents of diplomacy which he had shown while working in the West. When he was sent to Paris it was in the capacity of a military attaché extraordinary to try to establish even closer co-operation with the French. The timing of this visit could hardly have been more carefully judged. As Herzog arrived in Paris the Egyptians were about to bring to trial four Frenchmen who were suspected of being agents of both France and Israel, while it was whispered in the Chancelleries of Europe that the Israeli Military Intelligence chief had brought off a remarkable understanding with the Shah of Persia for a measure of collaboration between Aman and the SAVAK (Iranian Secret Police). To bring off such an arrangement with a Moslem country, despite Israel's confrontation with most of the Arab world, was no mean diplomatic feat, though of course what the two countries had in common was a wish to be kept well informed on what Russia was up to in the Middle East. The SAVAK had the reputation for being somewhat amateurish and crude in its bugging and counter-espionage techniques. The Shah wanted to assess this through his own private 'super-SAVAK' and as one Israeli commented: 'If the Shah could make a deal between Israeli Intelligence and his private Secret Service, doubtless he would feel better able to keep an eye on SAVAK.'

One of the main purposes of the Aman chief's mission to Paris was to seek aid in easing Israel's computerisation load. The Ministry of Defence view was that supplementary computer service was required, both from France and the United States, if Israel was to be in a position to win quickly any war that might be started in the Middle East. While France was officially maintaining a strictly neutral stance as regards the Middle East, there was still a good deal of unofficial support for Israel, notably in the Secret Service and the French Navy. It has been suggested that Pierre Mesmer, then French Defence Minister, by-passed de Gaulle in smoothing the path for the Israelis. It was not like that at all. De Gaulle usually knew what his Secret Service was doing in all its various branches, but he had a talent for discerning instinctively when it was better for him to remain in ignorance. Since his death various allegations have been made that he was hostile to Israel: this was far from being the case, and indeed one of his closest advisers on Secret Service matters was himself a Jew, that brilliant operator and administrator, Jacques Foccart. De Gaulle had no wish to see Israel crushed, though he was committed to a policy of friendship towards the Arabs, and especially to those who had been under French rule until recent years.

So Herzog had an arrangement for co-operation on computerised intelligence with the French Navy. It was to prove of tremendous value during the Six-Day War in helping the small Israeli Navy to play their part. But much more important was the aid which the Israelis obtained from the United States in the sphere of intelligence. President Johnson had already swung away from the tentative pro-Arab stance of the Kennedy administration which had always been frowned upon by the CIA. The Soviet pressure on Egypt had given both the White House and the State Department cause for concern. Fortunately for Israel at this time the US President's special adviser on national security was Walt Rostow who believed that the US policy towards Israel should serve as an effective check on Russia's backing of the Arab world. Thus Rostow reflected almost totally the views of the CIA hierarchy. So the discussions in Washington between the Israeli Secret Service chiefs and the CIA resulted in a secret agreement for concurrence in a contained war between Israel and Egypt with a tacit understanding that this would not infringe territorial lines between Israel, Jordan and Syria. In other words, the implied decision was that whatever war Israel fought, it would be on lines approved by the Americans for a limitation of the area of conflict. It was generally believed that this plan would deter the Russians from direct intervention, and it also had another purpose which was, from the American point of view, to retain good relations with Jordan and Saudi-Arabia, both of which could be described as anti-Nasser. Nasser had himself paved the way towards his own ultimate downfall by having gone out on a limb in refusing to call a meeting of the Defence Council of the Arab League on the grounds that Egypt was 'not prepared to reveal her military secrets to governments in the pay of the CIA and the British Intelligence Services', directly insulting his fellow Arabs.

All the proceedings leading up to the Six-Day War were exceedingly devious and complex and probably never before in history have Secret Services so completely dominated a war situation. It was in fact a joint plan between the American CIA and the Israeli Secret Service, but with the latter not only holding the trump card, but having secret reservations. King Hussein of Jordan was urged by the United States to lend his influence for a pro-Western approach to Arab diplomacy in the event of Egypt losing a war with Israel in return for a US guarantee that Israel would not invade Jordan. While tacitly agreeing to this, Hussein felt bound to appear to be supporting Egypt before the fighting started, so on 30 May 1967, he signed a defence pact with Nasser, pledging support in the event of a war with Israel.

It was a dangerously circuitous proposition which had been arrived at by joint Israeli-American talks at Secret Service level, and the Israelis were well aware of the risks of its back-firing. The Mossad had been informed that, despite this undercover plan, the American State Department was still seeking some kind of arrangement with Egypt. This put the Israelis on their guard. They now knew that the CIA-Mossad-Aman plan which envisaged a quick, limited war against Egypt in the second week of June could be imperilled if the State Department came to an agreement with Egypt in the meantime. For the Mossad agent in Cairo had just reported that President Nasser was sending Zacharia Mohieddin on an exploratory mission to Washington on 5 June.

Each side—the United States and Israel—feared being double-crossed by the other. This situation largely arose because negotiations had been very loosely conducted by the Secret Services so leaving a large question mark against what the politicians might decide. The Israelis were concerned that at the last moment their secret agreement with the CIA might be compromised in some way by the State Department. Because of this it was decided to bring forward the date for launching the war to 5 June, the day on which Mohieddin was to leave for Washington, but to keep these plans secret. As the Americans relied on intelligence from the Mossad alone as far as Tel Aviv plans were concerned, they were kept in the dark about the timing of the war.

But while the Israelis had been suspicious of changes of face by the State Department, they had overlooked the possibility of the CIA trying to safeguard themselves against any Israeli change of plans. The CIA had all along to consider the risks of Soviet involvement in a Middle East war if Israel allowed the conflict to spill over into Jordan and Syria. True, there was a tacit understanding that this would not be so, but the CIA wanted to be in a position to be abreast of every Israeli move. It was for this reason that the spy ship, the USS *Liberty*, bristling with electronic equipment, was ordered to sail to the eastern Mediterranean close to the Sinai Peninsula to listen in to Israeli signals, as well, of course, as those of the Arabs. The *Liberty*'s assignment was to supply detailed intelligence on both Arab and Israeli movements on land, sea and air and signals traffic to the National Security Agency in Washington. But the Israelis had not been informed of this.

Now once war had been launched the Israelis had one tremendous advantage over the Egyptians in that they had broken Egyptian and Jordanian ciphers and codes, while the Arabs had not done the same with the Israeli ciphers. Thus the Israelis, thanks to their superior intelligence, were in a position to exploit this advantage by feeding false information by signals to the enemy. In a relay station in Sinai radio messages from Cairo to Amman were being blocked by the Israelis and, in the jargon of the Intelligence world, 'cooked' before being swiftly re-routed to Amman. The Israeli plan was to create the impression that the war was going well for the Egyptians. Throughout the first day of the war the aim was to feed these false signals to the enemy, thereby creating the maximum confusion in their ranks, and to black out and jam messages from Cairo to Amman telling King Hussein that the Israelis were gaining ground. Later Israel falsely informed Jordan by 'cooked' messages that the Egyptians were counter-attacking in Sinai and needed support from Hussein by an attack on Israeli positions in the Hebron area.

The Israeli signals plot worked to perfection. It was all very well for the theorists to suggest that if the Israelis limited the extent of the war and concentrated solely on Egypt, they would have the blessing of American neutrality and non-interference and lessen the risk of Russia joining in. But there were too many things which could go wrong with this plan, the worst being that it could prolong the war, not lessen its duration, and so increase the risks of intervention either by the Soviet Union or the United Nations, both of which would be detrimental to Israel. At best the CIA-Mossad arrangement was a gamble, admittedly a useful preliminary to the war, but the State Department's invitation to Egypt to send an envoy to Washington totally changed the complexion of things. So the revised plan was for a major deception exercise to be practised on Egypt and Jordan, and a devastating blow to be struck against the Egyptian air force while launching land attacks. If victory could be secured within the week, all risks of intervention would be removed.

Israeli planes attacked the UAR and claimed 374 enemy aircraft destroyed, mainly on the ground, within the first day. Then, freed from enemy air attacks, Israeli armoured units entered the Gaza Strip and made a three-pronged advance into the Sinai Peninsula, the Suez Canal and the Gulf of Aqaba. On 7 June Israeli forces occupied the old city of Jerusalem and attacked the

Jordanians west of the Jordan River. On 6 and 7 June they continued to send out false messages to the Jordanians and similar deception was practised on the Egyptians.

But on the night of 7 June the Mossad and Aman knew that their deception plan had been spotted by the Americans. The Israeli Ambassador was called to the State Department and told that the Israeli attack must be halted forthwith as a cease-fire was to be ordered by the United Nations at the request of the UAR. When the Ambassador protested, he was informed in diplomatic language, that the United States knew that Jordan had been lured into fighting by signal deception. It was obvious that, if *Liberty* continued with her transmissions, it could be disastrous for Israel as they would be able to reveal that the Israelis were in violation of a UN cease-fire order.

How did the State Department know? That was the question posed to Tel Aviv. Neither the Mossad nor Aman had been told about the dispatch of the *Liberty* to the eastern Mediterranean, but their sophisticated know-how about the strange new world of war communications told them that the United States could only have learned of the deception plan by a satellite-spy, or, more probably, a spy-ship. The Ministry of Defence was informed that the likely source of this leakage of vital information was a ship fairly close inshore in the Sinai Peninsula vicinity of the Mediterranean.

Now though there are various somewhat conflicting versions of what happened after this, the main outlines are undoubtedly clear. The Israelis certainly ordered an instant search for a spy vessel 'whatever flag it was flying', and the instructions were clear—that it must be put out of action. Israeli officials have stated that no written orders were issued, or signalled orders given, and this one can accept not only as true, but as logical. But there is little doubt that verbal orders were given. The presence of the *Liberty* relatively close inshore was a threat to Israel's war plan: if this ship continued to monitor Israeli signals and movements of forces on land, air and sea, there could be leakages from the State Department to the United Nations and, even worse, the latter, whose administrators were already biased against Israel, could pass on information to the Egyptians. Israel's espionage organisation had long since learned that this was exactly what the UN had done in the Congo and elsewhere in Africa. The war plan could have been ruined in this way.

The situation was complicated by the fact that the Israelis knew, from messages that had passed prior to establishing that an American spy ship was responsible for monitoring her signals, that US Naval Intelligence must by then have discovered that Israeli Intelligence had broken the *Liberty*'s ciphers, and so knew exactly what was happening. Thus there was no chance of Israel responding to the *Liberty* operation by effectively passing messages designed to confuse the United States. From the Israeli point of view the *Liberty* had to be put out of action; from the American viewpoint the ship had to be withdrawn from the area. But a signal from the Joint Chiefs of Staff authorising this withdrawal was never received by *Liberty*. It was sent by the CIA, but somehow or other was misrouted and arrived back in NSA headquarters. Another message was dispatched, intended to be routed through a CIA post in the eastern Mediterranean area, instead of which it was sent in error to another CIA office in Port Lyautey in Morocco. No explanation of this appalling muddle over top secret orders of great urgency ever seems to have been given. Did the Israelis have an agent inside the CIA who was able to cause the signal to be lost? Improbable, perhaps, but it is not an impossible solution to the mystery.

On 8 June 1967, the US Defence Department announced that the 'US naval communications ship, *Liberty*, was accidentally attacked today by Israeli torpedo boats and jet aircraft in the Mediterranean near the Egyptian coast. . . . Ten Americans were killed and 100 wounded, twenty of them seriously when the *Liberty* was hit by a torpedo. She was flying the United States flag at the time. Pentagon officials said that the *Liberty* was first attacked by a number of Israeli jets that made six strafing runs, followed 20 minutes later by three torpedo boats that fired at least two torpedoes. . . . Damage to the vessel was said to be widespread but superficial.'

In fact the following day these figures were amended somewhat to give the casualties as nine dead, twenty-two missing and seventy-five wounded. The *Liberty*, though reduced to crawling pace, sailed back to Malta to the Valletta base. Meanwhile there had been panic in Washington. At first the US chiefs of staff were goaded into proposing a 'quick, retaliatory air strike on the Israeli naval base which launched the attack.'[1] But this plan was rejected and wiser counsels in the White House and the State Department pointed out that a move such as this would have dire consequences all round. The Israeli plea that the incident was an accident of mistaken identity was accepted. Officially, the Israeli version was that the *Liberty* resembled an Egyptian supply ship, the *El Ksair*, and subsequently the US Government seemed reluctant to question these assumptions. Indeed, there was even indisputable evidence of an Israeli helicopter coming to the *Liberty* to offer assistance, medical or otherwise, and being told to go away by the US commanding officer.

If, of course, an open brawl had developed on the subject with an inevitable rupture of relations between the USA and Israel, this would have admirably suited the Russians, comforted the Egyptians and ruined the American policy of counterbalancing Soviet influence in the Middle East, not to mention totally sabotaging CIA–Mossad–Aman co-operation. Both Israel and the United States would have lost the initiative. No doubt the Director of the CIA and other advisers close to President Johnson deeply regretted that the *Liberty* had been sent to monitor the Israeli–Arab War. It would have been wiser at least to have informed Tel Aviv that monitoring would be carried out. Israel meantime had won a swift and relatively cheap victory by intercepting messages between Egypt and Jordan, changing their wording and re-transmitting them with the aim of misleading both their enemies and forcing them into disastrous moves to the advantage of the advancing Israelis. However Machiavellian this plan may have been, and however ruthless and brutal was the order to put out of action the ship of a friendly power, the Israelis had something more than the US State Department's last-minute flirtation with Cairo to worry about. They had discovered long before the CIA that the Russians also had a plan for getting rid of Nasser, for, while they had acquired useful allies inside the Egyptian government, they had never gained all the influence they desired. Their aim frankly was to jettison Nasser and manoeuvre the setting up of a government of Soviet puppets. This had been planned through the KGB and the allies of the USSR in Cairo were no less than the Minister of the Interior, Sharawi Gomaa, and the Defence Minister, Muhammed Fawzi. The Soviet plan was as devious in its way as the Israelis' ploy against the Arabs: by planting false information on the Egyptians that the Israelis were mobilising to attack as early as mid-May 1967, well before Tel Aviv had taken any decision, they hoped either to force Nasser's removal and pave the way for a pro-

Soviet government, or to push Nasser into a war which he would lose. The USSR plays a Secret Service game rather like chess: they constantly aim at covering themselves either by check-mate or stalemate. In this case their tactics make more sense when one realises that they had discovered that there was a CIA–Israeli plot to check Soviet influence in the Middle East, even if they did not know all of its implications. But they knew enough about military power and logistics to understand that if Israel attacked Egypt, the latter would be defeated sooner or later. The longer such a war took the better, even if the Israelis won, because time was on the side of the USSR and would enable the KGB to manipulate a coup against Nasser. And what decided the Israelis to act with total ruthlessness was the knowledge obtained from the Mossad that the KGB man in Cairo was actually working on Nasser's staff as an adviser on intelligence. The Mossad's advice was that any delay in winning the war, any risk of a cease-fire made a KGB-inspired coup in Cairo a distinct possibility.

After the attack on the *Liberty*, despite spasmodic demands in the United States for a thorough examination of the whole affair, both sides played it cool and maintained a low profile until the incident was more or less forgotten. Within a year there was a similar incident when the US spy ship *Pueblo* was captured by the North Koreans and this detracted attention from the *Liberty* affair. And in May 1968, the Israeli Government paid a sum of approximately £1,800,000 to the families of those killed in the attack on the *Liberty*. Later, following representations from the US Government, a further sum of slightly more than two millions was paid to the personnel who had been injured. The Israelis maintained an absolute silence over the details of the attack and the findings of any inquiry were never made public.

By the time the *Liberty* was put out of action the Israelis had attacked the Jordanian army west of the Jordan River, were driving on towards Damascus and had seen the entire Egyptian army in flight on all fronts, as well as capturing Sharm el Sheikh with their naval forces. King Hussein promptly accepted a cease-fire proposal and the day afterwards so did Egypt, with Syria capitulating the following day.

Thanks largely to a brilliant Secret Service and Military Intelligence system, Israel had won the most successful military victory of modern times in under a week for the loss of only 679 Israelis against several thousands of Arabs. But the war itself was really won on intelligence alone in under two and a half hours, for it was in this period that the Egyptian air force was almost completely destroyed, many of its planes caught on the concrete ramps during the 9–15 minutes in which they were serviced. Israeli Intelligence, preparing for every contingency, had ascertained not only when and for how long the Arab planes would be on the ground, but even which planes were real and which were dummies. One Israeli pilot told me: 'We were given every possible chance by our life-saving corps—the I-boys. When we went to the briefing room on the eve of our first take-off in the Six-Day War, we were given large photographic maps of the Egyptian airfields which showed us the positions of every plane, the real ones and the dummies. When we got to the airfields we knew exactly what to hit and how long we had to do it in. Better still, we could indulge in psychological warfare. We had the names of many of the Arab pilots and we were able to bamboozle them with "go home to your family" messages.'

Israeli Intelligence had even trained personnel to mimic the voices of the Egyptian Air Force dispatching team, so that if an Egyptian pilot whose plane had been hit, asked for instructions, the Israelis could cut into the conversation and tell him to bail out.

15

Testing Time for Shabak

The morality of, shall we call it for short, cold war is so infinitely easier than the morality of almost any kind of hot war that I never encountered this as a serious problem.

(RICHARD BISSEL, deputy director of plans, CIA, 4 May 1965)

DESPITE THE FACT that there have been three 'hot' wars between the Arab world and Israel since the early fifties, it should be realised that for all of a quarter of a century now the two factions have been living in a permanent state of cold war. There has never been the slightest possibility of Israel relaxing her efforts to maintain military superiority or national security. And in coping with this state of affairs and learning to live with it, the Israelis have had to adopt something of the philosophy which Richard Bissell mentioned in his NBC television interview in 1965 cited above.

Throughout this period Israel has been confronted with a constantly recurring series of carefully organised espionage activities directed against her. Some of these, as we have seen, have been implemented by the Soviet Union, but the vast majority have been carried out by one or other of her Arab neighbours. The brunt of the task of checking all this has been ably borne by the Shabak and, by and large, they have shown a remarkable efficiency in tackling the threat to Israel's internal security, especially in view of the 300,000 Israeli Arabs, all speaking Hebrew, inside Israel. On the other hand, as most Shabak officers would be the first to admit, their work owes a great deal to co-operation with the Mossad and Aman.

In November 1964, David Ben-Gurion, then living in retirement on a kibbutz in the Negev Desert, spotlighted some of the problems which Arab espionage posed for Israel when he presented a massive memorandum to the Israeli Government. This dossier ran to more than 500 pages and contained sensational revelations about the competing and interlocking activities of Israeli and Arab Secret Services. Ben-Gurion decided to produce his own report on the subject following the Lavon Affair and he dwelt at some considerable length on the activities of Colonel Osman Nouri, the Egyptian Intelligence chief, and Paul Frank, the former Israeli agent who betrayed his masters to the Egyptians. In the report Ben-Gurion also drew attention to the latest activities of Colonel Nouri in his new role as Egyptian Ambassador to Nigeria. Israel had been trying to establish good relations with a number of the newly independent nations of Africa and the former Israeli Prime Minister revealed that Nouri had played a part in organising opposition to the visit to Nigeria of Mrs. Golda Meir, at that time Israeli Foreign Minister. These efforts were unsuccessful: the Nigerian Government issued a statement warning against any subversive activities which were not in the country's interest.[1]

The Ben-Gurion report had the effect of drawing attention to the need for increased vigilance in dealing with spies, stressing how widespread the Arab networks were and how very often these were linked with Soviet agents. What perhaps had not been fully realised before was the need for vigilance against Israelis actively engaged in spying for the Arabs, not merely Arab Israelis, but Jews. This problem of treachery from within has been a growing headache for the Intelligence Services throughout the late sixties and seventies. It is not that this tendency is widespread; in fact, the reverse is true. But where it is uncovered, it does great damage to national morale. The number of professional traitors among Israelis is very small. What is worrying is a fringe of disaffected Sabras (native-born Israelis), especially among the young, who are exposed to Marxist propaganda, and sometimes take a hostile view because of ideological sympathies with the Soviet Union. Mr. Shmuel Tamir put it very succinctly when he declared, in his capacity as leader of the Free Centre group, that 'Israeli youth hears every day from persons in high office that Jewish settlement in Hebron and Rafan is oppressive colonialism. Such preaching finally pushed young people into resorting to all means against the oppressors. The spiritual vacuum now pervading the [Israeli] Labour Party prepared the ground for such evil harvests.'

And when the full extent of treachery among Israeli-born Jews was revealed to the public by one spy case after another, the Israelis were first filled with disbelief and then outraged horror. Chief-Inspector Shaul Rosolio, of the Reshud, who conducted the investigation against nearly fifty suspects in a Syrian spy ring, stated: 'I was more deeply shocked by this than by anything so far discovered. To learn that a young Jew born in Israel, a member of a kibbutz and a paratrooper as well, is a spy is hard to believe.'[2]

Nevertheless it would be wrong to give the impression that Israel has at any time been riddled with a fifth column, or that the vast majority of the population is not deeply patriotic. Such sacrifices as the Israelis have made and such battles as they have won are not achieved without burning patriotism. In any event the Reshud, which is the equivalent of Britain's Special Branch at Scotland Yard, has kept a tight watch on even the slightest manifestation of subversive activity. Shaul Rosolio, who is now Inspector-General, was himself trained by Scotland Yard officers in Palestine. Linked to Reshud are various anti-terrorist squads whose functions are to protect the kibbutzim and prevent bomb outrages.

Yet Marxist propaganda, cleverly exploited, has played havoc among some radical university students and discontented youth in Israel, and ever since the Six-Day War the Soviet Union has played on this. The Soviet aim has been to isolate Israel and to bring every influence to make her surrender the conquered territories, and their propagandists have compared the kibbutz system, democratic as it undoubtedly is, with old-fashioned colonialism. Moshe Dayan was renamed 'Moshe Adolfovitch' in the Russian weekly, *Krokodil*, and all manner of atrocities attributed to him.

Immediately after the Six-Day War the Israelis conducted the same thorough probe of their prisoners-of-war as they had after that of 1956. They were then able to exploit to the full their great advantage in having so many more prisoners than the enemy. The Secret Service was determined to use this advantage to win back from Egyptian and other prisons some of their own agents who had been captured. Some intensive bargaining with the Egyptians went on and among those who were freed were

Wolfgang Lotz and his 'wife', Waldraut, and Victorino Nino, the young French Jewess who had spent fourteen years in prison since she was sentenced for her part in the sabotage fiasco of 1954. Israel traded nine Egyptian generals, several hundred officers and 5,000 other ranks in exchange for these and a few other Mossad and Aman agents. They were luckier than Elie Cohen. At the same time the Israelis openly admitted that Lotz and Waldraut were their agents and Lotz was given an enthusiastic welcome by his Secret Service colleagues. The released agents had something like the status of national heroes. Their experience as spies and the suffering they had endured while in captivity had brought Wolfgang and Waldraut closer together. What had started as a marriage of convenience was now a very genuine bond between them. Waldraut had been converted to the Jewish faith and had even taken a Hebrew first name, Naomi. Lotz's divorce from his real wife was one of those misfortunes of the espionage game and shortly afterwards he was married to his German bride for a second time.

Israel's first warning of the ease with which spies could enter the country came in the case of the former German SS Lieutenant Ullrich Schonhaft who escaped from Germany after the war by purchasing the identity papers of a dead Jewish concentration camp prisoner, Gabriel Sussmann. He joined a party of Jewish displaced persons and made his way to Palestine. There he joined the Israeli Army and might even have progressed to the highest ranks, but for the fact that he was persuaded to spy for the Egyptians. He was arrested and eventually sentenced to seven years' imprisonment before being sent back to Germany. Another long-term spy trained by the Egyptians was Kaboerak Yaakouvian, from Armenia, who was not only instructed in Jewish ways and customs, but was actually sent to hospital to be circumcised. This was in the mid-fifties, when, furnished with a Nansen passport, he was first of all sent to Brazil where he was ordered to pose as a Zionist refugee from Egyptian oppression, taking the name of Itzhak Ben Salomon. He entered Israel at the end of 1960 and joined a kibbutz, later becoming an itinerant photographer around Tel Aviv.

When he was arrested in 1963 Yaakouvian had been consistently passing on information to Cairo since his arrival in Israel. But, thanks to co-operation between the Mossad and the Shabak, the Armenian's cover had been blown long before his arrest and for some time the Shabak had been able to feed false information to him.

Up to the time of the Six-Day War the situation *vis-à-vis* espionage against Israel was more or less contained. But after that war, with the 'open-door' policy being introduced in the territories taken over, a quite different problem confronted the authorities. There were far larger areas to control, more scope for spies to infiltrate and move around easily, and some Israeli Arabs who had previously been loyal enough citizens were persuaded to collaborate with the terrorists of Al Fatah and other organisations. At least, sometimes it was gentle persuasion, more often it was blackmail and terror tactics.

But the most serious threat of all, which was not fully uncovered until 1972, was a spy-ring in the Israeli-occupied Golan Heights adjoining the Syrian border which operated from shortly after the Six-Day War in 1967. The organiser of this ring was the leader of the Druse tribe, Shakib Yousef Abu Jabal, who was in Damascus at the beginning of the Six-Day War, but was later allowed to rejoin his family in his village inside Israeli territory. The ramifications of this spy-ring may never be fully known. For example, when letter bombs addressed to President Nixon and US Secretary of State Rogers were discovered in a post office below the Golan Heights, the possibility that they had been sent by members of the spy-ring was investigated; though nothing was proved, it is assumed that the gang received them from Syrian Intelligence officers ready for posting and that all they had to do was to stick on Israeli stamps and put them in the local letter-boxes.

Eventually Israeli investigators learned that the head of the spy-ring passed information across to the Syrians when he visited his orchards in the early morning. Suspicion was not aroused because it was quite normal for him to supervise the irrigation of his orchards before sunrise, but the information he passed on covered troop movements, police and military activity and even details of the sites of defence posts. The whole family of Shakib was involved in this spy-ring; members of it were ordered to visit various places in Israel and to report from as far distant as Eilat and the Sinai Peninsula. It was only after one of the tribal chief's sons was arrested in Eilat that the secret was discovered.

These revelations proved an acute embarrassment to the Druse community in Galilee and around Mount Carmel. Not only had the Druse people been loyal to Israel, but they had even supplied soldiers to fight the Arabs

In January 1970, a Rumanian Jew, Ilan Stil, aged twenty-eight, was found to have been involved in a plot to kill General Dayan, then Israeli Defence Minister, shortly before the Six-Day War. In a special court in Nazareth Stil was accused of spying for Syria and Iraq. It was then stated that a few days before the 1967 War started, Stil had been warned that a special messenger would give him a rifle with telescopic sights in order to kill Dayan, but he had backed down at the last moment.

Much worse was to come. The discovery of the Druse spy-ring and then the notorious so-called Galilee spy-ring of the early seventies gradually showed how extensive Arab espionage was and how it had increased three-fold since the Six-Day War and even involved more than a hundred Israelis, some of them members of the Army. First of all there were skirmishes with infiltrators in the Negev Desert and the southern region and a number of Egyptians were arrested. But it was the revelation that young left-wing Jews had joined with an Arab spy network in the plot to kill Dayan which shocked the country. Not only that, but other Israeli leaders were on a death list prepared by the Arabs and the Jewish members of the Arab spy-ring knew this. A senior police officer said at the time that 'the sabotage and spy-ring was the largest, best-organised and most dangerous we have come up against since the establishment of Israel in 1948.'

How much this spy-ring was pro-Arab and how much it was simply a part of the anarchist-destructionist philosophy of the late sixties may still be hard to determine. In any event the question was, from a security point of view, irrelevant, because the effects of the spy-ring and its aims were against the Israeli establishment. But it is important to see that the anarchist-destructionist philosophy which infected scores of universities, colleges and schools in the late sixties, which was allowed to create a political crisis in France and a reign of terror in parts of Germany, as well as a student-trade unionist quasi-terrorist alliance in Britain for a brief period, somehow also threatened the integrity of Israel. It was tragic, and to the older generations of Israelis seemingly impossible to believe, but it was the terrible price which Israel had to pay for being one of the few genuine democracies in the Middle East.

In the first round-up of suspects some thirty-eight people, four of them Jews, were arrested in December 1972. This followed on two spy cases in the previous month. On 1 November, Peter Fulman, a German electronics engineer who had emigrated to Israel a year previously, was sentenced to fifteen years' imprisonment by the Haifa District Court for spying for Lebanon. In the same period there was a round-up of Egyptian infiltrators into Israel. When it became known that Israelis were involved in the plot against Dayan's life, there was an immediate accusation of a communist conspiracy. However, the truth slowly emerged that the Israelis involved were far to the left even of the Israeli Communist Party and that their only close links were with student anarchist groups and Maoist and Trotskyite organisations. Indeed, even the label 'Maoist' was probably wide of the mark and too respectable for such ardent haters of the Establishment. It had its beginnings in Paris when in the late sixties the German extreme Leftist agitator, Daniel Cohn Bendit, who led the student riots in Paris, persuaded two young Israelis, Ehud Adiv and Dan Vered, to join the ultra-radical group which finally led them to serve their country's enemies. The group of which they were leaders had planned to abduct prominent Israeli figures to force the Government to release all the jailed terrorists of the Arab cause and to gain political concessions by carrying out spectacular acts of terrorism.

Ehud Adiv was a former Israeli Army paratrooper, twenty-five years old, and undoubtedly a leading figure in the spy network. His mother, a psychologist, said afterwards that he had been brought up with 'progressive and Leftist ideas' while a member of a founding family of Kibbutz Gan Shmuel. She said he had been in a paratroop unit which in 1967 had broken into the old city of Jerusalem. Of the thirty men who went into battle with him only six survived and her son had returned broken in spirit by the bloodshed. He had played for a leading basket-ball team and his absence from it for a month at the start of the season was linked to allegations that he was then in Damascus, where he met a Syrian colonel who operated from Athens giving instructions and codes.

Dan Vered, arrested with Adiv was aged twenty-eight, came from a wealthy family living near Tel Aviv and was described as 'a lonely intellectual who made a natural target for the Anarchists'. With Adiv and other Israeli Left-wingers he first founded the Israeli Communist Party and then the Maoist–Trotskyist Matzpen Movement as a direct result of the influence of Cohn

Bendit. This movement was politically about as anarchistic and incoherent as the mishmash of names in its make-up suggests.

By the end of 1972 it was clear to the Shabak that the number of people implicated in the Jewish-Arab spy-ring working in Israel for Syria was between 100 and 150 and that at least half a dozen Jews were key members of this organisation. Political tempers flared and right-wing and ultra-religious politicians blamed Mapam, the Marxist-Zionist party within Mrs. Golda Meir's coalition government, for creating conditions for subversion. Adiv was a student at Haifa University, regarded as one of the seats of student unrest in Israel, which was not surprising in that 480 of the 800 Arabs in Israeli universities were enrolled there. It was while he and Vered were at university that they deserted the Communist Party on the grounds that it was too moderate and together launched their 'Revolutionary Community Alliance' which supported Arab terrorism and called for the liquidation of the Zionist State.

The handsome Adiv, markedly popular with the girls, became friendly with Daoud Turki, an Arab Christian who ran a book-shop in Haifa, and it was the latter who finally drew Adiv and Vered into the spy network. When the case came to court in January 1973, those charged were Ehud Adiv, Dan Vered, Daoud Turki, who was accused of heading the ring, Subhi Naarani, a Bedouin, Anis Karawi, from a Galilee Arab village, and Simon Haddad, a fellow student at Haifa University. Haddad had been appointed co-ordinator of Arab affairs at the university. He was the only one of the six defendants not charged with going to Syria for sabotage training, and of acts abetting the enemy, but with the others he faced charges of being a member of a hostile organisation, and having had contact with enemy agents.

Thus both young Jews and Arabs had joined an underground organisation in Galilee intending to overthrow the Israeli Government and replace it with a revolutionary regime. Others were charged in groups later. Between 1968 and 1969 Turki had started to organise a Marxist society for the purpose of building the nucleus of a revolutionary regime in Israel. He wrote to Habib Khawarji, a former resident of Haifa living in Cyprus, asking for financial aid and he was then put in touch with a Syrian Intelligence agent who arranged funds. By the end of 1969 Turki had begun to recruit members for his sabotage organisation. He was told that the leaders would be sent abroad for training. In 1970 he attended a meeting of the Matzpen and met Adiv and Vered. In October of that year he had a meeting in Turkey with Khawarji and was informed that shipments of arms and explosives would be sent through groups infiltrating from Lebanon, and that information about their dispatch would be given over Damascus Radio by means of a code based on the Koran.

By the end of 1970 several members had been recruited into the organisation and all knew its aim was to conduct an armed struggle against Israel and to carry out sabotage against military bases. The organisation was structured in cells of three. All members had aliases and did not know other members of their cells. Turki himself had contact only with cell leaders. It was not until the summer of 1971 that Adiv was given the job of recruiting Jews to be sent abroad for training in sabotage. He flew to Greece in September and sent a telegram from Athens to Beirut signed 'Musa', his underground alias. Six days later he was visited by Khawarji. The telegram included details of the deployment of Israeli Army paratroop units, the location of armoured units, airfields, anti-aircraft defences and also patrol operations.

Adiv later went to Damascus and gave further information about the Israeli Army, including armoured and artillery units and radar installations. It was stated in court that he had been instructed to send his letters in invisible ink to Athens. At the Athens meeting Khawarji gave Adiv 700 dollars for the organisation. On his return Adiv persuaded Vered to go to Greece and gave him a sum of money for the journey. Vered went on to Syria and was trained in using weapons, explosives and codes. He brought back some £250 from Khawarji with instructions to Adiv that he was to visit Athens and Damascus. Adiv then spent ten days in Damascus and while there wrote a twenty-page report on the political, economic and military situation in Israel. He had further training in the use of explosives and weapons.

In March 1973, Daoud Turki and Ehud Adiv were both sentenced to seventeen years' imprisonment for treason by the district court at Haifa. Subhi Naarani and Anis Karawi, who played lesser roles, but who had prison records of other security offences, were jailed for fifteen years, and Dan Vered, the Jewish schoolmaster, for ten years. Haddad had a two year sentence and other defendants received lesser penalties. After the sentences had been pronounced all the prisoners, apart from Haddad, sang the 'Internationale' and clenched their fists.

Highly dangerous and well organised as this spy-ring was, it had been detected by the Shabak long before it was able to do any serious damage. The plan for the organisation's development was highly professional, but the personnel were amateurs and still desperately trying to learn the rudiments of espionage when they were caught. Even after instruction abroad Adiv and Vered failed to decode messages beamed to them on a record request programme from Radio Damascus. The only real professional among them was Turki, a veteran Arab communist. Eric Silver, writing in the *Guardian*, said 'Adiv and Vered emerged as the workhorses of revolution, trapped by the logic of their own doctrine as they drifted leftwards from dissent to treason. Like Kozo Okamoto, the Japanese gunman of Lydda, they believed that theorising was not enough. They scorned coffee-house radicalism and took to arms. When, as in Vered's case, doubts seem to set in with his marriage last year, it was too late to drop out.'[3]

Vered had been drawn into left-wing politics while studying in the United States. Adiv on the other hand had somewhat surprisingly been persuaded towards a pacifist philosophy following the Six-Day War. Perhaps there was a view just short of treason which all the spy-ring might have shared: it was expressed by a member of Adiv's mainly left-wing dominated kibbutz who said 'somehow we must find a way of living in peace with our Arab neighbours. We must come to terms with them, returning territory as the price of peace.' But whatever the dream may originally have been it was soon twisted to make the young Jews simply tools of terrorists who had no wish other than the ultimate destruction of Israel.

Spy threats during the early seventies came from several quarters—Syria, Jordan, Egypt, Iraq, the Soviet Union and Rumania. On 24 January 1973, a British electrical engineer accused of spying for Jordan was sentenced to twelve years by a Tel Aviv court. Paul John Gerald Glover from London pleaded not guilty, but the court found he had maintained contact with foreign agents, conducted espionage and passed information to the enemy. It was alleged that Glover, aged forty-two, had undertaken his espionage mission after a meeting in London in 1968 with the then military attaché at the Jordanian Embassy. This was followed by contacts with a number of senior officers who gave him espionage targets, a camera with a telescopic lens and

air tickets to Israel. Glover worked for a firm selling heavy
mechanical equipment which planned to expand business in
Israel and Jordan. This gave him the chance to cross the Jordan
River bridges. Glover was warned by the Israeli authorities
against meeting foreign agents, but he paid no attention. Few
spies would perhaps have been given the chance of such a warning; fewer still would have failed to heed it. But Glover passed on
to Jordan details of airfields in Israel, security fences, various
military imports and plans of military bases and training methods.

Another Briton who spied against Israel was 71-year-old Arthur
Paterson, who was jailed for eight years in 1971 after a trial last-
ing six months and held in secret by a Tel Aviv court. Paterson,
who was accused of spying for Egypt, protested his innocence
throughout, but three judges found him guilty, though, as one of
them put it, 'he was certainly a little old for the espionage game'.

Paterson arrived in Tel Aviv from Cyprus in the winter of
1966, claiming to be a teacher and a freelance journalist. His
objective was undoubtedly to penetrate the closely guarded
military establishment at Dimona, where the Israelis have carried
out their nuclear experiments. It may have been that at first
Paterson's age persuaded the Israelis that he could not possibly
be a security risk, for he was given an Israeli Government press
pass which, in the period prior to the Six-Day War, gave him
the opportunity to travel extensively throughout the territory. It
was only when his preoccupation with military installations was
noted that Shabak had him watched.

Cyprus has been a centre for mounting various espionage
operations against Israel for some years. It has been used to some
extent by the Egyptians, but far more by the Soviet Union.
Indeed, Nicosia is an important KGB headquarters in the Middle
East and has become the rendezvous for Soviet agents operating
throughout the area and especially in Israel. Symptomatic of
this is the size of the Russian Embassy in Cyprus which a short
while ago was reported to have a staff of more than a hundred,
including agents working with the Soviet Trade Mission, the
cultural centre, Russian news agencies and Aeroflot. The Israeli
Secret Service keeps a close watch on who passes in and out of
Cyprus and the long hand of the Mossad reaches as far afield as
Amsterdam, Hamburg, Oslo and Stockholm in its quest for the
starting points of espionage operations directed against the state.
Sometimes this enables arrests to be made swiftly—the very

moment a foreign agent sets foot inside the country. In March 1970, a Dutchman, Wilhelm Ruysch, was jailed for five years and recommended for deportation after serving his sentence for spying for the Arabs. Ruysch had been arrested the previous September when he arrived at Lydda airport from Paris.

Most agents of the Egyptian Secret Service are controlled from France and Switzerland, though in recent years Greece and Italy have been favoured as organisational centres. Often they are recruited from seamen and tourists, while in a number of cases Egyptian spies combine espionage with opium-pushing. The Syrian Secret Service works along with the other Arab services, but is less efficient than the Egyptian. Smallest of all the Arab Secret Services is that of Jordan, which is, however, extremely up-to-date in many respects.

Israel's task in combating this persistent espionage is made much harder because the spying by the Arab bloc is also reinforced by the information which Soviet agents in Israel pass on to Egypt and Syria. Much of the Soviet technique in espionage in the Middle East is concerned with making mischief, creating mutual mistrust and playing a game of 'divide and rule' with the great advantage that it is not the Soviet Union which has to do the ruling. But the Russians are also keenly interested in Israeli methods of intelligence work, for which they have a great respect, and they are anxious to learn all they can about research work being done by Israeli scientists. Above all the KGB is primed with the task of finding out what is coming into Israel in the way of information from the Zionists in the Soviet Union and how they can not only stop this flow of information, but cut all links between Israelis and Soviet Jews.

In June 1973, Rami Livneh, aged twenty-seven, the son of Avraham Levenbraun, a Jewish Communist member of the Knesset, belonging to the New Communist Party, was sent to prison for ten years by the Haifa District Court for being in contact with an agent of Al Fatah, the Arab guerrilla organisation. Livneh, together with another defendant, were the last of six Jews to be found guilty of belonging to a spy and sabotage ring operating from Syria. Of the thirty-two prisoners tried in four groups all were found guilty except for one who had been charged with knowing of the existence of the ring and failing to report it to the authorities.

The growth and development of the various Arab guerrilla and terrorist organisations during the seventies concentrated on what they called 'the liberation of the Arab lands of Palestine' and greatly exacerbated the espionage problem for Israel. The first and most politically influential of these organisations was Al Fatah, led by Yasser Arafat, a Kuwaiti businessman who gave up his work to devote himself to the Palestinian cause. The PFLP (Popular Front for the Liberation of Palestine) was somewhat more militant and led by George Habbash, a doctrinaire Christian doctor of medicine: it was responsible for starting the policy of attacks on airliners as a means of political blackmail. There were various splinter groups such as the PDFLP (Popular Democratic Front for the Liberation of Palestine), headed by Naif Hawatmeh, a Palestinian Christian educated in Jordan; the PAO (Palestine Arab Organisation) run by Ahmed Zaarour, who broke away from the PFLP; the extremist Popular Front General Council, led by Ahmad Jibril, and, finally, the Black September Organisation which was an offspring of Al Fatah.

The multiplicity of guerrilla and terrorist organisations may have been unhelpful to the Palestinian cause in the political and diplomatic field, but for the Israeli Secret Service it acquired considerable nuisance value and so made their work harder. Apart from this there was always the problem as to which of the organisations had been infiltrated and possibly even controlled by foreign countries. There was soon evidence of increasing Soviet support for the guerrillas. Reports from Mossad agents told of Soviet and Eastern European Intelligence aid to the Palestinians such as the assistance extended by the Czechs to the guerrillas who overpowered a train carrying Russian Jews from Czechoslovakia to Austria in September 1973. It was soon evident that a certain amount of technical help and guidance was being given by KGB agents to some of the more extreme guerrilla movements and there was even suspicion that in some instances this guidance was to ensure that the guerrillas would serve Soviet purposes as much as fighting the Israelis.

Early reports of Chinese involvement in the Palestinian guerrilla movements can now be rejected almost totally. They probably arose originally because China was the first major nation to grant diplomatic recognition to Al Fatah and to have provided training for Palestinian guerrillas at the Nanking Military Academy. But newspaper and radio reports of Chinese infiltration of the Palestine guerrilla movement have not only been grossly exaggerated, but in many cases just not true, even though originally China as well as Russia established close relations with Al Fatah. It must be remembered that China also has a great interest in Middle East oil and that she is anxious to counteract Soviet interest in this part of the world.

In March 1970, the London *Guardian*'s Beirut correspondent described how 'Fatah guerrillas can be seen on the hillsides of Jordan with a little Red Book and Chairman Mao's benign portrait smiles down from the wall of most Al Fatah campaign HQ.' In 1973 it was claimed in a Tel Aviv newspaper that 'Chinese volunteers were found in the Palestinian army camps in North Lebanon during an Israeli raid there. They provided light weapons, medicines and some instructors.'[4]

But the truth behind all these scares of Chinese intervention against Israel on the guerrilla front was very different. The Chinese had learned their lesson as a result of their openly aggressive and somewhat clumsy efforts at espionage in Africa in the early sixties. Chinese espionage operations in the Congo, masterminded originally by their Belgian network, were by most standards a failure. In Burundi diplomatic recognition was withdrawn from the Chinese, while in Malawi the autocratic Prime Minister, Dr. Hastings Banda, said he was 'less afraid of Queen Elizabeth II than I am of the Kubla Khan in Peking.' In the early sixties China suffered one setback after another in Africa from trying to compete too soon and too speedily with Russian infiltration. But the Chinese have rapidly learned from their mistakes and their standing today in Africa is much higher. After having adopted a low-profile approach in Egypt, the Chinese Intelligence established its Middle East headquarters in Damascus and possibly because of this began to take an increasingly critical view of Nasser. In 1965 they were foolish enough to allow themselves to be implicated in an Arab Communist plot to assassinate him and the Chinese Ambassador had to leave the country after the Egyptian police found links between the plotters and the head of the NCNA (New China News Agency) who was reported to have helped finance the coup. In the Yemen, however, the Chinese played a much more subtle game. They sponsored a Chinese Islamic Association, set up technical schools and helped to build a 144-mile road on which Chinese workers toiled alongside Yemenis. They have ingratiated themselves far better at all levels with the Yemenis than the Russians have done.

China gradually became disillusioned with what it regarded as 'bourgeois military Arab regimes' in the Middle East and Chinese support for Palestine guerrillas eased off in the early seventies when Peking's indictments of Israel seemed somewhat moderated. The Chinese even criticised Black September and the more extreme of the guerrilla movements. The private face of Chinese Intelligence is often totally different from the propagandist public voice of the Chinese Government. Partly because of setbacks in Africa, but also because there have been throughout history close links between the Chinese and the Jews (a number of Intelligence advisers and officers to earlier Chinese governments have been Jews), China's attitude to the Arab–Israeli confrontation in recent years has been somewhat ambiguous. Today there are signs that Chinese Intelligence has cautiously established links with the Israeli Secret Service in a joint effort to thwart Russian influence in the Middle East. In 1973 an Israeli double-agent was reported to have been effectively master-minding Israeli–Chinese intelligence operations in Africa. It is too early yet to see how all this will develop, but both the Chinese and the Israelis appreciate that they have many common interests.

There was no indication of change in Israel's security problems as far as spying was concerned even after the Yom Kippur War of 1973. Israel continued to show concern for all her agents who were held prisoner abroad and her determination to rescue them whenever possible, even to the extent of surrendering Arab spies and guerrillas. In March 1974, on orders from Tel Aviv, sixty-five convicted Arab guerrillas were released from prison to Egypt in exchange for an alleged Israeli secret agent caught two years earlier in Yemen. The Israeli, identified as Baruch Mizrahi, had been delivered to the Egyptians. The sixty-five Arabs were inhabitants of the occupied areas serving terms from ten years to life imprisonment for espionage and sabotage. An official statement issued in Tel Aviv said the exchange was in the framework of contacts maintained between representatives of the Israeli defence forces and the Egyptian Army, but in fact it only underlined the value the Mossad puts on one of its own agents.

The following year there was a further epidemic of espionage inside Israel, some of which dated back to the era of the Galilee spy ring. First of all on 21 May 1975, an Israeli Jew named Dannie Zail was accused of selling large quantities of arms and equipment stolen from the Israeli Army to an Arab sabotage group operating in Hebron and Bethlehem. Zail was reported to have been well paid and to have fled to Europe from Israel the previous January. He had come to Israel as an immigrant from Iraq in the early fifties, was thirty-six years old, married with no children and had worked as a shoe salesman in Tel Aviv. He became one of the founders of the Israeli Black Panthers, a group founded some five years earlier to demonstrate against the under-privileged status of 'Oriental Jews'. During the 1973 general election campaign in Israel he broke away from the Panthers and set up a new movement, the Black Revolutionary Force, but in the past year had fallen out with some of his colleagues and had begun to advocate violent revolution. Nevertheless, when these accusations were made officially against Zail, his former Jewish colleagues found it hard to believe that he was associated with any Palestine Liberation group.

Investigation showed that the group he was working for was the Hebron–Bethlehem group which operated under the PFLP, and as a direct result of this the Shabak were able to uncover four other cells on the West Bank and in East Jerusalem and some scores of arrests were made in May 1975. The latest network of Fatah and other agents—many of them young Palestinians working or studying in Europe—was originally discovered from documents captured by Israeli Commandos during a raid on Beirut in April 1973, in which three guerrilla leaders had been assassinated. More will be said of this raid later on, but suffice it now to say that this had been a highly successful Secret Service operation which led to the trapping of the entire network. It was a slow process, for it involved building up a long list of names from lists containing those of only a few of the spy ring. The Israelis wanted to be sure that they would not only catch those spies still inside Israel, but learn exactly who their enemies were in Paris, London, Geneva and Rome.

Among those detained on a visit to Israel was Adib Alwan, a post-graduate student at London University who had taken a degree in comparative literature at the Hebrew University of Jerusalem. Alwan was astonished to find the police waiting for him at Lydda airport. He was tried and sentenced to four years' imprisonment and was also brought forward in May 1975, at the trial of Muzana Kamal Nikola, a Christian Arab nurse who had been employed since 1969 by the Hertfordshire County Council Health Authority. She, too, was charged with being involved in the Al Fatah movement on two earlier visits to Israel in 1970 and 1971. It was claimed that she then 'took it upon herself to try to recruit certain inhabitants of Nazareth into Al Fatah' and that she submitted reports to an Al Fatah agent on her return to London.

Muzana Nikola, who was thirty-one, had been arrested in March 1975, when she brought her British fiancé, a Mr. Ryan Lomas, to meet her family in Nazareth. The allegations were that she was promised and given money (the sum of £80 was mentioned) for her work on behalf of Al Fatah and that she had made a full confession. Her counsel, Mrs. Felicia Langer, a well known communist lawyer in Israel, claimed that the two Secret Servicemen investigating the case had threatened that Miss Nikola's family would suffer if she did not confess and that Miss Nikola herself had not been allowed to eat, drink, sleep or mix with other prisoners until she signed the statement. The police denied this, but insisted that she had offered to work as an agent for Israel if the charges against her were dropped. Miss Nikola eventually received a relatively light sentence—much shorter than if she had been a Jewess. On the whole the Israelis were content to let off lightly most of the others charged at this time. They were well aware of a good deal of discord in the Arab ranks and especially in the terrorist cells. The leniency shown to the non-Jews in the espionage cases brought before courts was not merely useful propaganda, but in a few cases it actually enabled some Palestinian agents to be effectively 'turned'.

The Egyptians and the Syrians would dearly love to have full details of all the research being undertaken at Israel's top secret Dimona research station near Beersheba. So, too, would the Russians. The President of Israel, Dr. Ephraim Katzir, says that 'Israel has the nuclear power and technological knowledge required for our defence which should keep our enemies worried.' Dr. Katzir should know; he is himself a scientist. But this huge complex is heavily guarded and subjected to intensive security checks. Apart from the case of the West German, Peter Fulman, the only other serious spy trial connected with Dimona was that of Jean Sellam, a Frenchman also working for the Egyptians, who was sentenced by a Tel Aviv court to eighteen years' imprisonment.

16

Mirage Blueprints from Switzerland

The soul of the spy is somehow the model of us all.

(JACQUES BARZUN)

AFTER THE SIX-DAY WAR a number of changes were made at all levels of the Israeli Secret Service. Meir Amit retired with honour from his post as head of the Mossad, which he had held with such distinction, and departed for civilian life when he became Director-General of Koor Industries. He was succeeded by another Army man, Brigadier-General Zvi Zamir, who had been born in Poland in 1925.

At the time of his appointment as the new Memuneh, Zvi Zamir was stationed in London, not just as military attaché, but as head of a mission on behalf of the Ministry of Defence. When he was due to leave in 1968, he was asked at a cocktail party what his next post would be. 'I am going into the textile business,' he is reported to have said. Not perhaps as far off the mark as it might seem: in some circles in Israel the word 'textiles' covers all manner of Secret Service and the hush-hush research stations at Dimona are often referred to as the 'textile factories'.

Zvi Zamir arrived in Israel before he was a year old. Coincidentally he was educated at the same school in Tel Aviv as Meir Amit. When he was seventeen he joined Palmach and in 1946 was arrested by the British police in Palestine for his part in aiding the landing of so-called illegal immigrants. Eventually he joined the Israeli Army and in 1951 was appointed to the command of the Givati Brigade. A jovial character off duty, General Zamir is very much the dedicated army officer. It is perhaps typical of the man that in his entry in the Israeli *Who's Who* he describes his education solely with the words: 'Staff Colleges in Israel and the United Kingdom'.

In his approach to his Intelligence work Zamir was very much the modern military officer rather than the backroom civilian Secret Service chief. In this he differed from both Harel and Amit: he wanted to be able to make his own assessment of a situation before he delegated any authority. In planning he would leave nothing to chance. It was a habit he had acquired while being a commander in the field. He liked to make a personal foray to explore the terrain before making any dispositions and it is said that he learned a great deal about Arab guerrilla tactics in this way. In many respects Zvi Zamir was a 'loner' and he maintained a far lower profile than either of his predecessors as chief of the Mossad.

One of the Mossad's greatest concerns after the Six-Day War was that of trying to maintain a lead over Israel's Arab neighbours in air power. Under Zvi Zamir the Mossad had become a far-ranging and versatile organisation covering not only intelligence from abroad, but the strange new world of electronic and computerised espionage with all its gadgetry, as well as having a special section devoted to intelligence on nuclear developments all over the world. When Zamir, promoted to major-general, took over as Memuneh, he paid special attention to nuclear intelligence and appointed a number of scientists and technical experts to this special section. It is thanks largely to his efforts that in many respects the Mossad of today is as scientifically-minded as the Aman, with one of the world's greatest specialists on nuclear fission and allied problems, Brigadier Horev, as a member. The Israelis have also adopted a technique similar to that of the Chinese in obtaining nuclear secrets and keeping up-to-date on what is developing in that field outside their country: they have made a point of carefully recruiting the help of non-Israeli Jews all over the world who are either scientists or students in nuclear physics, while at the same time patiently collecting all available information in a legitimate manner from scientific journals and conferences and analysing the results. These tactics have enabled the Chinese to catch up with the Western World to the extent of now possessing a powerful nuclear deterrent. Israel's ability to produce such a weapon is now undoubted.

This has been one of the spheres in which the Israelis and the Chinese have actually helped one another—not officially, but discreetly through Secret Service channels. The 'third party intermediaries' involved in such deals have sometimes been non-Israeli

Jews working for the Chinese and occasionally even Albanians. Whatever may be their public utterances on the subject of the Middle East, the Chinese privately acknowledge that Israel is in effect an ally in all matters relating to the Soviet Union. This is a subject rarely touched upon by any writers on Middle East affairs, but such closely guarded contacts as the two Secret Services maintain have bonuses to both sides. On balance the Chinese may have gained most from these relatively low-key and cautious exchanges. The Israelis have always been quick to note dissensions in the Arab ranks and the Mossad has more than once exploited these. It was partly through intelligence leaked to the Chinese and some Iraqis that Iraq cut its links with the KGB and quarrelled with the pro-Soviet government of Syria. The Iraqi Secret Service today has both Chinese and Albanian Intelligence advisers.[1]

When General Zvi Zamir first took office, the new Memuneh was most concerned with the ban which the French Government had imposed on any further Israeli purchase of the latest Mirage aircraft. This threatened drastically to reduce Israel's lead in air power, especially in view of increased Soviet aid to Egypt. Ben-Gurion had always taken the view that Israel's survival depended upon air power and he had constantly stressed the importance of aviation intelligence on Isser Harel. Zvi Zamir inherited a long list of intelligence items concerning Mirages and Migs which had been given to the Mossad as matters of top priority. A certain amount of intelligence on Soviet aircraft was obtained from Mossad agents working in Iraq and assisted by disaffected Iraqi air personnel. This was long before the country had broken away from its pro-Soviet stance and the coming to power of Saddam Husseini, the anti-Russian and pro-Chinese leader of the Baathist Party in Iraq. Sometime before Zvi Zamir became Memuneh, an Iraqi pilot had been contacted by Mossad agents in Europe and asked whether he would find a means of flying a Mig 21 to Israel for a sum reputed to have been not far short of £8,000. This was an error of judgment on the part of the agent concerned, for the Iraqi countered by not only demanding ten times this sum, but threatened to report the offer of a bribe to the Iraqi security police, if this demand was not accepted. The Israelis had to be cautious in making such approaches because, apart from the problem of encountering greedy Iraqis, there was always the risk of their being double-crossed and an out-of-date plane being delivered to them. In this instance, the pilot was shadowed on his way back to Baghdad and the Iraqi security police received an anonymous telephone call that he had tried to sell one of their latest Soviet planes to Israel for £80,000. Not long afterwards he was liquidated by the Iraqis.

It is, of course, a dirty game—the buying of secrets from a foreign power—and the Israelis play it as ruthlessly as any of the major powers do. The Mossad kept a file of pilots in Arab territories who might be enticed to fly off to Israel with a Mig 21. As the list was compiled so a complete dossier on each individual was drawn up, recording the man's financial status, details of his family, his weaknesses and, above all, any indications that he would like to leave Arab territory. Finally the list was narrowed down to about half a dozen names of men who might usefully be contacted. But the Mossad still wanted more information. They dared not risk another rebuff, with the Arabs then stepping up their own security against the theft of planes. One Israeli Arab who knew Iraq well told the Memuneh: 'If you can examine carefully the spy who is most susceptible to bribes and most likely to betray secrets in the Middle East countries, he or she is very often a Christian. It is the Christian Arabs we often have to fear in the field of espionage more than the Israeli Arabs and the Arabs have the same problem: the Iraqi Christians are more likely to betray them than their own Moslems. Now in Iraq there are about a quarter of a million Christians. It is among them that you should look for a pilot who, because he is a Christian, can never hope for the same rewards as a Moslem pilot.'

This was not a question of religious prejudice on the part of the Israeli: he was realistically assessing a trend that has existed in the Middle East for more than a century. Wherever one finds a religious minority who suffer from some form of discrimination, there one can expect to find the potential spy or traitor. The instinct to spy, to betray and double-cross is inevitably part of the instinct for survival in such an environment. It also explains the deep-rooted corruption in the Christian Churches of the Middle Eastern countries—Coptic, Greek Orthodox, Catholic and every other denomination.

However, while it was not difficult to find an Iraqi pilot who was a Christian, the problem was that any Christian Iraqi in a post involving the handling of the latest type of Soviet aircraft would be under much more careful scrutiny than a Moslem. The

Iraqis were fully alive to the risks of one of their planes being taken out of the country, especially after the earlier incident. Added to this was the fact that no pilot would want to take the risk of flying such a plane over to Israel before making sure his family were safely out of the country. And exit permits were not easy to get in such circumstances. The Mossad finally settled upon the likeliest candidate after he had been contacted by three of their agents. This time the approaches were made not to put a proposition to the pilot, but simply to ascertain his feelings, his views on his job and his future, what he most desired for his family and other points which would help to finalise the dossier that had been started on him. He had no idea when these approaches for information were being made that the people he spoke to were Israeli agents. In one instance the Mossad agent posed as a Christian. If ever an operation had been planned to discover and analyse the soul of a spy, potential defector or potential ally, this was it.

Eventually the perfect excuse was found for the application for exit permits for this Iraqi pilot's family. There was urgent need for highly specialised medical treatment for one of his two children. This could not be obtained in Iraq, but was possible in London. Visas were eventually granted; the wife of the pilot and their two children were allowed to go to Britain. All was set for the flying out of the Mig 21. The Ministry of Defence was warned of the time of the plane's arrival so that no offensive action would be taken against it, and the Cabinet was informed of impending developments. Eventually the plane landed in Israel and from it vital information was obtained. Indeed, without this knowledge, it is doubtful whether the Israelis could have hit back so devastatingly with their aerial counter-attacks in the Yom Kippur War of 1973. Through the Mossad's persistence the Israeli air force knew exactly how to destroy this type of craft in the sky.

The Israeli Secret Service as a whole—both the Mossad and the Aman—played a tremendous part in enabling the Israelis to maintain air superiority. It was all achieved with a mixture of audacity, patience, diligent backroom planning and imaginative intelligence. The incident quoted was only one of the many ploys the Mossad made to obtain detailed intelligence on aircraft development by other powers. Some of this came from contacts inside the KGB itself and much more from keeping a close liaison on technical developments with the CIA and some other Secret Services.

At the same time there was an urgent need to know how European aircraft were being developed in the military sphere, not merely by the French, but by other nations. Close attention was paid to Switzerland because it was realised that technologically the Swiss had often been ahead of both combatants in World War II and that in some respects this superiority had been maintained since. The Israelis wanted to develop a plane that would combine all the latest technological devices of the Mirage aircraft. The Mossad's man in Berne urged that they should pay particular attention to a new aircraft programme for the Swiss Air Force. This involved the production by Sulzer Brothers of Winterthur of a Mirage III, with an engine specially developed for the mountainous terrain of Switzerland, where it was necessary to have an improved performance for the rate of climb and to shorten the distance for the take-off.

This presented no particular problem for the Israelis' production department, providing they could obtain full details of the design of the machine tools needed for the manufacture of the parts. It was this technical problem that was presented to Zvi Zamir and once again the Swiss network of the Mossad was set in motion. The quest for someone who would supply the blueprint details for the Swiss Mirage III was much more difficult than that for an Iraqi pilot who would fly out a Mig, but the technique applied so effectively in Iraq for tracking down a collaborator was used in Switzerland.

Here again psychology played a part in finding a likely ally. In World War II some of the Swiss—especially the German-speaking Swiss—were more pro-Nazi than the great mass of the Germans. Afterwards many of them had developed a guilt-complex about their attitude during 1939–45 and this was especially true when they learned of the horrors of the concentration camps, with the result that some Roman Catholics suddenly swung from a posture of anti-Semitism to one of sympathy for the Israelis. It was a psychological change of view which proved easy to manipulate. The Mossad did not take long before discovering one such German-speaking Roman Catholic Swiss who was sympathetic to their cause, and who actually felt that the French embargo on arms to Israel was grossly unjust.

He was Alfred Frauenknecht, a Swiss engineer employed by

the Sulzer Brothers of Winterthur. On 27 September 1969, it was announced in the press from Geneva that the Israeli Military Intelligence had obtained plans relating to the production of the jet engine used in the Swiss Air Force Mirage IIIs and that a Swiss engineer employed by Sulzer Brothers had been arrested in Berne and charged with military and economic espionage. The engineer in question, Alfred Frauenknecht, was said to have confessed to selling the plans for about £86,000.

Contacts between the Mossad and the arrested engineer were established in the spring of 1968. Since then some twenty consignments of plans had been passed to the Israelis via contacts in West Germany. The blueprints were originally supplied by Sulzer to a sub-contractor and should have been destroyed on return. It was stated at Frauenknecht's trial that the military-industrial complex of Israeli Aircraft Industries, one of the country's biggest employers, was well equipped to profit from this intelligence. The engine used in the Mirage IIIs supplied to the Swiss Air Force had more thrust than that of the Mirage III C of which the Israeli Air Force had sixty-five aircraft. Frauenknecht had obtained the astonishing quantity of two tons of documents and blueprints which had been driven away from the Sulzer factory in a van and passed on to the Israelis. On 23 April 1969, he was jailed for four and a half years at a Federal Tribunal. It was described by the judge as 'the worst case of espionage in Switzerland since World War II'.

Relations between Switzerland and Israel had never been too good and this trial marked a breaking point. The Israeli military attaché in Berne was asked to leave Swiss territory.

During this period both the Mossad and Aman were occupied by the problem of ascertaining what was being planned by the most militant and unrelenting of all Israel's enemies, the Libyan regime of Colonel Muamar Gaddafi.

Libya occupied a key position both geographically and politically in the Arab world. Situated between Egypt and Tunisia, it was a threat not merely to Israel, for which she professed a paranoic hatred, but to Arab unity as well. For Gaddafi was never tired of proclaiming that his country was the only reliable ally in the fight against Zionism and that President Sadat of Egypt was betraying the Arab cause and merely serving the interests of American capitalism. At the same time, Libya possessed some of the best harbours and port facilities in the whole of North Africa, the use of which the Russians coveted.

Thus Israel was not only concerned with keeping a look-out for Libyan-inspired plots against herself, but equally for information on intrigues by Gaddafi directed against Egypt and other Arab regimes. Exploitation of Arab disunity was an essential part of the day-to-day work of the Israeli Secret Service. President Sadat paradoxically owes his continued existence in part at least to intelligence supplied to him by the Israelis. It is true that such intelligence was not given to him directly, but through the CIA as intermediary, nevertheless it was intended for his consumption. On some occasions Sadat has responded by actually putting a check on some of the wilder of Gaddafi's anti-Israeli schemes, one such being his intervention to forbid the plot to torpedo a liner carrying Jews on a pilgrimage to Israel.

Libya had established contacts not only in the extremist Arab guerrilla movements of the Middle East and Africa, but in subversive organisations in Western Europe as well as developing special relations behind the Iron Curtain. Under Zvi Zamir's direction Israeli intelligence in the communist countries of Eastern Europe was directed to discovering what exactly the Libyans were planning. It was initially a difficult operation because the Mossad hierarchy could not specify what their agents had to look for. It speaks highly for the calibre of Mossad agents in Europe, both East and West, that they were able to unmask a wide range of unexpected activities.

For example, from Mossad inquiries in Sofia the Israelis learned that Dr. Salah Saraya and certain Egyptian officers were actually working for Gaddafi's Intelligence Service. Through this information being passed to the Egyptians via devious routes, Saraya and ninety-one others were eventually arrested and charged with planning the overthrow and assassination of Sadat. Again it was Mossad persistence in keeping a close watch on the perambulations of Gaddafi's special envoy, Major Jaloud, in Russia and Eastern Europe which revealed that the Libyans were seeking big arms purchases and that the Bulgarians had agreed to help in building fortifications along the Libyan–Egyptian borders. The Libyans have long had a territorial dispute with the Egyptians.

On the whole this Secret Service activity was largely a question of intelligence-gathering. But in the latter part of 1969 one key Mossad agent in Europe discovered a plot that was actually being planned against Gaddafi on behalf of the deposed king Mohammed Idris Al-Senussi of Libya. This immediately posed the possibility of unofficial intervention by Israel.

Libya had become an independent, sovereign, federal kingdom under the Amir of Cyrenaica, King Idris, on 24 December 1951, when the British Residents in Tripolitania and Cyrenaica and the French Resident in the Fezzan transferred their remaining powers to the federal government of Libya in accordance with decisions passed by the United Nations the previous year. The King was deposed and a Libyan Arab Republic set up in 1969.

What the Mossad agent in Belgrade discovered was the merest hint of a plot to launch a Commando-style raid on Libya with the aim of destroying the new regime and restoring King Idris to power. At first this seemed to be a counter-revolutionary plot by Arabs themselves. But inquiries of Mossad agents in Vienna and Prague quickly revealed that though pro-Senussi as regards the source of funds, the actual plot was being master-minded by British and French personnel. In the Israeli view a conglomeration of this kind was doomed to failure unless it was heavily financed and always providing the intervention of European agents was not too pronounced. One enterprising freelance Israeli agent was prepared to back this coup and he even managed to organise some of the supplies of arms without his status as an Israeli agent ever being discovered. British and French mercenaries were recruited for the operation for which arms were purchased from the Czech state-owned arms combine of Omnipol in Prague. The true reason for the purchase was concealed by shipping the arms from Prague to Yugoslavia from where they could be transferred via Douala in the Cameroons to Chad which had a common frontier with Libya. But the plans for delivering arms by this circuitous route were fraught with considerable risk of delays and the Mossad agent reported that they were unlikely to succeed.

He had intercepted a letter, dated 10 May 1971, from a Yugoslav intermediary to a firm of transit agents in Vienna confirming the receipt from 'Omnipol of 54 cases of military equipment ... which is stored in our transit storage in the Port of Ploce.' The arms listed were twenty machine-guns, sixty machine pistols, fifty hand grenades, four anti-tank grenade launchers, signal pistol with cartridges and parachute, some 36,000 cartridges, twenty shells for anti-tank grenade launchers, blasting fuse, safety fuse, fifty kilos of plastic explosives with detonators and blasting machine, electric detonators and 100 incendiary grenades. It was, as the Mossad agent reported, 'hardly likely to be enough to displace Gaddafi.' [2]

Nor was it: the coup was never launched and the last heard of the surplus arms was an attempt to sell them to some other mercenary force. Nevertheless, although this was a non-starter as far as the Israelis were concerned, the gathering of such intelligence put them in an excellent position to bargain with both the CIA, the British and French Secret Services. Few other Intelligence Services in the world—and certainly no other of this relatively small size—are able to help other Secret Services to the extent that the Israelis can and do. It gives them, of course, a strong bargaining position and paves the way for a great deal of reciprocal help. It was through the close watch which the Mossad maintains on all Gaddafi's machinations abroad that Israel learned that the Libyan leader was actually co-operating with the IRA and linking the Irish terrorists with the Palestine guerrillas. The Mossad's Paris and Hamburg networks reported meetings between IRA members and Libyan agents. A tip-off from Malta brought news of a consignment of arms in a ship in Tripoli harbour destined for delivery to the IRA. Both the CIA and the British Secret Service were informed and this resulted in the Eire Navy and coastguard service co-operating in seizing the Cyprus-based ship *Claudia* off the Irish coast with its cargo.

One wonders whether President Sadat, when he makes his denunciations of Israel, ponders on the fact that on more than one occasion he has owed his life to Israeli intelligence, tip-offs on plans to assassinate him, passed to his Intelligence officer via the CIA.

Israel both sells and exchanges intelligence with other powers when it is in her interests to do so. While much of this is done on a basis of friendly co-operation, mainly a matter of exchanging information, or, occasionally, bartering it, there are times when both the Mossad and Aman need to be hard-headed enough to demand a price for it. After all, as has been seen in this chapter, intelligence of the right kind very often costs big money and the Israeli Secret Service needs to recoup some of its outgoings. However, all this is conducted in a pragmatic manner rather than on a commercial basis. Intelligence which is actually sold does not necessarily go to the highest bidder. Indeed, there may well be no bidding at all, though sometimes there has to be. In the complicated espionage world of today one section of a country's Secret Service may be prepared to pay more than another section.

Two commodities eagerly sought by Mossad and Aman agents have been uranium and plutonium. These became a prime requirement after the Six-Day War partly to supply the top secret reactor at Dimona so that further experiments could be carried out, but also because the Israelis were the first of the small powers to appreciate the risks of being held to ransom by a terrorist gang in possession of a mini-nuclear bomb. There was only one answer to such tactics: Israel needed to have similar weapons to be able able to bargain terror against terror. In November 1968, a West German freighter carrying more than 200 tons of natural uranium left Antwerp for Genoa, stopping at Rotterdam en route. The uranium, which was strictly controlled by international agreement, was logged for sale to Italy, but the ship never reached Genoa. She appeared to have doubled back on her tracks in the Mediterranean and returned to Germany. Many weeks later after the Italians had reported the disappearance of the ship and its cargo to the European Atomic Energy Committee, a secret investigation was carried out by the Intelligence Services of four European countries and the CIA. By that time the ship had gone to sea again and when she was eventually located, she was flying a different flag, bearing a new name and manned by a new crew. It seemed clear that either the ship had been hi-jacked and the cargo removed, or an undercover deal had been carried out. Nothing could be proved, however, but CIA investigators were convinced that this was yet another brilliant coup by the Israeli Secret Service, in order to obtain uranium. One version of what happened was that early in 1968 the Israelis either rented or bought the West German freighter and provided the captain and crew for the voyage to Italy. The ship was met in the Mediterranean by an Israeli freighter and the cargo was transferred and taken on to Haifa. Then the German ship returned to Germany where the Israeli crew hastily dispersed, and presumably another crew took the freighter to sea again.

This story was first revealed in public by Paul Leventhal, a former US Senate expert on nuclear proliferation, in a speech at an anti-nuclear conference in Salzburg in April 1977. While providing no positive evidence, he claimed that the incident demonstrated 'a dangerous loophole in the safeguards system that must be closed immediately'. Euratom made inquiries about the German chemical firm which had bought the uranium in the first place, but, according to one of their officials, 'the firm had by then been closed down and there was nobody to prosecute.'

According to a former Norwegian Chief Prosecutor, Mr. Haakon Wiker, speaking in June 1977, an Israeli agent confessed to the Norwegian police that he had 'helped divert 200 tons of uranium to Israel nine years ago'. Investigators reported that the ship's log had oil poured over it, apparently in an attempt to obscure any references to the incident. It was also alleged that the security forces' reports on the affair had been withheld from Euratom. The mysterious intermediary behind the deal was a Levantine who called himself 'Yarisal' who took possession of the ship for £157,000 in cash.

Euratom officials could not inspect the Israeli reactor to make sure whether Israel had used the uranium to make 'thirty nuclear weapons', as the CIA alleged, because Israel had not signed the treaty that provided for inspection. Meanwhile the Israelis have made no comment on the matter.

Daring coups such as this cause some of Israel's Arab neighbours to look enviously on Israel's Secret Service. On the other hand Iraq, Saudi Arabia and some of the Sultanates have every reason to thank Israel for intelligence which has enabled them to suppress revolutionary agitators and trouble-makers. King Khaled ibn Abdul-Aziz of Saudi Arabia has particular cause to be grateful for the contacts which his security chief, Kamal Adham, who was trained by the CIA, has with intermediaries acting on behalf of Israeli Intelligence.

17

The Case of the Five Gunboats

Jews don't celebrate Christmas Eve. We were in Cherbourg on business.

(VICTOR ZIPSTEIN)

THIS WAS THE COMMENT of Admiral Mordecai Limon's French Jewish chauffeur when asked by a journalist if he had missed his Christmas dinner (traditionally held on Christmas Eve in France) on 24 December 1969, the night the Israelis tricked the French and sailed their gunboats to Haifa.

The 'Case of the Israeli Gunboats', as it came to be known, was largely planned by the Israeli Secret Service and was their swift and secret response to the irksome arms embargo and other frustrations which, under General de Gaulle's changed policy, were imposed by France on Israel. Official relations between the two countries had steadily worsened since the Six-Day War, even though a certain amount of co-operation between the Mossad and the SDECE continued. Then in 1968 de Gaulle imposed the embargo.

This created the greatest difficulties for Admiral Mordecai Limon, who in 1962 had been appointed a special envoy of the Israeli Government for Europe and was sent to Paris to arrange all Israel's military purchases from France. Born in Poland on 3 January 1924, Limon had spent most of his life in the land that is now known as Israel. In 1940, when the country was still under British mandate, he joined the Palyam as a sea captain organising the illegal entry of Jewish refugees. He captained many of the small craft which slipped through the British blockade after World War II when Jews from the concentration camps were desperately seeking a new life in the Middle East. So effectively did Limon carry out this work that when Israel achieved independence he was made an admiral in his country's new Navy. At the age of twenty-six he became its Commander-in-Chief until he retired from the service in 1954.

For a time after that he lived in New York with his wife and two young children, still dedicated to serving his country in various capacities. Then, on his return to Israel, he joined the Ministry of Defence as deputy director-general in charge of the department of emergency economic planning. There was some mirth among his friends when this posting was announced: 'Mordecai is up to something again,' they said knowingly. He had always had something of the 'Nelson touch' as a sailor, was a man of few words and intensely serious. But off duty he was popular, made many friends, played a good game of tennis and loved chamber music. Despite the tensions in relations with the French, Admiral Limon had made many friends in France, too, and was a welcome figure at receptions and cocktail parties.

It was this cool and efficient officer who, against all the odds, organised the sailing of the five gunboats from Cherbourg to Haifa, in defiance of the arms embargo, thus fooling the French by escaping under their very eyes from one of the most closely guarded harbours in the world. His experience as a Palyam operator stood him in good stead.

On 1 January 1970, the Israeli Government broke its public silence on the affair, following the French Government's request for the recall of Admiral Limon. The statement, made from the Israeli Foreign Ministry laid responsibility for it on the 'unwarranted' French arms embargo, saying that the whole cause of the trouble was 'in the maintenance of the unjustified embargo by France and not in its implementation.'

At one point it seemed as though the incident might lead to a complete diplomatic break between the two countries, but in the end the French were well content with Admiral Limon's departure. The 45-year-old Admiral flew back to Tel Aviv on 9 January. On his arrival he told the press: 'Regrettably, we are the only nation in the Middle East which is not getting arms.'

The gunboats incident was the culmination of a long series of frustrations for the Israeli arms purchasing mission. Israel had ordered (and the order had been accepted) fifty Mirage jets from France: these the French refused to deliver after the embargo was arbitrarily imposed. De Gaulle had now resigned from the Presidency, but under Pompidou there was an apparent indecisiveness in government circles on the subject. Unofficially, the Israelis would be urged to be patient and told that before long something would be done to make things easier for them, but public pronouncements made no reference to this.

French arms manufacturers had been equally angry about the embargo, none more so than M. Marcel Dassault, head of the French aircraft-producing firm bearing his name, who had been forbidden to sell the Mirages to Israel. In the hope that before too long the embargo would be lifted, Israeli pilots had been testing these planes at two bases near Marseilles. After the escape of the gunboats from Cherbourg an order was issued banning all Israeli personnel from Dassault factories and a guard was put on Mirages. Meanwhile the Arab states continued to obtain arms from far and wide.

The gunboats in question had been built in the naval base on the west side of Cherbourg's inner harbour. All the details of the purchase had been completed before the French slapped their arms embargo on Israel with the somewhat thin excuse that it was imposed in retaliation for the Israelis' use of the French-built helicopters in the commando raid on Beirut airport on 28 December 1968. After the ban was imposed the gunboats remained at Cherbourg, though all further work on them was stopped. Even then the Israelis behaved with great tact and, when craft were ordered away from the naval base to the other side of the harbour close to the car ferry, they carefully collected all the workmen's belongings left aboard, clothes, tools, bottles of wine and packets of cigarettes as well as many personal oddments and stacked them neatly on the quayside.

The Israelis were quite determined not to lose the gunboats and the Mossad were asked what they could do to help. A quick survey of the whole situation was then made by the Secret Service and no aspect of the problem was neglected. On the political and diplomatic side soundings were taken from Admiral Limon, the Israeli Ambassador in Paris and various politicians and civil servants in France: the outcome of these inquiries was that there was no chance whatsoever of the French Government being persuaded to turn a blind eye to any attempt by Israelis to smuggle the ships out of Cherbourg. Indeed, what disturbed the Israelis was that it seemed as though the French authorities were keeping a strict watch on them and were prepared for a possible attempt to defy the ban and sail the craft away.

Nevertheless the Mossad had some promises of guidance and advice, if not actual help, from inside France itself. One of the French helpers was paradoxically a man who had been very close to de Gaulle and who believed that the General, despite the arms embargo he had imposed, was always anxious that Israel should be adequately armed. Indeed, according to one source, it was de Gaulle himself in retirement who in an ambiguous phrase conjured up the formula for Israel to retrieve the ships. To the Israelis' most dependable adviser in France he was alleged to have said: 'Let the Israelis agree to the ships being sold to a neutral commercial company and then let Israel retrieve the craft from that company.'

Mossad inquiries in Britain were frustrated by one of their agents reporting on the influence of left-wing pro-Palestinians in the then Wilson Government. 'Wilson may himself proclaim his sympathy for Israel,' was the reply, 'but he will always be outgunned by the pro-Palestinians in his ranks. And Wilson will always survive rather than pay attention to his personal preferences.' This effectively ruined one Mossad plan which was that the gunboats might make a quick dash for a British port.

Whether or not General de Gaulle or the Mossad should be credited with the plan eventually adopted is neither here nor there. It could not have been implemented without co-operation between the Mossad and the Israeli Navy. It was then that the Israelis brought forward the plan for selling the ships to the 'Norwegian' oil exploration firm of Starboat Oil Company of Panama through a firm of London solicitors and with only an accommodation address in Norway—PO Box 25078, Soli-Oslo 2. This was to be one of the many examples of co-operation between Israel and Norway on an Intelligence level: the two nations admired one another, Israel being the small power surrounded by enemies who stood out in the Middle East, while Norway, despite the anomaly of Quisling, being far and away the most courageous of the Scandinavian nations in opposition to Hitler during its occupation in World War II. When the gunboats eventually arrived at Tel Aviv photographs showed that on the bridge they bore a plate bearing the designation 'Starboat' and a number.

The main complaint against Admiral Limon by the French Government after the incident was that he had accepted a refund of the price paid by Israel for them and given his agreement to their sale to the Starboat Oil Company of Panama, signing a letter that Israel renounced both their ownership and their use. What the French did not realise was that in the end it was Admiral Limon himself, the man affectionately nicknamed 'Moka' Limon in Paris, who directed the final operation. Indeed he took over where the Mossad left off. There was, however, another admiral involved. In November 1969, Rear-Admiral Benny Telem, deputy chief of the Israeli naval staff, went to France to take his wife to a Lyon hospital for a cataract operation. During his visit he managed to find time to visit Cherbourg which is, after all, a very long way from Lyon. Significantly, he spent two days at the port.

Both the Mossad and Israeli Naval authorities made a careful survey of the harbour. It was one of the most difficult in Europe from which to escape and was kept under the closest security scrutiny because it was the base for France's two nuclear submarines, the latter of which, *Terrible*, was launched only four days before the last of the Israeli gunboats. The inner harbour was guarded by police, the Army and trained dogs. Only a shrewd sailor with Limon's experience could have plotted such a risky enterprise and got away with it. And there is little doubt, as journalistic investigation by the French newspaper *L'Express* showed, that the Israelis did get away with it and that there was no collusion with the French authorities.[1]

It was Victor Zipstein, a French citizen and chauffeur to Admiral Limon, who confirmed the Admiral's moves on Christmas Eve 1969. He drove Limon to Cherbourg in a car bearing diplomatic licence plates—59 CD 59. The Admiral arrived in Cherbourg just in time for lunch on Christmas Eve. This he had with M. Félix Amiot, chief of the firm which had built the gunboats. During that day weather reports were bad: the forecast was of a strong SSE wind in the Bay of Biscay, rising to gale force. Despite this, Admiral Limon left his lunch party with M. Amiot and gave the secret order to the gunboats to sail that night, knowing that Christmas Eve was the ideal time to take advantage of any laxity in security.

The flotilla commander objected to these orders on the grounds of weather reports and the fact that one of his craft had not yet had sea trials. But luck was with the Admiral: just before 1900 hours, when the crew were planning to go ashore for dinner, a British meterological report suggested that the SSE wind would

drop and conditions would improve. On the strength of this
Limon ruled out all objections and repeated his orders. There
was an immediate round-up of all crews; all, except for one man,
who was ill, were ordered back to their ships, and at 02.30 hours
on Christmas morning the five gunboats slipped their moorings
and started up their engines.

At that time there was nobody about to watch their departure
other than Admiral Limon himself. He had checked into a hotel
not far away from the quay under the name of 'Monsieur Limon
of Paris', together with his chauffeur. They booked rooms and
asked for a call at 3 a.m., saying they had to drive back to Paris
at that hour. The rooms were paid for in advance, so nobody was
suspicious. Then, while the night porter was asleep, the Admiral
slipped quietly out of the hotel and went down to the quay to say
farewell to the gunboats' commanding officers and probably to
reassure them about the latest weather reports.

Much thought had been given to the best method of leaving
the harbour. Agents had made observations for days ahead on
movements in and around the naval base at night and one had
even made a dummy run in a small craft on two occasions. The
gunboats were moored in the inner harbour, whose exit to the
outer harbour was between two jetties, the western one, part of
the naval base, had a permanent naval guard, whose movements
had to be taken into account.

Normally, when proceeding to sea from this inner harbour, the
route lay to port, right under the guns of the naval dockyard, past
the chain of forts and then into the English Channel. But this
would have exposed the craft to observation from the naval gun
batteries, so they took the shorter, less exposed, but far more
dangerous course straight across the outer harbour, between the
Fort de l'Est and the submerged rocks of the tiny island on the
starboard side. It was a much narrower exit and there was less
than two fathoms of water in which to navigate. Indeed, on the
charts this route was clearly marked as dangerous and 'forbidden',
and in normal circumstances no sensible navigator would attempt
it. But the gunboats had been trimmed to a shallow draught,
careful soundings had been taken on the dummy runs and the
risks of a quick dash to sea this way seemed to be outweighed
by the advantages of surprise and keeping away from the gun
batteries.

Thus it was that the gunboats sailed away to Haifa from the

most closely guarded of all France's naval bases. It was a masterly operation which must have delighted Admiral Limon who never bothered to sleep that night, but had a light meal and then motored back to Paris. When the French discovered what had happened there was a furious outburst at the Elysée Palace: 'we have been made to look absolute fools,' was President Pompidou's comment. Two civil servants were suspended for what Pompidou somewhat obscurely and unfairly called 'intellectual complicity'.

At about this time the Mossad were also given another poser by the Ministry of Defence: to deal with a Soviet-built radar station which had been sited in a remote settlement on the Gulf of Suez. For some considerable time this radar station had been an obstacle to Israeli aircraft operating in the area and some officers had even urged launching an attack on the installation.

However, both the Mossad and Aman were agreed that by far the best plan, providing it could be carried out smoothly and secretly, would be to send in a Commando-Intelligence team to steal the radar station and airlift it back to Israel. As someone remarked, 'this is something even James Bond wouldn't contemplate', and, indeed, the feat did seem to be as improbable as any of the Secret Service exploits thought up by Ian Fleming. The radar station weighed seven tons and contained all manner of new equipment.

While credit for airlifting this radar station a few days after the incident of the gunboats must go to the Israeli Army, it was made practicable only through the planning of the Secret Service. As a result the carefully trained and briefed invading force managed to get within twenty-five yards of their target before they were detected. The object was to capture this radar station intact and airlift it and all its crew back to Tel Aviv. In fact two Egyptians were killed and four others taken prisoner. Within half an hour all the vital equipment, containing valuable information, was raised by pulleys into helicopters and taken back to Israel.

18

The Long Arm of
the Avengers

*And if the avenger of blood pursue after him, then
they shall not deliver the slayer up into his hand;
because he smote his neighbour unwittingly, and
hated him not beforetime.*

(JOSHUA, XX, 5)

THE TRADITION of 'The Avenger', of the *Goel*, as he is called in
Hebrew, is one that has been revived in recent years in the shape
of various 'auxiliary' or 'subordinate' groups, sometimes linked
to the Mossad. Their existence, however, is not officially declared,
or admitted and in some instances their activities have been dis-
owned. Nevertheless, these various groups have played a considerable role in Israeli Secret Service affairs and will undoubtedly
continue to do so.

'The Avenger of the Blood' was the man who, in accordance
with Jewish custom, had the right of taking vengeance on anyone
who had killed one of his kinsmen. Cities of refuge were appointed
for the protection of such self-appointed killers. Some of the unofficial assassination squads of today have taken ancient titles for
themselves such as 'The Avengers'; 'Masada', named after the
great rock on the edge of the Judaean Desert where the Zealots
made their last great stand against the Romans; 'Squad 101'
(also sometimes designated 'Squad 1001' as a confusion tactic);
the 'July Unit' and 'Wrath of God', usually more irreverently
called 'WOG'.

The Israeli Secret Service no more likes indulging in assassination as an instrument of carrying out its work than the Secret
Service of any other law-abiding democracy. That it has felt
compelled to adopt such tactics on the grounds of expediency and
self-defence is proof partly of the pressure of public opinion inside

Israel against Arab terrorism and a realistic assessment of the permanent state of guerrilla warfare to which the state is subjected. But it is also a measure of the feeling which Israel has of being forced to 'go it alone' by the rest of the world and the supine attitude of the Western powers towards the challenge of international terrorism. It can safely be said that unless Israel had adopted this ruthless stance—that of rooting out terrorists once they have been identified—Arab terrorism would have achieved far more successes and the Western World as well as Israel would have been the victims. Yet even the Mossad has had to suffer the criticisms of a noisy minority of 'do-gooders' inside Israel. Its response to all this has been quite simple and essentially practical: to drive home the lesson to the Palestinian terrorists and their allies that if they continue with these activities, they will themselves be killed.

These tactics were launched as early as 1956, by which time the Mossad had had every opportunity of seeing how Arab terrorism in Algeria, Tunisia and elsewhere was becoming almost a way of life. President Nasser had then agreed to train, equip and support in every way possible the Fedayeen, as they were then called—raiding parties committed to launching terrorist attacks inside Israeli territory. This particular terrorist movement was popularised in the Western press as a body of devoted Moslem patriots who were prepared to die for their cause, as indeed many of them did when they were caught by Israeli patrols, largely because Nasser made no attempt to have them adequately trained to meet a highly efficient opposition. It was Nasser and his aides who were the criminals who encouraged this senseless terrorism, directed as usual against the civilian population and it was they who skulked in safety behind the lines while the poor misled Fedayeen went to their deaths.

The Israelis realised this and decided with brutal logic that the obvious answer was to snuff out the director of these operations who, from the safety of Egypt, sent out these poor Jordanians and displaced Palestinians on their death missions. It did not take the Mossad long to discover that this was Lieutenant-Colonel Mustapha Hafez, head of Egyptian Intelligence in Gaza. On 11 July 1956, Hafez went to meet an informant, who was also a double-agent; the latter handed him a parcel and when Hafez started to tear off the wrappings, it exploded and killed him.

Thus the number one enemy was wiped out. But the Mossad

wanted to make sure that there was no ready-made successor to the job. Three days later Colonel Salah Mustapha, the Egyptian military attaché in Jordan and a number two in the Palestinian terrorist set-up, received a book which appeared to have come from the United Nations offices: he, too, was killed by a parcel-bomb.

These actions had an instantaneous result. They effectively checked further terrorist activities for some time to come and, for this reason, in the hope that such preventive action would save many innocent Israeli lives, the Mossad made the assassination of terrorist leaders a prime objective in their operations. As we have seen, such tactics were revived under Isser Harel's regime in the sixties when Israel was confronted by the menace of the German scientists working for Egypt. The Israelis had been the first Secret Service in modern times to use the tactical weapon of the letter-bomb, but whereas this technique has been indiscriminately used by others since, the Mossad always concentrated entirely on the real culprits. Yet they have learned that with the best of intentions this method can lead to the most appalling mistakes.

The first letter-bomb ever sent was posted by Martin Eckenberg, a Swedish engineer, who lived in London and dispatched it from there to a Swedish businessman in 1910. He was tracked down by Scotland Yard to his home in Clapham, made a full confession and hanged himself in Brixton Prison. It was not until after World War II that the parcel-bomb was reintroduced first by the Stern Gang in 1948 against the British and then by the agents detailed to eliminate the German scientists in Cairo. It was then that the tactics of the letter-bomb seriously misfired when a parcel-bomb addressed to Professor Wolfgang Pilz seriously injured his secretary, and another sent to the Heliopolis missile factory, killed five Egyptian technicians. These bombs may have alarmed German scientists, but, as we have seen, they provided considerable adverse publicity for Israel and gave Ben-Gurion a major political problem as well as forcing a change in the post of Mossad chief. Though since that day the Arabs have themselves employed the parcel-bomb tactic in their terrorist campaigns, using it effectively against the Israelis, the latter have abandoned this method entirely. Their discipline seems to have been strong enough for this ban on postal-bombs to have been imposed on unofficial avenger squads as well as on the men of the Mossad.

Not even the Palestinian letter-bomb campaign of the early seventies provoked a like response from the Israelis, despite the fact that Dr. Ami Shachori, a Counsellor in the Israeli Embassy in London, was killed by such a bomb.

It was in the early seventies that the Israelis began to amass evidence that the new campaign of terror being waged by the Palestinian Arabs was being aided and to some extent distorted for their own ends by a cosmopolitan consortium of anarchists, Marxist agitators and professional terrorists in Europe and Japan as well as the Middle East. The ramifications of this terrorist network were widespread across four continents. The PFLP cell in Europe was linked with such other terrorist organisations as the IRA, the Basques and the Bretons and they had an inter-related supply organisation so that, in emergencies, one cell would call on another for assistance. The anarchists and the Marxists exploited the situation to the full and they included the Japanese Red Army, a German cell known as the Second of June Movement and even an Italian organisation known as the Red Brigade.

On 30 May 1972, three Japanese terrorists killed twenty people at Lydda airport. One of the groups indulging in terrorist tactics of various kinds was Saiqa, which was financed and directed by the Syrian Secret Service and assisted by KGB 'advisers'. Its leader was Major Zuheir Mohsen, and one of its key posts was in Rome where its chief supply centre for explosives was stored. This was a highly disciplined, professional group which very nearly brought off the bombing of the Israeli Embassy in Paris.

The response of the Israeli Secret Service to all this was swift, positive and ruthless, but whereas the Palestinians and their bizarre allies indulged in indiscriminate acts of terror, often directed at non-Israelis for blackmail purposes, the 'avenger groups' of Israel concentrated solely on eliminating the organisers and perpetrators of terrorism. It is true that they made some grievous mistakes on occasions, but as a general rule it has been Israeli practice to go only for the real killers or their bosses. Some Western Intelligence Services have actually been sympathetic towards these tactics of the Israeli Secret Service and on occasions have helped them, even against the express wishes of their governments. This has been particularly true of the French Secret Service and, to a lesser degree, of the British as well. When Abu Daoud, one of the leading Palestinian terrorists, was arrested in France in January 1977, the French Intelligence acted without informing their government. It was the French Government which ordered Abu Daoud's release for fear of upsetting relations with the Arab states, especially those producing oil.

The Secret Services of the West know just as well as the Israelis that behind the Arab terrorist campaign is something much more sinister and that, the more successful its operations, the more likely it is to be turned against other objectives. Jews today, but tomorrow it could be Western politicians who show sympathy to Israel, or Northern Irish businessmen, or even trade union leaders who support some kind of a 'Social Contract'. The links between the Palestinian terrorists and the Red Army faction of the Baader-Meinhof group, the Provisional IRA and the Basque fighters for independence are so strong that it would be quite simple to switch from Israeli targets to British, French, German or Spanish targets any time. What they seem to have learned belatedly, and then thanks largely to information passed on to them by the Israelis, is that the Soviet Union is actually controlling many of the Palestinian terrorists. Black September, the main arm of Arab terrorism in the early seventies, though secretly run by Al Fatah, was also aided and in some instances directed by the KGB.

The Israelis set about their campaign of wiping out the principal terrorists first by compiling a dossier on them, their habits, weaknesses, background and favourite haunts, and then by infiltration and the ordering of reports from Mossad agents everywhere in Europe. It was from the latter that a horrifying picture of organised terrorism on a vast scale gradually emerged. There was no major city in the whole of Europe without its cell of terrorists; some, such as Rome, being mainly supply depots, others like Paris and Zurich being spy centres, while London and Amsterdam had two active recruiting agencies. The Mossad learned that Black September's communication system was linked to that of the KGB and that, when necessary, they could use this network to communicate between one country and another. And, whenever Black September, or any other Arab terrorist group, required outside assistance or technical aid, they could get it from the KGB. The chief KGB cell concerned with Black September had been operating from Cyprus for some years with the connivance of the Greek Cypriots until it was blown by the Mossad and forced to switch to Damascus.

Each act of terrorism provided the Israelis with new leads and they relentlessly followed up every clue. Fortunately the splits and schisms in the ranks of the terrorists have been carefully exploited by the Mossad and a great deal of intelligence has been extracted from disillusioned 'freedom fighters'. Many of them felt that the hi-jacking of planes was counter-productive to their long-term plans. On the other hand, the extremists who believed that their bombings and hi-jackings were invaluable propaganda for their cause, could point to the fact that many Western governments had been frightened by such actions.

The Mossad had been hunting Dr. Waddieh Haddad, military leader of the PFLP, for some years and in July 1970, there had been an abortive attempt to liquidate him in Beirut. But the man they were particularly interested in was not even an Arab. This was the elusive and altogether fascinating character generally referred to as 'Carlos', who, on the dossiers of most police forces of Western Europe was known as 'World Terrorist Number 1'.

The true identity of Carlos, sometimes called 'The Jackal' because of his resemblance to the central character in Frederick Forsyth's book, *The Day of the Jackal*, was only established a few years ago. He is Ilich Ramirez Sanchez, also known as Carlos Martinez, born in 1950, the son of a Venezuelan doctor of law who was himself a fervent and dedicated, but not an extreme left-winger. In the dossier compiled on Carlos there are the following terse facts: 'Occupation, terrorist; employer, usually Dr. George Habbash, chairman of the PFLP, but sometimes the Algerian Government; leased by the KGB for special assignments for Arab and other powers.'

Carlos's father named all his sons with the various names of Lenin—Ilich, Vladimir and Lenin. In 1966, when Carlos was seventeen, he was sent with his brothers to London where he lived in a succession of flats in the West End. This period of Carlos's life is still largely unexplained. It has been suggested that his father became somewhat disillusioned with the influence of English life on his sons and that he sent them briefly to France and then suddenly decided that their education was best finished in Moscow. It is this part of Carlos's story which does not ring altogether true: according to other sources he was hand-picked by the KGB while he was in London. He was eventually sent to the Patrice Lumumba University in Moscow from 1969–71, where, according to one cynical Mossad report, he 'majored in sabotage with minors in marksmanship and terror'. The Patrice Lumumba University is in effect a recruiting and training agency for non-Russian KGB agents and it is significant that while he was there Carlos learned Arabic, French and German.

It was only after he left Moscow in 1971 that there was any evidence of Carlos being employed as a terrorist. In that year he paid a brief visit to Paris, returning to London to take up a teaching post at the Langham Secretarial College in Mayfair, and then in the early part of 1972 went back to Paris to be assigned to Mohamed Boudia, whose organisation, *Parisienne Orientale*, was a front for the PFLP. Boudia, a theatrical producer by profession, was an Algerian veteran of the underground war between the Palestinians and Israel. By this time Carlos was affiliated with the KGB and his job under Boudia was to be contact man with various European terrorist groups including the IRA, Baader-Meinhof and the Japanese Red Army.

The Israelis, when interrogating the one surviving raider, Kozo Okamoto, after the Lydda airport attack, learned that the supplier of their weapons was one 'Hector Hirodikon', who had been in Tel Aviv and then disappeared. The Mossad sent a message to London asking one of their agents there to keep a close watch on arrivals at Heathrow. The reply they eventually received back was intriguing: 'Nobody of the name of Hector Hirodikon has checked back to London, but 'Adolf Granel', supposed to be a Chilean of German stock, has. Not only do we feel sure he is the same person who went out to Tel Aviv as Hector Hirodikon, but he is the spit image of Carlos Martinez.'

Thus the Israelis came on the trail of Carlos. But they decided that, in view of his international associations, he should not be put on the death list, but merely shadowed. The Mossad wanted to find out where all the other Carlos trails led to and how closely he was linked with the KGB. To achieve this they nominated Hani Kuda, a Syrian journalist who had carried out other assignments for them, to infiltrate Boudia's group. Unfortunately for poor Kuda, Mohamed Boudia took an instant dislike to him. He told Carlos he had some misgivings about the new member, ordered the Venezuelan to shadow him and to kill without hesitation if Kuda was found to be an Israeli agent.

The Israelis' first big strike by the 'avenger squads' was on 8 July 1972, in retaliation for the attack on Lydda airport. The organiser of this outrage was Ghassan Kanafani, a poet and novelist who had been the public relations officer for the PFLP in Beirut. Zvi Zamir, who by then had become Memuneh, gave the signal for action and two skilled Mossad agents were secretly put ashore in Beirut with a radio-controlled bomb which one of them wired to the engine of Kanafani's car. This was the first positively recorded example of the use of a radio-controlled bomb by the Israelis, which probably explains how there were two deaths when only one was intended. Kanafani was killed at once, as he started his car, and his seventeen-year-old niece, who unexpectedly happened to be with him, died also. A day or two later the Israelis struck again, but this time not fatally. Bassam Abu Sherif, who had been ordered to take over Kanafani's role, received a letter-bomb which exploded in his hands: he lost his right eye and was badly injured, but survived the accident.

This was before the 'avenger squads' had acquired their latter-day clinical efficiency. The handling of both these actions was severely criticised inside the Mossad and it was pointed out that both methods of 'elimination' left much to be desired. It was then firmly ruled that the use of the letter-bomb was especially to be deprecated as it could not only lead to the wrong person being killed, but there was no guarantee of anyone being wiped out.

It was, of course, the Black September gang's massacre of Israeli sportsmen at the Olympic Games in Munich on 5 September 1972, which was directly responsible for a stepping-up of elimination tactics by the Israeli Secret Service as well as a creation of unofficial groups pledged to avenge such outrages. The Munich massacre resulted in the murdering of eleven Israeli athletes, shocking the whole world into a realisation that this was the ultimate horror in a whole year of senseless atrocities against innocent people by the Palestinian gangs. Anger inside Israel was intense and immediately after this tragedy there was no lack of volunteers for the 'avenger squads'. Even the Prime Minister, Mrs. Golda Meir, who had not been in favour of desperate retaliation measures, authorised a full-scale counter-terrorist campaign. In a speech to the Knesset Mrs. Meir announced that Israel would use 'all the spirit and determination and ingenuity our people possess to track down Palestinian terrorists wherever we can find them.'

Zvi Zamir had been fully aware of the criticisms made against the handling of the Kanafani and Sherif actions and he urged that the Mossad's 'avenger squads' should be reconstituted. If further outrages were to be checked and the killers stamped out, the whole operation must be efficiently and coolly planned. Any hot-headed action which might result in innocent people being killed, indeed any bungling at all, would only play into the hands of the Arab terrorists. Major-General Zamir went himself to Munich to make his own on-the-spot assessment and he actually saw the final confrontation between the terrorists and the German police. As Zamir said on his return, 'If Israel does not act, nobody else will. We can expect no help from the West.'

General Aharon Yariv, the former chief of Aman, was asked to take on the duties of Intelligence adviser on anti-terrorist tactics and to work in conjuction with Zamir. From then on the whole question of the 'avenger squads' was put on a highly organised basis, with the full weight of the Mossad thrown behind the 'unofficial groups', if only to keep them under control. One of the first undercover assassination groups to be set up was that known as the 'Wrath of God' (WOG). This comprised some volunteers, both men and women, mostly former commandos and paratroopers, together with a back-up team of French, German and Italian Jews whose job it was to collect evidence and plan operations. But behind this unofficial team was the know-how of the Mossad and Shabak. The policy was that the Mossad would carry out the research work and fix the targets for assassination then WOG would take over. If things went wrong, WOG was regarded as being entirely on its own.

One of the first problems was fixing the targets. It was generally agreed that, while top priority should go to finding and killing the murderers of Munich, it would not solve the problem of terrorism simply to wipe out the Black September gang. The aim must be to prepare a list which included the backroom planners of murder and the various non-Arab intermediary figures who were aiding Black September and other terrorist groups. Five special sections were set up to handle the whole operation and the nucleus of a sixth section was prepared, unknown to the others, with the intention that it could immediately spring into action if any of the other sections were hopelessly compromised or blown. Thus the prime task of the first section, code-named Ayin, was to compile a dossier on each of the prospective victims, to locate them and plot their movements.

There was a minor fracas in Brussels on 11 September 1972, when an unidentified caller lured an Israeli agent to a café where he was shot and seriously wounded. The gunman was at first though to be a Palestinian guerrilla, but later reports indicated that he was probably a Moroccan who had once been employed by the Israeli Secret Service. Eight days later a letter-bomb posted by Arab guerrillas exploded and killed a diplomat in the Israeli Embassy in London. Black September claimed responsibility.

Then in October the Israelis hit back. On the fourth of the month a bomb exploded in an Arab bookshop in Paris. An 'avenger squad' calling itself Masada claimed responsibility, but Israel denied all knowledge of the group. This was certainly not the kind of vengeance which Zvi Zamir planned. On 16 October 1972, Wadal Adel Zvaiter, a Palestinian poet who had been held responsible for the bomb explosion aboard an El Al flight the previous August, was shot dead. He, too, had been involved in the Munich murders as well as other attempted aircraft bombings.

One of the leading Mossad operators in the tracking down of the terrorists was Moshe Hanan Yishai, whose real name was Baruch Cohen. Born in Haifa, he spoke Arabic fluently and fully understood the customs and outlook of the Palestinian Arabs. His great grandfather had been Chief Rabbi of Haifa in the latter years of the Ottoman Empire. In 1952 Baruch had enlisted in the Israeli Army Intelligence Corps where he had acquired such an excellent reputation as an Intelligence officer that he was one of the first to be recruited by the Mossad for special services overseas in tracking down Palestinian terrorists. In 1970 he had been sent to Brussels and eventually he was posted to Paris to establish links with the Arabs. Baruch Cohen had a way with the girls and it was through chatting up two women named Bardelli, who had been used by the Boudia Commando group for certain missions, that he learned something of the Palestinians' set-up in the West. Having seduced one of them, it did not take him long to discover who her masters were, and the whereabouts of the terrorists' hideouts. The two girls, daughters of a wealthy Moroccan, were given false passports and sent on an assignment to Tel Aviv by Boudia himself. As a result of Baruch Cohen's information they were both arrested and others in the same terrorist network inside Israel were rounded up as well.

The Palestinians tried to hit back, but their loss in key personnel was beginning to tell: there were signs of hastily improvised attacks and a loss of nerve. They temporarily revived the letter-bomb tactics, and on 10 November 1972, a bomb posted in India exploded as it was opened by the official of a diamond firm.

Before the end of the month fifty-two more letter-bombs addressed to Jewish firms in Europe were intercepted in Bombay and New Delhi, while the British intercepted twenty others and the Swiss five. On 28 December 1972, Black September sent a commando team into the Israeli Embassy in Bangkok, taking several diplomats and their wives as hostages. But within two days the team tamely accepted a safe-conduct flight to Cairo arranged by President Sadat.

On 8 December 1972, Dr. Mahmoud Hamshari, another Black September chief and link-man with Boudia, was killed by a bomb in his apartment in Paris. During this month, acting on information received about Carlos and Black September links with the KGB, a special Mossad hit team was sent to Cyprus for two purposes, to destroy the Palestinian–KGB team on that island and to eliminate Hassain Abad Al Chir, who was actually being financed by the KGB. A bomb was placed in his room at the Olympic Hotel in Nicosia on 25 January 1973, and triggered off by a Mossad agent operating a radio-transmitter. By this time the Israelis had gone a long way towards perfecting the technique of the radio-bomb and were carrying out experiments with the telephone bomb as well.

But on the following day the Israelis lost one of their ablest agents in another part of the world. Baruch Cohen, who had done so much to track down the chiefs of the Palestinian terrorists, and had been mainly responsible for the information leading to the killing of Hamshari, had been lured to Madrid on the promise of vital information by one of his Arab contacts. He was a little apprehensive as to whether this might not be a trap, for Spain was in many ways an ideal territory in which the Palestinian terrorists could operate. Israel had no diplomatic relations with the Spanish Government which had usually adopted a pro-Arab policy in the United Nations. But Cohen felt it was worth the risk. On the morning of Friday 26 January, he set out for his assignment. Within an hour he had been shot dead: his killer was none other than Mohamed Boudia, the man he was hunting down.

In March there were other incidents involving the Palestinians both in the USA and Cyprus. In New York two unexploded bombs were found in abandoned rental cars outside Israeli banks. A further search revealed papers with Black September letter-heads. Then on 12 March, an Israeli businessman, subsequently branded by Egypt as a 'Zionist Intelligence officer', was shot and killed outside his hotel in Nicosia. This time Black September openly claimed responsibility. Three days later the French police arrested two Arabs allegedly trying to smuggle explosives into France to blow up the Israeli Embassy. At last co-operation between the Mossad and French Intelligence was paying off.

On 6 April 1973, the Israelis hit back. Dr. Basil Al-Kubaissi, a professor at the American University in Beirut, was shot dead at point-blank range in Paris. He was believed to have been one of the organisers of explosives supplies for the Arab terrorists. Three days later the Mossad struck again, this time in Cyprus, and the victim was Al Chir's successor as Palestinian link-man with the KGB, Zaiad Muchasi. Once again the bomb technique was employed. The killing was intended to underline the warning that the Black September–KGB network in Cyprus had been blown.

The indiscriminate nature of the Palestinians' terrorism in 1973 actually helped the Israelis. It certainly swung public opinion towards them and silenced the early criticism about a civilised country using 'murder squads'. People began to see that, if the Israelis were taking the law into their own hands, at least they were getting results in the war against world-wide terrorism, which was more than could be said of the supine Western governments who could not agree among themselves as to how to tackle the problem. One singularly ill-conceived outrage of the Palestinians was when on 16 April 1973, a shot was fired through the bedroom window of the home of the New Zealand Chargé d'Affaires. Painted on the house were the words 'Black September': the Jordanian Ambassador had once lived there. And on 27 April an Italian employee of El Al airlines was shot and killed outside a department store in Rome. The police arrested a Lebanese citizen who said he was a member of Black September and had been ordered to kill the Italian because he was an Israeli spy. In this period Arab 'liquidators' disposed of at least three Mossad agents by killings which were made to look like accidents.

Then in March 1973, the Mossad planned what was to be their biggest and most successful 'avenger squad' operation. This was a reprisal for an Arab attempt to blow up the Israeli Embassy in Nicosia. The operation had been planned from the PLO headquarters in Beirut, not from Cyprus, and the Israelis decided it was time to launch a major onslaught in the Lebanon, aimed at invading the PLO headquarters and capturing their secret files,

while at the same time wiping out three prominent Black Septembrists—Mohamed Yusif Najjar, Kemal Adwan and Kamal
Nasser.

This raid was planned in meticulous detail before it took place
on 13 April. Two weeks before, an advance party arrived in
Beirut. All were Mossad agents, but carefully chosen so that they
did not resemble typical Jews, and all had forged passports. One
arrived in the name of Dr. Dieter von Altnoder, a West German
businessman travelling from Rome; another was Gilbert Rimbert,
a Belgian salesman. Both booked in at the Sands Hotel and it was
recalled afterwards that Dr. von Altnoder made inquiries about
facilities for night fishing from the beach of the nearby Ramlet-
el-Beida. Three others arrived at the Coral Hotel in Beirut shortly
afterwards. One had a French passport in the name of Charles
Boussart, describing himself as a management consultant, and
the other two had British passports in the names of George Elder
and Andrew Witchloe. Later another 'Briton' booked in at the
Atlanta Hotel in the name of Andrew Macy, saying he had
arrived from Frankfurt. This advance party, acting individually,
made all the arrangements for the raid, watching the PLO headquarters and noting the daily pattern of movements in and out of
the building, and taking similar action in respect of the apartments of the three victims to be. Under the pretext of night fishing, the beach at Ramlet-el-Beida was also surveyed and marked
down as the 'reception area' for eight commandos.

The commandos were taken by sea to within swimming distance of the beach and, in frogmen's attire, they went quietly
ashore, bringing with them water-proof packages containing
clothes, explosives and radio-transmitters as well as the equipment of professional burglars. The advance party covered their
arrival and provided the commandos with cars. Then the team
split up and set about their missions with admirable precision,
efficiency and economy of time and effort. Within a span of two
hours the Israelis had tracked down and shot dead all three of
their targets: the chief PLO spokesman in Beirut, the leader of
Black September and the organiser of Septembrist operations in
Israel. All documentary evidence in the apartments of the victims
and filing cabinets in PLO headquarters were removed after the
guards had been killed by silenced pistols. There was an element
of television drama in this operation when an Israeli helicopter
descended and took aboard the documentary evidence. All the

agents made their getaway smoothly and without interference, actually driving back to the beach, leaving their cars and making their rendezvous with the stand-by team at sea. It was another example of how the Israeli Secret Service, more than any other Secret Service in the world, is backed up superbly by its armed forces, naval as well as military.

There was a brief announcement in Tel Aviv of 'an action carried out by commando units who arrived in Beirut by road and sea and returned without losses', mentioning that three Al Fatah agents were killed. But that was all and no mention, of course, was made of Secret Service operations. Nevertheless the operation was hailed by the Israeli Cabinet as a massive triumph for the Mossad and Major-General Zamir became almost a folk hero. This quiet, unobtrusive, wiry chief of Intelligence had proved himself to be just as effective as the famous Isser Harel. What was more he had not only personally supervised the 'avenger squad' organisation, but on a number of occasions actually travelled abroad to observe how operations were carried out. This was a tremendous boost to morale among his daredevil agents, for what other Intelligence chief in the whole world took such risks? A Secret Service chief going 'into the field'? It was as revolutionary an idea as a commander-in-chief venturing into the firing line.

It is touches like this which, in its short history, have given the Israeli Secret Service a quality of *élan* and *panache* not possessed by any of its rivals in the field of Intelligence. The Russians are painstaking, ruthlessly efficient, and eternally vigilant, always getting results, yet their methods are still cumbersome and even crude in comparison with those of the Israelis. Their Intelligence hierarchy is remote from their operators and the latter are controlled by fear rather than comradeship. The Israelis have managed to combine in their own set-up the ruthlessness and military approach of the Russians, the flair and *ésprit de corps* of the old-fashioned amateurs of the British Secret Service (prior to 1945, not today) and the intelligence and imagination which have always been a marked feature of French Intelligence. To these qualities they have added the enthusiasm of a young nation, backed up by all the know-how of a tightly knit and ancient religious community.

The full implications of the raid on Beirut did not become obvious to the Lebanese authorities for some time. Their first reaction was that there had been a parachute landing purely by the military; then they discovered about the beach landings and the mysterious tourist who was interested in night fishing. A check was immediately made on hotel registers, but it took a long time for British, Belgian, French and German names to be linked with agents of the Mossad. Interpol and the police of Britain, France, Belgium and West Germany were consulted and it was then discovered that the passports queried were all forged. There were protests from the British and French Foreign Offices to the Israeli Government, but the Israeli Foreign Ministry were able to fob them off with the reply that they knew nothing at all about men masquerading under these passports. They knew perfectly well that the true identity of their agents had never been established.

To strike back in Arab territory was one thing, but the Israelis were well aware that any vengeance killing carried out in Europe or in a non-Arab territory was something quite different. In those cases it was not only essential for the killer not to be discovered, but for his identity to remain a mystery and for all traces of Israeli involvement to be obliterated. Occasionally, if only to boost morale back in Israel, details of such killings were leaked to the press: it was some comfort to the victims of terrorist attacks if they knew that the enemy was being eliminated. But because of the general need for secrecy in such operations most killings carried out by 'avenger squads' were master-minded by a team which took care not only of the get-away, usually by car, but the cover up as well. They also learned that it was just as important to employ women as members of the killer section as men, despite the fact that sometimes it was necessary not merely to eliminate an enemy by a radio-controlled bomb from a distance, but at close quarters to ensure total success. Great care was taken in selecting the actual detailed killers: it was vital that they adopted a totally professional stance and were not squeamish. For all these reasons particular attention was always paid to the method used for killing. The radio-controlled or telephone bomb was employed whenever the 'avenger squad' could be sure that this would get the right victim and when it was necessary to operate well away from the target. But sometimes it was necessary to kill from point-blank range and for this type of killing the Israelis chiefly used a .22 calibre long-barrelled semi-automatic Beretta, normally used for target practice, but specially modified to carry bullets with a very light powder loading. This weapon is especially effective at short range. It had been tried out by Israeli security guards in El Al flights.

The Israelis themselves had adapted the .22 Beretta so that it had an exceptionally light trigger mechanism and was ideal for use by a female. Their second 'avenger squad' weapon was the bomb set off by radio or telephone through a hypersonic signal when the victim is known to be within range. In many respects this latter weapon is the safest and deadliest of all, but when it was tried out on Dr. Mahmoud Hamshari in Paris in late 1972, it did not kill him outright. He was fatally wounded when he answered a telephone call which triggered off the bomb, but lived long enough to be able to tell the French police exactly what had happened—that the bomb went off when he picked up the telephone and that the bomb itself was placed under the telephone table. This discovery by the French police alerted the Arabs to the surprise attack by telephone and radio-bombs, but the Israelis also learned about the discovery of their technique and have since only used this weapon sparingly.

On the whole the Mossad has kept an increasingly tight control over its operators and, to illustrate this, an amusing story is told. A young Palestinian Arab had been sent to Europe on a mission about which the Israelis had no details. They ordered an 'avenger squad' to keep tabs on him. On his way from Paris to the South of France the young Palestinian stopped at an *auberge* for a meal. The Mossad agents immobilised his car while he had a lengthy lunch and telephoned Paris for instructions from their boss.

'We are all ready to scrub him out,' they elatedly informed their chief.

'Don't be so bloody eager,' replied the area chief tersely. 'So far we haven't anything positive against him. He hasn't killed anyone. You've only got to shadow him. You have no right to kill him, and you haven't even any right to tamper with his car. So put it right before he finishes his lunch.'

The Mossad man who tells this story somewhat ruefully added later that the Palestinian left the *auberge* before they could put things right. 'But, when we saw he was having trouble, we went up and asked him if we could lend a hand. He was terribly grateful because I don't think he knew much about cars. He certainly didn't suspect anything and even wanted to pay us for our trouble. But we drew the line at that!'

In the killings of Abdel Hadi Nakaa and Abdel Hamid Shibi

in Rome on 7 June 1973, the technique of the car bomb was reintroduced. So by 28 June 1973, the Israelis had eliminated thirteen key Arab terrorists. On that day they made the number fourteen when at long last they tracked down and finally killed with a car bomb Mohamed Boudia, the head of *Parisienne Orientale*. The Arabs had had some successes; Colonel Yosef Alon, the Israeli air attaché in Washington, had been shot dead as he came out of the garage at his home and the killer was never found. It was suspected that the Black Septembrists had paid a member of the Black Power organisation a considerable sum of money to carry out this attack. But the main Arab success had been in extending their links with other terrorist organisations, chiefly through Carlos, and in protecting the last few key men of the Black Septembrists.

Chief among the latter was Ali Hassan Salameh, the terrorist leader responsible for the Munich massacre and its organising genius. He was the son of Hassan Salameh who had been one of the Arab guerrilla fighters against the Jews before Israel was founded in 1948. Salameh had managed to keep his movements secret for a number of years and the gaps in his dossier were as numerous as those in that of Carlos. He had been associated with the Saiqa guerrilla group and had been trained by the Russians in 1972 in a village outside Moscow, though no positive proof of subsequent relations with the Soviet Union had been obtained. In any event Salameh was a seasoned guerrilla fighter long before this, having been involved in the incident in May 1970, when Black September hi-jacked the Sabena airliner at Lydda airport and having helped plan the Japanese terrorist massacre at the same airport. He was one of the senior Intelligence officers of Al Fatah.[1]

Meanwhile Carlos had changed the name of the *Parisienne Orientale* to the Commando Boudia when he took charge of this cell after Boudia's death. His link-up man was Michel Moukardal, whose cover was that of a jewel merchant travelling between Beirut and Europe. But it was Carlos himself who set up the meetings with the Baader-Meinhof group and Yutaka Furuya, the operations officer of the Japanese Red Army organisation, who sometimes called himself Suzuki, and some envoys of the Irish Republican Army. The first man on Carlos's death list was Lord Sieff, head of Marks and Spencer, and a great supporter of Zionism. The Israelis were hot on the trail of Carlos, but his talent for swiftly changing his identity, his passports and his women made him hard to locate with any regularity. Again it is the experienced Mossad operator who has the apt comment: 'We can cope with any spy, any terrorist except the compulsive lecher. You find him out through one woman and then, lo and behold, he is off with another one and when you catch up with her he has moved on to someone else. And you can be sure that the woman who is left behind never has any idea who her successor might be.'

Heartened by their success up to the end of June 1973, the Israelis decided to launch a European-wide search for Ali Hassan Salameh, who they regarded as the chief of operations of all Black September activities. The Palestinians were now very much on their guard for further Israeli assassination attempts and they made a point of keeping on the move. The Mossad had tracked Salameh from Germany to Paris where he had hidden out in a small hotel on the Left Bank. Two Israeli agents were keeping watch on him and awaiting further instructions when suddenly he gave them the slip. Salameh had been tipped off that the Israelis were 'bugging' him and, pretending over the telephone to make a rendezvous with a friend, he slipped out of the hotel by a side-door.

Now it is fairly clear that from this moment on someone deliberately led the Mossad on a fool's errand and, for once, the whole, normally smooth-working 'avenger squad' was seriously compromised. Perhaps there had been too much complacency; maybe the avengers had become careless. But certainly the Palestinians' counter-intelligence led the Israelis on a disastrous mission to Scandinavia. A tip had been given to a Mossad agent in Switzerland that members of Black September were re-grouping after the attacks on their leaders and planning to move to Scandinavia where they intended to set up 'safe houses' in both Oslo and somewhere on the outskirts of Stockholm. From these bases they would plan new attacks on aircraft and Israeli embassies in Northern Europe. The report seemed reasonably factual, it gave names and made sense in the light of what had happened. The Israelis knew that Sweden was a favourite haunt of the terrorists.

But some of the Intelligence analysers in Tel Aviv were worried about the tip. They thought it was almost too good to be true. As one of them said: 'It was all too flip, especially as we got three reports all at once, including one from Geneva about a Black Septembrist leaving for Denmark, another from Zurich about the move to Sweden and another from Paris saying that Salameh had left France and was on his way to Denmark or Norway. What made me suspicious was that no other Intelligence Service —neither the British, the CIA nor the French—had any inkling of this. There was no confirmation. Even the report we got in Paris was from an agent who had just returned from Switzerland. The Swiss Intelligence were, as usual, totally uncooperative. It is always difficult for an Israeli to operate inside Switzerland because of that silent hostility of officialdom. An Arab terrorist may get away with it, but a Mossad man is always followed and frustrated at every turn. And the Swiss Intelligence never cooperate.'

The Israeli was right in his hunch. There was an attempt to set up the 'avenger squads' and to lure them away from the real targets. But the powers-that-be, probably feeling that one more big push would quickly eliminate the other names on the death list, decided to make one more effort to locate Salameh and his allies. Meanwhile some of the last 'avenger squad' had been sent on leave; they had spent months tracking down the terrorists, often risking their lives and just missing being captured on a number of occasions. So the Mossad made their second mistake by operating with a hastily picked new team. It is true that this included some who had been on similar assignments, but none of them had operated in Scandinavia. Nevertheless the Mossad decided that at least one member of the team must have knowledge of the terrain. They chose a girl named Marianne who had dual Swedish and Israeli nationality and who had emigrated to Israel two years previously and worked in an Israeli Intelligence office. She had actually volunteered to go and act as an agent.

It was not long before the trail led directly to Norway, first to Oslo and then about a hundred miles north to the tiny Norwegian inland resort of Lillehammer, not far from the Swedish border. A more unlikely spot for espionage activities could hardly be imagined; it was small, everyone knew everyone else and the presence of strangers could not fail to be noticed, even though it was a small tourist area. And, by their own normally meticulous standards, the Mossad made another mistake: hitherto they had usually operated with a mere two agents moving in to locate suspects, even when they could easily be lost in the total anonymity of a vast city. They sent no fewer than ten to Lillehammer!

There were, of course, special circumstances. The view of the Mossad chiefs was that the sooner all those names on the death list could be ticked off, the safer Israel and the non-Arab world would be, and that it was highly desirable that the 'avenger squads' could complete all their missions by the end of the year. Time, they argued, was on the side of the Palestinians, not of Israel. The other special circumstance was that for once the Mossad would be operating in a territory which was well disposed towards Israel and where they had close, unofficial contacts with the Norwegian Intelligence. The situation in Norway was in many respects ideally suited for a Mossad-controlled operation, whereas in Sweden and Denmark there were pro-Arab sympathisers and even spies inside the police and Intelligence Services. Perhaps it was for this reason that Major-General Zvi Zamir took the brave decision to supervise the whole operation personally and went to Oslo for this purpose. It is perhaps worth while recording that the chief of Britain's MI6 had a similar opportunity on at least three occasions between 1937 and the outbreak of war in 1939, when there were plots to eliminate Hitler, but not only did he fail to give a personal lead, he vetoed every proposal. A Secret Service killing then might have saved a lot of lives and six years of war. Israel's Intelligence chiefs have without exception all been men of great personal bravery with the confidence to take dangerous decisions. And by deciding to go to Norway to supervise this dangerous mission, fraught as it was with all manner of diplomatic shoals and hazards, Zvi Zamir should not be blamed too much if things went wrong.

The 'avenger squad' in Lillehammer soon located the alleged Black Septembrist courier who was supposed to have left Geneva with messages for Ali Salameh. He was followed and watched as he met an Arab at a local café. But it was on the vital question of establishing positive identification that the Mossad team slipped up. For this they relied too much on newly recruited, inexperienced sub-agents. There was from all accounts a dispute on the subject. However, a majority of the team identified the Arab as Ali Salameh.

The attempt to locate Salameh coincided with the hi-jacking of a Japan Airlines plane travelling from Amsterdam to Tokyo. This was carried out by Arab and Japanese terrorists and Israeli

Intelligence believed that the plane might be directed for some operation over Israel itself. In fact the plane was taken on to Dubai and then Benghazi where the hi-jackers blew it up. This incident must have provided a further excuse for urgent action in Lillehammer. For this reason Tel Aviv flashed a message to the 'avenger team's' headquarters in Oslo to go ahead with the killing of Salameh.

On the evening of 21 July 1973, the man the team believed to be Salameh was walking hand in hand with a woman when a car drew up alongside them. A man and a woman jumped out and fired a volley of shots at him. The Arab was killed immediately and the woman, who was Norwegian, was unhurt.

But the man the Mossad agents had killed was not Ali Salameh, but Ahmed Bouchiki, a Moroccan waiter at a local health farm.

19

Disaster at Lillehammer

Experience, the name men give to their mistakes.

(GEORGE BERNARD SHAW)

THE CATASTROPHE at Lillehammer included not merely killing the wrong man, but the detection and arrest of the 'avenger squad'. It was in fact the nadir of the Israeli Secret Service, not so much because of the incident itself, but of all the other factors in the case. Zamir had been on the spot; thus the head of the Mossad was himself personally involved in a Secret Service blunder. This inevitably meant that all the criticisms and doubts which had been prevalent towards the end of Harel's reign regarding the activities of the Mossad were once again voiced by members of the Knesset. Also the arrests made by the Norwegians, the publicity attaching to the subsequent legal proceedings and the counter-propaganda put out by the Arabs did not help the Israeli cause.

'In the end it was Norway, a good friend of Israel and hardly a traditional backcloth for Israeli–Palestinian violence, that put a stop to it,' wrote Colin Smith.[1] He was referring to the Mossad-controlled 'WOG' teams in Europe. Smith described Bouchiki as 'a Moroccan disc jockey connected with Al Fatah', and another report called him 'the PLO representative in Scandinavia'. The pro-Arab press insisted that he was an innocent victim, that he had never in any way been associated with any guerrilla movement. Certainly he was not Ali Salameh, but throughout the Israeli campaign against the Black Septembrist killers the latter had found their defenders, especially in Britain and France. Lady Richmond had written to the British press claiming that Dr. Basil Al-Kubaissi was 'a harmless Iraqi scholar', while another letter writer, Eleanor Aitken from Cambridge, stated that 'Kamal Nasser . . . hated violence. Palestinians gave him the nickname "Addanir"—Voice of Conscience.'[2]

In France, too, there were murmurings against what the pro-
Arabists called 'Israeli terrorists' and it was forcibly brought
home to Tel Aviv that the wave of encouragement which Israel
had received when first embarking on the vengeance killings was
now receding fast. Added to this was the pressure being brought
upon Israeli diplomats, most notably in Britain and France, that
terrorism in their territories had got to stop. In Britain this
message was irrelevant and uncalled for, as no attempts at
vengeance killings had been made in that country, but in the
seventies both Tory and Labour Prime Ministers had allowed
themselves to be influenced by the hard core of pro-Arabist Civil
Servants in the Foreign Office. On the other hand, the killings
in France of Palestinian terrorists had aroused a certain amount
of anger among the parties of the Left and the Communist fellow-
travellers.

In so small a place as Lillehammer it did not take the Norwegian
police long to learn that a party of foreigners in hired self-drive
cars had arrived in the resort. Messages were exchanged between
Lillehammer and Oslo and a watch was kept on all travellers
between the two places. For once the getaway plans were not
effectively carried out. Almost everything that could go wrong
went wrong, despite the fact that the Norwegian Intelligence
was secretly co-operating with the Mossad as it had been in the
case of the five gunboats. David Tinnin in his book, *Hit Team*,
states categorically that 'there is little doubt that the Norwegian
Intelligence Services covertly assisted the Israelis. They refused
to co-operate with investigation by their own police, and refused
to assist the state prosecutors when the six Israeli agents were
brought to trial. Journalists covering the story were pointedly
warned off, not only by the Norwegian Intelligence, but by the
security forces in their own countries.'[3]

There was no question but that this particular 'avenger squad'
had been weakened by the inclusion of one or two newcomers.
Two of the squad—Dar Ert (or Aerbel), a Danish-born Israeli
who had had little experience, and Marianne Gladnikoff, the
Swedish girl—were traced and arrested within a few hours. Four
others were caught within a day. The situation might have been
even worse as none of them seems to have been able to warn
either Major-General Zamir or his aides in Oslo that the whole
plan had misfired. They only heard the news on the radio and
then, probably with the assistance of allies in Norwegian Intelli-

gence, escaped from Oslo by an unknown route before the police caught up with them. If the head of the Mossad had been arrested, the catastrophe might have been total.

Unquestionably the operation had been deliberately infiltrated and upset by a double-agent, possibly even by two or three double-agents, with each supplying confirmation for the others' planted information. Inquiries since suggest that this luring of the Mossad teams to northern Europe was not altogether unconnected with the Egyptian–Syrian moves towards the attack on Israel which was launched some weeks later. It was more than just a decoy movement to lure the 'avenger squads' away from their real targets; another motive was to distract the Mossad's attention from war preparations. No doubt, in Palestinian minds, the greatest success of all was the fact that Zvi Zamir went to Oslo. But apart from all this the operation was most untypically bungled by amateurs who left clues all over the place. For example, when the Norwegian police found two people with Canadian passports in the names of Leslie and Patricia Roxburger, they spotted among their possessions the ex-directory telephone number of the Mossad man in Oslo, who happened to be security officer at the Israeli Embassy. This in turn led the police to the Mossad man's apartment where two other Israeli agents were found.

How many got away from Norway without being arrested is still not clear. Certainly all the key members of the 'squad' and those directing it escaped. But those remaining were brought to trial and in due course found guilty and sentenced for 'participation with foreknowledge in a second-degree murder'. The Norwegians knew full well that the real killers had got away and their tolerant, indeed benevolent, system of justice benefited the accomplices. Sylvia Rafael and Abraham Gehmer were sentenced to five and a half years in prison. Dar Ert got five years, Marianne Gladnikoff was convicted of being involved in manslaughter and given a thirty-month sentence and Zwi Steinberg, the principal getaway driver, one year. One man was acquitted.

There was a curious incident during the trial which reveals something of the dilettantism of the Lillehammer operation. Dar Ert told the court that he had asked his interrogator to check his evidence by calling 'Miko' in Tel Aviv at a certain number. At this point the other prisoners protested that the court should be closed to the press and the public. It was a somewhat stupid point to make as by that time the journalists had rushed out to put through their own calls to this Tel Aviv number. All they got was a pre-recorded voice stating that 'this is no longer a working number' in English. The probability was that the more experienced agents among the prisoners were trying to warn Dar Ert to be careful what he revealed in open court.

Luckily for the Israelis and those of their 'avenger squad' who were sentenced, they were operating in one of the benignest countries in Europe, for the Norwegians mix quixotic courage with a passion for tolerance and leniency towards ill-doers. In fact none of those sentenced served longer than two years in jail, some very much less.

These were the days of seering experience for the Mossad. It was not long afterwards that Major-General Zvi Zamir retired and became the chairman of a building company. Others were more fortunate: the Mossad man in charge of the whole operation, who escaped from Norway, not only survived in his profession, but was asked to join the Special Mossad Committee of Inquiry into the Lillehammer affair. Others were given a second chance in the light of experience gained. But one member of the squad was peremptorily dismissed for having identified the wrong man.

Marianne Gladnikoff was set free after fifteen months and, after a brief visit to Israel, returned to Sweden. Gehmer was released together with Sylvia Rafael after some twenty-two months and both retained their posts with the Mossad. Sylvia Rafael is especially worthy of mention as an example of the new emancipated female secret agent, the modern and much more efficient counterpart of Mata Hari. Indeed, to mention Sylvia in the same breath as Mata Hari is almost to insult her: she is in every respect her superior, professional throughout, attractive, yet the equal of any male agent, and a delightful personality.

Sylvia is the 'pin-up girl' of the Mossad and people of many nationalities who have met her testify to her real life personification of the kind of female spy all film producers dream about. I quote from a Norwegian who interviewed her on a number of occasions: 'Sylvia Rafael was, shall we say, not so dedicated and ruthless an operator as the "Hit Team's" chief female killer—the one we did not capture. That we know from outside evidence. But I am willing to bet that she was a better all-rounder, a shrewd digger of information and in the long run a more efficient spy. When we interviewed her, we suddenly found that she was also interviewing us! She had the gift to turn a question put to herself into a question to us. Sometimes we fell for it. She was chic, attractive, with a terrific personality and eyes that looked at you and made shooting stars flare across your own eyes. A sweater, ski pants, a locket on a chain and a passion for surrounding herself with beautiful things—that was Sylvia.'

He might also have added that Sylvia's sense of humour was one of her chief attributes. During her spell in prison she passed the time by playing the guitar, studying psychology and Hebrew (which previously she had understood only slightly) and writing a diary which she illustrated with her own amusing sketches. Excerpts from the diaries were later published in Israeli, South African and Norwegian newspapers.

When the Norwegian State Prosecutor went to hospital following an accident, Sylvia sent him a greetings card of sympathy, signing it '005$\frac{1}{2}$ The Spy Who Came in from the Cold'. The '5$\frac{1}{2}$' was a subtle reminder of her five and a half years' sentence which ultimately she did not serve in full. When she got back to Israel her sudden notoriety had preceded her and she was given a reception marked by flag waving, flowers and dancing when she visited the kibbutz Ramat-Hakovsh which voted her an honorary member while she was in prison.

All the members of the 'avenger squad' who had been in Norway were closely guarded for some time afterwards as their identities had in some cases been blown and they were obvious targets for reprisals. There were attempts by the Palestinians to copy the Israelis by launching revenge assassinations, but it is a mark of the Shabak's efficiency as well as the Mossad's that they never succeeded. Indeed, it was soon clear to the Palestinians that to go ahead with such plans would inevitably lead to further decimations in their own ranks.

A story appeared in the press in 1976 that the Israeli authorities had offered $300,000 to stop publication of a book about 'an alleged Israeli attempt to kill a Palestine guerrilla which ended in the death of the wrong man'.[4] The Norwegian newspaper *Aftenposten* stated that the offer was made by an Israeli, linked to his country's embassy in Paris, to the book's two authors, Dag Christensen of *Aftenposten* and David Tinnin of *Time Magazine*. The newspaper went on to say that Israel tried to prevent publication because the book gave a far from flattering picture of the efficiency of the Israeli Secret Service in the murder at Lillehammer. Israel Radio made an instant reply to this allegation, claiming there was 'little in the book which had not been published before apart from a love interest between two members of the Israeli group'. They added that there was little point in trying to stop publication, but that *Aftenposten* might have been misled for publicity purposes.

It is hard to quarrel with the Israel Radio claim because, apart from pin-pointing the story of the killing of the wrong man, there is nothing in the book that does any serious harm to the Israeli cause or to their Secret Service. This view has been confirmed to me in private by knowledgeable Israelis who accepted that—to quote one of them who actually knows two members of the 'avenger squad'—'basically the material in the book is accurate and not at all harmful'. Some people who read the book complained that is was anti-Arab in its content: Eleanor Aitken wrote from Cambridge to the *Sunday Times* that 'The label "Black September" which David Tinnin seems to apply indiscriminately to all victims of Israeli official terrorism since Munich raises doubts about his impartiality.' In any event some of the information about the Lillehammer catastrophe had already appeared in newspapers and at least one other book, while the trial itself had been covered by the press.

The Mossad soon formed a fairly accurate picture of what went wrong at Lillehammer and how it was through the machinations of an Arab agent posing as a friend of the Israelis who not only directed the team to the wrong man, but also tipped off the Norwegian police. The agent in question is safely in Switzerland where he seems to have the devoted protection of Swiss Intelligence as well as that of the Arabs. This is yet another example of the curious one-sidedness of Swiss Intelligence in the Arab–Israeli dispute.

Ali Hassan Salameh may well have praised Allah that it was not he who was gunned down in Lillehammer, but the Mossad gave him very little respite afterwards. They were soon on his trail when news came that he was living in Beirut. On 10 December 1974, three PLO offices in Beirut were severely damaged by rocket attacks. Four people were reported to have been injured. The rockets, equipped with timing devices, had been strapped to the roof racks of three cars parked near the PLO headquarters.

The cars had been rented by four men, holding British, Irish, Mexican and West German passports, who had left the country before the attacks. It was suspected that this was the work of the Israelis and two days later the office of the agency which had rented a car to the man with the West German passport, was destroyed by a bomb.

During the civil war in the Lebanon another 'avenger squad' was sent to that city to hunt down Salameh. In the middle of 1975 he was traced to an apartment in Beirut and watch was kept on it. One night the silhouette of a man they believed to be Salameh was seen through a window by the Mossad assassin bending over his rifle with its telescopic sights. He fired, but the 'silhouette' turned out to be a dummy. By this time Black Septembrists were taking new measures in evasion tactics. A year later, on 7 October 1976, the Israelis finally caught up with Salameh, who was now operating under the code-name of Abu Hassan and closely linked to the mysterious Carlos. He continued to indulge in his taste for expensive silk shirts and fashionable suits which partly proved to be his undoing. He had acquired an extensive and highly paid network of agents who protected him, sometimes even getting advance information of Mossad moves. He changed his address frequently, but still master-minded terrorist coups all over the Middle East and further afield.

On this last occasion Salameh was shot, critically wounded and taken to hospital, but, though first reported as killed, he survived to carry on with his work.

Latterly it has become much harder for the Mossad to track down and eliminate the remaining leaders of the Palestinian groups. Except for the killing of Mahmoud Saleh, head of the PLO office, in Paris on 4 January 1977, the Israelis have not had much success. Carlos has survived despite the fact that in their search for him the Israelis have had assistance from American, British and French Intelligence Services. After lying low for a considerable time, Carlos himself became a professional assassin on 30 December 1974, when he is believed to have fired the shot which seriously wounded Lord Sieff, and followed this up with a personal hand grenade attack on the Israeli Hapoalim Bank.

At this stage the Mossad entered into one of their periodic unofficial secret conferences with other Intelligence Services. They compared notes with the British DI6 and French security agents and found that the quest for Carlos was to some extent complicated by the fact that he was supposed to have a double, directed by the KGB, who could be used at any given moment either as a decoy or another killer. The Mossad suggested that the best way to catch Sanchez would be to keep a tail on the Japanese Red Army contact in Paris. Shortly afterwards the French, acting on this proposal, arrested the Japanese at Orly airport. In his possession were three passports and several hundred thousand dollars in forged currency, but after three weeks' close questioning he gave away no worthwhile clues. It was not surprising, for Furuya, the Japanese in question, was convinced his fellow terrorists would find some way of rescuing him. Carlos was his ally: he sent members of his Commando Boudia to the Hague to inspect the French Embassy for the Japanese Red Army. On 13 September 1974, three Japanese terrorists invaded the Embassy. After five days the French gave in to them and Furuya was released and flown to Syria with $300,000 in ransom money.

Meanwhile Carlos had also master-minded various attacks on pro-Israeli institutions in Paris, including right-wing French daily newspapers. Convinced that he had the measure of the French, he organised an attack on an El Al flight at Orly airport, believing the Israeli Foreign Minister to be aboard. It was one of the most daring attacks by terrorists ever launched, the weapons used being two RPG-7s, but they missed the El Al plane and hit a Yugoslav airliner instead. Yugoslav dissidents were blamed for the incident. Three days later another attempt was made to fire an RPG at an El Al plane at Orly, but this was thwarted by the French security. None the less the terrorists managed to take hostages and even negotiated their escape. Shortly afterwards Carlos was reported as having been seen in London and there was a security alert at Heathrow airport.

But in London Carlos had talkative girl friends and once again he had to be on the move. The French claimed to trace him to Bangkok, but the Mossad, with their persistent, relentless efficiency, never undermined by countless setbacks, told them that Carlos was still in Paris. The French officer in charge of these operations muttered something about a double for Carlos being used once more.

'A double?' queried the Israelis. 'Maybe yes, maybe no, but Carlos Sanchez exists and what is more everything points to the fact that he is being professionally directed by the KGB. He is on loan to the PFLP, while being used for other operations as well. He has at least four passports in different names and different nationalities. His Commando Boudia has as many Europeans as Arabs among its members.'

Carlos's next operation was to plant a quarter of a million dollars in counterfeit currency inside Israel and to sell it on the black market. But the plot was rumbled and his agents were caught. In June 1975, the French—again thanks to a Mossad tip—arrested Moukarbal, Carlos's go-between. He talked and betrayed Carlos, though somewhat reluctantly, leading the police to his apartment. It was a singularly clumsy operation by the French DST agents, as Carlos was quick on the draw and killed Moukarbal and the agents. He escaped through a window and disappeared to Eastern Europe for a spell. From then on he has been constantly hunted by the Mossad, in Czechoslovakia, in Switzerland, where he re-emerged in Zurich, and in Austria. In December 1975, Carlos again hit the headlines when he led the raid on OPEC headquarters in Vienna. He is now being hunted by the Mossad, the British SIS, France's DST and SDECE and SAVAK, the Iranian Secret Service, Iran is detested by the Palestinians because the Shah still insists on selling oil to Israel.

Raids carried out by Mossad agents in Vienna and Berlin, after which the Austrian and German police were warned, revealed that quantities of a nerve gas, tabun, developed by the Nazis in World War II, had fallen into the hands of terrorist groups. It was later established that a parcel which contained an explosive charge wired to a phial of the gas had been discovered by the American postal authorities. The parcel had been sent from an Arab country and the *Boston Globe*, which reported the affair, linked this deadly weapon with the terrorist, Carlos.

The story of the gas phial in the post is just a little too slick; there seems no doubt that one was sent, that the CIA were tipped off and the incident received publicity. But the person who posted it from an Arab country was probably an Israeli agent who was trying to seek publicity for the discoveries which the Mossad had made in Vienna and Berlin. On 27 February 1976, police in gas masks raided the Vienna home of Johann Konigstorfer, alias John Kuz, seizing him and his fiancée, a Hilton Hotel hostess. In the cellar of the house occupied by the girl's unsuspecting mother, they found the deadly nerve gas in bottles and cans. It had been air-freighted from West Berlin by its producer, Richard Konigstorfer, the 25-year-old brother of the Vienna suspect.

The other elusive Arab terrorist tracked down by the Israelis was Abu Daoud, a member of the inner council of Black September. He was wanted by them for a number of terrorist crimes and was said to be wanted by the West German police for his role in the Munich killings. Daoud claimed to have been in Sofia at the time of the attack on the Israeli Olympic team, but according to Mossad informants he had gone to Munich early in 1972 to plan the whole affair, using an Iraqi passport in the name of Saad-a-din-Wali. Because he spoke German he was able to make contact with one of the people who had planned the building of the Olympic village and through him got information on its lay-out. In February 1973, he was caught and sentenced to death in Jordan for his part in a failed commando raid aimed at kipnapping the entire Jordanian Cabinet. The sentence provoked a wave of protests throughout the Arab world and from the USSR. The attacks on the Saudi Arabian embassies in Khartoum and Paris were launched partly with the intention of forcing Abu Daoud's release. In September 1973, King Hussein ordered his sentence to be commuted to life imprisonment and shortly afterwards he was set free.

Then in January 1977, Abu Daoud, still travelling under his Iraqi alias, went to Paris to attend the funeral of Mahmud Saleh, the Palestinian who had been shot dead outside his bookshop on the Left Bank of the Seine. The French DST, acting in collusion with the Mossad, moved swiftly; they arrested him without the authorisation of President Giscard d'Estaing, or the Foreign Minister or the Minister of the Interior. The Arab states immediately denounced this as an 'unfriendly act', while Israel asked France to hold Abu Daoud pending a request for his extradition. What acutely embarrassed the French Government and the President was that Giscard d'Estaing had been seeking the role of arbitrator in the Middle East since his election in 1974 and had closely co-operated with President Sadat. It was feared in governmental circles that the arrest would harm talks between PLO representatives and Israeli peace campaigners which had been secretly taking place in France. There was also the incredible fact that the day before he was arrested, Abu Daoud had been welcomed as an official member of a Palestinian delegation by the Foreign Affairs Ministry.

Behind all this was secret agreement between members of the Mossad and the French DST that something ought to be done, not merely about Abu Daoud, but the increasing number of terrorists who came in and out of France with impunity. All this was not unconnected with their mutual concern about Carlos and the stepped-up co-operation between terrorists of several nations. Both the Mossad and the DST viewed the secret Palestinian talks with scepticism, if not downright mistrust, and they would have been quite happy to see them break down: to arrest Abu Daoud was one way to achieve this. What, however, was not so clear was whether the Israeli Cabinet wished to see the talks break down. There was evidence that the Prime Minister and others had actually encouraged the contacts being made.

But in terms of international law and order, not to mention considerations of honour and respect for treaties, there can be no question that when on 11 January 1977, the French released Abu Daoud and let him go to Algiers, they gave a boost to terrorism and failed to back up the Common Market countries' agreed concerted policy against terrorism.

Various changes in the Israeli Secret Service were made during the years immediately following the Lillehammer disaster. Major-General Zvi Zamir was eventually followed as chief of the Mossad by Major-General Yitzhak Hofi in September 1974, though, according to custom, no official announcement was made and the appointment was kept secret. This round-faced veteran officer is a native-born Israeli, just over fifty years of age. He was already a Palmach officer in his late teens and he served in the 1948 War of Independence as company commander in the first battalion of Palmach's crack Yiftah Brigade. After independence he made the Israeli Army his career, becoming the first instructor at the Officers' Training College and he then served under Generals Yigal Allon and Moshe Dayan as Operations Officer, Southern Command.

Eventually Hofi was given a battalion command in the Givati Brigade, after which he taught in the new Command and Staff College. Before and during the 1956 Sinai campaign he was deputy commander of the Paratroop Brigade under Ariel Sharon, from whom he learned a great deal which stood him in good stead later. The two men were about the same age and each took a keen interest in the techniques of military intelligence. Brigadier-General Ariel Sharon had been active in Haganah as a youth and took part in 'Operation Dany' in 1948. He was Regimental Intelligence Officer in the War of Independence and later appointed Intelligence Officer to the Central and Northern Commands. In 1952 he went to the Hebrew University to undertake special studies. Put in charge of the celebrated 'Unit 101', he went on numerous reprisal operations, being wounded in one of them. Later 'Unit 101' became part of the Paratroop Regiment and Sharon was made its commanding officer, again undertaking a number of reprisal raids. In between these operations he studied law. During the Six-Day War Sharon was head of the Brigade group which broke through Egyptian fortified positions in Um Katel, Abu Ageila, Bir Hassna and to the Mitleh Straits.

Major-General Hofi was eventually appointed Paratroop Brigade Commander, a factor which was undoubtedly of some considerable influence when the highly successful Entebbe raid was made in 1976. A study course at the US Army Command and General Staff College was followed by his appointment from 1965–68 as Chief of Staff 'G' Branch Operations Department and in connection with this Hofi was praised by the Chief of Operations, Major-General Ezer Weizmann for his 'great contribution to victories' in the Six-Day War. It was in 1968 that he was promoted to Brigadier-General as deputy chief of Operations and in the following year he became a Major-General as Commander of the Training Branch. Thus Hofi has had all-round experience in the Israeli Army and one of his special talents is a rare gift of being able to impart difficult instructions to others and at the same time to inspire them to carry these out efficiently. He is both a gifted instructor and a morale booster, vital talents for the head of a Secret Service which has always got to be on a war footing.

In the summer of 1972, Hofi took over the Northern Command from General Mordecai Gur (who became military attaché in Washington) and he commanded the northern front in the 1973 war. Before that war Hofi, who had become something of an authority on intelligence, repeatedly warned of the probability of a Syrian attack and demanded reinforcements. Some of these he got and the war might otherwise have gone much worse for Israel. By January 1974, he was Chief of Operations and, following Chief of Staff David Elazar's resignation in April of that year, he replaced him for a brief period until General Gur took over. It has been said that the Israeli Army desperately wanted Hofi to stay with them, but he resigned in July 1974, and shortly after this became the new Memuneh.

There was never any shortage of volunteers for 'avenger squads' operating against Arab guerrillas. The successes of the Israeli Army had created a *mystique* and an aura around the special branches which undertook semi-Secret Service missions. In July 1975, it was reported that a former Israeli paratroop officer was trying to form volunteer death squads to operate against Arab guerrilla bases in Southern Lebanon.[5] The Israeli newspaper, *Ma'ariv* confirmed this. It identified the officer only as 'Lieutenant Eitan H', describing him as tall and athletic and said to have served on the Suez Canal front in the 1973 war under the command of Major-General Ariel Sharon, who had by this time been promoted. The mysterious officer involved in this recruitment scheme was in fact anxious to cast his net rather wider in search for talent, seeking volunteers to form the 'July Unit', an acronym for 'fight to the death', to wipe out guerrillas. He told the newspaper that he was not trying to establish a partisan group, but one which would have the blessing of the Israeli security authorities. It also stated that he had asked General Sharon to command the force. By this time General Sharon was an opposition member of the Knesset, but it was understood that the new Defence Minister, Shimon Peres, had asked him to return to active service for 'special duties' which had not then been publicly defined.[6]

Perhaps in the light of the continual battle between Israelis and Arabs in the terrorist war, these comments by Abu Daoud in an interview in Algiers on 14 January 1977, will illustrate the theme of this chapter, 'I arrived in Paris as an official delegate of the PLO. The French DST knew that one of my main aims was to expose the assassin of Mahmoud Saleh. We were making an inquiry into the killing. That was my mission. The DST and the Israelis knew that I was beginning to shed some light on the question. The DST are implicated in the affair and are covering for the Israelis. I tell you, if I had photographs in front of me, I could point out to them the person who killed Saleh. . . . So, of course, I was arrested by the DST, which is most irregular, and in co-operation with the Israelis. . . . I did not do Munich. I mean, just look at the Israeli demand for extradition. The French showed it to me. It mentioned a name—not even the name of my Iraqi passport, but the name of Mohamed Daoud Audeh, saying

quite simply that that person was a member of a terrorist organisation. For us that name is like Smith or Jones in England. We
have three people of that name in our office in Algiers alone. I
have never used that name, but they could have arrested hundreds
of Palestinians or Arabs who do bear it.'[7]

These were sophistries. Abu Daoud ('Father of David') was the
code-name in the Palestinian movement of Daoud Silwani, who
was named after the village from which he came. The West
German police are in no doubt whatsoever that this man visited
Munich twice before the massacre took place, the second time
only a few days before and that he was the main planner of the
outrage.

As for the other elusive terrorist, Carlos, he was last reported
to be moving around the Persian Gulf in 1977. Early in January
that year he was seen in Dubai which he visited on a Jordanian
passport. His base is believed to be Baghdad, where he was given
sanctuary following his Vienna coup in December 1975. But he
is also believed to have close links with Yugoslav terrorists among
the anti-Tito front and has more than once slipped into Belgrade
unobserved.

20

Lessons of the
Yom Kippur War

We are never deceived; we deceive ourselves.

(JOHANN WOLFGANG VON GOETHE)

IN THE MEDIA the view has constantly been reiterated that all the kudos which the Israeli Secret Service won for itself in the Six-Day War was almost totally lost by its failings in the Yom Kippur War. This is, however, very far from being the truth. Admittedly, wrong interpretations of intelligence were made before the war of 1973 was finally launched by the Arabs, but it would be quite wrong to suggest that this was due to poor intelligence.

The truth was that the Israeli Intelligence system was working just as smoothly in the early autumn of 1973 as it had been on the eve of the Six-Day War, but the administrative machinery responsible for acting on that intelligence was beginning to creak. There was obviously scope for changes in this direction and it was to the credit of the Israeli Government that they acted as speedily as is possible in a democracy.

One of the important points to bear in mind in any assessment of the Israeli Secret Service is that, though at times it may act as ruthlessly and authoritatively as, say, the KGB, or its rivals in the Middle East, it belongs to a democratic state. This fact is sometimes overlooked, but even the Mossad has to some extent to take public opinion into account. There have been times when Israel's intelligence system, excellent as it is, has been criticised in the Israeli press, and there has often been a witch-hunt for scapegoats in this field. The Lavon Affair showed how a Secret Service can go so far and then suddenly find itself out on a limb, with its critics baying for sackings and resignations. And one of the factors which militated against the Israeli Secret Service in the autumn of 1973 was that at that moment critics of both the

Mossad and Aman were highly vocal in circles close to the Government.

There was a certain amount of justification for such criticism for it must have seemed at the time that the Israeli Secret Service had been paying far too much attention to hunting down terrorists in Norway in the previous July and too little to watching movements just the other side of the border. In the desire to find a scapegoat after the Yom Kippur War of 1973 it was all too easy to assert that if the Mossad had been more alert and less anxious to trail individual killers, all might have been different. And there is absolutely no doubt that Black September laid a perfect smoke-screen for detracting attention from the real threat to Israel.

But, as will be seen, this was only part of the story and the deductions drawn from it are unjust to the Mossad, which, in fact, never lost sight of the major issue. The real criticism that can be legitimately made is that there was a lack of adequate co-ordination of intelligence reports in 1973 and nothing approaching the same degree of co-operation between the Mossad and Aman as there had been in 1967. The latter had shown a tendency to cast doubt on some Mossad reports which, as was subsequently revealed, were correct. While one reason for this was the mistrust of the Mossad felt by some members of the Israeli Cabinet after the Lillehammer disaster, there had also been a lamentable lack of self-confidence in the hierarchy of Aman in this vital period. A possible reason for this was that Aman had changed their chiefs far more frequently than the Mossad. It is one of the great failings of the Intelligence Services of all armed forces that they change their directors far too often. In wartime the British Naval Intelligence Division was for the best part of half a century one of the most formidable intelligence organisations in the world. Between the wars it sank to abysmal levels of incompetence because, due to a futile Service bureaucratic custom, the post of Director was changed almost every year, and sometimes more frequently. As often as not it went to the man next in line for this type of promotion, not to the one most suitable for the job. In one instance it actually went to a man who was blatantly pro-German at a time when Hitler was our prospective adversary.

Israel never fell into quite the same error. Almost all her Military Intelligence chiefs have been men of high intellectual capacity. Nevertheless their appointments have often been far too brief. This particularly applied to the relative newcomer at the head of Aman in 1973, Major-General Eliyahu Zeira.

Things might have been very different if one of the most efficient and reliable senior agents of Israeli Intelligence had not been killed in Sinai during the Six-Day War. This was a tremendous loss, for not only were his reports given the greatest credence, but his opinions and interpretations weighed enormously with the senior officers in Aman and the Mossad.

The facts from all sides—Israeli, American and other independent observers—seem to indicate that there was ample intelligence coming into Tel Aviv as early as May 1973, that the Egyptians were preparing for a war in the very near future. Aerial photographs showed additional defences, ramparts and bunkers being built and that there were constant movements up to the west bank of the Suez Canal. Early that month some highly competent junior officers in Aman took the view that war was imminent. But Major-General Zeira did not agree. It was a critical misjudgement, common sense should have made him pay more attention to the opinions of the war forecasters, if only because the Six-Day War, while admittedly giving Israel the advantage of a greater aerial warning space, had deprived her of such an advantage on land approaches. And it was on land rather than in the air that Israel had reason to fear her adversaries.

Drew Middleton, the *New York Times* correspondent, stated that 'as early as 24 September 1973, the United States, the CIA and the NSA (the latter specialising in electronic intelligence) were convinced that the major Arab attack was coming and warned Israel. The Israeli Command rejected the warning. They were too confident in their knowledge of the Arabs and underestimated their potential enemies' ability to keep secrets.'[1]

This was partly true, but somewhat unfair. With the benefit of hindsight, US civilian and military intelligence experts later 'studied with dismay the errors of the Israelis in evaluating their own information and the material made available to them by Western Intelligence Services', as Drew Middleton recorded. But the United States does not appear to have had all that faith in its own reports prior to the Yom Kippur War; certainly it made no effort to impress their accuracy upon the Israelis. If the Israelis had lessons to learn from the Yom Kippur War, so too had the Americans. For it would seem that somebody, somewhere in the States Department or the White House deliberately ignored the warnings of the CIA and the NSA just as much as Major-General Zeira refused to accept the reports coming in to him.

Much later the *New York Times* published brief extracts from a secret report which stated that 'the US Intelligence community acknowledged that it failed to predict the 1973 Arab–Israeli War and that several Intelligence agencies even predicted there would be no war only hours before hostilities broke out.'[2] The *New York Times* added that this report was compiled by the Committee charged with advising the National Security Council on war and critical situations. The Committee had met on the very day that the Arab forces were to attack Israel and they stated that 'we can find no hard evidence of a major co-ordinated Egyptian–Syrian offensive across the Canal and into the Golan Heights area'.[3]

General Dayan himself seems to suggest in his biography that the Israelis and the Americans shared the same viewpoint at the time. He writes 'at the beginning of October 1973, the Israeli Intelligence Branch [presumably Aman] reported that the Egyptians were engaging in military exercises but not preparing to launch a war. This was not only the view of the Israeli Intelligence, but also of American Intelligence Services.'[4] He then goes on to cite the fact that a CIA bulletin dated the day before the attack stated that 'the exercise and alert activities may be on a somewhat larger scale and more realistic than previous exercises, but they do not appear to be preparing for a military offensive against Israel'.

Both sides undoubtedly blamed each other for their failure to see exactly what was happening—American and Israeli—but the truth is that on the lower levels, at least, each side had the right intelligence. It was the interpreters who got it wrong. Dayan himself does not make this clear. Dr. Ray Cline, former Director of the State Department's Intelligence section and once a senior CIA officer, blamed the Intelligence breakdown as being partly the result of Secretary of State Henry Kissinger's 'unwillingness to accept the conclusions reached by the Intelligence Community'.[5]

In May 1973, though Zeira did not agree with his own junior Intelligence officers that war was imminent, the Chief of Staff, Lieutenant-General David Elazar, supported the expectation of war and recommended preparations to be made. These preparations were in fact carried out by the government of Mrs. Golda Meir, but the alarm proved to be false on this occasion and the cost of it in terms of transport and supplies was more than fifty million pounds. As far as can be ascertained, however, the Government did not reproach the Chief of Staff as they were aware that it was not always easy to assess the risk of war. And on 21 May, Moshe Dayan, then Minister of Defence, went on record as telling senior members of the General Staff 'a renewal of the war in the second half of the summer must be taken into account . . . we, the Government, say to the General Staff, please prepare for war, as those who are threatening to begin [it] are Egypt and Syria'.

In his brilliantly analytical thesis on the Yom Kippur War, Michael Handel, of the Hebrew University of Jerusalem, makes the point that 'in almost all cases of strategic surprise, intelligence officers familiar with the surprise theory and decision-makers who had all the signals and data necessary to foresee a coming attack, failed to make the right decision'.[6] He goes on to point out that these failures 'stem from the flow of information (signals or noise) through three "noise barriers", each adding its own distortion to further complicate the perceptual–conceptual framework of decision-makers. Consequently, available signals become weakened and shrouded in noise. Decision-makers must then do their best to improve the signal-to-noise ratio (i.e. amplify signals and reduce noise).'[7]

In January 1973, Egypt and Syria started planning and co-ordinating a combined war effort against Israel, and in the following month the Egyptian War Minister Ismail visited Damascus for military discussions with the Syrians. Now as far as has been ascertained from authoritative sources, Israeli Military Intelligence had no information on any of this until after the 1973 war. Yet the Mossad almost certainly had some inkling of what was going on and one can only conclude that at somewhere dangerously close to Cabinet level, or just below it, someone or some people rejected Mossad intelligence as well as that of Aman. It is clear that though Zeira consistently rejected war warnings, both the Chief of Staff and the Minister of War declined to accept his advice.

Yet on 18 May at a meeting of the Knesset's Committee on Security and Foreign Affairs on the possibility of war, Zeira was still asserting that an attack by the Arabs was improbable. The following day Sadat paid a lightning visit to Damascus for a mere seven hours in the greatest secrecy. Throughout the latter part of May and the months of July and August there was increasing evidence from the Mossad of joint Egyptian–Syrian talks at all levels in the military sphere. Where there seems to have been real failure was in the interpretation of these moves by the Israeli military as being indicative merely of a war of nerves by the Egyptians. Some senior Army officers actually believed the Egyptian aim was to force Israel to spend vast sums of money and to cause her economic disruption through calling up reserves. Yet by 12 September, Sadat and the Syrians had signed battle plans for 'Operation Badr', the code word for the Yom Kippur attack.

On 23 September, Henry Kissinger became US Secretary of State and the following day Israeli intelligence reports told of a massive concentration of Syrian troops with tanks and artillery batteries along the border. Then on 27 September the United States, without informing the Israelis, put a SAMOS reconnaisance satellite into orbit to monitor the Middle East area.

The following day attention was somewhat distracted from these developments by the news that Arab terrorists had held up a train with Jewish immigrants from Russia en route to Vienna. This guerrilla gang demanded that the Austrian Government should close down the Jewish transit immigration camp in Schenau, which the Austrians agreed to do. While the Israeli Government was occupied with this problem, all leave for the Egyptian Army was being cancelled.

By the end of the month there was clear evidence that SA-6 units had been distributed among the armoured divisions of the Egyptian Army. There was plenty of intelligence coming in from all sections of the front and clearly a substantial part of the Egyptian Army was in battle formation close to the Canal. The Israeli Deputy Chief of Staff expressed his concern about the evaluation of these reports by Military Intelligence, especially regarding the disposition of troops along the Syrian border. The interpretation was that this was another 'exercise' in a war of nerves. From that view Zeira could not be shaken. Israeli Naval Intelligence on the other hand rated the chances of war as being high, stressing that the Russians had sent in two electronic spy ships close to Israel's shore. As a result the Israeli Navy was ordered to be fully prepared for all eventualities.

In a situation like this in a modern war the attacking power has all the initial advantages largely because of the 'noise barriers' of the other side's signals. Israel had this advantage in 1967; she suffered because the initiative was with the Arabs in 1973. When an enemy's signals are too clear, too explicit and obtained too easily, deception can reasonably be deducted. In this case the Israelis were hampered by the fact (only discovered after the war) that only eight high Arab officials knew in advance of the time and points of attack. The Egyptians and the Syrians had had some disagreements right up to the last moment as to the exact hour and day for the attack to be launched. The final date and time was only decided on 3 October, three days before the war started.

Thus there were excuses for Israeli Intelligence not being absolutely sure as to when an attack would be launched. There were, however, few excuses for Major-General Zeira to insist, as he did on 1 October, that Egyptian troop concentrations were part of an extensive exercise that would last until 7 October. For, though the Egyptians had not agreed upon the timing of the attack until 3 October, one Mossad report suggested that the Egyptians had been pressing for an attack at 1800 hours on 6 October, but that the Syrians were not in agreement.

But the most positive and dramatic intelligence came from a middle-aged, mild-mannered Mossad operator who arrived at Lod airport on the evening of 4 October. This highly skilled agent who travelled far and wide across Europe and the Middle East had the cover of a professor of languages and was regarded by most of his colleagues as so absent-minded that he lost umbrellas and books almost daily. In fact, nobody could guard secrets more carefully: in his brief-case, which he never let out of his sight, was a complete set of photostats of the Egyptian–Syrian war plans right down to the last detail, including the date and time of attack. The photostats even gave the code-name for the operation—'Badr', an oblique reference to the battle which Mohammed and his allies won as a preliminary to their seizure of Mecca.

Zvi Zamir had no doubt at all about the accuracy of this Mossad agent's information and he pressed this viewpoint on the Prime Minister. But both she and Dayan felt at that time that the Arabs were deliberately feeding false information to the Mossad. Again vital evidence was neglected, despite the additional information that on that same day the Russians had launched Cosmos 596, one of their spy-satellites, and that this was in a position to monitor the Israeli–Arab battlefields. Clearly, the

Soviet Union was using this device to transmit vital information to Egypt.

At 3 a.m. on 6 October Israeli Military Intelligence received a firm indication that the attack would probably come at 1800 hours that day. There had also been reports of the Egyptians employing excavators for earth-removing operations along the northern section of the Suez Canal. Once again a junior Intelligence officer urged that there was enough evidence to suggest that all these manoeuvres were not just an exercise, but a cover for a coming attack. On 5 October other Intelligence reports had told how the Russians had evacuated their advisers and families from the war zone. By the end of the day there was a lengthy dossier of offensive preparations in Egypt, with evidence that the Egyptians were moving heavy bridging and water-obstacle equipment to the Canal. Still the view was that the chances of war were small.

Yet all the conditions for an attack by the Arabs were ideal. The night of the sixth offered the best conditions for building bridges and passing tanks across the Canal, while the records of the Suez Canal Company showed that water currents between the banks of the Canal were not adverse on that day. It was the evening of the Yom Kippur holiday in Israel, just the kind of occasion for the Arabs to take their adversaries by surprise. But the 'no war' evaluators countered this argument by saying that, as it was then the second week in the fast period of Ramadan, the Egyptians would be unlikely to fight as their troops would not be in peak condition.

On the whole it was the junior officers who were convinced something was afoot, especially from evidence from the Bar Lev Line, but their seniors insisted it was 'just training'. There was one lesson which the Egyptians had learned from the Six-Day War: this time they were determined not to be trapped by their own communications system. In 1967 the Israelis had won the war so quickly by more or less infiltrating and 'running' the enemy's signals system. This time the radio signals emanating from the Egyptians all suggested a massive exercise, but to prevent the kind of eavesdropping that had happened prior to and during the Six-Day War the Egyptians had developed a comprehensive network of buried telephone cables.

Egypt and Syria finally attacked at 1400 hours on 6 October without the expected aerial preparation. The evaluators of Military Intelligence had believed Egypt would only attack if she had sufficient air power to knock out the Israeli Air Force and bases first. But right up to the last moment the Israeli Chief of Staff was in a dilemma. A substantial body of opinion believed that an Arab attack was imminent. It was Zeira who emphatically refuted this view and General Elazar, though he felt uneasy, did not want to make another costly misjudgement in putting the country on a war footing, so he accepted Zeira's opinion. Even then the Egyptian and Syrian forces opened fire along the entire front line four hours and five minutes earlier than the most reliable military intelligence report had suggested. This meant that for the first twenty-four hours Israel was completely taken by surprise, especially in that area where no effective measures had been taken to ensure against a Syrian attack.

In the end Israel made a brilliant recovery and turned the tables. Yet, but for the American airlift of arms to Israel in October 1973, the Israelis might have lost the war. As Elizabeth Monroe has diagnosed 'in simple terms only American or (better still) Soviet–American pressure, either exercised directly or channelled through the United Nations, can produce even short-term alleviations of the contest for the same lands [Palestine]. By joint pressure these two great power mentors brought off the successive ceasefires of 22 and 24 October, 1973. Great power "interference" is a *sine qua non* at the cease-fire or disengagement level and becomes all the more so should peace-making materialise.'[8]

After the war there was an immediate quest for a scapegoat for the narrow escape which Israel had had. There was no question that poor intelligence evaluation was to blame, though at the time it was not generally realised that the actual intelligence received was adequate. It has been said that 'an "imperfect" intelligence system is safest, since by its description, decision-makers are wary of information distributed to them' and that 'beyond an unspecifiable level of efficiency in a communication system, improvements in intelligence can be a negative factor in policy making'.[9] A small country such as Israel, surrounded by enemies within easy range and dependent upon hastily mobilised reserves must depend upon a first-class intelligence system as its front line of defence in modern warfare. When that intelligence system is misused or ignored, then defeat and disaster threaten it.

The Government set up the Agranat Commission of Inquiry to

investigate the lack of preparedness before the Yom Kippur War. It was required specifically by its terms of reference to examine two subjects—first, intelligence information on the enemy's moves and its evaluation, and, secondly, the state of preparation by the Israeli Army. Apart from there being some desire to find a culprit and pin the blame, world press opinion had forced the need for such an inquiry and for its findings to be made known. There had been, to take one of many examples, this kind of comment by Drew Middleton in the *New York Times* 'Israel's intelligence service—in the past regarded as the best in the Middle East and the equal of the larger services—is under severe criticism because of its failure to assess Arab intentions correctly before the October war.'[10]

As a result of the Agranat Commission's report four officers in the Intelligence branch of the Army were relieved of their posts. The Commission's verdict on Major-General Zeira was that 'in view of his grave failure he cannot continue in his post as Chief of Military Intelligence'. At the same time they found that Zeira's deputy, Brigadier Aryeh Shalev, Lieutenant-Colonel Yona Bendman, who was in charge of the Egyptian desk in the Intelligence Research Department, and Lieutenant-Colonel David Gedalia, Chief Intelligence Officer of Southern Command, should not be retained in their posts. That was drastic enough, possibly in some cases a little unfair. But when it came to expressing opinions on higher ranks the true views of the Commission became somewhat blurred. For example Lieutenant-General David Elazar, the Chief of Staff, had already left that office, while on the subject of the Minister of Defence, General Dayan, the Commission stated that 'we have not felt called upon to give our views on what can be considered the Minister's parliamentary responsibility. . . . The question is whether the Minister of Defence was negligent in carrying out his duties on matters that were within his area of responsibility. . . . We reached the conclusion that by standards of reasonable behaviour required by the one holding the post of Minister of Defence, the Minister was not required to issue orders for precautionary measures additional to or different from those proposed to him by the General Staff in accordance with joint assessment and consultation between the Chief of Staff and the Chief of Intelligence.'

This may have exonerated the Minister of Defence, but it was a somewhat mild judgement compared with the harsh verdict on the Intelligence officers. After all, there had been doubts on the part of the Chief of Staff, even if the Director of Military Intelligence was convinced his assessment was correct. It is still somewhat surprising that Dayan, an astute and imaginative operator in the military sphere, had not read the danger signals, especially in view of his own lengthy army experience. For the first time the halo was in danger of being removed from the head of this national hero.

Major-General Shlomo Gazit became the new head of Military Intelligence and there was immediately an overhaul of the whole system of collecting, assessing and evaluating intelligence. It was suddenly realised that Ben-Gurion had anticipated the dangers of a purely monolithic intelligence service, without allowing enough scope for the development of varying opinions. In 1963 Ben-Gurion, then Prime Minister, had appointed the Yadin-Scherff Committee to examine the means of improving Israel's Secret Service. This report, presented on 31 July 1963, had proposed that (1) the intelligence research unit of the Ministry of Foreign Affairs should be strengthened; (2) the Mossad should be given more scope to develop its own intelligence evaluation system (presumably mainly in relation to military problems); (3) there should be no reliance on any one branch of the Secret Service— i.e. Mossad, Aman, etc.; (4) a special adviser on intelligence should be assigned to the Prime Minister.

Few of these proposals had been implemented and, when they were, hardly in the way in which the Committee intended. The Agranat Commission found that the coverage of the four agencies of Israeli Intelligence overlapped at points, but that this was not necessarily a bad thing. Indeed, it was not: one of the reasons for failure of evaluation prior to the Yom Kippur War was undoubtedly that more attention had been paid to the Military Intelligence unit than to the others—the Mossad, Shabak, and the Centre for Research and Strategic Planning of the Ministry of Foreign Affairs. And well might the Agranat Commission arrive at the conclusion that Israel's field and tactical intelligence had been neglected for years. Not for lack of intelligence, let it be noted, but it was not provided with the same amount of information, maps and aerial photographs which were provided for the Chief of Staff and others. In short, the evaluators were often being asked to carry on with their work without being kept fully in the picture. Those who were actively supplying intelligence from the field were not being fed back with the kind of information that would help them in making judgements.

Many changes were made in the personnel of all the Intelligence Services in the following year. The new Prime Minister, Mr. Yitzak Rabin, one of the heroes of the Six-Day War, signified the appointment of a new head of the Mossad for the first time in six years when he and the Chief of Staff, General Gur, held a farewell reception party for the outgoing Memuneh, General Zvi Zamir, on 1 September 1974. At the time of this party the name of the new Memuneh was kept strictly secret. It was, however, clear by now that there had been a grave lack of co-ordination between the Mossad and Aman and that this was in part due to a feeling by some Army officers that the Mossad was indulging in too much filibustering. One of the chief criticisms emerging from the inquiry into the events of 1973, according to the Agranat Commission, had been that the only intelligence advice submitted to the Chief of Staff and the Minister of Defence was that of the Military Intelligence branch. An experienced all-round operator like David Ben-Gurion would never have allowed such a state of affairs to occur. Of all Israel's Prime Ministers he was undoubtedly the one who understood the problems of Intelligence best, even if in doing so he had laid himself open to the hazards of having his finger too deeply in the espionage pie.

There was some hard thinking both at Cabinet and Prime Ministerial levels after the Agranat Report had been received. One suggestion that was keenly discussed was that of the introduction of officers assigned to a permanent doubting role of devil's advocate in order to challenge possibly wrong assumptions. Another proposal was for the computerising of all data that might programme forthcoming trouble so that any real threat to the state might be promptly and automatically drawn to the attention of the Government.

On 19 May 1975, Prime Minister Rabin announced that a special adviser on intelligence had been appointed as a safeguard against further mishaps such as the wrong assessment of Arab moves before the Yom Kippur War. He was Major-General Rechavam Zeevi, who had been a General Staff Officer during the Six-Day War when Rabin was Chief of Staff. In fact the Agranat Commission had recommended the appointment of an expert who was not a regular army man to help the Prime Minister to keep in touch with activities by the various Secret

Services. Much later Professor Yigal Yadin, a member of the Commission, expressed regret in a newspaper interview that the recommendation had not been implemented. This might have precipitated the Prime Minister's announcement.

General Rechavam Zeevi was a Sabra of the fifth generation, having been born in Jerusalem in 1926. He joined the Palmach in 1944 and in 1950 was appointed Intelligence Officer of the Southern Command, often spending months in the Negev Hills mapping out the region. It was in fact an imaginative, even a quixotic appointment, and perhaps for this very reason it was a sound choice. How many other nations would have opted for the unconventional in making such an appointment, for in effect Zeevi was being made devil's advocate to the Prime Minister. Zeevi was noted in the Israeli Army for his unconventionality, his slow speech and his mischievousness. He was nicknamed 'Gandhi' because, when in a settlement training group, he appeared one day disguised as Mahatma Gandhi wrapped in a bed-sheet and dragging a goat behind him. Zeevi joined the General Staff as early as 1952 and some years later was sent abroad for what were then described as 'advanced studies'. In 1960 he went to the USA, while in 1964 he went on foreign aid missions to African and Asian countries. The full reasons for the appointment of General Zeevi may not yet be clear, but it might be added that according to reports from outside Israel he is known to be a shrewd judge of espionage techniques behind the Iron Curtain and at the same time to have a partiality towards and a deep understanding of Bulgarian immigrants to Israel. This may have been an eccentric appointment, but Zeevi brings a breath of fresh air and imagination to a role that needs to be raised beyond the limits of bureaucracy. He at least would understand that Israel needed to be ready for war on the Day of Atonement (Yom Kippur) more than any other day in the year.

In any criticisms of Israeli intelligence evaluation in this war, it must be conceded that the continued processing of this intelligence swiftly enabled Israel to take the initiative after the first two disastrous days which saw the Egyptians consolidating their positions along much of the east bank of the Suez Canal and advancing some miles into Sinai. An Israeli counter-attack, based to a large extent on sound intelligence reports, established a major bridgehead on the west bank of the Canal, pushing well inland and destroying many of the SAM missile sites as well as enforcing aerial superiority. Indeed, the tide turned very quickly in Israel's favour and it must always be remembered, when Israeli aggression is sometimes criticised, that here is a small country which not only confronts the Arab nations, but is always frustrated from complete victory by a racially prejudiced United Nations which inevitably imposes a cease-fire at the very eve of Israeli victory. So it was in 1967, so, much more so, was it in 1973. The Israelis had the Egyptian Third Army trapped in a pincer movement in the southern end of the front when a UN Security Council resolution imposed a cease-fire. Not only this, but at that very moment the Israelis had counter-attacked the Syrians so strongly that they had advanced to within twenty miles of Damascus.

If Israel hits back in unconventional and sometimes seemingly piratical tactics against her enemies in both the Middle East and Africa, the Western World, bogged down in its provincial and outdated morals, should try to appreciate the reason for this. When tiny little England faced the might of imperial Spain in the sixteenth century, she achieved victory through piracy. When the American revolutionaries fought against George III in the eighteenth century they depended upon a ruthless Intelligence Service which often adopted piratical methods. Israel not only has to fight the Arab states, but the whole apparatus of the United Nations as well, dominated as that megalophonous body is by the combined charlatanry of the communists and their Third World followers. Only the Secret Services of the world fully understand what a political-syphilitic monster the United Nations has turned itself into: in their own secret jargon they refer to anyone working inside the UN as being 'in the pudding club'.

21

The Entebbe Raid

The mission in Uganda, in one short hour, strengthened the backbone of the Jewish people and of the whole free world. This was the time when the fate of a nation was determined in one hour by a small body of brave men.

(SHIMON PERES, Israeli Minister of Defence)

THERE HAVE BEEN many Israeli Secret Service operations which have been outstandingly successful, but perhaps none has so captured the imagination of the outside world, or won the hearts of neutral peoples, as that generally known as the Entebbe Raid.

It was an astonishing epic of military adventure and enterprise carried out in a spirit of medieval buccaneering by a team trained in the arts of both the military and espionage. Hardly had the operation been carried out than countless journalists set about reconstructing the whole story in lively and dramatic prose and at least half a dozen authors set out to produce an 'instant' book. Within weeks of the raid paperbacks were pouring from the presses and within a few months Hollywood had put on the market a full-length film on the subject, featuring such stars as Charles Bronson, Peter Finch, Burt Lancaster, Kirk Douglas and even Elizabeth Taylor, playing the part of a Jewish mother.

It was on Sunday, 4 July 1976, that an Israeli Secret Service plan was put into action when a raiding party sent by aeroplane escaped from the African bush with more than a hundred hostages detained by President Idi Amin of Uganda. This was 'Operation Jonathan', the most spectacular operation ever launched against the forces of terrorism.

But to trace the origins of the Entebbe raid one has to go back to before Idi Amin's rule in Uganda. Israel had been quietly trying to win friends in this part of Africa for several years, competing with Egyptian, pan-Arab, Russian and Chinese influence in north and east Africa. Relations between Israel and Uganda had initially been good. Israel had not only given generous aid to Uganda, but had helped train the Ugandan army and even supplied it with equipment. During this period Lieutenant-Colonel Baruch Bar-Lev spent five years in Uganda as head of the Israeli Defence Ministry's mission to the country. He was highly popular in Kampala, was consulted on various problems and sometimes given snippets of intelligence on African affairs, while he became a close associate of Idi Amin before the latter came to power. Indeed their friendship was sufficiently close for Amin to be invited to stay in Israel and to have special treatment there for a rheumatic condition.

In the early seventies the President of Uganda at that time, Milton Obote, suddenly turned against the Israelis, largely to play along with some of his pro-Egyptian neighbours, and he even threatened to throw the Israeli advisers out of the country. It was Idi Amin, then Chief of Staff of the Ugandan Army, who defended them and stood out against the President. And it was Bar-Lev who repaid Idi for this support by warning him of Obote's plot to arrest him on a trumped-up charge. The respective families of Idi and Bar-Lev were on visiting terms. Years later Bar-Lev must have looked back somewhat quizzically at the time when his intervention saved Idi from death or imprisonment. For shortly after Amin came to power Bar-Lev began to realise that any relationship with the new President must be unpredictable.

In 1971 the Israelis sold Uganda one of their own Commodore jet planes as a personal aircraft for the President. The sum charged was half the normal selling price, and even then the Israelis agreed to accept the money in instalments. Then in 1972 Amin broke relations with Israel in a sudden fit of inexplicable anger and ordered the Israeli advisers out of the country. Nevertheless the President continued to use the jet and at the same time refused to make any further payments on it, despite repeated requests from Tel Aviv either for the money or the return of the aircraft.

It was on 27 June 1976, that Air France airliner 139 took off from Athens for Paris carrying some 246 passengers. The flight had started off from Tel Aviv that morning and had taken aboard a large number of Israelis. The latter noticed with some concern that the security arrangements at Athens airport were somewhat lax and that there had been no adequate screening of the passengers joining the flight there. Less than two hours after the plane left Athens a message was received in Tel Aviv which stated: 'Air France Flight No. 139 which left Israel this morning and landed at Athens en route to Paris disappeared after take-off. All contact has been lost, but it is known that the plane turned south-eastwards.'

It was swiftly realised in Tel Aviv that this was not just another hi-jacking, serious as that might be. In view of the large number of Israelis on board and the indications that the aircraft was heading for the heart of Africa, the Israeli Cabinet, backed up by Secret Service reports, felt that this was a direct challenge to Israel, an act of terrorism that could not just be bought off by handing over ransom money or Arab prisoners. There had been rumours on the underground grapevine for some weeks that a spectacular hi-jacking was being planned and that Carlos was in some way associated with it. Reports suggested that this hi-jacking would be carried out by an international team including Arabs and Europeans.

Security at the Israeli airports had been tightened; a close watch was being maintained on all El Al flights. Yet when the attack came it was directed against an Air France plane known to be carrying more than a hundred Israelis. And the passengers were informed over the aircraft address system: 'This is Captain Basil Al-Kubeisi of the Che Guevara Force of the Commando of the Palestinian Liberation Forces. This plane has been hi-jacked. If you behave quietly, nothing will happen to you.' The words were English, but the accent was not that of an Arab: most of the passengers were sure the speaker was a German.

Later a young German woman also informed the passengers that the hi-jacking operation was under the control of 'the Che Guevara Group and the Gaza Unit of the Popular Front for the Liberation of Palestine'. Though there were Arabs among the hi-jackers it was evident that those in command were German. It was also fairly certain that they were close associates of Carlos. The chief of the hi-jackers, Wilfred Boese, was a member of the Baader-Meinhof gang and well known to the police of a number of European countries. He was known to have had links with the PFLP. His principal accomplice on the aircraft was a German girl who wore a wig and insisted on being addressed as 'Halima'. One of the two Arabs among the hi-jackers was later identified as Ja'il el-Arja, who had represented the PFLP in Latin America.

The Mossad had a dossier on him showing his connections with Carlos.

Flight 139 first landed at Benghazi and the knowledge that they were in the territory of the notoriously unpredictable and violently anti-Israeli Colonel Gaddifi hardly reassured the passengers. This news reached Tel Aviv fairly quickly and a special Cabinet meeting was called forthwith. The Prime Minister, Itzhak Rabin, acted with commendable speed: he delegated each of his ministers to undertake specific tasks in relation to the hi-jacking, and of these that assigned to Shimon Peres, then Minister of Defence, was perhaps the most important. His long experience of Intelligence ensured that he would keep closely in touch with the Aman and the Mossad on the subject. Naturally one of the first things he did was to ensure that the Israeli and French Intelligence Services kept on the same wave-length quite apart from diplomatic exchanges between the two Foreign Offices.

The aircraft was next reported as having left Benghazi and to be flying in the direction of Khartoum. In fact, four hours after midnight on 28 June the news came that it had landed at Entebbe in Uganda. By this time the French Government had said they would take every possible step to ensure the safety of all passengers, but this sounded rather unrealistic when it became known that the aircraft had landed in the territory of the mad dog of African politics, President Idi Amin Dada of Uganda.

Gradually, the Israeli Secret Service was beginning to build up a picture of the type of hi-jacking operation this was. They were convinced that the hi-jackers, or at least one of them, was knowledgeable about flying, could read air maps and understood the rudiments of air navigation. Equally, they were sure that this was a joint operation between European and Arab terrorists on a pattern similar to other operations of its kind. The vital question was: what would the terrorists' demands be?

All the Intelligence Services of Europe were alerted by this hi-jacking and most were concerned by the apparent international make-up of the terrorist group. The French were convinced that Sanchez was one of the men behind it and that Dr. Waddieh Haddad, military leader of the PFLP, was master-minding the operation. On the other hand the West German Intelligence 'thought that gangsters were involved in the hi-jacking of the Jumbo; or, because the operation was so professionally executed, that it was a "brilliant tactic of the Israeli Shin Beth", with the intention of discrediting the Palestinians'.[1]

Dr. Haddad had been hunted by the 'avenger squads' for some years. It was also reported that other more mysterious agencies wanted to remove him as well. When he was entertaining Leila Khaled, the 'pin-up' girl of the Palestinian hi-jackers, in July 1970, both of them narrowly missed death when six Soviet-built anti-tank rockets were fired by an electronic timing device from a rented room across the street. But it seems probable that this may have been a devious attack by an Israeli 'avenger squad' with captured Soviet weapons aimed at discrediting the Russians, or letting them take the blame for the attack. Not unnaturally Dr. Haddad himself allowed this story to be used as propaganda for the Palestinian cause. In the day-to-day battle silently being waged between East and West and Arab and Israeli today, victory often depends upon the effectiveness of the lie and the counter-lie. Recruitment to one cause or the other certainly rises or falls according to the successes or failures in the propaganda war.

It was certain that everything had been done in Uganda to assist the hi-jackers and that some details of this operation had been secretly passed to the Ugandans long before the plane landed. At Benghazi the plane had had to circle over the airport for some time before it was allowed to land, whereas at Entebbe the landing was made immediately, almost as though it was being signalled to come in at once. Passengers on the aircraft afterwards reported that they saw the hi-jackers waving to the Ugandans in such a way, and receiving waves back, that the arrival of the plane must have been anticipated.

This was amply confirmed by the swift arrival of Idi Amin Dada on the scene, chatting in an ostentatiously friendly fashion with the hi-jackers. The passengers aboard were encouraged when the French Ambassador to Uganda arrived at the Entebbe airport and talked with the terrorists. Soon afterwards the French Embassy in Kampala, however, announced that the talks had produced no results. It was another day before the hi-jackers stated their demands for the release of the passengers: the freeing of fifty-three so-called 'freedom fighters' held in prisons in France, Israel, West Germany, Kenya and Switzerland. All fifty-three were to be flown to Entebbe in a special plane which would then be used to fly out the hi-jackers. It was laid down that Air France was to be responsible for flying to Entebbe all those who were imprisoned in Israel. The other countries would have to make their own arrangements to fly the released terrorists to Uganda. Two final points were made: France would have to appoint a special envoy to negotiate with the hi-jackers and the represen- tative of the PFLP in any talks with the French Government would be the Somali Ambassador to Uganda. The deadline for finalising negotiations was 1400 hours on the following Thursday afternoon and, if agreement was not reached by this time, savage reprisals would follow.

But by this time Israel had already set in motion a plan to counter the terrorists. True, it was in the initial stages little more than the embryo of an idea that this was the moment to make a dramatic gesture to launch a devastating blow against hi-jacking and similar acts of terrorism, involving hostages. But for a long time the Mossad had been working on the various possibilities for such a move in the light of known hi-jacker tactics. Meanwhile Prime Minister Rabin laid down that the Israeli Cabinet must be seen to be following normal democratic processes in the first instance.

By making this latter point a matter of diplomatic policy the Israelis ensured some semblance of unity among the governments involved. The West German Government had taken the lead in urging a common front among all the governments concerned and the French Government had stated that France rejected the demands of the hi-jackers. World opinion, however, was sceptical about this so-called unity. Franch was suspected of being liable to cave in ultimately because of its pro-Arab stance, while many remembered that Israel had also given in to terrorist demands on two previous occasions when Israeli citizens were held hostage.

In the intense heat of an Ugandan summer 257 people, men, women and children, were ushered off the plane into the terminal building at Entebbe airport where they were herded together in conditions of extreme discomfort while the building itself was ringed by Ugandan troops. On the third day of captivity the hi-jackers ordered the separation of the hostages into groups, though they denied that this was in any way connected with their respective nationalities. Meanwhile Idi Amin paid yet another visit to the hostages and told them that he could 'do nothing until Israel agrees to the terms put to her'.

*

Time on this occasion was to some extent on Israel's side. In those days before the deadline set by the terrorists the Israelis lost no opportunities either in the diplomatic sphere or in the Intelligence world. In the latter there were, as always, contacts with the Americans, the French and the British. Rabin's hope was that somehow Israel could save the lives of the hostages and come out of the affair without what would appear as abject surrender. The chances seemed slender, especially as on this occasion another sovereign state was co-operating with the hi-jackers. The Israeli Cabinet took the view that, grave as was their responsibility for the lives of more than one hundred of their nationals, the long-term prospects for Israel were appalling if the rescue depended on the freeing of criminals and terrorists from their prisons. It would be tantamount to an invitation to further and increased terrorism.

One move that was made was for Lieutenant-Colonel Bar-Lev to put through a personal telephone call to Idi Amin in the somewhat forlorn hope that, on the basis of their previous friendship, something might be achieved. After a fairly lengthy talk all that emerged in the end were these tape-recorded words of Idi Amin: '. . . They [the terrorists] are ready to explode it [the plane] . . . You can help me if you tell your government to release these persons, those whom you call criminals. It's better to save the lives of more than 200 people. . . . They said they are going to kill completely. They'll begin with blowing up the plane and then they'll kill everyone at once with explosives. They said that if any plane comes over Uganda, they'll blow up everything immediately.'[2]

This conversation and the implications of Idi Amin's remarks seemed at first to rule out any chance of an effective rescue operation. 'Operation Jonathan', as the rescue plan was eventually code-named, already existed as a blueprint to be ready for just such an eventuality, and it made provisions for alternative versions of the plan. The task was to ascertain all the facts to fit into the framework and then to decide what were the chances of success. In brief, the main plan was to send a plane carrying troops who would rescue the hostages and deal with the hi-jackers.

Israel's Army and Secret Service are not hamstrung by too much bureaucracy or emphasis on that self-destroying military myth, the divine right of seniority. All ranks had the opportunity to press plans and suggestions over the heads of their immediate superiors to the C-in-C, the Memuneh, head of the Aman, etc.

In turning 'Operation Jonathan' into a practical proposition this was a tremendous advantage: some excellent ideas came from minor agents in the field and non-commissioned soldiers and airmen.

Advantages were weighed against disadvantages. Entebbe was more than 2,500 miles from Israel; on the other hand there were many Israelis who had first-hand knowledge of Uganda, of the lay-out of the airport itself and of the Ugandan Army and Air Force. Idi Amin was about to go off to Mauritius for the meeting of the Organisation of African Unity; this allowed two days more for planning, as it was felt that nothing would be likely to happen while Idi was out of the country, though in Africa such deductions are apt to come unstuck. Encouraging news came from Mossad agents in Kenya that there was a prospect of assistance there, even though no approaches had been made to the Kenyan Government. Better still, another report from Kenya was that Mossad agents had been infiltrated into Uganda.

Meanwhile an exercise of 'Operation Jonathan' was conducted in a remote part of Israel when paratroops landed in a mock rescue in realistic conditions. All they had to do was to follow the blueprint, while observers made notes of mistakes that might need to be corrected and improvements for any future operation. One suggestion made at the time was that if the rescue plane arrived at Entebbe while Idi Amin was in Mauritius, it might be worth while trying to trick the Ugandan troops on the ground that Idi was returning in this plane. The first idea was to make an effigy of him and one was hastily mocked up and dressed in Ugandan Uniform (as the Israelis had been advisers to the Ugandan Army such a uniform was easy to come by), to be brought out of the plane when it landed. But this plan was changed so that a particularly outsize Israeli paratrooper was made up to look like Amin; they even found a Mercedes car which was sprayed black to make it look like Idi's very own model. This, too, was to have been transported in the rescue plane. But careful research suggested this plan was not practicable and that in any event the rescue attempt could not be mounted before Idi Amin returned.

Another advantage, though a minimal one, perhaps, was Lieutenant-Colonel Bar-Lev's intimate knowledge of Uganda and of Idi Amin's character and probable reactions; he also knew Amin's habits and ailments. The Colonel's dossier on Amin which he gave to Intelligence was invaluable at filling in gaps in their own information. Because behind 'Operation Jonathan' an enormous amount of marginal information needed to be gathered and assessed; often some seemingly trivial point proved to be of vital importance. For example, it was known that Amin had conceived the mad idea of having a miniature plane built for his young son so that the youngster could pilot it himself around the grounds of his home at a height of not much more than twenty or thirty feet from the ground. One imaginative member of the Mossad team analysing the Amin dossier proposed that Israel should hastily construct such a model plane—or at any rate a make-believe toy—and offer it to Amin as a gesture of goodwill, getting the escape plane to tow the toy plane behind it. 'That way Amin will never allow his forces to shoot down our plane,' was the argument. 'It could work as well as the Trojan horse.'

'A Trojan horse, yes,' was the reply of another officer, 'but a Trojan plane, no. It might just work if we could actually make the kind of miniature plane that Amin wants in so short a time, but if he discovered that it was only a mock-up too soon. I wouldn't give much for the chances of the hostages.'

But plans were going ahead and intelligence was coming in all the time from Uganda and Kenya. Israel, playing for time, announced through the French Ambassador to Uganda just as the deadline was up, that she was ready to negotiate with the hi-jackers. The next day 101 of the hostages were released at Entebbe, leaving only those with Israeli citizenship and some Jews of other nationalities still in the hands of their captors. More intelligence was gleaned from those released, most notably the French passengers from whom the Mossad agents managed to obtain quite a lot of information. Major-General Rechavam Zeevi, who had been appointed as special adviser on intelligence to the Prime Minister after the Yom Kippur fiasco, also played a vital role at this stage. Not only was he able to advise on intelligence received from all branches of the Secret Service, but to give his own appraisal to the Cabinet. He was in Paris at this time and he controlled and analysed the various statements made by released passengers. He was also able to maintain the closest links with the Quai d'Orsay.

Negotiations for the release of the Israelis dragged on and, while some of the Cabinet were against the rescue plan because they feared that if it failed, the deaths of more than a hundred of their fellow-countrymen would be laid at their door, the fact that the hi-jackers now gave the impression of making further demands swung opinion in favour of 'Operation Jonathan'. Israel had wanted the exchange of prisoners for hostages to take place in France, especially as France was the country legally responsible for the safety and well-being of them. Meanwhile the new deadline set by the hi-jackers was 1100 hours GMT on Sunday, 4 July.

Israel was fortunate that she had a young, enthusiastic Army which possessed a spirit of adventure allied to patriotism. When the British Government was confronted by the prospect of a British subject seized by Amin and under sentence of death merely for having been 'disrespectful' to the Ugandan President, it was the chiefs of the Armed Forces who insisted that no rescue operation could be mounted. British chiefs of staff from the time of the timorous 'it can't be done' Lord Alanbrooke, who so tried Churchill's temper in wartime, have invariably been defeatist and wholly unco-operative in such emergencies whether at Suez, or the Ian Smith challenge when he declared UDI. But the Israeli military chiefs, backed up by the Navy, were pressing for action and eager to carry out a rescue attempt. It was the Cabinet they had to convince. Fortunately the Army was backed one hundred per cent by the Secret Service.

Nothing was left to chance. Even Amin's flight movements to Mauritius were monitored, while a reconnaisance plane listened in to radio traffic with a plane which had left Tripoli for Entebbe. As a result of this they were able to report that it looked as though Arab reinforcements for the hi-jack team were being flown into Uganda. The Israeli Navy dispatched a spy ship filled with electronic gear to the Indian Ocean and close in to the coast of East Africa. This ship became a vital communications centre and also monitored messages from Mauritius to Nairobi and Kampala as well as picking up signals from Mossad agents.

The chief—indeed, some said the only—problem of 'Operation Jonathan' was how to make a quick landing of troops to carry out the rescue before the captors took action against the hostages. The returning passengers in Paris had enabled the Secret Service to build up an accurate picture of the terminal hall where the Israelis were herded together, its proximity to the landing strip and some idea of how it was guarded. This information was supplemented by further intelligence from inside Uganda by the agents who smuggled themselves in from Kenya. One agent hired a small boat from Port Victoria, pretending to go on a fishing expedition, made his way by night through the group of small islands in the north-east corner of Lake Victoria and landed secretly on Ugandan soil. In this instance he passed himself off as a Sudanese and, posing as a virulent anti-Semite, obtained information about the number of troops at Entebbe airport, how they were disposed, their daily timetable and the exact location of Ugandan Air Force planes. This story was considerably exaggerated later in the German weekly *Der Spiegel* by an account of Israelis hiring motor-boats at Kisumu in Kenya, sailing across Lake Victoria to the Ugandan shore close to Entebbe airfield.

As a result of all this the military planners in Tel Aviv were able to report that, providing they could land at Entebbe, without arousing suspicion, the rescue of the hostages would be a relatively simple operation. By this time they were able to work out the timetable of the rescue from the moment of landing. 'But,' stressed the chief of operations, 'this timetable is OK for now. It doesn't mean it will be OK for tomorrow, or the day after. We must have up-to-date intelligence all the time right up to the last moment.'

Wonders were worked in the amount of intelligence that was obtained over the next twenty-four hours. It looked as though about one hundred Ugandan soldiers were actually stationed at the Entebbe airport. Further news came in that the Ugandan force included Russian-built Mig-17s and Mig-21s as well as tanks. To supplement the news coming in from agents a team was dispatched to Nairobi to make contact with allies inside Jomo Kenyatta's own discreetly named secret service, the General Service Unit. The tentacles of the Mossad had now extended into Kenya and Uganda, making full use of some of their African and Sudanese sub-agents.

There was, however, extensive and intensive activity by the Israeli Secret Service in Kenya. If there was to be a rescue attempt, re-fuelling of the planes for the return journey was essential and the Nairobi airport was the obvious place for this. To re-fuel in the air was a dangerous operation, especially as it would offer opportunities to any unfriendly planes to intervene and create an 'accident'. But as secrecy was so essential in any approach to the authorities at Nairobi, it was decided that the best plan was for the Secret Service to come to an understanding about the refuelling and protection while it was done, from the Nairobi police hierarchy and Kenyatta's GSU. Fortunately

Israel's relations with Kenya were good and the Mossad had an effective network in the area. An added bonus was that relations between Uganda and Kenya were strained.

Afterwards the Nairobi correspondent of the *Los Angeles Times* reported that 'Israeli agents who had been in Nairobi several days made arrangements for the complex operation. An Israeli tourist said, "There were many Hebrew-speaking young men in my hotel and they were not tourists. The hired cars of his temporary aides were parked closely together outside the Israeli envoy's home." An Israeli Boeing 707 fitted out as a field hospital was waiting at Nairobi for the returning people.'

A hint of the secret nature of the talks between the Israelis and some of the Kenyan authorities occurred when Yehuda Ofer's book, *Operation Thunder*, was serialised in the Kenyan *Sunday Nation*. The *Weekly Review*, a Nairobi magazine, reported in its issue of 18 October 1976, that George Githii, editor-in-chief of the *Nation* group of newspapers, who controlled the policy of the *Sunday Nation*, had been asked on 12 October to stop the serialisation on the ground that it was 'against national security'. The demand was said to have been made by Kenya's Commissioner of Police, who at the same time asked Mr. Githii to stop writing anti-Arab stories.

In some ways luck assisted the Secret Service. For example, the Entebbe airport had been built by an Israeli firm, Solel Boneh, and details of its lay-out and construction were easily obtainable from the firm's engineers. True, it had been enlarged later by an Italian firm, but details of this were also forthcoming. On-the-spot reports from Entebbe indicated that the terminal building where the hostages were kept had not been booby-trapped. After the released passengers were interviewed in Paris by the Israeli interrogation team, at least one, and probably more of them were re-interviewed later after undergoing hypnosis treatment. This was said to have been particularly effective when linked to the polygraph lie detector.

No possible sophisticated device of modern espionage was neglected. At the use of some of these one can only guess and deduct, but it seems probable that some satellite-recorded photographic data on Entebbe was obtained by the Israelis, possibly through the Americans. It also seems certain that the Israelis themselves may have indulged in some aerial espionage over Entebbe from a very great height by the use of disguised planes.

There could well have been some degree of co-operation in the field of aerial reconnaisance with South Africa, or even with BOSS, the South African Secret Service. Certainly backroom boys supplied psychometrical and astrological data. A psycho-metric reading on Idi Amin was taken and close attention was paid to the constantly monitored Israel 'foundation chart' which had been kept up-to-date since the creation of the state in 1948. Experience had shown that it was astonishingly accurate in regard to both the Six-Day and the Yom Kippur wars and so its indica-tions as regards the Entebbe raid were carefully examined. The signs were good: one astrological deduction made was that at this time 'Jupiter p. IS (Israel chart) is close opposition Uranus r. IS and Neptune p. is stationary conjunction ASCr IS, these last two aspects symbolising a successful aviation event since Neptune and Uranus are both connected with aviation and either or both may be involved in this type of event.'

The rehearsal of the rescue operation went smoothly. This con-firmed the original opinion that three Lockheed C-130 Hercules craft should be used for the action. The chief of the Operations Branch, General Yekutiel Adam, was in charge of planning, and assisted by Brigadier-General Dan Shomron, chief of the Infantry and Paratroop Corps. The men chosen for the mission were the élite of Israel's paratroop guerrilla forces and led by one of their most brilliant young officers, Lieutenant-Colonel Jonathan Netanyahu, after whom the operation was code-named.

Two factors swung the whole of the Israeli Cabinet behind the rescue plan eventually: one was the fact that, though Israel had indicated that she would negotiate on the terms laid down by the hi-jackers, the latter had stepped up their demands; the second that reports suggested that execution of the hostages would be carried out on Sunday, 4 July, and that this would be aided and abetted by Idi Amin's dictatorship. Eventually at sunset on the Jewish Sabbath, Saturday, 3 July, the three planes took off from Tel Aviv, flying SSE along the Red Sea at a very great height, with the hope that they would be mistaken for civil aircraft flying towards South Africa. No doubt there was some effective radar-blocking, probably directed at Entebbe where the men in the control tower certainly failed to give a prompt alarm which could have ruined the whole operation.

Then about a minute after midnight on Sunday, 4 July, the first of the Hercules craft landed smoothly at Entebbe and the assault troops dashed straight for the terminal building. The Mossad had done well to cover up the operation and to lure the Ugandans as well as the hi-jackers to believe that Israel was still hoping to negotiate. Telephone conversations to this effect had been made to France in the full knowledge that they would be monitored and passed on to the enemies of Israel. One senior French Intelligence executive had told his opposite number in the Mossad: 'Always use that line to the Quai d'Orsay, or to the Hotel ————. You can then be sure your conversation will be bugged and every word will get back to the PLO. In this country we in the SDECE always have to fight against our own enemies in Government circles.'

The full story of the rescue of the hostages has been told at great length by many authorities. Suffice to say here that it was one of the most spectacular rescue operations in history. Within minutes the hostages were released, sheperded to the aircraft and the control tower was put out of action. Only four Israeli lives were lost in an operation in which they expected something like twenty per cent casualties. Three were civilians and the only military casualty was that of Lieutenant-Colonel Netanyahu, who was killed in cross-fire from the control-tower. 'Operation Jonathan' lasted for fifty-three minutes, two minutes less than the time taken in the rehearsal exercise. All the terrorists except one were killed.

No time was lost in flying on to Nairobi where the planes refuelled and then returned triumphantly to Tel Aviv.

There was, however, one incident which marred the occasion. Nobody was quite sure about the identity of the terrorist who escaped. He was said to have been with Amin at the time of the raid. Yehuda Ofer wrote that he was 'the Peruvian anarchist, Antonio Bouvier, who was the leader of the terror group at Entebbe'.[3] But some suspected he was Carlos Sanchez. In the Israeli film made by Menahem Golan about the raid, which had the full backing of the Israeli Cabinet and Ministry of Defence, Carlos was introduced as a character. 'No one knows for sure whether the Jackal was involved and if he was the man who escaped,' said Golan.

On a lighter note there was the post-raid rescue of the jet aircraft supplied to Amin by the Israelis in 1971 and for which he still hadn't paid. Shortly afterwards news came from Tel Aviv that this plane had been flown back to Israel. There were murmurs of 'another Secret Service coup', despite the fact that Amin in an effort to save face claimed that it had been returned on his orders. The Israeli radio repeatedly broadcast Amin's message. No doubt the Mossad had cleverly engineered the whole affair, even if they could claim that the operation was not carried out by Israeli agents. In fact, Amin had been hoodwinked by two American pilots. One of them, Peter Demos, told how he duped the Ugandan security forces and flew to Tel Aviv via Cyprus. He said he was contacted 'by an agent in Zurich and paid to retrieve the plane'.[4] He ferried another plane to Uganda and then persuaded Amin to allow him to test fly the President's personal jet. On the first test flight there were armed guards aboard; on the second run he and his American co-pilot flew alone and headed off north. Once again the Israelis had outwitted not only Amin, but even his own dreaded Secret Service, the SRC (State Research Centre).

22

The Strange World of
Psychic Espionage

*Secret PSI research associated with state security
and defence is going on in the USSR.... the
dangers of the possible misuse of PSI should not
be overlooked.*

(DR. MILAN RYZL)[1]

ISRAEL'S FIGHT FOR SURVIVAL depends increasingly on her Secret
Service and this has been even truer since the Yom Kippur War.
Several factors have contributed to this apart from the one already
stressed—that of a small nation surrounded by enemies living in
a perpetual state of cold war—and one such factor is the steady
improvement of the Secret Services of the Arab states.

Sadat's Secret Service chief, former Air Force General Hosny
Mubarak, is an outstandingly good organiser of intelligence who
has done much to modernise Egypt's espionage and counter-
espionage and has had a fondness for electronic spying devices.
What might be called the 'capitalist Arab states' nearly all come
under American influence and receive backing from the CIA. In
Saudi Arabia the whole security service has been organised by an
American finance company who have set up a private company,
Interset, to do this. The Saudi-Arabian Secret Service has also
been equipped with every modern electronic and computer device,
not perhaps to be compared with Israeli standards as yet, nor
having the highly skilled native analysts possessed by Tel Aviv,
but none the less highly competent. Just as there are contacts
between the CIA and the Saudi-Arabian Secret Service, so, too,
there are contacts between the Saudis and the Israelis in the field
of intelligence: the fact is that both countries have some mutual
enemies in the Arab camp.

One of the key men in the Saudi-Arabian intelligence set-up is

Sheikh Ghassan Shaker, a very wealthy businessman who is also a Cambridge graduate. Shaker, who comes from Jeddah, has great influence in the City of London and has figured in various deals there. His wealth can be measured in three-figure millions and it is whispered in the City that the Bank of England looks upon him favourably. Shaker is a realist and the result of this has been that Saudi Arabia has had not only the benefit of CIA advice, but sometimes of Israeli intelligence passed on to them via the CIA.

In recent years Egypt has greatly improved its counter-espionage organisation and a number of Israeli agents have been caught. The first major breakthrough was in November 1972, when Moheb Abdul Ghaffar, a former Egyptian Ambassador to Denmark, was sentenced in Cairo to ten years' hard labour for spying for Israel. Ghaffar had served for some time as Egypt's military attaché in West Germany. He appeared before a military tribunal, accused of 'communicating with a foreign state with the intention of harming Egypt militarily and politically and divulging state secrets to a foreign power'. In this case few details were revealed, but the gist of the evidence was that Ghaffar confided in 'an Intelligence officer of a Western state who had close contacts with Israel.'

In November 1974, an Egyptian military court sentenced a Palestinian and his Egyptian wife to death by hanging after finding them guilty of spying for Israel. Ibrahim Shalim and his wife, Inshirah, were said to have been arrested the previous August for being in possession of a US-made radio transmitter. The prosecution stated that they used it to report on 'any military moves indicating a new war in the region'. Their eighteen-year-old son received five years on the same charge and two younger sons were sent to a juvenile home. Again on 30 November 1976, a supreme military court in Cairo condemned to death a Palestinian, Samir el Tamini, for spying for Israel. It is interesting to note that el Tamini had been arrested as long before as October of the previous year.

It could be deducted from all this that, though Israel may have had traitors in her own camp, equally the Arabs have had some in theirs. This has been a see-saw situation, with left-wing Israelis sometimes taking a pro-Arab view, and with some left-wing Arabs being disenchanted with Sadat's anti-Soviet policy and swinging over to the Israeli cause. In the Middle East it is perhaps easiest to seek traitors among the totally illogical and the semi-educated. But there are sometimes firmer bases for establishing a secret alliance and one such was set up in the late summer of 1976 when Shimon Peres made an arrangement with Lebanese Christians and Moslem moderates for the purpose of destroying the power of the Palestinian guerrillas in Lebanon. Peres paid a number of secret visits to Lebanon to make such an arrangement, the spadework for which was done by the Mossad. Plans included the training of Lebanese troops, an Israeli naval blockade of ports controlled by Moslem leftists, supply of arms to Lebanese rightists and efforts to train villagers in Southern Lebanon should Palestinian guerrillas seek to re-establish bases there.

But the other factors which have made the development of a highly efficient Secret Service so vital to Israel have been the international co-operation given to the Palestinian terrorist movement and the steadily increasing hostility of Russia. Reports of huge arms supplies to Egypt from the USSR, despite the ostensibly cool relations between the two countries, and the creation of a large reserve of Russian arms in the Egyptian Western Desert have not helped matters. The Israeli Secret Service believes that Russia is prepared to encourage yet another Middle East war, if Israel does not retreat to her pre-1967 borders. Late in 1976 all intelligence reports pointed to the establishment of huge Russian military stores and equipment not only in Egyptian territory, but in Libya, too.

Sadat, like Nasser before him, may give the impression to wishful thinkers in the Western World that he is anti-communist, but this has never prevented Egypt from choosing a long spoon to sup with the devil they know may help them. Often it has been the KGB who has passed information to Egypt indicating the activities of Israeli spies. One such case was that of Ifeba Amer Selim, an Egyptian who had worked in the Paris office of the Arab League, who in December 1974, was tried and executed for spying for Israel.

In combating the internationalist aspect of the terrorism directed towards Israel (and its international nature was an important part in the psychological warfare waged by the Arabs), the Mossad set great store on its co-operation with other Secret Services. This was particularly well illustrated in September 1976, when co-operation between the security services of Israel, Holland and India broke a European self-styled 'Maoist' gang training to hi-jack airliners with the PFLP. Lydia Janssen, a 23-year-old Dutch woman, was arrested at Ben-Gurion airport in Jerusalem on the eve of the Jewish New Year. According to the Israeli police, she confessed that she had come on a reconnaissance mission. She and a male member of the gang, Marius Nieuwburg, had been sent to check Air France flights from Paris to Bombay by way of Tel Aviv for a future sabotage operation. On the basis of a tip from Interpol the Indian police arrested Nieuwburg in Bombay, while the Dutch police raided houses in Amsterdam, Breda and Nieuweroord in quest of other members of this international gang. The Dutch woman was one of a group of sixteen who had been given training in handling weapons and explosives at a PFLP base in South Yemen, thirteen of them being Dutch citizens. They belonged to the 'Red Youth' organisation which had established links with various international revolutionary movements, including the IRA.

Soviet espionage directed against Israel is, however, a many-sided operation and it goes far beyond the mere helping of the Palestinian Arabs' cause, or that of Egypt or Syria. The Russians are eager to learn something of Israel's intelligence methods and techniques, because they have been highly impressed by the technological developments of the Israeli Secret Service in the past decade. Then again, they are desperately anxious to find out what kind of intelligence is being passed out by Zionists in the Soviet Union. Though the Russians have made a point of not employing Russian Jews in key technological posts in the USSR, or in the Secret Service, for several years past, they have not been able to stamp out completely the previous Jewish monopoly in scientific learning. Just as Israel has used Jews who can be passed off as Arabs to spy in Arab territories, so, too, they are able to employ Jews who can pass as non-Jewish Russians in the Soviet Union. And if the Russians have tended to ban Jews from posts in the KGB and other security services, some of the other East European communist states have not followed suit. There are still a number of Zionists in key positions in Intelligence in Rumania, Bulgaria and Czechoslovakia who are able to act as agents of the Mossad as well.

For a long time to come the menace of international terrorism may pose more problems for the Israeli Secret Service than even the possibility of war. But for the Israelis' response to this growing problem, the situation today might be very much worse for the

whole civilised world. But the fact remains that the very diverse
and international nature of organised terrorism gives it an advantage which ultimately could pose threats greater than those of war.
This was illustrated early in 1977 when a hidden microphone was
placed in the home of a West German scientist because of fears
that he would pass on information about nuclear equipment to
terrorists. The tip that he might do just this was passed on to the
West German Intelligence by the Mossad. The fact that there was
a real risk of a leakage of information was admitted by the
Minister of the Interior in Bonn, Professor Maihofer.

The man in question was Dr. Klaus Traube, manager of the
Interatom nuclear equipment firm and supervisor of a fast-
breeder reactor project, one of the few West Germans in a position to release, in the words of Professor Maihofer, 'the danger-
potential of atomic energy to the public's detriment . . . he had
been in a position to give terrorists instructions for attacks from
outside as well as for infiltration'. Professor Maihofer added that
a series of bomb attacks on French nuclear installations early in
1975 had been a vital factor in the decision to 'bug' Dr. Traube,
who had been in contact with Hans-Joachim Klein, who took
part in the attack on the Vienna headquarters of the Organisation
of Petroleum Exporting Countries in December 1975.

There can be no question at all from a strictly Western
military point of view that Israel, and especially the Israeli
Secret Service, could be worth a great deal to the NATO powers,
more than enough, if included in that alliance, to offset the growing supremacy of the Russians. Already Israel has many answers
to questions which the Western Intelligence Services have failed
to solve, often in fields which seem to be in the realm of science
fiction. One of these is the strange new world of psychic espionage.

Paradoxically, the Soviet Union, though supposedly based on
no-nonsense strictly materialistic principles, has for many years
taken the keenest interest in this subject. Scientists, occultists and
even amateurs who dabble in the sphere of the paranormal, are
swiftly brought within the Soviet official orbit, whether they are
Russians, Bulgarians, Rumanians or Czechs. At the same time a
great deal of Soviet espionage is being devoted to discovering
what other powers are doing in this sphere. Generally speaking,
the Western World has been sceptical of any serious study of
psychic espionage. It is said that the United States is fifty years
behind the Soviet Union in its systematic and scientific examina-

tion of what can broadly be described as the paraphysical, yet in Israel and China there is a growing realisation that it is a matter of national security for this gap to be closed.

On 21 December 1976, the Soviet authorities stamped down firmly on a planned three-day symposium in Moscow on Jewish culture, some forty-five Jewish activists reportedly being arrested as 'ringleaders'. The security sweep by the KGB netted the entire thirteen-man Moscow organising committee and many more Jewish activists were arrested in Soviet provincial cities. This was reported in the world's press at the time, but one thing was not mentioned: one of the symposiums said to have been prepared by the Jews was on the subject of 'the international study of the paraphysical phenomena, covering telepathy, psychokinesis, extra-sensory-perception and Kirlian photography'.

Among the foreigners refused entry visas for some of these meetings were Israelis who had been prepared to present several addresses on these subjects. A number of participants arriving from provincial cities were deported from Moscow. Others were prevented from coming and only three reached the conference. Members of the organising committee detained included Professor Benjamin Fain, Leonid Volvovsky, Pavel Abramovich, Vladimir Prestin, and Arcady May. Another Jewish activist, Alexander Lerner, was taken into custody with his wife. Some fifty Jews were gathered at the suburban flat of Grigory Rozenshtein, one of the detained speakers. Two of the papers delivered by Mr. Rozenshtein covered 'the role of mysticism in Jewish history'.[2]

Psychic espionage aims, in effect, to make a devastating short cut through the normal processes of espionage and counter-espionage. Any nation which manages to acquire a distinct lead in this sphere could achieve something like total superiority in a war. So far no nation has acquired this lead, not even the Soviet Union which has the undoubted edge in the extent of its research and experimental work. But the Israelis have taken this sufficiently seriously to have monitored what the Soviet Union and other communist countries are doing in this field. What has impressed the Israelis is the fact that it is not only Soviet Russia which is developing the theme of psychic espionage, but her Eastern European allies as well.

The versatility of the Jews in scientific as well as cultural fields is well known, but their pre-eminence in what is now referred to as PSI is not generally appreciated. One of the most remarkable

of their early practitioners in psychic and paranormal experimentation was Stefan Ossowiecki, who was born in Russia in
1877, and who found he had psychic gifts and developed these
with the aid of a Rabbi. In 1917 Ossowiecki was imprisoned for
political crimes and in 1921, when he was set free, he went to
Poland. There he developed his psychic talents to the full and
carried out a number of telepathic experiments, including one
long-distance transmission. A journalist in Cracow made a drawing at his home, sent a copy of it to scientists at Marienbad while
at a distance of 400 miles Ossowiecki telepathically drew the same
picture in the sand.

Ossowiecki never accepted any monetary rewards for his work
and during World War II he used his talents to help the Polish
underground. 'Documentary accounts speak of him locating
specific bodies in mass graves. . . . On the day of the Warsaw
Uprising he remarked, "I see that I shall shortly die a terrible
death. But I have had a wonderful life!" '³ Before the end of the
war he was executed by the Nazis. In the annals of the Jewish
underground movement the name of Stefan Ossowiecki is still
honoured and one paraphysical laboratory inside Poland today is
named after him and actually services Israel with intelligence
gleaned through PSI techniques. So highly is the PSI-work
carried out by this agency regarded that, in case it is eventually
located by the KGB, a duplicate laboratory working on parallel
lines has been set up in Western Europe.

Such work is more effectively carried on outside Israel for a
number of reasons. First, there is the undeniable fact that Israel
is not only a democracy, but a small and compact nation where
gossip spreads as fast as it does in a village. Anything unusual or
bizarre in the realm of intelligence needs to be experimented with
outside Israeli territory. A great deal of this experimentation can
fairly easily be conducted under the guise of other aspects of the
paranormal—faith healing, psychometry and extra-sensory perception. But there are other reasons for working outside Israeli
territory: psychic research is still a comparatively new science
and it can only be developed by a free exchange of ideas with
international bodies. American research in this field is nowhere
near as advanced or as intensive as in the USSR, but at least
American scientific studies are freely available for others to study.
It is also fairly certain that only among the Eastern European
communist states is psychic espionage being developed and put

on a military basis. So Israel's espionage in this field is mainly directed to that quarter.

The International Association for Psychotronic Research is based in Prague and its president is a Czech, Dr. Zdenek Rejdak. Other leading members come from Bulgaria, Britain, France, Yugoslavia, the United States and the USSR. According to an Israeli source, the Russians are eager to take full advantage of such international bodies to spy on what others are doing, but unwilling to give away much more than morsels of information on their own work. Dr. Milan Ryzl, a scientist who lived in Prague until 1967, when he went to the USA, has made a prolonged study of all aspects of the paraphysical and PSI. In Prague he set up his own paraphysical laboratory. One day shortly before he left the country the Czech secret police visited him: 'they wanted me to report to them on the psychic research going on in countries I visited. . . . I am a scientist, not a spy, so I decided to get out and go to America.'[4]

An Israeli specialist in PSI and in its applications in intelligence told me: 'Our main contacts in this sphere are mainly behind the Iron Curtain. There is no particular secret about that because that is where psychic espionage is being practised. The Russians, as one would expect, are in the lead as regards the extent of the work carried out. They have military-controlled research centres into the paraphysical at Moscow, Leningrad, Omsk, Irkutsk, Vladivostock, Khabarovsk and Sartov of which we know for certain. We have had reports of secret establishments for this purpose being set up in Siberia and at the Durov Institute there are many specialists studying telepathy and conducting experiments in ESP. All this is controlled either by the military or the KGB. We have had some details of Soviet submarines conducting telepathic experiments.

'But in Czechoslovakia, Poland, Rumania and Bulgaria there are many centres for developing psychic espionage and counter-espionage. Our contacts in these countries are excellent for the very good reason that the Jews led the field in this type of research before World War II, notably in Czechoslovakia and Poland. News from concentration camps was sometimes obtained by clairvoyant means and telepathy. The Czechs used PSI long before the war and it was a Jew who helped compile the Czech Army handbook on ESP in 1942—*Clairvoyance, Hypnotism and Magnetism*.'

The young Jew who was in part responsible for this handbook

escaped from Czechoslovakia in 1946 and made his way to Vienna where he served the Israeli cause until his death in 1971, often using clairvoyancy and ESP, as well as psychometry to ascertain the whereabouts of missing persons and in some instances enemy agents.

The Israelis have found that there is widespread indifference and scepticism in Western Europe about the development of psychic espionage, even if in the USA there is a little more enthusiasm. But Dr. Ryzl has made it quite clear that he regards Soviet experiments in this direction as menacing: 'the military and the Secret Police in the USSR display an unusual, disproportionate interest in parapyschology. Some years ago a project was begun in the USSR to apply telepathy to indoctrinate and "re-educate anti-social elements". It was hoped that suggestion at a distance could induce individuals, without their being aware of it, to adopt the officially desired political and social attitudes. . . . The dangers of possible misuse of PSI should not be overlooked.'[5]

The Israelis have not overlooked this and they probably now have a closer insight into what the Russians are doing in psychic espionage than any other nation. 'This isn't just a question of telepathy or ESP alone,' my Israeli contact told me. 'The USSR is spending vast sums of money in developing research and experimentation in some very sinister directions. Their telepathic research for instance is being devoted to what they call the transference of behaviour impulses—the subluminal conditioning of a person's character. We know they are concerned with developing this technique to try to control agents and even to create traitors. There is some evidence that they have experimented with this technique in the Middle East. One young Israeli who was studying at a European university was marked down by the KGB as a possible candidate for "subluminal control". He was invited to various telepathic seances organised by a Bulgarian and he at once suspected something devious was being practised on the participants. In these seances a third person was introduced, known as "The Interpolator". He was not only bugging the telepathy exercises of the two people involved in transferring messages by ESP, but, one suspects, trying to distort this work in some way. The young Israeli then recalled that when he had first been recruited to come along to these meetings with other young students, he had been questioned quite a lot about his home, family and background. One of the questions put to him concerned his father and he realised that he had supplied the information that his father worked in a military establishment in Tel Aviv.

'This proves nothing, you may think. Well, the young Israeli reported his suspicions. He couldn't in any way confirm them because he was not knowledgeable in this field. But we followed up his report by making inquiries from agents in Sofia and Leningrad. Surprise, surprise, we found that the Russians were working on means of monitoring—or bugging, if you like—telepathic communications, and one of the aims of this was to distort the flow of messages. You can compare this to radar; "The Interpolator", as they call him, creates a kind of jamming of the thought waves. But of course it can also be used for playing tricks with the sub-conscious mind. This is the kind of way in which psychic espionage could be applied in the case of a man like Lee Harvey Oswald, who murdered President Kennedy. I am not saying this was the case then, but Oswald had been to Russia. What we are now convinced of is that some of the extremist terrorist and anarchist groups of young people have been subjected to a kind of telepathic control.'

Another aspect of Soviet development of PSI is that of Kirlian photography, so named after Davidovitch Semion Kirlian, its 78-year-old inventor. This is a revolutionary form of photography which investigates the supposed human 'aura' and the energy field emitted by all living things. The Russians have experimented with Kirlian photography in various ways, for detecting diseases in the early stages, for selecting better seeds for planting and also as a new means of lie-detection in interrogation. It has proved more accurate and effective than any other lie-detector techniques and the Israelis are also examining the application of Kirlian photography in Intelligence.

To monitor Soviet experiments in this field is a tremendous undertaking and in the normal way for any Secret Service to attempt this would be so costly it would hardly be worth while. The Israelis have cut the cost by ensuring that the monitoring is only done by trained psychic researchers and by setting up paraphysical laboratories where information passed through from agents behind the Iron Curtain can be assessed. The agents gathering such intelligence are themselves practitioners in this field. As my Israeli contact told me: 'The really big clamp-down on psychic and paraphysical data in the Soviet Union has not yet come. At the moment they are still as anxious to learn from the West as they are to guard their own motives for research. Their policy seems to be that they are prepared to leak a certain amount of information to the West in the hope that they will get something in return. To some extent they are highly successful in this, largely because the Western World as a whole is still lukewarm towards the menace of psychic espionage in the long term. So the result is that this type of research is left to scientists and others who have no connection with Intelligence. They see no reason why they should not exchange information with the Soviet Union. Thus at the moment it is not too difficult to get a general picture of what is going on in the USSR and Eastern European countries, providing the monitoring of such intelligence is conducted solely by scientists in this particular sphere of research.

'Our best sources are in Bulgaria where the secret police use trained clairvoyants to assist them in crime detection. The Bulgarians have some of the finest clairvoyants and telepathy experts in the game. They also have Institutes of Suggestology and Parapsychology in Sofia and Petrich.'

Israel's own Uri Geller is, of course, already world famous through his demonstrations of psychic phenomena. The Russians set up a special committee to study him and his experiments three years ago. 'We found out that they were doing this in a round-about way from Paris,' said my contact. 'At the same time we discovered that they were developing a new form of music to help induce and maintain a state of trance—heliphonic music.'

It is possible to set alongside this Israeli evidence of the Soviet Union's development of psychic espionage some positive confirmation from other sources. The authors of *PSI: Psychic Research Behind the Iron Curtain* have written 'top-calibre Soviet scientists had already made significant breakthroughs in psychic research, a field usually ignored by Western science.... By the time our trip through Russia, Bulgaria and Czechoslovakia was over, our originally slender baggage had grown to three hundred over-weight pounds of research material.' Dr. Ryzl, when visiting Soviet PSI laboratories in 1967, said he was told by a Russian that 'when suitable means of propaganda are cleverly used, it is possible to mould any man's conscience so that in the end he may misuse his abilities while remaining convinced that he is serving an honest purpose . . . the USSR has the means to keep the results of such research from the rest of the world, and, as practical applications of these results become possible, there is no doubt the Soviet Union will do so.' This was before Dr. Ryzl left Czechoslovakia for America which may suggest that he was then being treated as a confidant.

Israel is already far ahead of the Western World in these techniques, but this is in no small measure due to the fact that during the past century Jews have led the world in much of this research and have shown a remarkable talent for it. There is no better example than the telepathist Wolf Messing, a Polish Jew who fled from the German advance in Poland in 1939 by escaping to the Soviet Union hidden under a cart-load of hay. He had little to offer the Russians other than his own telepathic talents which, if somewhat reluctantly at first, they accepted as being worthy of consideration. Eventually he was given personal audiences by Stalin. By the 1950s he was one of the best known men in Russia and the one man who was able to use his telepathic talents to get through the guards into Stalin's presence without being challenged. In his autobiography, *I am a Telepathist*, Messing refers to the occasion when he managed to walk out of a building past guards ordered to stop him at all costs: 'I am sure the guards would not have let me pass if I had directed at them the sug-gestion to let me pass as myself, but, using my mental power, I made them see in me the high official whom they would let through without a pass. Similarly, a man under hypnosis can be told to shoot a rabbit when in fact he would be shooting at a man.'[6]

During World War II Messing was officially evacuated to Siberia for his own safety, but he still offered advice to the authorities and was on countless occasions proved to be accurate in his divinations. When his autobiography was published by *Sovietskaya Rossiya* in 1967, the book was suddenly withdrawn, though no official reason for this was given. Messing is as cele-brated as a stage artist as a serious telepathist and researcher, and long before he escaped from Poland to Russia he had travelled all over the world giving exhibitions of his talents. He is not an orthodox Jew, but he has retained a devotion to his race, as was exemplified before World War II when he refused a reward from a Polish count for locating some missing family jewellery, but asked for the count's influence to be used with the Polish govern-ment to have a law infringing the rights of Jews to be annulled. This was in fact done.

'Just as there was a space race between the super-powers, eventually there will be a race in PSI,' my Israeli contact continued. 'The West hasn't woken up to the urgency of this yet. All we can hope is that that race ends in a stalemate. Only then will there be any safety. We must somehow ensure that we attain the same kind of deadlock in the sphere of psychic espionage that we have in nuclear warfare, with no side daring to run the appalling risks of releasing this type of secret warfare to the full. Certainly our aim is to make sure that there is such a deadlock and stalemate and that the Western World as a whole and not just Israel benefits from this.'

This digression into what is still largely an unexplored area of espionage and counter-espionage as far as the Western World is concerned is yet another example of how the Israeli Secret Service is very often not only diligently trying to ensure the survival of her own people, but doing much of the work which is essential to the survival of the whole Western World.

There are many who will take a contrary view and equate Zionism with militant nationalism and not all who do this are necessarily pro-Soviet. Therein lies Israel's dilemma: she is beset with the problem of living with enemies in both camps—the Western World and the Soviet Union's orbit. Yet it is hard to see how Western civilisation as we know it can survive in the long run without the co-operation of Israel's Secret Service. Already the West has benefited to a remarkable degree from a certain amount of co-operation in this respect, just as Israel has acquired certain advantages from the assistance of Western Intelligence. What should be borne in mind is that the work of a Soviet spy placed inside Israel is directed not only against that country but against the West as well. The greatest Soviet espionage success, so far as is known, was the placing of a top agent in the Ministry of Foreign Affairs, and it was the Western World, perhaps even more than Israel, which suffered from this. The man, a Swiss Jew, had formed part of Leopold Trepper's Rote Kapelle ('Red Orchestra') network in Belgium before World War II. After having been thoroughly trained in Russia he was sent to Israel as a 'sleeper agent' after the war and his talents were so remarkable that two Israeli ministries fought over which should take his services. Eventually, and disastrously, it was the Israeli Ministry of Foreign Affairs which secured him. When he was finally caught enormous damage had been done.

One thing is certain: persecution of the Jews continues today as virulently inside the Soviet Union as ever it did in Nazi Germany: there is only one difference, the Russians are prepared to tolerate the Jews as long as they prove themselves to be good Soviet citizens. This may seem a distinct advance on the Hitlerian attitudes, but there are no accurate figures on how many Jews have been eliminated in the Soviet Union. Worse still, the Soviet Secret Service goes to the most bizarre lengths to plant anti-Jewish propaganda round the world. One of the most mysterious of these operations is the attempt to show that it was the Jews who smuggled the Czarist millions and jewels out of Russia during the Revolution and that it was a Jew, Aaron Simonovitch, secretary to the notorious Rasputin, who not only organised this, but enabled the Russian Royal Family to be rescued from Ekaterinburg. Nor do the Russians just rely on rumours; they back them up with forged coded messages (of which a number have come into my possession) purporting to show how the Czar and his family were not murdered by the Bolsheviks, but enabled to escape by a diabolical American–Japanese–British–Jewish plot. The notorious 'Chivers Papers', which are alleged to be in American CIA archives, include all manner of faked telegrams, alleged accounts of rescue operations and 'proofs' that members of the Russian Royal Family are still alive today.[7] That there was an attempt to rescue the Royal Family is now undoubted and it is equally certain that the events at Ekaterinburg were not as described in the 'White Russian' report by Judge Nicholas Sokolov. But the detailed dossier on the bogus rescue concocted by Soviet Intelligence is just blatant propaganda, but sufficiently cleverly and semi-factually manufactured as to have provoked exhaustive inquiries into the subject both in the USA and Britain.

From the same 'Disinformation Section' of the KGB has also come the smear on Henry Kissinger, alleging that he was formerly a secret service agent working for the Polish Intelligence! Naturally, the Russians are clever enough to use right-wing organisations and personnel to spread these stories, always providing sufficient bogus factual detail to give them some substance. It was the Chinese Secret Service which first scotched that canard, informing both the Americans and the Israelis of its origins.

But the propaganda of hate, the spreading of false information will continue, just as it did under the Czarist regime, under the Nazis and today under the Brezhnev administration, as long as there are sufficient fools in the world to accept the nonsense about the Protocols of the Elders of Zion, about the rescuing of the Czar and the stories about Henry Kissinger. Only when sanity prevails over romantic credulity will the propaganda cease and persecution stop. Until then Israel will need to have one of the world's finest Secret Services.

Notes,
Bibliography
and
Index

Notes

CHAPTER 1
1 Joshua ii, 1–21.
2 Numbers xiii, 3.
3 Numbers xiii, 17–26.
4 See *The Romance of the Last Crusade*, Vivian Gilbert, W. B. Feakins, New York, 1923, pp. 183–5.
5 See *History of the Commonwealth and Protectorate*, vol. III, S. R. Gardiner, Longmans, London, 1894–1903.
6 See *A History of Russia*, Graham Stephenson, Praeger Publishers, New York, 1970, and *Azeff: The Spy, Russian Terrorist & Police Stool*, Boris Nicolaievsky, Doubleday Doran, New York, 1934.

CHAPTER 2
1 *Story of My Life*, Moshe Dayan, Weidenfeld & Nicolson, London, 1970.
2 *Ibid.*
3 *Days of Fire*, Shmuel Katz, W. H. Allen, London, 1968.
4 Cited by William Stevenson in *A Man Called Intrepid*, Macmillan, London, 1976.
5 *SOE in France*, M. R. D. Foot, HMSO, London, 1964.
6 The failure to undertake at least a token rescue operation has always been played down by all the Allies. From French Resistance sources alone the British and French Governments had ample reports, as early as the spring of 1943, that more than 110,000 Jews had been deported from France alone to Auschwitz and that of this number less than 14,000 were then alive. Ultimately the figure of those who survived is said to have been barely 2,800. As Leon Poliakov wrote in *Harvest of Hate*, 'just being alive was a kind of defiance in a Jew as one can gather from the innumerable SS sayings, such as "You leave here only through the chimney." '

CHAPTER 3
1 *Shield of David: The Story of Israel's Armed Forces*, Weidenfeld & Nicolson, London, 1970.
2 *Sunday Times*, 15 September 1946.
3 *Sunday Times*, 1 June 1947.
4 For further details of the building up of the Israeli Air Forces see *The Israeli Air Force*, Robert Jackson, Tom Stacey, London, 1970.

CHAPTER 4
1 *Daily Telegraph*, 28 October 1952.

CHAPTER 5

1 *Story of My Life*, Dayan.
2 *The Israeli Army in Politics: the Persistence of the Civilian over the Military*, Amos Perlmutter, University of California, 1968.
3 *Story of My Life*, Dayan.
4 *The Israeli Army in Politics*, Perlmutter.
5 *Ibid.*

CHAPTER 6

1 This is the identity given by most sources, including newspaper reports after Elie's arrest. However, it may even be that Elie had two 'covers' and that at some stage in the operations one of them was 'blown', as E. H. Cookridge has this to say in an article entitled 'Amid This Susurration of Spies', *Daily Telegraph Magazine*, 23 July 1976: 'He [Cohen] appeared in the Syrian capital as Harnhan Attasi, an American-naturalised member of a wealthy Syrian family, who had settled many years before in Detroit.'
2 *Elie Cohen: Our Man in Damascus*, Ben Hanan. See also *L'Espion Que Venait d'Israel: L'Affaire Elie Cohen*, E. Ben Dan.
3 *Sunday Times*, 30 May 1965.
4 Cited in *Elie Cohen: Our Man in Damascus*, Ben Hanan.

CHAPTER 7

1 *The Final Solution: The attempt to exterminate the Jews of Europe, 1939–1945*, Gerald Reitlinger, Vallentine Mitchell, London, 1953.
2 Cited by Gerald Reitlinger.
3 Article entitled 'Nazi Hunter has 250 more targets' in *Insight* column of the *Sunday Times*, 21 April 1963.
4 Article entitled 'The Avenger', by René MacColl, *Daily Express*, 30 April 1964.
5 Article entitled 'The Secret Lifeline for Ex-Nazis on the Run', by Antony Terry, *Sunday Times*, 23 July 1967.
6 Article entitled 'How I Caught Mass Killer', by Professor Tuviah Friedman, *Sunday Graphic*, 29 May 1960.
7 *Ibid.*

CHAPTER 8

1 *The House on Garibaldi Street; the capture of Adolf Eichmann*, Isser Harel, André Deutsch, London, 1975.
2 *Ibid.*
3 *Ibid.*
4 *Ibid.*
5 Victor Alexandrov, writing in *Israel Star*, 2 December 1960.
6 Cited by Ladislas Farago in extracts from his book *The Bormann File*, appearing in the *Daily Express*, 30 November 1972.
7 *The House on Garibaldi Street*, Harel.
8 *The Capture of Adolf Eichmann*, Moshe Pearlman, Weidenfeld & Nicolson, London, 1961.

CHAPTER 9
1 Article entitled 'Israel: Trends in Intelligence', by C. L. Sulzberger in the *New York Herald Tribune*, 23 October 1974.
2 *Story of My Life*, Dayan.
3 See article in *Psychology Today*, 18 March 1975. Christopher Macy, editor of this magazine, then stated that the classified documentation on pigeon-training had come to him from the USA. 'We quoted the military contract number [Air Force contract 33 (615) 2301] to prove their authenticity.'
4 See article entitled 'Spotting the truth in a bead of sweat' by Simon Winchester, in the *Guardian*,

CHAPTER 10
1 Article entitled 'The Secret Service Nasser Fears', by Denis Sefton Delmer, *Sunday Telegraph*, 14 January 1962.
2 *Ibid.*
3 Gehlen's Memoirs were serialised in the German newspaper, *Die Welt*, 10 September 1971.

CHAPTER 11
1 Some of the background to the activities of the German scientists in Egypt is given in *La Chasse aux Savants Allemands*, by Michel Bar-Zohar, Librairie Arthème Fayard, Paris, 1965.

CHAPTER 12
1 *The House on Garibaldi Street*, Isser Harel.
2 *Days of Fire*, Shmuel Katz.
3 *The House on Garibaldi Street*, Harel.

CHAPTER 13
1 Article entitled 'Amid This Susurration of Spies', *Sunday Telegraph Magazine*, by E. H. Cookridge, 23 July 1976.
2 All quotations in this paragraph are taken from *The Times* report of the case, 15 January 1862.

CHAPTER 14
1 *CIA: The Myth and the Madness*, Patrick McGarvey, Saturday Review Press, 1972.

CHAPTER 15
1 The Ben-Gurion memorandum caused something of a sensation at the time and some of it was leaked to the press. See 'Israelis Study Spy Report' by Terence Prittie, diplomatic correspondent, in the *Guardian*, 3 November 1964.
2 'Spy Ring Staggers Israel', *Sunday Telegraph*, 17 December 1972.
3 *Guardian*, 26 March 1973: article by Eric Silver, entitled 'Tightrope that Bust'.
4 *Ha'aretz*, Tel Aviv, 22 February 1973.

CHAPTER 16

1 See *A History of the Chinese Secret Service*, by Richard Deacon
(Frederick Muller, London, 1974): one of the men responsible for a
changed outlook towards the Israelis was Kao Liang, who became secretary
of China's delegation to the United Nations, and who was a go-between
for the diplomats and their African contacts. He is one of the ablest
operators in the Chinese Secret Service. China's aim in Africa has been
to check Russian influence and to spy on all Russian missions; to this
extent its aims coincide with those of the Mossad. The Chinese NCNA
helped to finance the abortive coup against Nasser in 1965. In Khartoum
in the early seventies, the Chinese Intelligence Service was credited with
having established some unusual links with both the French Intelligence in
neighbouring territories, north and south, and with Israel. In the largely
unreported civil war that has been waged for years in the Sudan there
were at times some incredible groupings of rival interests: Egypt, France,
Russia, Israel and China, each aided by mercenaries.
2 These Israeli statements were checked against information from other
sources and found to be correct. There was a letter from a company in
Yugoslavia handling the shipment which confirmed that the cargo had
been flown from Prague by a special flight of Czechoslovakian airlines, as
described by the informant: for the record the transit permission was No.
33512–887, 5.4.71, and the name of the agent who had authority to dispose
of the goods was cited together with his address. Translation of a cable
concerning this transaction read: 'Transit authority Nr. 3351–2/887
[indecipherable] 5/7 concerns various arms and ammunition from CSSR
to Chad port of destination Douala. Permission sent to frontier authorities
Ploce and InterEuropa.'

CHAPTER 17

1 There was nevertheless an impression in French governmental circles
that there had been bungling in their own ranks. Two French officials,
General Bernard Cazelles, permanent Under-Secretary for Defence, and
Engineer-General Louis Bonte, head of the international section of the
armaments department, were suspended, while shortly afterwards another
officer resigned and joined the French armaments firm of Dassault.

CHAPTER 18

1 The *Daily Telegraph* of 15 September 1972, reported from their
Jerusalem correspondent that Ali Salameh was 'the brains behind the
Munich Olympic murders' and that he 'headed the European wing of
the Palestine guerrilla organisation, the Black September group. . . . Israeli
sources say this group aims at carrying out spectacular and daring operations in Europe, the Middle East, Africa and North America. Its spearhead
is believed to consist of "a suicide squad" of a few dozen terrorists ready
and eager to sacrifice their lives.'

CHAPTER 19

1 *Carlos: Portrait of a Terrorist*, by Colin Smith, André Deutsch, London,
1976.

2 Letter by Eleanor Aitken, headed 'A Poet's Death' in the *Sunday Times* of 26 September 1976.

3 *Hit Team: The exciting Story of Israel's Strike Against Arab Terrorists in Europe*, by David Tinnin, Weidenfeld & Nicolson, London, 1976.

4 *Guardian*, 11 August 1976, citing the Norwegian newspaper, *Aftenposten*.

5 *Guardian*, 9 July 1975.

6 One of the problems in identifying some of Israel's commando heroes is that many of them go under code-names for security reasons and a number of them have been called 'Rafael' or 'Eitan', and sometimes the names are combined together. Apart from this mention of 'Eitan H', William Stevenson in *90 Minutes at Entebbe* (Bantam Books, New York, 1976) refers to one of the Entebbe raid team: '.'. "Rafael" is his *nom de guerre*.' In *L'Oeil de Tel Aviv* by Steve Eytan there is mention of 'Rafoul', '... *le plus célèbre des parachutistes et le plus discuté, l'homme qui monte les opérations de représailles en territoire ennemi.*' This refers to Rafael (sometimes called 'Rafool' because of his daredevil exploits) Eitan, who was born in 1929 in a kibbutz in the Yezreel Valley. As a youth he was a Palmach officer and between 1949 and 1954 he was discharged and rejoined the Israeli Army twice. In between he studied military history in Tel Aviv. He made a name for himself as a daring fighter, commanding various reprisal raids against Arab terrorists with the motto 'After Me'. After a course at the Staff and Command College he was appointed deputy commander of a paratroop brigade and then given time off to study in the US. In the 1967 War he commanded a paratroop brigade and fought in the Gaza Strip and Sinai. He was wounded in Kantara for the third time in his military career. Later he was promoted to Major-General and since April 1974, he has been Commander of Northern Command.

7 Interview with Abu Daoud by Mo Teitelbaum, *Sunday Times*, 16 January 1977.

CHAPTER 20

1 *New York Times*, 21 May 1974.

2 *New York Times*, 12 September 1975.

3 *Ibid.*

4 *Story of My Life*, Dayan.

5 *Ibid.*

6 *Perception, Deception & Surprise: the Case of the Yom Kippur War*, Michael I. Handel, Hebrew University of Jerusalem, The Jerusalem Papers on Peace Problems.

7 *Ibid.*

8 *Adelphi Papers*, no. 111: *The Arab–Israeli War, October, 1973, Background & Events*, International Institute of Strategic Studies, London, 1975.

9 *Blitzkrieg and Conquest*, G. B. Williams.

10 *New York Times*, 21 May 1974.

CHAPTER 21

1 *90 Minutes at Entebbe*, Stevenson.
2 From the transcripts of telephone calls made by Lieutenant-Colonel Baruch Bar-Lev to Idi Amin, issued by the Israeli Information Office.
3 *Operation Thunder*, Yehuda Ofer, Penguin Books, Harmondsworth, 1976.
4 Cited in a message from Arthur Chesworth in the *Daily Express*.

CHAPTER 22

1 Article by Dr. Ryzl entitled 'Parapsychology in Communist Countries of Europe', in the *International Journal of Parapsychology*, vol. X, No. 3, 1968.
2 'KGB Swoop on 45 as Moscow Jews Meet', *Daily Telegraph*, 22 December 1976.
3 Cited in *Psychic Discoveries Behind the Iron Curtain*, Sheila Ostrander and Lynn Schroeder, Bantam Books, New York, 1971.
4 *Ibid.*
5 'Parapsychology in Communist Countries of Europe', *International Journal of Parapsychology*, vol. X, No. 3, 1968.
6 'About Myself', in *Science & Religion*, 1965, and see also Messing's autobiography, *I am a Telepathist*, Smena, 1965.
7 Photostats of the mysterious 'Chivers Papers' still appear in various parts of the world in an effort to convince people that they actually exist either in US State Department archives or in those of the CIA. No official admission of the existence of these papers has ever been given. Some of the extracts consist of coded messages from the Russian Soviet authorities, some from the US State Department. 'Chivers' is the unexplained code name for the so-called operation to rescue the Czar and his family. Some samples of the messages are as follows: 'The plan is now in readiness . . . the aid of Simonovitch has been finally secured at a high cost'; there is a reference to a stay at 'a safe place of refuge' and to the fact that the Czar 'will not be known without his whiskers and with his hair so long'. . . the GDs [Grand Duchesses] were most compliant and snipped off each other's hair'. And on 16 February 1919 is this alleged message from the Secretary of State to the White House: 'Chivers in Turkish waters in accordance with route planned. Outside our jurisdiction.'

Bibliography

Allon, Yigal: *Shield of David: The Story of Israel's Armed Forces*, Weidenfeld & Nicolson, London, 1970.

Bar-Zohar, Michel: *La Chasse aux Savants Allemands*, Librairie Arthème Fayard, Paris, 1965.

Ben Dan, E.: *L'Espion Qui Venait d'Israel: L'Affaire Elie Cohen*, Librairie Arthème Fayard, Paris, 1967.

Ben Hanan, E.: *Elie Cohen: Our Man in Damascus*, ADM Publishing House, Tel Aviv, 1967.

Ben Shaul, Moshe (ed.): *Generals of Israel*, Hadar Publishing House, Tel Aviv, 1968.

Dayan, Moshe: *Story of My Life*, Weidenfeld & Nicolson, London, 1976.

De Gaury, Gerald: *The New State of Israel*, Derek Verschoyle, London, 1952.

De Gramont, Sanche: *The Secret War: The Story of International Espionage Since 1945*, André Deutsch, London, 1962.

Dekel, Efraim: *Shai: the Exploits of Hagana Intelligence*, Yoseleff, 1959.

Eisenberg, Dennis & Landau, Eli: *Carlos: Terror International*, Corgi Books, London, 1976.

Elon, Amos: *The Israelis: Founders & Sons*, Weidenfeld & Nicolson, London, 1971.

Eytan, Steve: *L'Oeil de Tel Aviv*, Paris, 1970.

Franklin, C.: *Spies in the 20th Century*, Odhams, London, 1967.

Friedman, Tuvia: *The Hunter*, Gibbs & Phillips, London, 1961.

Harel, Isser: *The House on Garibaldi Street*, André Deutsch, London, 1975.

Ind, Allison: *A History of Modern Espionage*, Hodder & Stoughton, London, 1965.

Jackson, Robert: *The Israeli Air Force*, Tom Stacey, London, 1970.

Joesten, J.: *They Call it Intelligence: Spies & Spy Techniques Since World War II*, Abelard-Schuman, London, 1963.

Katz, Shmuel: *Days of Fire*, W. H. Allen, London, 1968.

Laqueur, Walter: *The Struggle for the Middle East: The Soviet Union & the Middle East 1948–68*, written under the auspices of the Centre for Strategic and International Studies, Georgetown, Routledge & Kegan Paul, London, 1969.

Lotz, Wolfgang: *The Champagne Spy*, Vallentine Mitchell, London, 1972.

Marchetti, Victor & Marks, John D.: *The CIA & the Cult of Intelligence*, Jonathan Cape, London, 1974.

McGovern, W. M.: *Strategic Intelligence & the Shape of Tomorrow*, Bailey & Swinfen, Folkestone, U.K., 1961.

Monroe, Elizabeth: Adelphi Papers, No. 111, *The Arab–Israeli War, October, 1973; Background & Events*, International Institute of Strategic Studies, London, 1975.

Ofer, Yehuda: *Operation Thunder: the Entebbe Raid: the Israelis' Own Story*, Penguin Books, Harmondsworth, 1976 .

Pearlman, Moshe: *The Capture of Adolf Eichmann*, Weidenfeld & Nicolson, London, 1961.

Perlmutter, Amos: *The Israeli Army in Politics: the Persistence of the Civilian over the Military*, Committee for Middle East Studies, Institute of International Studies, University of California, Berkeley, 1968.

Smith, Colin: *Carlos: Portrait of a Terrorist*, André Deutsch, London, 1976.

Stevenson, William: *A Man Called Intrepid: the Secret War*, Macmillan, London, 1976.

Stevenson, William: *90 Minutes at Entebbe*, Bantam Books, London, 1976.

Teveth, Shabtai: *Moshe Dayan: the Soldier, the Man, the Legend*, Weidenfeld & Nicolson, London, 1972.

Tinnin, David B.: *Hit Team: the Exciting Story of Israel's Strike Against Arab Terrorists in Europe*, Weidenfeld & Nicolson, London, 1976.

Wiesenthal, Simon: *The Murderers Among Us*, William Heinemann, London, 1967.

Index

Aaronson family, 16–18
Aaronson, Aaron, 16–18
Aaronson, Alexander, 17
Aaronson, Sara, 17–18
Abdullah, King of Jordan, 92, 122
Abel, Hans, 89, 91, 103
Abramovich, Pavel, 291
Abwehr, the, 41, 134
Adam, General Yekutiel, 283
Adenauer, Dr. Konrad, 93, 155
Adham, Kamal, 214
Adiv, Ehud, 192–9
Adwan, Kemal, 234
Agranat Commission of Inquiry, 265–8
Al Ard, Magd, 83
Al Chir, Hassain Abad, 232–3
Alexandrov, Victor, 110, 302
Alexandrovitch, Grand Duke Sergei, 15
Al Fatah, 190, 197–9, 201–2, 226, 235, 238, 243
Al-Kubaissi, Dr. Basil, 233, 243
Allenby, General (later Field-Marshal), 10
Allon, Yigal, 40, 253
Alon, Col. Yosef, 238
Al-Senussi, King Mohammed Idris, of Libya, 211
Alwan, Adib, 201
Aman, the, 57–60, 68–9, 75, 120–2, 124, 126, 140, 164, 171, 176, 179, 181, 204, 258–60, 267–8
Amer, General Ali, 85
American Emergency Committee for Zionist Affairs, 34
American War Crimes Office, 97
Amin, Professor Omar (*see also* von Leers), 134
Amin Dada, President Idi, 271–2, 274–80, 283–5, 306

Amin el-Hafez, General, 83–4
Amiot, Félix, 219
Amit, Meir, 170–4, 203
Angleton, James, 169–70
Antaryessian, Hagop, 53
Anti-Defamation League, 170
Arafat, Yasser, 198
Arazi, Yehudi, 39, 43, 46
Arbush, Ali, 161
Argentinian Secret Service, 110–13
Ariel, Dr. Shmuel, 35
Arrighi, Batonnier Paul, 87
'Avengers', the, 222–42, 255, 275
Avigur, Shaul, 38–9
Avriel, Ehud, 42
Azeff, Ievno, 14–15, 20, 64, 301
Azia, Achmed Daoud, 160
Azzar, Samuel, 69–70

Baader-Meinhof Group, 226, 228, 238, 273
Baathist Party, 81, 83–4, 86–7, 205
Bach, Gabriel, 156
Balfour, Lord, 16
Bardelli sisters, 231
Barjot, Admiral Pierre, 118
Barker, General, GOC Palestine, 47
Bar-Lev, Lt.-Col. Baruch, 272, 277, 306
Basque Fighters, 225–6
Bauer, Dr. Fritz, 104–6, 110, 112
Bazri, Joseph, 68
Beer, Israel, 163–6
Be'eri, Isser, 54, 69
Begin, Menahem, 35, 50
Beirut, Secret Service raid on, 201, 233–5
Belkind, Na'aman, 17
Bendit, Daniel Cohn, 192–3
Bendman, Lt.-Col. Yona, 266
Ben-Gal, Joseph, 153–7

Ben-Gurion, David, 15, 29, 41, 43, 47–51, 56–8, 61, 63–6, 72–4, 105, 112, 116, 123, 147, 155, 158, 164, 168, 186–7, 224, 267–8
Ben-Gurion report on intelligence operations, 187, 303
Bennett, Max, 70
Bergson Group, 34
Beridze, Anastasse, *see* Tauber, Adolf
Bernadotte, Count, 48
Bevin, Ernest, 35, 62
Bissell, Richard, 186
Bitar, Salah, 83
Black Power Organisation, 238
Black Revolutionary Force, 201
Black September Organisation, 198, 200, 226, 229–34, 238–9, 241, 243, 249, 252, 304
Blake, George, 165
Blake, Admiral Robert, 12
Bodganovitch, Governor of Ufa province, 15
Boese, Wilfred, 273
Bonds for Israel, 170
Bormann, Martin, 93, 99–100
BOSS, 283
Bouchiki, Ahmed, 242–3
Boudia, Mohamed, 228, 231–2, 238
Bouvier, Antonio, 284
Brandner, Ferdinand, 135, 138, 142
Brenner, Willi, 133
British Secret Service, 51
British Royal Commission Report on dividing Palestine into three parts, 25
British White Paper on Jewish Immigration, 29–30
Byroade, Hector, 63

Caceres, Simon de, 12
Caffery, Jefferson, 63
Canaris, Admiral Wilhelm, 41
Carlos, 227–8, 238, 249–51, 253, 256, 273–4, 284, 304
Carvajal, Antonio Fernandez, 12
CERVA, 132–3, 137
Cherbourg gunboats affair, 215–21
Chinese Intelligence, links with

Israelis and Arabs, 198–200, 204–5, 299, 304
'Chivers Papers', 299, 306
Christensen, Dag, 247
Churchill, Peter, 33
Churchill, Winston, 22, 29, 30, 61–63, 167
CIA, 58, 64, 66–7, 79, 85, 92–3, 118–19, 127, 133, 141, 165, 169–170, 178–80, 182–4, 208, 210, 212–14, 240, 251, 259–60, 286–7, 299, 306
Clérisse, Raimond, 91
Cline, Dr. Ray, 260
Cohen, Aharon, 161
Cohen, Baruch, 231–2
Cohen, Elie, 68, 77–88, 139, 142–3, 173–4, 189, 302
Cohen, Nadia, 78, 87–8
Cookridge, E. H., 165, 302–3
Commando Boudia, 238, 250–1
Cyprus, espionage activities in, 196, 226, 232–3
Czech Intelligence Service, 289, 293–4

D'Andurain, Countess Marguerite, 89–92, 94, 99, 134
D'Andurain, Vicomte Pierre, 89–90
Dani, Shalom, 107, 112–14, 116
Danon, David, 148
Daoud, Abu, 225–6, 252–3, 255–6, 305
Dar, Col. Abraham, 68–71
Dassault, Marcel, 217, 304
Dayan, General Moshe, 26, 48, 64–67, 72, 74–5, 119, 123, 129, 167–8, 188, 191–2, 253, 260–1, 266–7, 301–3, 305
De Gaulle, President Charles, 124, 175, 177, 215–16, 218
Delmer, Denis Sefton, 134–5, 303
Demos, Peter, 285
D'Estaing, President Giscard, 175, 252
DI 5, 60
DI 6, 58, 249
Dinaburg, Professor Ben-Zion, 16
Dirlewanger, Oscar, 133

Dollfuss, Austrian Chancellor, 163
Doron, Uriel, 42
Dreyfus, Capt. Alfred, 12, 14
DST, 251–3, 255
Dulles, John Foster, 61, 135

Eban, Abba, 116
Eckenberg, Martin, 224
Eden, Anthony (later Lord Avon), 29, 61
Egyptian Intelligence Services, 136, 142, 150–1, 223, 286
Eichmann, Nikolaus, 110, 115
Eichmann, Otto Adolf, 91, 94–6, 100–2, 103–17, 147, 156
Eichmann, Vera, 106, 108–9
Eisele, Dr. Hans, 145
Eisenhower, President Dwight D., 61, 64, 67, 101, 135, 169
Eitan, Major-Gen. Rafael, 305
El-Arja, Ja'il, 273
Elazar, General David, 254, 260, 265–6
Eleazar, founder of the Zealots, 11
El Hayek, Kassam, 161
El Makdah, Hassan, 161
El Muad, Maflah, 161
Elon, Amos, 52
El Tamini, Samir, 287
Enigma Chain, 37
Entebbe Raid, 254, 271–85
Ert, Dar, 244–5
Eshkol, Levi, 61
Eskenazy, Dr. Alfred, 28
Evron, Ephraim, 169–70
Eytan, Steve, 125, 305
Eytan, Walter, 104

Fahrmbacher, General Wilhelm, 134
Fain, Benjamin, 291
Farouk, King of Egypt, 131
Fawzi, Muhammed, 183
Federation of Jewish Philanthropies, 170
Feinberg, Avshalom, 17
Foccart, Jacques, 177
Foot, Prof. M. R. D., 33, 301
Forrestal, James V., 50

Frank, Paul, 68, 70–1, 73, 187
Frauenknecht, Alfred, 208–9
French Intelligence Services, 118, 124, 175, 212, 225, 235, 240, 249, 274, 284
Friedman, Prof. Tuviah, 100–2, 302
Friedman-Yellin, Nathan, 31
Frondizi, President of Argentine, 111–12
Fulman, Peter, 192, 202
Furuya, Yutaka, 238, 250

Gaddafi, President Muamar, 209–212, 274
Galilee Spy Ring, 191–5
Gazit, Maj.-Gen. Shlomo, 267
Gedalia, Lt.-Col. David, 266
Gehlen, General Reinhard, 73, 92–93, 133, 135–6, 141, 173, 303
Gehlen Organisation, 133, 135–6, 141, 144, 173–4
Gehmer, Abraham, 245–6
Geller, Uri, 296
General Service Unit (Kenyan Secret Service), 281
Ghaffar, Moheb Abdul, 287
Ghorab, General Youssef, 144
'Gideon' secret society, 155
Gilbert, Major Vivian, 10–11, 301
Ginsberg, Pino, 42
Githii, George, 282
Givli, Col. Benjamin, 68–9, 74, 122
Gladnikoff, Marianne, 244–6
Gleim, Leopold, 133
Glover, Paul John Gerald, 195–6
Goebbels, Dr. Josef, 134
Goercke, Heidi, 152–3
Goercke, Professor Paul, 132–3, 137, 152–4
Golan, Menahem, 284
Goleniewski, Col. Michael, 165
Golomb, Eliahu, 38
Gomaa, Sharawi, 183
Goren, Yoel, 107
Gur, General Mordecai, 254, 268

Habbash, Dr. George, 198, 227
Haddad, Simon, 193
Haddad, Dr. Wadieh, 227, 174–5

Hafez, Lt.-Col. Mustapha, 223
Haganah, 11, 23–32, 34, 38–9, 41–4, 46–50, 52, 55, 57, 63, 69–70, 102, 112, 118, 139, 164, 171, 175–6, 253
Haganah B., 24
Halperin, Isser, *see* Harel, Isser
Hamshari, Dr. Mahmoud, 232, 237
Handel, Michael, 261, 305
Harel, Isser, 54–9, 68, 103–5, 107–8, 111–15, 131–2, 146–8, 155, 157–8, 169, 171, 205, 224, 235, 243, 302–303
Harkabi, General Y., 121–2
Harris, Marshal of the RAF, Sir Arthur, 34
Hashan, Abdullah, 83
Hashomer, the, 21–2
Hassan, Hassan Abd el Hassied, 161
Hawatmeh, Naif, 198
Hebrew cryptography, 37–8
Hebron–Bethlehem Group, 201
Hecht, Reuben, 149
Heikal, Mohammed Hassanein, 76
Heilbronner, Prof. André, 28
Hermann, Lothar, 109
Herod, King, 11
Herzog, Brig.-Gen. Chaim, 60, 121, 176–7
Himmler, Heinrich, 102
Histadrut, 63
Hitler, Adolf, 30–2, 36, 92, 102, 134–5, 140, 218, 241, 258
Hofi, Maj.-Gen. Yitzhak, 253–4
Horev, Brigadier, 204
Horrocks, Gen. Sir Brian, 176
Horthy, Admiral, 102, 113
Hussein, King of Jordan, 178, 180, 184, 252
Husseini, Saddam, 205

'Ibis' and 'Cleopatra' projects, 146
Ibn Saud, King, 90
Institute of Technology, Haifa, 162–3
International Association for Psychotronic Research, 293
INTRA, 137, 149
Intrepid Network, 34

IRA, Provisional, 212, 225–6, 228, 289
Iraqi Secret Service, 205
Irgun Zvai Leumi, 24–5, 28–30, 34–36, 38, 40–1, 43, 45–6, 48–50, 63, 79, 148–9
Ismail, Egyptian War Minister, 261
Israeli Black Panthers, 201

Jabal, Shakib Yousef Abu, 190
Jabotinsky, Vladimir, 24, 29
Jaloud, Major, 210
Janssen, Lydia, 289
Japanese Red Army, 225, 228, 238, 250
Jerusalem, Mufti of, 28, 96, 135
Jet-Propulsion Study Institute in Stuttgart, 136, 142, 147
Jewish Agency, 31–2
Jewish Brigade, 40–1, 171
Jewish Defence Committee, 170
Jewish Documentation Centre, 97
Jibril, Ahmad, 198
John, Dr. Otto, 93
Johnson, President Lyndon B., 170, 178
Joklik, Otto Frank, 152–8
Joseph, Dr. Dov, 48
Joshua, the son of Nun, 9
July Unit, 222, 255

Kamil, Hassan, 142, 148–9, 153–4
Kamil, Mme. Hassan, 149
Kanafani, Ghassan, 228–9
Karawi, Anis, 193–4
Katz, Shmuel, 31, 148, 301
Katz, Willy, 46
Katzir, Dr. Ephraim, 202
Kennedy Administration, 169, 178
KGB, operations against Israel, 79, 150, 159, 165–6, 173, 183–4, 196–8, 205, 207, 225–8, 232, 250, 288–92, 294, 299
Khaled, Leila, 275
Khaled ibn Abdul-Aziz, King of Saudi-Arabia, 214
Khalil, Aldin Mahmoud, 136
Khawarji, Habib, 193–4
King David Hotel, bombing of, 36

Kirlian, Davidovitch Semion, 295
Kissinger, Dr. Henry, 260, 262, 299–300
Klein, Hans-Joachim, 290
Kleinwachter, Dr. Hans, 150, 152–3
Klement, Ricardo (see Eichmann, Otto), 103–4, 106, 108–15
Knetch, Jurgen, 133
Kohlman, Litzi, 168
Konigstorfer, Johann, 251
Konigstorfer, Richard, 252
Kook, Hillel, 34
Kraus, Ulrich, 133
Kreisky, Dr. Bruno, 98
Krug, Frau, 149
Krug, Heinz, 149, 153
Kuda, Hani, 228
Kultz, Hélène, 89, 91

Landor, David, 156
Langer, Mrs. Felicia, 202
Laskov, Gen. Chaim, 73
Lavon Affair, 61–75, 169, 174, 187, 257
Lavon, Pinhas, 63–75
Lawrence, T. E., 83, 90
Lemoine, Jules, 103
Lerner, Alexander, 291
Levenbraun, Avraham, 197
Leventhal, Paul, 213
Levin, George, 33
Liberty, USS, attack on by Israelis, 179–84
Libyan Intelligence Service, 210
Libyan plots, 210–12
Liebl, Veronika, see Eichmann, Vera
Lillehammer Affair, special inquiry into, 246
Limon, Admiral Mordecai, 215–21
Livneh, Rami, 197
Lloyd, Lord, 29
Lloyd, Selwyn, 119
Lochamei Herut Israel (LHI), 30, 34, 48–50
Lonsdale, Gordon, 80
Lotz, Waldraut, 143, 189
Lotz, Wolfgang, 139–45, 173–4, 189
Lubentschik, Naftali, 31

Lubow, Dr. Robert, 128

Maihofer, Professor, 290
Mapai Youth Movement, 63
Mardor, Munya, 43
Martinez, Carlos, see Carlos
Marzouk, Dr. Moussa, 69
'Masada' avenger squad, 222, 231
Masterman, Sir John, 159, 162
Matzpen Movement, 192, 194
May, Arcady, 291
Meir, Mrs. Golda, 42, 187, 193, 229, 266
Memuneh, office of the, 58, 75, 202, 268
Mendès-France, Pierre, 62–3, 124
Mengele, Joseph, 98, 112, 115
Mercier, Mâitre Jacques, 87
Mesmer, Pierre, 177
Messerschmitt, Willy, 136–8
Messina, Cdr. Jorge, 111
Messing, Wolf, 297, 306
Middleton, Drew, 259, 266
Mig espionage, 205–7
Mirage aircraft, quest for and espionage on, 205–9
Mizrahi, Baruch, 200
Mohieddin, Zacharia, 179
Mohsen, Major Zuheir, 225
Monheim, Admiral Fawzi, 144
Monroe, Elizabeth, 265
Moses, 9–10
Mossad, the, 38–41, 43, 45–6, 49, 52–60, 67–8, 76–80, 92–3, 103–5, 107, 114, 131–3, 136–8, 168–70, 179, 195, 206–7, 210–13, 215, 224, 229, 232, 235, 244–5, 258, 267–8
Mossad Le Aliyah Beth, 38
Moukarbal, Michel, 238, 251
Moukhabarat-el-Amma, 127
Moukhabarat-el-Kharbeya, 127
Moyne, Lord, 29–30
Mubarak, General Hosny, 127, 286
Muchasi, Zaiad, 233
Mustapha, Col. Salah, 224

Naarani, Subhi, 193–4
Najjar, Mohamed Yusif, 234
Nakaa, Abdul Hadi, 237

Nasser, Lt.-Col. Gamal Abdul (later President), 61–4, 68, 70, 101, 119–120, 131–6, 142, 145, 148, 167–170, 175, 178–9, 183–4, 199, 223, 288, 304

Nasser, Kamal, 234, 243

Nazi War Crimes Centre in Israel, 101

Ne'eman, Yuval, 60, 120–4, 130, 172, 174

Neguib, General, 61, 70

Netanyahu, Lt.-Col. Jonathan, 283–4

Neumann, Waldraut, see Lotz, Waldraut

Nieuwberg, Marius, 289

Nikola, Muzana Kamal, 201–2

Nino, Victorino, 69–70, 174, 189

Nissenthal, Jack, 32–3, 127

Nixon, President Richard, 190

Norwegian Intelligence, 218, 241, 244

Nouri, Col. Osman, 70–1, 73, 187

NSA (National Security Agency), 125, 127, 259–60

Obolensky, Governor of Kharkov, 15

Obote, President Milton, 272

Ochrana, the, 13–16

Ofer, Yehuda, 282, 284, 306

Okamato, Kozo, 195, 228

Olympic Games massacre at Munich, 229, 252, 304

OPEC headquarters, raid on, 251, 290

'Operation Badr', 262–3

'Operation Eichman', 103–17

'Operation Jonathan', 271, 277–80, 284

Osman, General Fouad, 144

Ossowiecki, Stefan, 292

Palestine Liberation Organisation (PLO), 170, 233–4, 243, 248, 255, 284

Palmach, the, 38, 112, 203, 254, 269

Palyam, the, 38, 40, 175, 215

PAO, 198

Parisienne Orientale, 228, 238

Paterson, Arthur, 196

Pauker, Anna, 46

Pavelic, Ante, 111

PDFLP, 198

Pearlman, Moshe, 116, 302

Peres, Shimon, 65–6, 72, 75, 255, 271, 274, 288

Perlmutter, Amos, 65, 75, 302

Peter, Dr. Friederich, 98

PFLP, 198, 201, 225, 227–8, 251, 273–4, 276, 289

Philby, H. A. R. (Kim), 70, 85, 163–4, 166, 168

Pilz, Wolfgang, 149, 156, 224

Plehve, W. K., 15

Poale Zion, 15, 21

Polish Secret Service, 165

Pompidou, President Georges, 216, 221

Popular Front General Council, 198

Prestin, Vladimir, 291

Priester, Karl Heinz, 134

Protocols of the Elders of Zion, 13, 300

Psychic espionage, 290–7

Rabin, Yitzhak, 268, 274, 276–7

Rabinowitz, Aharon, see Yariv, Maj.-Gen.

Radio Damascus, 82–3, 86

Rafael, Sylvia, 245–7

Rahab, the harlot of Jericho, 9

Rahman, Col. Abdel, 143

Rajakovic, Erich, 97

Rauff, Walther, 98

Raziel, David, 24–5, 29, 31

Red Brigade, the, 225

Reilly, Sidney, 18, 139

Reitlinger, Gerald, 95, 302

Rejdak, Dr. Zdenek, 293

Rekhesh, the, 39–40, 43, 46, 57

Reshud, the, 60, 188

'Revolutionary Community Alliance', 193

Rogers, US Secretary of State, 190

Rose, Peretz, 32–3, 127

Rosenblum, Sigmund, see Reilly, Sidney

Rosolio, Chief-Inspector Shaul (now Inspector-General), 188
Rostow, Eugene, 170
Rostow, Walt, 170, 178
Rothschild, Edmond de, 21
Rozenshtein, Grigory, 291
Ruysch, Wilhelm, 197
Ryzl, Dr. Milan, 286, 293–4, 296–7, 306

Sadat, Col. Ahmar (now President of Egypt), 127, 144, 209–10, 212, 232, 252, 261–2, 286–7
Saif, Salem, 83
Saiqa guerrilla group, 225, 238
Salameh, Ali Hassan, 238–43, 248–249, 304
Saleh, Mahmud, 249, 252, 255
Samir, Ali, 151
Sanchez, Ilich Ramirez, see Carlos
Sanger, Eugen, 136, 147–9
Sarayan, Dr. Salah, 210
Saudi Arabian Secret Service, 127, 286
SAVAK (Iranian Secret Service), 177, 251
Schonhaft, Lieut. Ulrich, 189
SDECE, 215, 251, 284
Second of June Movement, 225
Selim, Ifeba Amer, 288
Sellam, Jean, 202
Shabak, the, 57, 59, 161–2, 175, 186, 190, 195, 201, 230, 247, 267
Shachori, Dr. Ami, 225
Shai, 38–40, 46, 54, 56, 69, 79
Shaker, Sheikh Ghassan, 287
Shalev, Brig. Aryeh, 266
Shalim, Ibrahim, 287
Shalim, Inshirah, 287
Shaltiel, David, 39, 171–2
Sharett, Moshe, 13, 64–5, 72
Sharon, Maj.-Gen. Ariel, 253–5
Sherif, Bassam Abu, 229
Shertok, Moshe, see Sharett, Moshe
Sheruth Bitakhon, 49
Sheruth Bitakhon Klali, 57
Shibi, Abdul Hamid, 237
Shiloah, Reuven, 56
Shinar, Dr., 104

Shin Beth, 37–51, 55–8, 60, 63, 65, 67, 70, 73–4, 132, 275
Shitreet, Bechor Shalom, 23
Shomron, Brig.-Gen. Dan, 283
Shukeiry, Ahmed, 170
Shulsky, Shlomo, 21
Sieff, Lord, 238, 249
Silver, Eric, 195, 303
Simon the Apostle, 11
Simoni, Yehuda, 113
Simonovitch, Aaron, 299
Sinclair, Col., 90
Sipyagin, 15
Sitte, Professor Kurt, 162–3
Six-Day War, 120, 125–6, 167–85, 188, 195–6, 203–4, 213, 215, 254, 257, 259, 264, 268, 283
Slotin, Dr. Louis, 27–8
Smith, Colin, 243, 304
SOE, 33
Sokolov, Judge Nicholas, 299
Spears, Brig.- Gen. Sir Edward (later Major-Gen.), 34
'Special Brigade of Blue Falcons', 113
Special Services Unit, 64–5, 67–8
'Squad 101', 222
SRC (Ugandan Secret Service), 285
Stangl, Franz, 97, 99
Starboat Oil Co. of Panama, 218–219
Steinberg, Zwi, 245
Steinmetz, Charles Proteus, 23, 37
Stephenson, Sir William, 22–3, 27–28, 32, 34
Stern, Avraham, 25, 29–31, 53
Stern Gang, 30, 224
Stil, Ilan, 191
Strauss, West German Defence Minister, 148
Suez Crisis (1956), 77, 101, 118–19, 132, 140
Suleiman, General Salaam, 144
Suleiman, Sheikh, 90
Sulzberger, C. L., 118, 123, 303
Sussman, Gabriel, 189
Swindani, Col. Ahmed, 86
Switzerland, Israel's relations with, 148, 240, 248

Syrian Army coup d'état (1961), 175
Syrian Intelligence, 190, 197, 225

Tabachnik, Shlomo, 29
Tabet, Kamel Amine, *see* Cohen, Elie
Tamir, Shmuel, 187
Tangier, immigrant traffic through, 44–6
Tank, Kurt, 142
Tauber, Adolf, 110
Tavin, Yaacov, 35
Telem, Rear-Admiral Benny, 219
Thalalat, 138
Thurloe, John, 12
Tinnin, David, 244, 247–8, 305
Torquemada, Juan de, 12
Traube, Dr. Klaus, 290
Trepper, Leopold, 298
Trumpeldor, Joseph, 16
Tubiansky, Major Meir, 69
Tuchman, Barbara, 172
Turki, Daoud, 193–5
Tzalh, Shalom, 68

Ulbricht, Walter, 173
Unit 101, 254
Unit 131, 66, 68–9
US Land Warfare Laboratory, 130

Vassilyev, A. T., 14
Vatican City, smuggling of ex-Nazis to safety, 94, 103
Vayda, Mme Claire, 35
Veesenmayer, Col., 102
Vered, Dan, 192–5
Vespasian, Emperor, 11
'Voice of Israel', 39
'Voice of the Arabs', 62
Volvovsky, Leonid, 291
Von Leers, Dr. Johannes, 133–4
Voss, Dr. Wilhelm, 131–3

War of Independence, 41, 53, 64, 120–1, 140, 164
Watson-Watt, Sir Robert, 32
Wauchope, General, 24
Wavell, Gen. Sir Archibald (later Field-Marshal), 25
Weizmann, Chaim, 22, 24–5, 28, 32, 69
West German Intelligence, 104, 135–6, 141, 144, 274, 290
Wiesenthal, Simon, 89, 96–100, 102
Wilson Government, 218
Wingate, Capt. Charles Orde, 25–8
Wingate, Mrs. Lorna, 27
Wingate, Sir Reginald, 25
Wisliceny, Dieter, 95
'Wrath of God', 222, 230, 243

Yaabi, Yehuda, 116
Yaakouvian, Kaboerak, 189
Yadin, General Yigal, 49, 164, 269
Yadin-Scherff Committee, 267
Yariv, Brig.-Gen. Aharon (later Maj.-Gen.), 60, 170–4, 230
Yom Kippur War, 200, 207, 257–70, 283–6

Zaarour, Ahmed, 198
Zail, Dannie, 200–1
Zameret, Shmarya, 40
Zamir, Maj.-Gen. Zvi, 60, 203–5, 208, 210, 228–31, 235, 241, 243–6, 253, 263, 268
Zealots, the, 11
Zeevi, Maj.-Gen. Rechavam, 268–9, 279
Zeira, Maj.-Gen. Eliyahu, 259–63, 265–6
Zionist Organisation, 22
Zipstein, Victor, 215, 219
Zorea, Gen. Meir, 116
'Z Team', 107
Zvaiter, Wadal Abdel, 231